Astrology, Almanacs, and the Early Modern English Calendar

Astrology, Almanacs, and the Early Modern English Calendar is a handbook designed to help modern readers unlock the vast cultural, religious, and scientific material contained in early modern calendars and almanacs. It outlines the basic cosmological, astrological, and medical theories that undergirded calendars, traces the medieval evolution of the calendar into its early modern format against the background of the English Reformation, and presents a history of the English almanac in the context of the rise of the printing industry in England. The book includes a primer on deciphering early modern printed almanacs, as well as an illustrated guide to the rich visual and verbal iconography of seasons, months, and days of the week, gathered from material culture, farming manuals, almanacs, and continental prints. As a practical guide to English calendars and the social, mathematical, and scientific practices that inform them, *Astrology, Almanacs, and the Early Modern English Calendar* is an indispensable tool for historians, cultural critics, and literary scholars working with the primary material of the period, especially those with interests in astrology, popular science, popular print, the book as material artifact, and the history of time-reckoning.

Phebe Jensen is Professor of English at Utah State University, USA. She is also the author of *Religion and Revelry in Shakespeare's Festive World* (2008).

Alison A. Chapman (Foreword) is Professor of English at the University of Alabama, Birmingham, USA.

Astrology, Almanacs, and the Early Modern English Calendar

Phebe Jensen

FOREWORD BY ALISON A. CHAPMAN

LONDON AND NEW YORK

First published 2021
by Routledge
2 Park Square, Milton Park, Abingdon, Oxon OX14 4RN

and by Routledge
52 Vanderbilt Avenue, New York, NY 10017

Routledge is an imprint of the Taylor & Francis Group, an informa business

© 2021 Phebe Jensen

The right of Phebe Jensen to be identified as author of this work has been asserted by her in accordance with sections 77 and 78 of the Copyright, Designs and Patents Act 1988.

All rights reserved. No part of this book may be reprinted or reproduced or utilized in any form or by any electronic, mechanical, or other means, now known or hereafter invented, including photocopying and recording, or in any information storage or retrieval system, without permission in writing from the publishers.

Trademark notice: Product or corporate names may be trademarks or registered trademarks, and are used only for identification and explanation without intent to infringe.

British Library Cataloguing-in-Publication Data
A catalogue record for this book is available from the British Library

Library of Congress Cataloging-in-Publication Data
A catalog record has been requested for this book

ISBN: 978-1-4724-8183-2 (hbk)
ISBN: 978-1-315-61579-0 (ebk)

Typeset in Sabon
by codeMantra

For my mother, Lucy Johnson Jensen

Contents

List of figures   xiv
Foreward, by Alison A. Chapman   xix
Acknowledgements   xxiii

Introduction   1

PART I
Backgrounds   15

1.1 Astrology   17
Ptolemaic judicial astrology 18
Astrological medicine 25
Lunar prognostications 28
Egyptian days 29
Brontologies 29
Esdras or dominical letter prognostications 30

1.2 Calendars   34
The Julian calendar 34
The compotus *36*
Late medieval calendars and the folded almanac 39
Calendars in print: pre-Reformation primers 40
Calendars in print: prayer book calendars, the
   Reformation, and the saints 43
The Gregorian reforms 50
Clog almanacs and xylographic calendars 51

1.3 Almanacs and prognostications   57
Multi-year almanacs 57
Single sheet imported almanacs 58

Annual prognostications 59
Annual book form almanacs and prognostications, 1540–1571 60
The Watkins and Roberts monopoly, 1571–1603 64
The English Stock, 1603–1640 67
The university press almanacs 70

1.4 Related publications and controversies   74
Perpetual almanacs 75
Astrological guides 78
Controversies 82
Mock almanacs 88

Colour plate section appears between pages 94 and 95

PART II
How to read an early modern almanac   95

2.1 The almanac   97
Physical format 97
Rubrication 98
Title pages 98
    Images and borders 98
    Title and year 101
    Compilers 102
    Leap year, meridian, and pole arctic 102
    Epigraphs 104
    Printers and privileges 105
Declarations 106
Law terms 107
Chronologies 108
Zodiac Man 108
Elections 109
The calendar 112

2.2 The Prognostication   118
Title page 118
To the reader 118
Calculating prognostications 120
Formatting prognostications 123

    Revolutions and the four seasons 124
    Eclipses 124
    Monthly prognostications 124
  Additional astronomical and astrological content 126
    Planet and star tables 127
    Planetary hours 128
  Additional miscellaneous content 129
    Principal fairs 130
    Calendar history 130
    Travel and geography 130
    Tide tables 131
    Itineraries, rhombs, and latitude 131
    Catalogues of shires and choreographies 132
    Measurement 132
    Advertisements 133

PART III
Early modern calendars   137

3.1 The four seasons   139
  Introduction 139
  Spring 142
    Astronomy and astrology 142
    Allegory 142
    Pastimes, activities, and labors 144
    Complexion, qualities, and disease 146
  Summer 147
    Astronomy and astrology 147
    Allegory 148
    Pastimes, activities, and labors 149
    Complexion, qualities, and disease 150
  Autumn 151
    Astronomy and astrology 151
    Allegory 152
    Pastimes, activities, and labors 154
    Complexion, qualities, and disease 154
  Winter 155
    Astronomy and astrology 155
    Allegory 156
    Pastimes, activities, and labors 157
    Complexion, qualities, Weather and disease 157

3.2 The planets and seven days of the week   162
Introduction 162
Sunday: The Sun 163
Monday: The Moon 165
Tuesday: Mars 167
Wednesday: Mercury 169
Thursday: Jupiter 171
Friday: Venus 173
Saturday: Saturn 175

Colour plate section appears between pages 178 and 179

3.3 The twelve months   179
Introduction 179
    Labors and agricultural tasks 179
    Zodiac, astronomy, and astrology 180
    The ages of man 180
    Physic 181
    The church calendar 181
    Fairs 182
    Law terms 182
    Festive traditions and pastimes 183
    The saints in the calendar 183
January 185
    Labors and agricultural tasks 185
    Zodiac, astronomy, and astrology 187
    The ages of man 187
    Physic 188
    The church calendar 188
    Fairs 189
    Law terms 189
    Festive traditions and pastimes 189
February 191
    Labors and agricultural tasks 191
    Zodiac, astronomy, and astrology 193
    The ages of man 193
    Physic 195
    The church calendar 195
    Fairs 197
    Law terms 197
    Festive traditions and pastimes 197

March 199
    Labors and agricultural tasks 199
    Zodiac, astronomy, and astrology 201
    The ages of man 201
    Physic 202
    The church calendar 202
    Fairs 203
    Law terms 203
    Festive traditions and pastimes 204
April 206
    Labors and agricultural tasks 206
    Zodiac, astronomy, and astrology 208
    The ages of man 208
    Physic 208
    The church calendar 210
    Fairs 211
    Law terms 211
    Festive traditions and pastimes 211
May 213
    Labors and agricultural tasks 213
    Zodiac, astronomy, and astrology 214
    The ages of man 215
    Physic 215
    The church calendar 216
    Fairs 217
    Law terms 218
    Festive traditions and pastimes 218
June 221
    Labors and agricultural tasks 221
    Zodiac, astronomy, and astrology 222
    The ages of man 222
    Physic 222
    The church calendar 224
    Fairs 225
    Law terms 225
    Festive traditions and pastimes 225
July 227
    Labors and agricultural tasks 227
    Zodiac, astronomy, and astrology 229
    The ages of man 229
    Physic 230

xii *Contents*

  Church calendar 230
  Fairs 231
  Law terms 231
  Festive traditions and pastimes 231
August 233
  Labors and agricultural tasks 233
  Zodiac, astronomy, and astrology 235
  The ages of man 235
  Physic 236
  The Church calendar 236
  Fairs 237
  Law terms 237
  Festive traditions and pastimes 237
September 239
  Labors and agricultural tasks 239
  Zodiac, astronomy, and astrology 240
  The ages of man 241
  Physic 241
  The Church calendar 243
  Fairs 243
  Law terms 244
  Festive traditions and pastimes 244
October 245
  Labors and agricultural tasks 245
  Zodiac, astronomy, and astrology 246
  The ages of man 248
  Physic 248
  The Church calendar 249
  Fairs 249
  Law terms 249
  Festive traditions and pastimes 249
November 251
  Labors and agricultural tasks 251
  Zodiac, astronomy, and astrology 253
  The ages of man 253
  Physic 254
  The church calendar 254
  Fairs 255
  Law terms 255
  Festive traditions and pastimes 255

December 257
    Labors and agricultural tasks 258
    Zodiac, astronomy, and astrology 259
    The ages of man 259
    Physic 260
    The church calendar 261
    Fairs 262
    Law terms 262
    Festive traditions and pastimes 262

3.4 Sample calendars, 1518–1640   267
January 267
February 267
March 269
April 270
May 272
June 273
July 274
August 274
September 277
October 278
November 279
December 280

Bibliography   283
Primary bibliography 283
Secondary bibliography 294

Index of Saints and Holy Days   307
Index   312

Figures

Black and white images

I.I	Ptolemy and Jester, Anonymous, *A Mery Pronosticacion for the Yere of Chrystes Incarnacyon a Thousande Fyve Hundreth Fortye & Foure* (1544), Title Page	3
1.1.1	Ptolemaic Universe, William Blagrave, *The Mathematical Jewel* (1585), 7	18
1.1.2	Armillary Sphere, Anonymous, *The Kalender of Shepeherdes* (1528), P3v	19
1.1.3	Spring Equinox Horoscope, John Harvey, *An Almanacke or Annual Calendar* (1589), Title Page	23
1.2.1	December calendar, Catholic Church, *Hore Beate Virginis Marie* (Paris, 1520, STC 15926), A7v-A8r	41
1.2.2	Almanac for seventeen years, Catholic Church, *This Prymer of Salysbury Use* (Paris, 1532, STC 15978), A7v-A8r	44
1.2.3	Almanac for 1537, Catholic Church, *This Prymer of Salysbury Use* (Paris, 1532, STC 15978), A5v-A6r	45
1.2.4	January Calendar, John Foxe, *Acts and Monuments of Matters most Speciall and Memorable* (1632), v.1, A2r	49
1.4.1	Zodiac Man, Leonard Digges, *A Prognostication Everlasting of Ryght Good Effecte* (1556), Title Page	77
2.1	Sun, Moon, and Armillary Sphere, John Securis, *1581. An Almanacke and Prognostication*, C1r	100
2.2	Law Terms, Thomas Bretnor, *Bretnor. 1615. A Newe Almanacke and Prognostication*, A3r	107
2.3	Elections for Physic and Phlebotomy, George Osborne, *Osborne 1622. A New Almanacke and Prognostication*, B3v-B4r	110
2.4	Elections for Husbandry, George Osborne, *1622. A New Almanacke and Prognostication*, B4r	111
2.5	January Calendar, William Cuningham, *A Newe Almanacke and Prognostication* (1558), Alm.A3v-A4r	112
2.6	Good and Evil Days, Thomas Bretnor, *Bretnor 1617. A Newe Almanacke and Prognostication*, C7v	116

Figures xv

2.7	Winter Solstice Horoscope, William Cuningham, *A Newe Almanacke and Prognostication* (1558), Pro.A3v-A4r	121
2.8	Weather and Planetary Aspects, George Gilden, *Gilden. 1621. A New Almanacke, and Prognostication*, B7r	125
2.9	Calendar for the Year, John White, *White 1633: A New Almanack and Prognostication*, C4r	128
3.1.1	*Lente (Spring)*, Engraving, Philips Galle, after Maarten van Heemskerck, 1563	143
3.1.2	*Lente (Spring)*, Engraving, Pieter van der Heyden, after Pieter Bruegel, 1601–1652	145
3.1.3	*Zomer (Summer)*, Engraving, Philips Galle, after Maarten van Heemskerck, 1563	149
3.1.4	*Zomer (Summer)*, Engraving, Adriaen Collaert, after Maerten de Vos, 1570–1618	150
3.1.5	*Herfst (Autumn)*, Engraving, Philips Galle after Maarten van Heemskerck, 1563	152
3.1.6	*Herfst (Autumn)*, Engraving, Jan Saenredam, after Hendrick Goltzius, 1590–1600	153
3.1.7	*The Four Seasons: Winter*, Engraving, Martin Droeshout, 1620–1630	156
3.1.8	*Winter*, Engraving, Philips Galle, after Maarten van Heemskerck, 1563	158
3.1.9	*Winter*, Engraving, Jan Saenredam, after Hendrick Goltzius, 1590–1600	159
3.2.1	Planetary Rulers, Book of Magic, Manuscript, Folger Shakespeare Library V.b.26 (1), ca. 1577–1583, 63	163
3.2.2	The Sun, *De Zone en Zijn Invloed op to Wereld*, Engraving, Johan Sadeler (I), after Maerten de Vos, 1585	164
3.2.3	The Moon, *Luna, de Maan, En Haar Kinderen*, Engraving, Harmen Jansz Muller, after Maarten van Heemskerck, 1566–1570	166
3.2.4	Mars, *Mars En Zijn Planeetkinderen*, Engraving, Anonymous, after Hans Sebald Beham, after Georg Pencz, 1531	168
3.2.5	Mercury, *Mercurius en Zin Planeetkinderen*, Engraving, Anonymous, after Hans Sebald Beham, after Georg Pencz, 1531	170
3.2.6	Jupiter, *De Planeet Jupiter en zijn Kinderen*, Engraving, Harmen Jansz Muller, after Maarten van Heemskerck, 1638–1646	172
3.2.7	Venus, *Here Begynneth the Kalender of Shepardes* ([1518?], STC 22410), L3v	174
3.2.8	Saturn, *The Kalender of Shepeherdes* (1528, STC 22411), R4v	176

xvi *Figures*

3.3.1	January, William Cuningham, *A Newe Almanacke and Prognostication* (1558), Pr.B2v	185
3.3.2	Janus, January Roundel, Canterbury Cathedral	186
3.3.3	February, Misericord, Worcester Cathedral, fourteenth century	192
3.3.4	February, James Gesner, *An Almanacke and Prognostication* (1555), Single Sheet Broadside	192
3.3.5	February, Catholic Church, *This Prymer of Salisbury Use* (Rouen, 1555, STC 16068), A3v	194
3.3.6	March, William Cuningham, *A Newe Almanacke and Prognostication* (1564), Pr.A6r	200
3.3.7	Aries, Richard Roussat, *Arcandam* (Paris, 1542), K1r	201
3.3.8	April, Misericord, St. Mary's, Ripple, Worcester, fifteenth century	207
3.3.9	April, Catholic Church, *This Prymer of Salisbury Use* (Rouen, 1531, STC 15971), [A4v]	209
3.3.10	May, Thomas Buckminster, *A New Almanacke and Prognostication* (1567), A8r	214
3.3.11	May, Catholic Church, *Hore Beate Virginis Marie* (Paris, 1520, STC 15926), [A4v]	215
3.3.12	June, William Prid, *The Glasse of Vaine Glory* (1600), A6v	221
3.3.13	June, Catholic Church, *This Prymer of Salysbury Use* (Paris, 1529, STC 15961.5), B2v	223
3.3.14	July, Glass Roundel, ca. 1450–1475	228
3.3.15	July, Misericord, Worcester Cathedral, fourteenth century	228
3.3.16	August, Catholic Church, *Hereafter Followeth the Primer* (1555, STC 16071), B1v	234
3.3.17	August, Misericord, St. Mary's, Ripple, fifteenth century	234
3.3.18	September, Thomas Buckminster, *A New Almanacke and Prognostication* (1567), B5r	239
3.3.19	September, Catholic Church, *Enchiridion, Preclare Ecclesie Sarum* (Paris, 1530, STC 15965), B1v	242
3.3.20	October, William Prid, *The Glasse of Vaine-Glorie* (1600), A8v	246
3.3.21	October, Catholic Church, *This Prymer of Salisbury Use* (Rouen, 1556, STC 16076), B3v	247
3.3.22	November, Misericord, Great Malvern Priory, fifteenth century	252
3.3.23	November, William Cuningham, *A Newe Almanacke and Prognostication* (1558), B5r	252
3.3.24	December, Detail, Four Seasons Tapestries, Hatfield House, Hatfield, Hertfordshire	257
3.3.25	December, William Prid, *The Glasse of Vaine-Glorie* (1600), A9v	258

Figures xvii

3.3.26	December, Catholic Church, *Enchiridion, preclare ecclesie Sarum* (Paris, 1530, STC 15965), B4v	260
3.4.1	January, Anonymous, *Here Begynneth the Kalender of Shepardes*, ([1518?], STC 22410), B5r	268
3.4.2	February, Michael Nostradamus, *An Almanacke for the Yeare of Oure Lorde God, 1559*, A2v	269
3.4.3	March, Buckminster, *A New Almanacke and Prognostication* (1567), A7r-A7v	270
3.4.4	April, John Securis, *1576. An Almanacke and Prognostication*, A3v	271
3.4.5	May, Thomas Hill, *A New Almanack* (1572), Single Sheet Almanac, Detail	272
3.4.6	June, J.D. *A Triple Almanacke for the yeere of our Lorde 1591*, B3v-B4r	273
3.4.7	July, William Prid, *The Glasse of Vaine-Glorie* (1600), A7r	275
3.4.8	August, Trevelyon Miscellany, Manuscript, Folger Shakespeare Library, V.b.232, fol. 11r, 1608	276
3.4.9	September, Church of England, *The Booke of Common Prayer* (1611), A6r	277
3.4.10	October, Thomas Bretnor, *A New Almanacke* (1616), B4v-B5r	278
3.4.11	November, William Beale, *Beale 1631, A Almanacke*, A8r	280
3.4.12	December, John Booker, *M.D.C. XL Almanack Et Prognostication* (1640), B7v	281

Chart

| 1.1.1 | The Signification of the Astrological Houses | 22 |
| 3.3.1 | Labors of the Months and Zodiac Signs | 180 |

Color plates

1.1 Brontology, Manuscript Almanac, British Library, BL Addl. MS 17,367, 16th century
1.2 Zodiac Man, Catholic Church, *Hore Beatissime Virginis Marie* (Paris, 1530, STC 15968), ✠9v
2.1 April and May, Clog Almanac, Chetham's Library, Manchester
2.2 September and October, Guilaume Brouscon, Xylographic Nautical Almanac on Vellum ([Brittany, 1546?]), F11r
2.3 October, Clog Almanac owned by Archbishop William Laud (1636), History of Science Museum, University of Oxford

xviii *Figures*

- 3 Single Sheet Almanack, Thomas Hill, *A New Almanack* (1572)
- 4.1 Title Page, Cuningham, William, *A Newe Almanacke and Prognostication* (1558), A1r
- 4.2 Title Page, Gabriel Frende, *Frend. 1598. An Almanacke and Prognostication*, A1r
- 5.1 Almanac Title Page, Richard Allestree, *Allestree. 1626. A New Almanacke and Prognostication*, A1r
- 5.2 Prognostication Title Page, Richard Allestree, *Allestree. 1626. A New Almanacke and Prognostication*, C1r
- 6.1 Almanac Title Page, Arthur Sofford, *Sofford. 1633. A New Almanacke and Prognostication*, A1r
- 6.2 A Catalogue of all the Shires, John White, *White. 1633. A New Almanacke and Prognostication*, C2r
- 7.1 Declaration, Jeffrey Neve, *Neve. 1621. A New Almanack, and Prognostication*, A1v
- 7.2 Chronology, George Gilden, *Gilden, 1621 A New Almanacke, and Prognostication*, A2r
- 8.1 Zodiac Man, Arthur Hopton, *Hopton. 1608. An Almanacke for this Present Yeare of Our Redemption*, A2v
- 8.2 Vein Man, Thomas Rudston, *Rudston. 1607. A New Almanacke and Prognostication*, A2r
- 9 Labors of the Month, Leaden Font, Church of St. Augustine, Brookland, Kent, UK
- 10 Labors of the Month, Anglicus Bartholomaeus, *Batman vppon Bartholome, His Booke De proprietatibus rerum* (1582), after 141v
- 11 Spring, The Four Seasons Tapestries, Hatfield House, Hatfield, Hertfordshire
- 12 Summer, The Four Seasons Tapestries, Hatfield House, Hatfield, Hertfordshire
- 13 Autumn, The Four Seasons Tapestries, Hatfield House, Hatfield, Hertfordshire
- 14 Winter, The Four Seasons Tapestries, Hatfield House, Hatfield, Hertfordshire
- 15.1 March (Pruning), Wall Painting, Easby Church
- 15.2 June, Edmund Spenser, *The Shepheardes Calender* (1586), fol. 22v
- 16.1 August (Virgo), Petit-point Silk Panel, Hardwick Hall, 16th century
- 16.2 November (Sowing), Wall Painting, Easby Church

Foreward

In late August 2019 when I was reading a preliminary draft of this book, Hurricane Dorian began ominously building strength far out in the Atlantic Ocean. Having spent much of my childhood on various back bays along the Gulf Coast of the United States, I have a horrified fascination with the destructive potential of these storms, and I maintain a carefully curated set of bookmarks in my internet browser so I can keep an eye on things. Weather Underground offers good tracking maps on its Hurricanes and Tropical Cyclones page. The National Hurricane Center has satellite and radar imagery and aircraft reconnaissance information. The National Weather Service page provides charts of wind history, tide surge, and rainfall. And my local news outlet has a discussion board where users can weigh in on the latest forecast data. Each morning as Dorian ground across the Bahamas, bounced off the Florida then Georgia then South Carolina coastlines, and finally drifted off northwards, I poured coffee and clicked through my private array of hurricane-related predictive tools. And then I read another chapter of this book.

This conjoined exercise—tracking Hurricane Dorian and reading *Astrology, Almanacs, and The Early Modern English Calendar* —brought into sharp relief how much effort we human beings put into trying to predict the future and how fortunate we moderns are compared to our early modern peers. Our advantage comes from the astonishing technology of the modern world. Meteorological scientists send P-3 Orion aircraft through the eyes of hurricanes to collect data. Doctors take MRI scans of the body to understand how disease tissues will develop. Banks and insurance companies use actuarial algorithms and AI to fine-tune their levels of risk. Those such as myself who work in higher education use statistical predictions to help us guess which students are in danger of dropping out and what six-year graduation rates will be. In contrast to all of these digital and technological marvels, early modern men and women had the almanac. These small, cheap books were packed with information about when the holy days would fall, what the weather would be like, when to bathe or prune fruit trees, when the law courts opened, when the next high tide would occur, what dire effects the next eclipse would bring, etc. As Jensen points out, almanacs were the single most useful books of the early modern world. It is hardly a surprise, then, that they were also the most popular, published in volumes that far outstripped anything else in early modern England. When we consider the numbers of English almanacs and the extraordinarily wide variety of uses they served, the true surprise is that this book is the one of the first to provide a working introduction to them.

Why have almanacs been so neglected? As Jensen suggests in her introduction, one of the primary reasons has to do with the inaccessibility of their contents. Most scholars of the early modern period enjoy studying works that have an allusive or linguistic richness or that offer a window onto human subjectivity. Presented with a choice between poring over an early modern diary or an early modern table of calendrical data, few of us will choose the table. Moreover, the technical information in early modern calendars and almanacs is often of a particularly arcane nature. We no longer have to calculate for ourselves the framework of each year (e.g., the date of Mother's Day or whether a friend's birthday next year will fall on a Friday or a Tuesday). Men and women of the sixteenth and seventeenth centuries still needed to be able to make these calculations. To help them, almanacs included information that is mystifying to most modern readers such as the epact, the circle of the sun, and golden number. Reading an early modern almanac is like trying to read a partially encrypted message. One of Jensen's most generous contributions is that she decodes the information in early modern almanacs so that modern readers can understand precisely what they are seeing and why it was so useful and compelling to its original readers. Jensen has provided a way for us to take these texts on their own terms instead of on ours.

Secondly, scholars have overlooked almanacs because these works were inextricably tied to the larger discourse of astrology. Although there were some non-astrological calendars and almanacs in the period, the vast majority of them either include specific astrological information or are broadly indebted to astrological ways of thinking. It is fitting then that astrology figures so prominently in this book and that Jensen gives it the careful attention it deserves. Because astrology enjoys little credibility today, most people are at best patronizing when they encounter its early modern manifestations. Like Isaac Newton's interest in alchemy, references to astrology in sixteenth- and seventeenth-century works can seem regrettable holdovers from the medieval past. However, this attitude of pained tolerance does not do justice to the role astrology played in the early modern worldview. As evidenced by my own fixation on Hurricane Dorian, human beings have a deep need to make sense of their world. Astrological almanacs helped satisfy this need. The fact that we regard their predictions as valueless is beside the point. Like us, the people who wrote and read almanacs were using the best tools at their disposal to peer into the future and thereby to protect themselves, their families, and their communities against life's frightening vicissitudes. We should remember, too, that those who compiled almanacs and offered astrological predictions were synthesizing huge amounts of information, ranging from planetary aspects to eclipse charts, and making complex calculations. In their own way, almanac-makers were the cutting-edge data analysts of their world. They put that data analysis to uses that do not seem important to us, but this should not diminish their skills or achievements.

Setting aside astrology's flaws as a predictive system, we have much to learn from it as a way of seeing the world. Jensen reminds us that astrology is premised on an idea of interconnectedness, a point that is worth dwelling on here. The precise nature of this interconnectedness is so alien to us that it can seem absurd. Take, for instance, the common notations in early modern almanacs about when to cut one's hair and when to let blood. Almanac makers included these because most people took it for granted that their bodies were interlaced into a cosmic web of influences. The body's liquid tides pulsed just like those in the oceans, and so just as mariners needed to know when and where to drop anchor, people needed precise information about when and where to apply the scalpel. Likewise, the wheeling planets were believed to tug at each filament of hair so managing one's health involved looking outwards toward the night sky as well as inwards towards the pangs of joints and the stirrings of organs. This sense of time and space as being thick with meaning also undergirds Part III of this book where Jensen describes the symbols and figures associated with the days, weeks, and seasons. Autumn brought in mythological figures such as Bacchus and Ceres. Tuesdays were associated with Mars and Fridays with Venus. Each month was populated with saints. For early moderns, time itself was densely peopled.

The modern world is currently rediscovering some of these earlier assumptions about interconnectedness although they are oriented in a very different way. To return to Hurricane Dorian, this storm—like others in recent years including Harvey, Michael, and Florence—was more destructive because it moved so slowly. Storms are slower than they were a century ago because the winds and currents that drive them have slowed, and most scientists believe that this is function of warmer global temperatures, which can, in turn, be linked to human activity. Two hundred years ago, the idea that human beings and hurricanes exerted reciprocal influence upon one another would have seemed laughable. Since then, our awareness has begun to shift, and it has done so in a way that can give us more insight into the early modern astrological worldview. By helping us decode almanacs and understand the complexities of the calendar, this book opens up a world in which every aspect of terrestrial life participated in larger networks of planetary, lunar, and astral influences and in which religion and nature animated one another. As I read this book, I felt a lightly ironic sense of relief that my daily regimens do not mirror early modern ones: I do not check an almanac before showering, nor do I worry that my Tuesday commute might be more dangerous because of the day's Martial associations. But I also felt a wistful tug that we have lost the early modern assumption that the cosmos was a communal, interconnected place. In this sense *Astrology, Almanacs, and Early Modern Calendars* has much to teach us about how men and women in earlier centuries understood their roles in a wider and differently textured world.

Alison A. Chapman
University of Alabama at Birmingham

Acknowledgements

It's a pleasure to acknowledge the institutions and individuals who have supported this project over many years. Final research was made possible by short-term fellowships at the Folger Shakespeare Library and The Huntington Library, and by travel and research grants from the Utah State University College of Humanities and Social Sciences and the USU Department of English. Many thanks to the friends and colleagues who supported the project by writing letters of support, reading drafts, sharing research or citations, or listening to me enthuse about almanacs: David Houston Woods, Erika T. Lin, Lowell Gallagher, Arthur Marotti, Julie Sanders, Marissa Greenberg, Laura Gelfand, Jessica Frazier, Anston Bosman, Frances Gage, Debapriya Sarker, Emily Rose, Heather Wolfe, Camille Seerattan, Caroline Duroselle-Melish, Gillian Woods, Jennifer Duncan, Alison Shell, David Loewenstein, and Mary Floyd-Wilson. Claire Harlan was an enthusiastic and careful undergraduate research assistant; Emma Crumbley helped immeasurably with the book's final preparation. I owe a special thanks to Erika Gaffney, whose email query about a possible book on calendars for Ashgate turned a project on time-reckoning in a new direction. Without Erika's enthusiastic support at the early stages of the project, this book would never have been written. My most profound scholarly debt is to my co-conspirator Alison Chapman, who has inspired me with her scholarship, delighted me with her friendship, and honored this book with a Foreward.

Full credit for the images in *Astrology, Almanacs, and the Early Modern Calendar* can be found elsewhere in the book, but here I gratefully acknowledge the generosity of those individuals and institutions who helped me stretch my budget by waiving copyright fees, providing high resolution images free of charge, assisting my own photography efforts, or otherwise bartering deals that enabled me to include material from their collections: the Rare Book & Manuscript Library at the University of Illinois, Champagne-Urbana, with special thanks to Dennis Sears; Dominic Strange at misericords.co.uk; and The Huntington Library, Lambeth Palace Library, Chetham's Library, The Museum of the History of Science, the Rijksmuseum, Amsterdam, and Canterbury Cathedral Archives. I am especially grateful to

xxiv   *Acknowledgements*

the Folger Shakespeare Library for generously allowing me to use my own photographs, taken in their reading rooms, without charge.

   Many thanks to the friends and family who have supported this project and its author for many years: Lolita Chakrabarti, Jennifer Collins, Lucy Merrill Cotter, Mark Damen, Ken Franklin, Laura Gelfand, Natalie Jensen, Carol McNamara, Brian McCuskey, Kristine Miller, Mary Palmer, Sally Prager, Jim Ray, Ralph Seymour, Elizabeth Stainton, Betsy Tanner, Kym Tiffany, Frances Titchener, and Alice Truax. As always my greatest debt is to Paul Crumbley, and to our daughters, Nell and Emma, dragged in their youth to libraries, churches, and cathedrals to see the vestiges of historical time-reckoning. This book is dedicated to my mother, Lucy Jensen, librarian, artist, and bibliophile, whose joyful love of rare books and Renaissance engravings inspired my own.

Introduction

Astrology, Almanacs, and the Early Modern English Calendar was first conceived as a handbook to English calendars in the sixteenth and early seventeenth centuries, and that remains its primary purpose. It teaches modern readers how to decipher Tudor and early Stuart calendars, outlines the evolution of the calendar, describes the form calendars took in early printed books, and tracks their development in the early modern printed almanac. The final part of the book is an illustrated guide to the seasons, months, and days of the week that synthesizes material from almanacs, prayer books, material artifacts, and farming guides in order to recuperate the visual and verbal iconography of time reckoning in the period. The book's primary goal is to help scholars and students of early modern England unlock the vast cultural knowledge contained in calendars, and thereby to support further study and original scholarship on other topics in the field. It strives to be a helpful book that, like almanacs, will be used as much as read.

But calendars are far too complex to be understood in isolation from the culture that produced them. Calendars are man-made systems that divide up the unruly cycles of the natural world created by the spinning of the earth, its rotation around the Sun, and the movement of the Moon and other planets. Though tied to the astronomical realities of life on earth, the divisions created by any given calendar are arbitrary, devised by particular cultures in accordance with cosmological and theological beliefs of the time, in order to serve religious, social, and political needs.[1] Tudor and Stuart calendars specifically, like their late medieval antecedents, can only make sense to modern readers who understand the basic cosmological and medical theories that undergird them, especially the Ptolemaic astrology that made calendars of much richer and varied use to early moderns than the bare and basic calendars of the twenty-first century. For this reason, a guide to calendars inevitably became a guide to early modern popular astrology as well.

But calendars in early modern England are also not fully contained in the familiar twelve-month grids that annually align the days of the week with the date of the month, indicating holidays and leap year. From the medieval period onward, calendars in the *compotus* tradition had been structured as "anthologies," in Faith Wallis' useful description, which attracted ancillary documents including treatises on time reckoning, medical guides, and humble poems on calendrical and other matters.[2] That additional material both extended the information in calendars, and gave readers the tools they needed to use those calendars fully. From the mid-sixteenth century, calendars and such accompanying documents were most frequently found in England in the annual printed almanac. These almanacs might be thought of as extended calendars. The almanac supplemented those familiar twelve-month grids with additional information necessary for understanding the time reckoned in a given year. That information was astrological, astronomical, historical, agricultural, medical, and also religious, for early modern English calendars register the tectonic religious shifts of the Reformation.[3] Material on those (and many other) topics was squeezed into the thirty-six or forty-eight pages of the standard early modern annual printed almanac and prognostication, the book-form in which calendars most frequently appeared in early modern England after the middle of the sixteenth century.[4] In the end, then, this handbook to calendars and popular astrology in early modern England has also become a guide to the early modern printed almanacs in which such calendars appear.

As a handbook, the rhetorical stance throughout this book is primarily explanatory, not argumentative. However, the book does have an agenda: it is that almanacs, and the popular, Christianized, Ptolemaic astrology they communicate, deserve greater attention in early modern studies, perhaps especially in the study of Shakespeare and the work of his literary contemporaries. That agenda repeats the hope expressed by Bernard Capp in 1989 in his magisterial *Astrology and the Popular Press: The English Almanac 1500–1700*, the indispensable guide for anyone working in this area: to "persuade specialists that, in almost every field, almanacs constitute a neglected source well worth further investigation."[5] That hope has been subsequently realized in a rich body of work on almanacs by scholars including Alison Chapman, Adam Smyth, Katherine Walker, and Louise Curth.[6] But obstacles remain that have kept both almanacs and popular astrology on the sidelines of contemporary scholarship.

The first obstacle concerns the general reputation of the annual combined almanac and prognostication, which has had bad press from the moment the genre evolved in England in the fourth decade of the sixteenth century. In its day, the almanac was derided as a pathetic low level publication filled with errors, written by hacks, cheaply printed, and fully deserving of its ignominious repurposing every January 1st for lining book-bindings or privy paper.[7] That derision can be seen in the title page woodcut of the first English mock almanac, the anonymous *A Mery Pronosticacion* (1544); which replaces a standard image of Ptolemy pointing to the stars with the image of a jester surrounded by loons (Figure I.I).

Figure I.1 Ptolemy and Jester, Anonymous, *A Mery Pronosticacion for the Yere of Chrystes Incarnacyon a Thousande Fyve Hundreth Fortye & Foure* (1544), Title Page. The Huntington Library, San Marino, California, RB 56465.

Such mockery grew in quantity and scornfulness in the Elizabethan and Jacobean period, when the compilers of almanacs became a particular target. In Sir Thomas Overbury's *Sir Thomas Overburie His Wife* (1616), for example, the "Almanacke-maker" is an ignorant charlatan who admires Ptolemy and Tycho Brahe but cannot understand them, who mis-predicts the weather ("for his judging at the uncertainty of weather, any old Shepheard shall make a Dunce of him"), and is exposed annually when his predictions lose all credibility "at the yeeres end, for time brings truth to light" (G1v-G2r). Richard Brathwaite's *Whimzies* (1631) similarly takes aim at compilers' pretensions to learning: "Horizons, Hemispheares, Horoscopes, Apogaeums, Hypogaeums, Perigaeums, Astrolages, Cycles, Epicycles are his usuall dialect; yet I am perswaded they may bee something to *eate*, for ought he knows" (A8v). By the start of the seventeenth century, the almanac had become a cultural shorthand for the ephemeral and unreliable; in John Marston's *Jack Drum's Entertainment* (1601), one character describes another's affections as "uncertaine as an Almanacke, as unconstant as the fashion, Just like a whiffe of Tabacco, no sooner in at the mouth, but out at the nose."[8] Famously, the first director of the Bodleian Library refused to allow "baggage bookes" such as almanacs and plays into his collection.[9] Mock almanacs included an *Astrologicall Prognostication* for 1591 by "Adam Fouleweather, Student in Asse-tronomy," and a number of works adopt the bird motif of *A Mery Prognostication:* Thomas Dekker's *The Raven's Almanacke* (1609), Thomas Middleton's *The Owles Almanacke* (1618), and the Poor Robin almanacs first published in the 1660s.[10] The almanac's credibility has not been helped by its subsequent evolution in nineteenth century America into a dubious annual collection of folk wisdom, execrable verse, and scientific nonsense.

In addition to the almanac's sorry reputation, a second set of obstacles to its integration into early modern studies concerns accessibility. The first difficulty with access is a straightforward one: almanacs are hard for a modern reader to decipher. When seen in an exhibition or rare book repository, it is easy to marvel over their tiny size, their rubrication, the intriguing images of Zodiac Man, the horoscope charts, and the calendars that mark the location of the Moon to the degree and minute. But understanding these charts and their utility for their early modern owners demands knowledge of early modern astrological praxis that is not usually taught in graduate school. A second accessibility issue is more complex, a function of the methodology of literary and historical scholarship in the digital age. The vast majority of early printed almanacs are available on Early English Books Online (EEBO), the database that, in making the primary printed material of the early modern period available to scholars worldwide, has transformed and enriched our understanding of early English culture. But as scholars of the digital humanities well know, the structure of such databases influences the nature of the evidence they present. Given the sheer quantity of cultural material available on EEBO, the keyword search has become a standard tool for finding material on a given subject. Yet the annual almanacs do not turn up in keyword searches on EEBO because they are not—not a single one of them—available in fully searchable XML format.[11] One reason for this exclusion is that the books chosen for digitization by the Early English Text Creation Partnership are determined by their inclusion in the New Cambridge Bibliography of English Literature. A product of its time, that bibliography favors works by the learned, the famous, the academic, the notorious, and the literary; almanac compilers, though often well credentialed as physicians or university-trained mathematical practitioners, do not rate in such a hierarchy.[12]

The effect of the exclusion of almanacs from full text in EEBO has been to shade them in a kind of digital invisibility cloak that distorts the almanac's actual place in early modern cultural discourse. A good example of such distortion concerns the printed vernacular debates about astrology that began with William Fulke's *Antiprognosticon* of 1560. Because of its author's stature, Fulke's pamphlet, like every single other vernacular attack on astrology before 1640, is available in searchable full text; anyone conducting a keyword search for astrology or related terms will turn up its devastating denouncement of astrology, partially aimed at the almanac. But it will not turn up any of the important responses to those attacks. For one thing, those mostly occur before the seventeenth century in almanac prefaces or letters to the reader, which are not available in full text. John Chamber's *A Treatise against Judicial Astrologie* (1601) is available in searchable full text, but the massive 555-page response by Sir Christopher Heydon, *A Defence of Judicial Astrologie* (1603), is not. When it comes to popular astrology, then, an accident of database organization means that only one side of the argument is fully represented in the most important resource for tracking its discussion in print culture.

So the structural organization of EEBO—itself the product of the history of intellectual inquiry in the field—skews our understanding of attitudes towards astrology and the role of almanacs in cultural discourse. Because they are not searchable in full text, the only way to know what is in early modern almanacs is to read them. This introduces two more accessibility problems. First, early modern almanacs are rubricated. But cheap red ink fades, and it was apparently often not dark enough to register on the microfilms of early printed books that later became the basis for EEBO. As a result, almanacs are often simply—literally—illegible when found in that resource. They are fully accessible only in the archives. The final accessibility problem is one of plenty, rather than dearth. There are close to a thousand separate editions of annual almanacs extant from roughly 1540 to 1640; at that point, the numbers become even more absurdly inflated.[13] Despite invaluable guides to this material in Capp's *Astrology* and the still useful earlier bibliography by Eustace Bosanquet, it is difficult to sort through all these almanacs.[14] Scholars specializing in the field recognize that "almanacs as a genre are far too diverse to be summed up in a single

6 *Introduction*

article," yet much of the work on almanacs attempts exactly that.[15] Though the available single chapter overviews of almanacs are scholarly sound, and keep almanacs on the academic radar, such brief treatments cannot hope to suggest the range of the genre.[16] The tendency to generalize about almanacs has obscured the fact that they change over time; an Anthony Askham almanac for 1552, a William Cuningham almanac for 1564, a Gabriel Frende almanac for 1598, and a John Booker almanac for 1640 differ significantly from each other due to changes in the social, religious, technological, scientific, and economic conditions in which they were produced.

Another significant obstacle to the full consideration of almanacs in early modern culture is connected to astrology's larger neglect in early modern historiography and literary studies. In 2001, Anthony Grafton and William R. Newman wrote that "[f]ew historians are willing, even now, to give astrology its due."[17] That issue has in many ways been redressed in the past twenty years. Astrology has indeed been given its due in work by Glyn Parry, Lauren Kassell, Steven Vanden Broeke, Brian Copenhaver, H. Darrell Rutkin, Ann Geneva, and Mark Dawson; by a superb collection edited by Brendan Dooley, *A Companion to Astrology in the Renaissance* (2014); by Robin B. Barnes' *Astrology and Reformation* (2016); and by Grafton's earlier monograph, *Cardano's Cosmos: The Worlds and Works of a Renaissance Astrologer* (2001).[18] In addition to Capp's *Astrology*, Keith Thomas's *Religion and the Decline of Magic* (1979) supplied an expansive, still useful overview of astrology's scope and social significance. Over the years, literary scholars have contributed to the field, mostly by focusing on debates over the art and its representation in English literature, as in the work of Carroll Camden, Johnstone Parr, Don Cameron Allen, and Harry Rusche.[19] But literary scholarship concerning astrology has never been extensive, and it does not always reflect awareness of the different branches of astrology and the art's technical aspects. Unfamiliarity with astrology has led to significant misinterpretations of almanacs, calendars, and astrological references in literary texts. For example, literary scholarship does not always accurately register the distinction between the conjuring, summoning of spirits, and spell-casting of famous Renaissance magi such as Cornelius Agrippa or John Dee, on the one hand, and the relatively straightforward Ptolemaic astrology of the almanac on the other. As Barnes has written, the "ideas and methods" of the latter "were not magical for the simple reason that they were not operational; they sought not to manipulate or control nature, but merely to understand and adapt to it."[20] Admittedly, the line between magic and science was a movable one in the early modern period, drawn differently by practitioners than it was by critics, and the boundary between magic and astrology was especially difficult to fix.[21] The mathematical data thrown up by the practice of "exact astrology" was certainly used by conjurers, and also in alchemy—both operational arts.[22] Yet the astrology of the almanacs had little to do with those more esoteric practices. That failure to discriminate different kinds (and uses) of astrology is reflected in explanatory notes to Shakespeare and other early modern literature that routinely characterize basic Ptolemaic astrology as a subset of magic or medieval "superstition."[23] On the other hand, the claim that almanacs were harmless because they reflected "natural" rather than "judicial" astrology is also misleading. Those terms, though part of early modern polemic concerning the art, do not delineate actual astrological practice; the field is not divided into natural and judicial "branches."[24] The prognostications in almanacs were arrived at through judicial astrology, which involved the judgment of horoscope charts, though compilers were usually careful to avoid reporting on controversial subjects. These and other misconceptions have led to a misunderstandings of the references to popular Ptolemaic astrology that permeate both almanacs and early modern literature.

Astrology, Almanacs, and the Early Modern English Calendar seeks to remove such misconceptions while providing a guide to early modern English calendars that situates them firmly in the early history of printing and popular science. In Part I, four chapters provide resources for understanding early modern texts concerning astrology, calendars, and almanacs. The first chapter, "Astrology," describes the practices of judicial astrology concerning calendars (known as revolutions), the lunar astrological medicine associated with calendars (connected to Zodiac Man), and other non-astrological prognostications that appear frequently in medieval and early modern calendars. The second chapter, "Calendars," provides accounts of the Julian calendar, medieval *compotus* calculations and manuscripts, the late medieval folded medical almanac that was in many ways a precursor to the early modern almanac, and the printed primer calendars of the early sixteenth century that brought calendars to an ever widening market and register the impact of Protestant reform. Miscellaneous calendars such as clog almanacs and xylographic calendars are briefly discussed at the end of this chapter. The third chapter, "Almanacs and Prognostications," covers the history of printed works in these genres in sixteenth- and early seventeenth-century England, focusing especially on the economic and political factors—including the incorporation of the Company of Stationers and Elizabethan and Jacobean regulatory mechanisms—that shaped these printed works. The fourth chapter, "Related Publications and Controversies," describes material useful for contextualizing the astrological almanac in the larger culture of popular scientific belief. This chapter discusses perpetual almanacs and guides to astrology, as well as the most pointed book and pamphlet attacks on almanacs, ending with an overview of Tudor and early Stuart mock almanacs. Part I as a whole is designed as a resource to be consulted with the help of the book's index, to whatever extent is dictated by readers' interests and prior knowledge. Its goal is to provide the vocabulary, cosmological theories, and historical context needed to understand the almanacs, calendars, and astrological practices illustrated in the second and third sections of *Astrology, Almanacs, the Early Modern English Calendar*.

8 Introduction

Part II, "How to Read an Early Modern Almanac," attempts to crack open the annual combined almanac and prognostication for modern readers. All efforts have been made to avoid the standard rhetorical ploy of the mock almanacs: the sonorous pronouncement of the obvious (almanacs have two title pages!). But at the same time, this part of the book takes almanacs seriously as material objects worth careful attention—books that organize vast amounts of material into different (and changing) graphic forms. Making almanacs legible and comprehensible in this way is, it is hoped, a first step for them to be considered in all their typographical, visual, and textual richness, as important works worth considering within the larger history of the book.[25]

The third and final part of *Astrology, Almanacs, the Early Modern English Calendar* is designed as a reference guide to the qualities and cultural associations attached to the various increments of time as these were organized in early modern calendars: the seasons, the days of the week, and the months. Deeply indebted to earlier work on early modern English calendars by Alison Chapman, C.R. Cheney, David Cressy, and Ronald Hutton, this section of the book synthesizes almanacs, prayer books, Thomas Tusser's *Five Hundred Points of Good Husbandry* (a calendrically organized guide to farming), and other popular printed works.[26] The goal here is to reconstruct the annual year as it was visually and textually experienced in the period by merging information concerning astrology, astronomy, agriculture, medicine, and commerce. Its sources are primarily printed books, but also continental engravings which, as Anthony Wells-Cole, Tara Hamling and others have shown, provided templates for domestic decoration, some of it concerning astrology, the seasons, or the labors of the months.[27] There are few surviving examples of calendar imagery from material objects in late medieval or early modern England, but some are gathered here, including images from stained glass windows, misericords, needlepoint, and the Four Seasons tapestries at Hatfield House. The final section of Part III is a series of sample calendars from January to December, given in roughly chronological order, with January taken from a c. 1518 edition of the *Kalender of Shepherds*, and December from a 1640 John Booker almanac.[28] This overview provides readers with a sense of the graphic variations in early modern calendars over time.

Part III of *Astrology, Almanacs, the Early Modern English Calendar*, then, attempts to draw attention to the time reckoning material of the astrological almanac by showing how it articulated a coherent understanding of the annual year. Again, efforts have been made to reduce the ponderous pronouncement of the pedestrian (the weather is miserable in February, and people get colds!). Readers are warned that a love of doggerel (or at least sturdy tolerance) is essential for the study of calendars and almanacs. The primary goal of this section of the book is to provide a resource for scholars seeking the cultural associations—visual, literary, historical, and iconographical—that early moderns might have attached to a particular date, day of the week, month, or time of the year.

All three parts of *Astrology, Almanacs, and the Early Modern English Calendar* register the essentially utilitarian nature of the early modern printed almanac. Almanacs were extraordinarily popular largely because they were so extremely useful. The combination of usefulness and ubiquity put almanacs into a position in their culture that somewhat resembles the twenty-first century smart phone. Almanac owners could use these small pamphlets as devices with which to check the weather, verify holidays, ascertain the day of the week on a given date, self-diagnose medical complaints, gather tips on diet, look up dates in history, plot legal action, plan shopping excursions, find directions, keep track of expenses, and jog their memories about how many pints are in a gallon and gallons in a peck. That utility and ubiquity might have been one source of the widespread derision; as with smart phones, everyone complained about almanacs, everyone understood the fools they made of their owners, yet almost everyone (including the critics) owned one.

It is easy from a modern perspective to understand the usefulness of calendars, which are essentially utilitarian instruments. Astrology, at least the astrology of the almanacs, was equally practical. Yet despite its quotidian uses, the astrology of the almanacs had another advantage: it connected their owners to nature, the larger cosmos, and even (or so its compilers claimed) to the divine. It is possible the humble almanac was, in this way, an empowering artifact. An almanac provided a cheap but effective key to reading the book of nature as it was conceptualized in the Christianized Aristotelianism of late medieval and early modern England.[29] That cosmology posited a connected world, in which a merciful God embedded various clues to help human beings support the precarious life of the mortal body: to avoid treacherous weather, choose the safest times for medical treatment, eat wisely to support mental and physical health, travel safely by land or water, etc. Almanac compilers read the skies in order to interpret the connections between the mutable sublunar world and the immutable supralunar spheres of the stars and planets, and God's intentions as expressed in astral signs. They then translated that information into easily understood guides for daily life. This information gave ordinary people tools with which to interpret nature, which could be used to keep themselves safe (and well-organized). The almanac was humble, but it was also ambitious; its modest subject was, as Capp puts it, "the whole of Creation"[30] In this way, almanacs connected the ordinary workaday world with the cosmos, as well as with the more specific social, economic, philosophical, medical, and religious information contained within its pages.

Astrology, Almanacs, the Early Modern English Calendar invites its readers to reap the benefits of this wealth of information, even if it means becoming—as this book's author certainly has—like Sordido in Ben Jonson's *The Comicall Satyre of Every Man Out of his Humor* (1600), "A Wretched Hobnail'd Chuffe, Whose Recreation, Is Reading of *Almanacks*" (A2r). Jonson may have mocked almanacs, but like Thomas Middleton—who made fun of them onstage in *No Wit No Help Like a Womans* (first published in 1657), and even more extensively in *The Owles Almanac* (1618)—chances are he also owned one. Fundamentally utilitarian in their own time, almanacs can be equally useful for scholars today who seek to understand the mentality of those ordinary (though literate) people in sixteenth- and seventeenth-century England, who purchased early modern astrological almanacs and used their calendars to guide them through the days, weeks, months, and seasons of the early modern annual year.

Notes

1 General work on calendars includes E. G. Richards, *Mapping Time: The Calendar and its History* (Oxford: Oxford University Press, 1998); Gerhard Dohrn-van Rossum, *History of the Hour* (Chicago: Chicago University Press, 1992); David S. Landes, *Revolution in Time: Clocks and the Making of the Modern World* (Cambridge, MA: Harvard University Press, 1983); Arno Boorst, *The Ordering of Time: From the Ancient Computus to the Modern Computer*, trans. Andrew Winnard (Chicago: University of Chicago Press, 1993). On the Jewish calendar see Elisheva Carlebach, *Palaces of Time: Jewish Calendar and Culture in Early Modern Europe* (Cambridge, MA: Harvard University Press, 2011).
2 Faith Wallis, "Medicine in Medieval Calendar Manuscripts," in *Manuscript Sources of Medieval Medicine*, ed. Margaret R. Schleissner (New York: Garland Publishing), 105–143, esp. 109.
3 Indispensable book-length works on early modern English calendars are C.R. Cheney, *Handbook of Dates for Students of English History* (Cambridge: Cambridge University Press, 1995); David Cressy, *Bonfires and Bells: National Memory and the Protestant Calendar in Elizabethan and Jacobean England* (Berkeley: University of California Press, 1989); Ronald Hutton, *The Rise and Fall of Merry England: The Ritual Year 1400–1700* (Oxford: Oxford University Press, 1994); and Ronald Hutton, *The Stations of the Sun* (Oxford: Oxford University Press, 1996). On the impact of the Reformation on the English calendar see especially Alison Chapman, "Now and Then: Sequencing the Sacred in Two Protestant Calendars," *Journal of Medieval and Early Modern Studies* 33, no. 1 (2003): 91–123; Alison A. Chapman, "The Politics of Time in Edmund Spenser's English Calendar," *Studies in English Literature* 42, no. 1 (2002): 1–24.
4 The term "almanac" is used throughout this book as a shorthand to refer to the standard, combined almanac and prognostication that emerged in mid sixteenth century England. A fuller account of the history of the genre, and the relationship between the almanac and prognostication portions of these publications, is provided in Chapter 1.3, "Almanacs," and Part II, "How to Read an Early Modern Almanac," below.
5 Bernard Capp, *Astrology and the Popular Press: English Almanacs, 1500–1800* (Ithaca, NY: Cornell University Press, 1979), 13.
6 Alison Chapman, "Marking Time: Astrology, Almanacs, and English Protestantism," *Renaissance Quarterly* 60, no. 4 (2007): 1257–1290; Katherine Walker, "'Daring to Pry into the Privy Chamber of Heaven': Early Modern Mock-Almanacs and the Virtues of Ignorance," *Studies in Philology* 115, no. 1 (2018): 129–153; Katherine Walker, "Early Modern Almanacs and the Witch of Edmonton," *Early Modern Literary Studies* 18 (2015): 1–25; Adam Smyth, *Autobiography in Early Modern England* (Oxford: Oxford University Press, 2010); Adam Smyth, "Almanacs and Ideas of Popularity," in *The Elizabethan*

Top Ten: Defining Popularity in Early Modern England, eds. Adam Keyson and Emma Smith (London and New York: Routledge, 2013), 125–133; Louise Curth, *English Almanacs, Astrology, and Popular Medicine* (Manchester: Manchester University Press, 2007).
7 Smyth, "Almanacs and Ideas of Popularity," 127. See also Carroll Camden, "Elizabethan Almanacs and Prognostications," *The Library* 12 (1931), 83–108, especially 100–108; Capp, *Astrology*, 231–235.
8 John Marston, *Jacke Drums Entertainment*, in *The Plays of John Marston in Three Volumes, Volume Three*, ed. H. Harvey Wood (Edinburgh: Oliver and Boyd, 1939), 1189.
9 Thomas Bodley, *Letters to Thomas James, Keeper of Bodleian Library* (Oxford: Clarendon Press, 1926), 222.
10 In *A Countercuffe given to Martin Iunior* the author (possibly Thomas Nashe) claims he is writing "a very famous worke, Entitled, THE OWLES ALMANACKE" (London, 1589, A2v) but no such publication in the Marprelate series has survived. The Poor Robin series had it both ways, providing standard calendrical information that made it a usable almanac, while simultaneously making fun of the genre. On the substantive and sustained attacks in works against astrology, see Chapters 4 and 5, below.
11 Some perpetual almanacs are digitized, such as some editions of the *Kalender of Shepherds* and Leonard Digges perpetual almanac, first published as *A Prognostication of Right Good Effect* (1555). Among the annual almanacs, however, only three are listed on EEBO as having full-text availability (all fragments).
12 "About EEBO and the Text Creation Partnership," eebo.chadwyck.com).
13 This very rough number counts the separate editions in Alfred W. Pollard and G.R. Redgrave, *A Short-Title Catalogue of Books Printed in England, Scotland, and Wales* (London: Bibliographical Society, 1976–1991), hereafter cited as Pollard & Redgrave. The count includes only the annual almanacs and prognostications (not multi-year or perpetual almanacs). On that distinction, see Chapman, "Marking Time," 1269–1270, and Chapter 3, "Almanacs," below.
14 Capp, *Astrology*, 347–386; Eustace F. Bosanquet, *English Printed Almanacs and Prognostications: A Bibliographical History to the Year 1600* (London: Chiswick Press, 1917); Bosanquet, "Notes on Further Addenda to English Printed Almanacks and Prognostications to 1600," *The Library*, 4th series, 18 (1937): 39–66.
15 Chapman, "Marking Time," 1259.
16 See, for example, Lauren Kassell, "Almanacs and Prognostications," in *The Oxford History of Popular Print Culture, Volume I, Cheap Print in Britain and Ireland to 1660*, ed. Joad Raymond (Oxford: Oxford University Press, 2011), 431–442; in the same volume, Simon Schaffer, "Science," 308–416; R. C. Simmons, "ABCs, Almanacs, Ballads, Chapbooks, Popular Piety and Textbooks," in *The Cambridge History of the Book in Britain, Volume 3, 1400–1557*, eds. Lotte Hellinga and J.B. Trapp (Cambridge: Cambridge University Press, 2008), 504–513; Mary Erler, "The Laity," in *A Companion to the Early Printed Book in Britain, 1476–1558*, eds. Vincent Gillespie and Susan Powell (Cambridge: D. S. Brewer, 2014), 134–149.
17 Anthony Grafton and William Newman, *Secrets of Nature: Astrology and Alchemy in Early Modern Europe* (Cambridge, MA: MIT Press, 2011), 5. Lynn Thorndike does consider astrology throughout his magisterial eight-volume *A History of Magic & Experimental Science* (New York: MacMillan, 1923–1958).

12 Introduction

18 Glyn Parry, *The Arch-Conjuror of England: John Dee* (New Haven, CT: Yale University Press, 2011); Lauren Kassell, *Medicine and Magic in Elizabethan London: Simon Forman: Astrologer, Alchemist, and Physician* (Oxford: Clarendon Press, 2005); Steven Vanden Broecke, *The Limits of Influence: Pico, Louvaine, and the Crisis of Renaissance Astrology* (Leiden: Brill, 2003); Brian Copenhaver, "Astrology and Magic," in *The Cambridge History of Renaissance Philosophy*, eds. C.B. Schmitt et al. (Cambridge: Cambridge University Press, 1991), 264–300; H. Darrel Rutkin, "Astrology," *The Cambridge History of Science, Volume 3, Early Modern Science*, eds. Katherine Park and Lorraine Daston (Cambridge: Cambridge University Press, 2008), 541–561; Mark Dawson, "Astrology and Human Variation in Early Modern England," *The Historical Journal* 56, no. 1 (2013): 31–53; Brendan Dooley, ed., *A Companion to Astrology in the Renaissance* (Leiden: Brill, 2014); Anthony Grafton, *Cardano's Cosmos: The Worlds and Works of a Renaissance Astrologer* (Cambridge, MA: Harvard University Press, 2000). See also Eugenio Garin, *Astrology in the Renaissance: The Zodiac of Life*, trans. Carolyn Jackson and June Allen (London: Routledge and Kegan Paul, 1983); Robert S. Westman, *The Copernican Question: Prognostication, Skepticism, and Celestial Order* (Berkeley: University of California Press, 2011); and Ann Geneva, *Astrology and the Seventeenth Century Mind: William Lilly and the Language of the Stars* (Manchester: Manchester University Press, 1995). See more recently H. Darrel Rutkin, *Sapientia Astrologica: Astrology, Magic and Natural Knowledge, ca. 1250–1800* (Cham, Switzerland: Springer, 2019).
19 Keith Thomas, *Religion and the Decline of Magic* (New York: Scribner, 1971); Carroll Camden, "Astrology in Shakespeare's Day," *Isis* 19 (1933): 26–73; Camden, "Elizabethan Astrological Medicine," *Annals of Medical History* 2 (1930): 217–226; Don Cameron Allen, *The Star-Crossed Renaissance: The Quarrel about Astrology and its Influence in England* (Durham: Duke University Press, 1941), 147–189; J. C. Eade, *The Forgotten Sky: Astrology in English Literature* (Oxford: Oxford University Press, 1984); Moriz Sondheim, "Shakespeare and the Astrology of his Time," *Journal of the Warburg Institute* 2, no. 3 (1939): 243–259; and Johnstone Parr, *Tamburlaine's Malady and Other Essays on Astrology in Elizabethan Drama* (Tuscaloosa: University of Alabama Press, 1953). See also William Wilson, *Shakespeare and Astrology: From a Student's Point of View* (Boston, MA: Occult Publishing Company, 1903); Parr, "Edmund's Nativity in *King Lear*," *The Shakespeare Association Bulletin* 21 (1946): 181–185; Harry Rusche, "Edmund's Conception and Nativity in King Lear," *Shakespeare Quarterly* 20, no. 2 (1969): 161–164.
20 Robin B. Barnes, *Astrology and Reformation* (Oxford: Oxford University Press), 10.
21 See Brian Copenhaver's useful overview of the issues concerning the differentiation, "Astrology and Magic," *passim*.
22 Parry, *Arch-Conjurer*, 10.
23 For example, Gloucester's repetition of the language of a typical early modern almanac prognostication in *King Lear* has been glossed as evidence of his "superstitious belief in the role of heavenly bodies as augurs of misfortune" (Greenblatt, *Norton Shakespeare*, 2353n), and as evidence that "[e]clipses were represented by superstitious men like Gloucester as auguries of evil," *The Tragedy of King Lear*, ed. Jay Halio (Cambridge: Cambridge University Press, 1992), 116n. On this issue see Phebe Jensen, "Causes in Nature: Popular Astrology in King Lear," *Shakespeare Quarterly* 69, no. 4 (2018): 205–227.
24 On that distinction see H. Darrell Rutkin, "Understanding the History of Astrology (and Magic) Accurately: Methodological Reflections on Terminology and Anachronism," *Philosophical Readings* 7, no. 1 (2015): 42–54; and Chapter 1.1, "Astrology," below.

25 From a large and growing literature considering early modern books as interactional objects see Juliet Fleming, *Graffiti and the Writing Arts of Early Modern England* (Philadelphia: University of Pennsylvania Press, 2001); Jennifer Anderson and Elizabeth Sauer, eds., *Books and Readers in Early Modern England: Material Studies* (Philadelphia: University of Pennsylvania Press, 2002); William H. Sherman, *Used Books: Marking Readers in Renaissance England* (Philadelphia: University of Pennsylvania Press, 2008); Adam Smyth, *Material Texts in Early Modern England* (Cambridge: Cambridge University Press, 2017); and the essays collected in "The Renaissance Collage: Toward a New History of Reading", eds. Juliet Fleming, William H. Sherman, and Adam Smyth, a special edition of the *Journal of Medieval and Early Modern Studies* 45, n. 3 (2015).
26 See above, n. 6.
27 Anthony Wells-Cole, *Art and Decoration in Elizabethan and Jacobean England: The Influence of Continental Prints, 1558–1625* (New Haven: Yale University Press, 1997); Tara Hamling, *Decorating the Godly Household: Religious Art in Post-Reformation Britain* (New Haven: Yale University Press, 2010).
28 Following Martha W. Driver, the title for the *Kalender of Shepherds*—the popular miscellany and perpetual almanac printed with multiple titles and texts from the late fifteenth to the mid-seventeenth centuries—is here and throughout standardized to *Kalender of Shepherds*, and shortened to *Kalender* in parenthetical citations. Driver, "When is a Miscellany Not Miscellaneous? Making Sense of the 'Kalender of Shepherds.' *The Yearbook of English Studies* 33 (2003): 199–214.
29 On the Aristotelian account of the book of nature, the appeal of that cosmology, and its complex displacement with the advent of the new science, see Lawrence Principe, *The Scientific Revolution: A Very Short Introduction* (Oxford: Oxford University Press, 2011), and Mary Thomas Crane, *Losing Touch with Nature: Literature and the New Science in Sixteenth Century England* (Baltimore: Johns Hopkins University Press, 2014).
30 Capp, *Astrology*, 13.

Part I
Backgrounds

1.1 Astrology

The astrology included in sixteenth-century almanacs and prognostications involved two different areas of astrological praxis, both of which derive from the work of the second-century CE mathematician Claudius Ptolemaeus. Ptolemy established the contours of the Ptolemaic universe in the thirteen-volume *Almagest*, and laid out the major principles of astrology in the single-volume *Tetrabiblos* (also known as the *Quadripartitum*).[1] The centrality of Ptolemy's *Tetrabiblos* for the astrology of the early modern almanac reflected a wider movement—joined by Lutheran astrologers and supported by some religious leaders, especially Philip Melanchthon—that sought to clear away from astrological practice elements of medieval and Arabic astrology deemed superstitious. As Ornella Faracovi has written, the sixteenth century saw an effort "to reform astrology by returning to the classical works, de-emphasizing magic, and focusing instead on the physical influences of the stars and planets on living things in the sublunar sphere."[2] Although based on a Ptolemaic model of the universe, this reformed astrology was not in conflict with emerging Copernican theories but, in fact, benefited from them, as the Copernican model of the universe improved the accuracy of astronomical predictions, and, therefore, (theoretically at least) of astrological prognostications.[3]

Ptolemaic astrology—understood as part of natural philosophy and supported rather than threatened by the Copernican revolution—was the basis for the astrology in early modern English calendars, including the printed almanac. The prognostication portions of annual almanacs were the result of one branch of Ptolemaic judicial astrology, known as revolutions. But the material in the almanacs concerning Zodiac Man and elections for physic and husbandry reflected a lunar astrological practice that developed in the middle ages. Though lunar astrology also followed guidelines established in Ptolemy's *Tetrabiblos*, it did not involve casting figures or horoscopes. Other calendrical prognostications that appeared in medieval manuscripts had nothing to do with Ptolemaic astrology. These included (1) the Days of the Month prophecies (sometimes called lunar prognostics or lunaria), (2) the Egyptian Days, (3) brontologies (prognostications by thunder), and (4) Esdras or dominical letter prophecies. All of these prognostications lingered in early modern calendars and perpetual almanacs. Because of their

18 *Backgrounds*

longevity, they should be understood as part of early modern calendar culture, but they must also be distinguished from the astrological prognostications, based on Ptolemy, that retained scholarly credibility through the early modern period.

Ptolemaic judicial astrology

Astronomy, according to Ptolemy in the *Tetrabiblos*, was the study of the movements of the celestial bodies. Astrology was the study of the influence of those movements in the sublunar sphere. Modern readers probably find no particular difficulty in distinguishing between astronomy and astrology, but the terms, though not exactly interchangeable, were not always used precisely to differentiate the two practices in popular use in medieval and early modern England.[4]

Ptolemaic astrology followed the Ptolemaic model of the universe (derived and refined from earlier classical models) and the originally Aristotelian distinction between the supralunar and sublunar spheres.[5] That model can be seen in Figure 1.1.1, from William Blagrave's *The Mathematical Jewel* (1585).

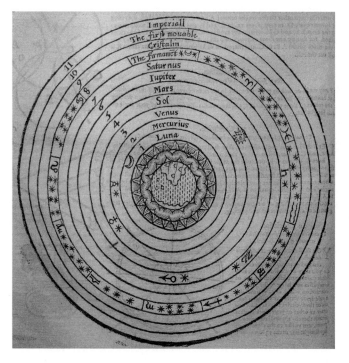

Figure 1.1.1 Ptolemaic Universe, William Blagrave, *The Mathematical Jewel* (1585), 7. Photograph by Phebe Jensen, from the collection of the Folger Shakespeare Library, STC 3119.

Astrology   19

The Earth is at the center of the universe. On it can be seen the heaviest of the four elements, earth, covered with the second heaviest, water. The earth is surrounded by stylized clouds representing air, and the lightest element, fire, is represented by the ring of fire believed to exist just beneath the sphere of the first planet (the Moon). The seven planets are represented in concentric circles, from nearest to farthest from Earth: the Moon, Mercury, Venus, the Sun, Mars, Jupiter, and Saturn. These are both labeled and marked with the traditional planetary symbols (still in use today). The eighth sphere, labeled "the firmament," represents the fixed stars. The symbols here (also still in use) denote the stars that reside in the narrow band against which all seven planets (including the Sun) make their apparent journey around the earth. That path is known as the *ecliptic*; the stars that lie along that path are the twelve constellations of the Zodiac. (We now know this plane is actually the plane of our solar system, since the Moon and all the planets rotate around the Sun on approximately the same plane as the earth.) As in Figure 1.1.2, graphic representations of the universe often cut away the other stars in the firmament, leaving the narrow band of the twelve Zodiac signs so that it appears "in manner of a girdle, or as a garlande of floures" wrapped around the earth (*Kalender*, J8r). In reality,

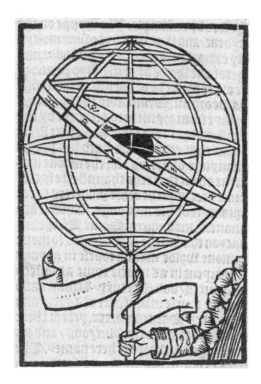

Figure 1.1.2 Armillary Sphere, Anonymous, *The Kalender of Shepeherdes* (1528), P3v. The Huntington Library, San Marino, California, RB 69440.

the twelve constellations are not neatly spaced across this 360-degree girdle, but astrology divides the twelve signs into twelve equal thirty-degree increments that are used to calculate the location of the planets.

According to Aristotle, the supralunar universe—everything above the ring of fire—is eternal and never changing, but everything in the sublunar world is mutable. There, the four elements that comprise all matter are forever commingling and transforming as they are acted upon by the qualities of heat and cold, moistness and dryness. That matter includes the human body, which is made up of the four bodily humors that correspond to these four elements: black bile with the earth, phlegm with water, yellow bile with air, and blood with fire.

Judicial astrology is predicated on the "major premise" of astrology: the belief that the planets and the stars influence the mutable sublunar world.[6] That principle is anchored in the obvious fact that two of the planets, the Sun and the Moon, have discernible effects in the sublunar sphere: the Sun in heating, cooling, the generation of plants, etc. and the Moon on the tides. The deductive reasoning here is that though the influences of the Sun and Moon are more easily perceived, the other planets also exert influences on the sublunar world. That influence—at least in the kind of astrology practiced by sixteenth-century almanac compilers—is physical. More specifically, judicial astrology operates on the assumption that the configuration of the stars at key moments influences matter in the sublunar world, including the physical bodies of human beings. The influence depends on the location of the planets and the Zodiac relative to the Earth and to each other.

The first step in making a prognostication is to create a map of the universe at a particular moment. That map is the horoscope chart. The moment for which a horoscope chart is cast would depend on which of the four general areas the astrological practitioner is working. These areas, as defined by the fourteenth-century scholar Albertus Magnus yet still applicable in the early modern period, include (1) nativities, (2) horary questions, (3) elections, and (4) revolutions. For nativities, horoscopes would be cast for the moments of conception and birth. Nativity charts allowed the astrologer to assess an individual's temperament and complexion, and also to identify future challenges (and the possibility of good fortune) over the course of a life. Nativities were widely cast, disseminated, and studied, but also often resisted on religious grounds. For the second area, interrogatories or horary questions, astrologers would cast a figure for the moment at which a client asked a question. This practice became the stock in trade of the professional astrologer, but it was also the practice subject to the greatest controversy, as it was seen as an Arabic innovation of Ptolemy's principles. In the third area of practice, elections, astrologers would cast a horoscope for timing a particular event or initiating an important action: starting a journey, getting married, or scheduling a coronation, a topic on which Elizabeth I consulted John Dee. These three areas of judicial astrology had little to do with almanacs or calendars, though almanacs did traffic in a different kind of elections associated with lunar astrological medicine.

That leaves the fourth and final area of astrological praxis defined by Magnus: revolutions. This is the area in which almanac compilers operated. With revolutions, astrologers compiled horoscope charts that yielded generalized predictions for humankind. As these were general rather than individual predictions, they escaped some (though not all) of the opprobrium leveled at nativities, interrogatories, and elections. The most important chart in the study of revolutions was the horoscope of the year, taken at the moment of the Sun's entry into the first point of Aries, at the Spring Equinox. That horoscope also was believed to predict, more specifically, the inclinations in the Spring quarter of the year. Almanac compilers often refined their forecasts by also considering horoscopes cast for the start of the other three seasons: the Summer Solstice, the Autumn Equinox, and the Winter Solstice. Another set of charts that would be factored in when assessing revolutions were those cast for relevant eclipses. This analysis followed the guidelines in *Tetrabiblos* concerning when, where, and for how long the effects of an eclipse would be felt, based on the location, duration, and extent of the eclipse.

In order to fully comprehend the information in astrological almanacs, it is useful to understand the methods used by astrologers in creating the horoscope chart—also known as a figure. A horoscope chart is a snapshot of the universe taken at a particular moment in time from a particular vantage point on the earth. Blagrave's diagram (Figure 1.1.1) can help clarify the protocol in erecting figures or casting horoscopes.[7] This diagram apparently presents a snapshot of the Ptolemaic universe at a particular moment (though it may well be an imagined or contrived moment). Imagine that the geographical location of the event being charted is at the very top center of the earth (in the twelve o'clock position). From that perspective, the celestial objects on the Eastern horizon are in the 9:00 position, and the celestial objects on the Eastern horizon at 3:00. The 12:00 position for the diagram as a whole is the zenith in the visible sky; everything in the lower half of the diagram is under the earth.

To cast a figure, the astrologer essentially maps the configuration of the universe at a particular moment, such as we can imagine in Blagrave's diagram, onto a horoscope chart, such as the one on the cover of John Harvey's almanac for 1589 (Figure 1.1.2). That chart provides twelve separate triangles representing thirty degrees each. These are the twelve astrological houses. The houses begin with the first house at the ascendant—the nine o'clock position in the diagram. They then proceed counter-clockwise: the second house begins at 8:00, the third at 7:00, and so on, so that the final house (the twelfth) begins at the ten o'clock position on the diagram. Each of these houses has a traditional signification. The theory of the twelve houses does not appear in Ptolemy's *Tetrabiblos*; it was an innovation of

22   *Backgrounds*

House	Signification
First	Life
Second	Hope (Gain)
Third	Brethren
Fourth	Parents
Fifth	Children
Sixth	Health or Sickness
Seventh	Marriage or Wife
Eighth	Death
Ninth	Religion, or God
Tenth	Heaven (Kingdom)
Eleventh	The Good Spirit (Benefactors)
Twelfth	The Evil Spirit (Prison)

Chart 1.1.1 The Signification of the Astrological Houses. Lambeth Palace Library, London, [ZZ]1589.3.05.

medieval Arabic astronomy, yet one that mostly escaped the purging of Arabic accretions to Ptolemaic astrology (at least until the seventeenth century). Pico della Mirandola and other critics of astrology attacked the astrological houses as arbitrary and fantastical, yet most astrological practice in the sixteenth century depended on them. There were differences of opinion on their signification of the houses, but the general scheme in Chart 1.1.1, taken from Claude Dariot's *A Briefe and Easie Introduction* (1598) with slight variations from Thomas Blundeville's *M. Blundeville His Exercises* (1594), is relatively consistent in vernacular publications in England in the sixteenth century.

To understand how astrologers created a horoscope chart, imagine superimposing the diagram in Chart 1.1.1 (the twelve houses) over Blagrave's diagram of the universe (Figure 1.1.1). A planet is said to be *in* a Zodiac sign when it appears before the fixed stars of that constellation, as seen from the Earth. With that in mind, it is clear that in the chart created by merging these two diagrams, the first house (at nine o'clock) has within it both the Moon, in Leo, and Mercury, in Cancer. Continuing to move (as the houses do) counter-clockwise, it is evident that Venus (in Virgo) is in the second house and Mars (in Scorpio) is in the fourth house. Jupiter is near the boundary of the fifth and sixth houses, and either in Capricorn or Sagittarius; Saturn is in the seventh house, in Aquarius; and the Sun is in the eighth house, in Pisces. Other information not included in Blagrave's diagram of the universe that would be added to a completed chart would indicate (by degrees) where exactly within the houses each sign and planet falls, and also the location of the dragon's head and the dragon's tail—the position in the Zodiac where the Moon crosses the Sun's orbit twice a year.

All that information can be seen in the completed chart for the horoscope of the year in Harvey's 1589 almanac (Figure 1.1.3).

Astrology 23

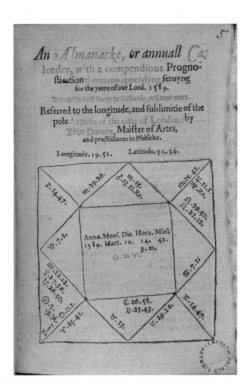

Figure 1.1.3 Spring Equinox Horoscope, John Harvey, *An Almanacke or Annual Calendar* (1589), Title Page. Lambeth Palace Library, London, [ZZ]1589.3.05.

Above the chart, Harvey indicates the place and time for which the chart was calculated: London, latitude 51.34 (north), and longitude 19.51 (west), at 2:41 in the afternoon on March 10th, the moment the Sun entered the first point of Aries that year. (Harvey has, unusually for almanac compilers, used the prime meridian proposed by the renowned fifteenth-century astronomer Regiomontanus, in Budapest.) The chart then maps the location of the twelve Zodiac signs, the seven planets, and the dragon's head and dragon's tail (the spot where the Moon transits the ecliptic) into those twelve houses, using the standard astronomical and astrological symbols. The numbers following the symbols give the more precise indications of their location within the houses. It is not really possible to confirm the location of the planets in the Zodiac with the naked eye; that calculation must be done mathematically or with an ephemerides.

Though casting a horoscope took great mathematical skill and depth of knowledge, the interpretation of the chart was equally if not more demanding. An astrologer would interpret the significance of the dispersal of the stars and the planets into the twelve houses, considering which planets or

Zodiac signs had more power given their relative position in the chart, and also factoring in the planetary aspects. The interpretation would consider the essential qualities of the Zodiac signs and the planets. Each planet was considered to be good or evil, masculine or feminine, hot or cold, moist or dry; the exception is Mercury, whose changeable nature makes him good with good influences, bad with bad influences, masculine or feminine when under the power of masculine or feminine stars and planets, etc. The ultimate source for these qualities is Ptolemy's *Tetrabiblos*, but that information was widely disseminated in scholarly epitomes and encyclopedias and, after the advent of print, vernacular printed guides. The skilled interpreter must assess, synthesize, rank, and take into consideration all the variables by which astral influence is mitigated or empowered. For example, if the evil, hot, dry, masculine planet Mars is in the beneficent, cool, moist sign of Libra, his effects might be softened, whereas they would be enhanced in an evil, hot, dry constellation, such as Scorpio. The significance of that configuration would depend on where in the chart they occurred; if dangerous Mars was in Scorpio in the ninth house—the house of religion or God—it might suggest dire changes in religion or danger to religious figures. In addition, the relative position of the houses vis-à-vis the planets and signs is also important. The most powerful positions in the chart are the first, fourth, seventh, and tenth houses, known as the four Angles (East, the bottom of heaven, West, the middle of heaven). And an astrologer must take into consideration planetary aspects, or angular positions between planets, which can enhance or diminish planetary influence. The aspects considered included conjunctions, where planets were in the same house; opposition, when they were at 180 degrees; sextile, or 60 degrees apart (objects in the first and third houses, for example); square, at 90 degrees (objects three houses apart); and trine, at 120 degrees (four houses apart). All these factors added up to a dizzying number of variables and a huge amount of interpretive play in the system.

Understanding that a horoscope is a schematic, spatial representation of the universe is helpful for grasping both the relationship between calendars and astrology, and also the understanding of what a calendar was in the late medieval and early modern periods. A horoscope chart represents the universe at one particular moment in time. In this sense, it is a specialized kind of calendar, one that registers both the definition of calendar as the record of an event, as well as the idea of a calendar as a system for keeping track of days, months, and years. The kinship between horoscopes and calendars highlights a fundamental difference between modern and pre-modern ways of thinking about time. All calendars are graphic representation of astronomical realities, but because in the modern world we have little use for information regarding the location of the Sun or Moon in the Zodiac or planetary aspects, and because modern calendars include very little astronomical data in the first place, that is easy to forget. But in the early modern period, astronomical information was given in the astrological terms that were useful to everyday life—increasingly so, as astrological literacy flourished in the late sixteenth and early seventeenth centuries. The inclusion of horoscopes in early modern calendars suggests the greater precision, specificity, and quantity of astronomical detail that was considered to be relevant to a calendar in early modern England.

Astrological medicine

The prognostication portions of early modern almanacs were calculated using judicial astrology. But almanacs also reflect less-studied principles of lunar and planetary astrological medicine. Guidelines for these practices appear in hundreds of medieval manuscripts, including encyclopedias, receipt books, and miscellaneous collections with a medical orientation, some in Latin, others in the vernacular. Lunar astrology was part of mainstream medieval medicine, taught in the universities and followed by physicians as well as barber surgeons and other practitioners. It is closely linked with late medieval calendars, especially those in the medieval folded almanacs described in Chapter 1.2; as Hilary Carey notes, "the folded almanacs provide data needed for the practice of lunar astrology without making provision for a full medical astrology that included the consideration of longitudes for planets other than the moon."[8] Lunar astrological medicine eventually migrated into the early modern printed almanacs, where it complemented the prognostications based on horoscopes for revolutions and eclipses.

The central figure for the practice of lunar astrological medicine was Zodiac Man, sometimes called *Homo Signorum*, a diagram that appears throughout the folded medical almanacs as well as in many books of hours and other medieval medical manuscripts (early modern printed examples can be seen in Figure 1.4.1 and Plate 8.1). Zodiac Man detailed one central principle of lunar astrological medicine: that the body of man was a microcosm whose parts corresponded to the macrocosm of the universe. The correspondences were simple. The first Zodiac sign, which the Sun enters at the start of the astrological year, is Aries; Aries rules the head. The rest of the Zodiac band is mapped onto the human body, traveling down from the head in the order of the astronomical year: Taurus rules the neck and throat; Gemini rules the shoulders, arms, and hands; Cancer rules the breast and lungs; and so on down to Pisces, which rules the feet. This image and its correspondences could be "found throughout the Middle Ages, in astronomical, theological, philosophical and medical treatises and encyclopedias"; it "represented the epitome of an exact 'science,' culminating centuries of practice of its peculiar techniques."[9]

The Moon was a particularly powerful planet in lunar medicine for two separate reasons. First, its power over the tides was imagined to also effect the ebbing and flowing of the internal tides of men, including the blood, phlegm, yellow and black bile. As the closest planet to the earth, the Moon also was believed to act as a kind of transmitter for the rays of the more distant stars and planets—a prism that intensified and directed those other planetary rays to the earth.

The principle undergirding the use of the Zodiac Man diagram concerns the first power of the Moon, to influence internal bodily fluids. The idea is that when the Moon is in a sign ruled by a particular part of the body, it exerts an especially powerful tidal (so to speak) pull that must be considered in phlebotomy, purging, administering medicines, and bathing. Zodiac Man was especially important to consider in bloodletting, since blood would infuse the part of the body corresponding to the sign of the Moon's location: bleeding under those circumstances could kill you. A related chart which sometimes appears in the folded medical almanacs and early modern printed almanacs is Vein Man, a diagram which identifies the location of major veins for bleeding and so supports the principles of Zodiac Man (Plate 8.2). Though Zodiac Man was particularly important for bloodletting, it was also used for other elections; treatment with purging, medicine, or bathing for a malady in a particular part of the body might be timed depending on the Moon's location.

In addition to considering the location of the Moon via the principles of Zodiac Man, lunar astrological medicine also dictated the importance of lunar phases. These rules, which appear in the *Tetrobiblios*, are described, for example, in the fourteenth-century calendar compiled by Nicholas of Lynn, in a "Canon for discovering the apt time for letting blood." Citing the pseudo-Ptolemaic *Centiloquium*—a hundred sayings that guided astrological practice in the middle ages and later—these instructions note, for example, that the humors of the human body "go out from the innermost parts to the exterior parts in the first and third phases of the moon."[10] Again, the principle is that it is dangerous to bleed when the blood is flowing too freely—in this case in response not to the Moon's location, but to where the Moon is in its synodic cycle.

In addition to the location of the Moon and its phases, a third set of data that allowed for astrological judgments without horoscopes concerned the planetary hours. The concept that a planet reigns in every hour may have originated in Babylonian astrology. The planetary hours are determined using the unequal hours—not the equal clock hours, which are consistently sixty minutes long throughout the year.[11] The length of the unequal or planetary hours varies depending on the season, since they are found by dividing the hours of daylight and the hours of nighttime on any given day into twelve equal units. The planetary hours are sixty minutes long only twice a year, on the Spring and Autumn Equinoxes. Otherwise, in Summer, the planetary daytime hours are longer than sixty minutes (and nighttime hours shorter), and in Winter, the planetary nighttime hours are longer than sixty minutes (and daytime hours shorter). Calculations were necessary to map the planetary hours into the equal twenty-four hours kept by both the clock and the early modern almanac, as was a very precise understanding of the liminal periods of dawn and twilight.

The way that planets were assigned to reign in each particular hour was straightforward. The first (unequal) hour of the first day (Sunday) was assigned to the Sun. Whichever planet ruled the first hour, also ruled that day, though that power would be enhanced or mitigated by the other planetary rulers over the course of the day. The sequence continued by moving inward (according to the Ptolemaic system) from the Sun, so that the second hour of the first day was ruled by Venus, the third by Mercury, and the fourth by the Moon. The sequence then leapt back out to the farthest planet, Saturn, which ruled the fifth hour, then moved back inward to Jupiter, which ruled the sixth hour, and Mars, which ruled the seventh hour. The Sun ruled the eighth hour, and the cycle began again. By this scheme, the first hour of the second day falls to the Moon, or Monday; of the third day, to Mars (Tuesday or *dies Martis*); of the fourth day, Mercury (Wednesday or *dies Mercredi*); and so on. The names of the days of the week are linked to the tradition of the planetary hours. The principle is that the planets cast their benign or evil influence over the hours or days which they ruled. To assess the benefits and risks, a practitioner would take into consideration the characters of the planets, which were described in a wide range of manuscript and, later, print sources including almanacs and encyclopedias.

The planetary hours provided a way to assess the influence of the planets without knowing their precise location in the Zodiac, and also without casting a horoscope—that is, it required lower mathematical or technical training and information. The planetary hours had many uses, especially in prognosticating the progress of a disease. That could be assessed by considering the planetary hour at the decumbiture, or time of the initial onset of disease, as well as the planetary ruler at various moments in a disease's cycle (periodicity), and especially at the time of most extreme crisis.[12] The planetary hours were also useful for assessing the time for medical interventions. One of the important principles relevant here, which reappears in early modern almanacs, concerns the Galenic four capacities: digestive, retentive, attractive, and expulsive. A good physician would identify which of these capacities needed comforting or support, and time interventions accordingly. Since each planet was associated with one of these capacities, knowing which planet reigned at a particular hour was useful for establishing dietary guidelines and determining when to purge, bleed, bathe, or administer medications.[13]

Data about the location of the Moon and its phases, as well as the planetary hours, could also guide elections other than medical ones. Some of the folded almanacs, described in Chapter 1.3, and many of the later annual almanacs use this information to provide guidance on the best time for other tasks, especially the tasks of husbandry: sowing, reaping, trimming vines, and cutting timber. In later almanacs that information was often used to produce guidance on enterprises that depended on the elements of water or earth, including travel by land and sea. At times, the data was extended to provide guidance on other kinds of elections. It is easy to see that advice concerning the best time to cut one's hair (which appears regularly in almanacs) is an extension of the guidance given for cutting other sublunar material, such as timber. It is perhaps less easy to see, from a modern perspective, how the location of the Moon could be helpful in determining the most auspicious date for one's wedding.

For understanding early modern calendars it is important to note that lunar astrology provided the basis for elections, though these elections were not the same kind that were determined by the casting of horoscopes. In this sense, the astrology of calendars can perhaps be thought of as poor man's astrology, since the information needed to make prognostications was much more accessible than the mathematically precise horoscopes cast by professional astrologers. It is quite possible that when some writers (such as John Calvin) defended natural astrology, they were thinking in particular of the lunar astrology represented by Zodiac Man. That tradition, which outlined propitious times for bloodletting, taking medicine, sowing, reaping, pruning, slaughtering animals, and other activities specifically concerned with sublunar bodies, were attached to calendars in the middle ages, and remained central to printed almanacs in the sixteenth and seventeenth centuries.

Judicial astrology and lunar astrological medicine were both parts of learned tradition. But other prognostications associated with calendars and almanacs that first appear in medieval manuscript sources linger in later almanacs and related publications. The four most commonly seen in early modern calendars are lunar prognostications based on the day of the Moon, the Egyptian Days prognostications, brontologies or predictions based on thunder, and Esdras or dominical letter prophecies.

Lunar prognostications

Lunar prognostications, also called lunaria, flourished in late medieval vernacular manuscripts, including books of secrets.[14] These prognostications are not the same as those based on the Moon's phases or location in the Zodiac, though they often appear in collections with that more properly astrological material. Instead, lunar prognostications make recommendations for elections based solely on the age of the Moon. Though the Moon's cycle is approximately 29.5 days, the advice is always given in 30 day increments. Though the prophecies for each day vary, they are consistently linked to biblical events. A sense of this material as it appeared in the sixteenth century can be seen in *De Cursione Lune*, ascribed to Aristotle and printed by Robert Wyer in 1528, which describes "the course and disposicion of the dayes of the Moone in laten and in Englisshe whiche be good: and whiche be badde" (title page). The material in Latin in this publication provides prognostications based on the mansions of the Moon (its place in the Zodiac). The material in English tracks the origin of "good" and "badde" nature of the days to the Bible: "The fyrst day of the moone Adam / Our forne father in to this world cam / That day is good withouten synne / All thynges for to be gynne." Other days receive their character from their association with Cain, Abel, Noah, Shem, Jacob, Isaac, Mary Magdalene, etc. (A4v). A sixteenth-century prose version of similar material is later published in Godfridus' *Boke of Knowledge of Thynges Unknowen*, discussed in more detail in Chapter 1.4. Later compilers of astrological almanacs have nothing but scorn for such lunar prognostics; Arthur Hopton, for example, attacks Godfridus by name for his lunar prognostications in "a little foolish booke, called the *Booke of Knowledge*" (*Concordancy*, 74). Hopton substitutes a more scholarly prognostication conducted according to the mansions of the Moon, not its age (75–77).

Egyptian days

Another calendar tradition with uncertain roots but great staying power was lore concerning good or evil days anchored to particular dates in the Julian calendar. These were sometimes called the Egyptian Days, to reflect (it seems) the punishment of the Egyptians for their mistreatment of God's chosen people as recounted in the Old Testament. In a medieval poem edited by Linne Mooney, "The Compendium of Astrological Medicine," evil days for bleeding are referred to as "the dismall days" that were recognized "When God chastid Egypcians."[15] These Egyptian or evil days have remarkable longevity, but they are also utterly inconsistent, as Keith Thomas has noted: neither medieval nor early modern sources agree on the specific dates. For example, Hopton confidently provides a list in the *Concordancy of Years*; the evil days of January, for example, are "The 1.2.4.5.10.15.17.19" (71). But these lists are not consistent in early modern printed material. Even if they were consistent, the Egyptian Days would inevitably clash with astrologically calculated good or evil days for particular elections (bleeding, purging, traveling, etc.) based on the ever-changing location of the Moon, its aspects with other planets, and its phases. Yet as their appearance in Hopton's *Concordancy* suggests, the Egyptian Days continue to be invoked well into the seventeenth century.

Brontologies

Another surprisingly long-lived calendrical tradition concerned prognostications based on the occurrences of thunder in the twelve months of the year. This was an ancient practice which David Juste and Howard Chiu have "traced back to cuneiform tables of the neo-Assyrian period (ca. 1000–612 BC)"; it survives in a number of classical and medieval manuscripts in languages including Greek, Latin, Hebrew, Aramaic, and Arabic.[16] An early medieval tract outlining this scheme titled *De Tonitrius* was attributed to the Venerable Bede; it appeared among his works printed in Cologne in 1537 and Basel in 1563.[17] Brontologies also appear in an unusual sixteenth-century English folding almanac, now BL Addl. MS 17367, which includes (among other things) a xylographic calendar with saints, images for the twelve Zodiac signs with basic descriptions of their qualities, circular charts indicating the number of daylight and nighttime hours for each month, and the twelve labors of the month. In Plate 1.1, the November calendar from this manuscript, the left side of the image is a labor for that month (slaughtering livestock, a labor usually associated with December). The image to the right illustrates the text at the top of the page: "If yt thunder In November yt syngnyfyeth In that yere shalbe grete plenty of good corne and gret myrthe Among the peopyll." Brontologies appear in books of secrets, including Godfridus' *Boke of Knowledge,* and in a work attributed to Aristotle, *Here Begynneth the Nature, and Dysposycyon of the Days in the Weke* (1554). Like the Egyptian Day prophecies, the brontologies also persevere: brontologies appear in the *Erra Pater* prognostications of the sixteenth and seventeenth centuries (discussed in more detail in Chapter 1.4), and in Gervase Markham's *The Second Booke of the English Husbandmen* (1614).

Esdras or dominical letter prognostications

A final prognostication tradition involves predictions based on the day of the week on which holidays fall in a particular year. Some of these prognostications were based on the day of Christmas, but later versions were usually based on the day of the week of New Year's Day. Since these can be indicated using the dominical letter—in an "A" year, New Year's Day is a Sunday, in a "B" year, a Monday, etc.—these prognostications are also sometimes called dominical letter prognostications. As Hardin Craig has shown, in the medieval period these are frequently called Esdras prophecies as they are "attributed to the prophet 'Esdras,' or Ezra." Craig has discovered these prophecies in multiple medieval manuscripts in Greek, Latin, Old English, and Middle English.[18]

The Esdras prophecies continue into the sixteenth century in the *Erra Pater* series, but also in other books such as an anonymous perpetual prognostication printed in 1550 and 1585, *The Husbandmans Practice*, and I.A.'s *A Perfyte Prognostication Perpetuall* (c. 1556). Some of this material was later absorbed into seventeenth-century editions of Godfridus' *Boke of Knowledge*. At a higher end, it appears in two of the three manuscript miscellanies compiled and illustrated by Thomas Trevelyon. In the Trevelyon manuscript at University College London, for example, a year on which New Year's Day is a Sunday (an "A" year) presages "good fruet," "stor of honey," "good corne," but also that there will be "great morning," "yongemen shall dye," and there will be "change of prences."[19] These predictions are illustrated in Trevelyon's inimitable way. In the Trevelian Great Book of 1616 at the Wormsley Library, there is a different, also beautifully illustrated, dominical letter prognostication; there, the prediction for an "A" year includes a cold moist Winter, a hot Summer, good "corne" and "fruits," lots of wine, honey, and "garden fruits," but also "Many yong people will dye," "great morning," "Great Warres," and "Newes of kyngs" and "Prelates of the Church."[20]

Notes

1 On Ptolemy's works and their dissemination in the medieval West through Latin translations of Arabic translations of Greek manuscripts, see F.E. Robbins, ed., and translator, *Ptolemy: Tetrabiblos* (Cambridge, MA: Harvard University Press, 1940), vii–xv; Edward Grant, "Cosmology," in *The Cambridge History of Science, Volume 2, Medieval Science*, eds. David C. Lindberg and Michael H. Shank (Cambridge: Cambridge University Press, 2013), 436–455; Edward Grant, *Planets, Stars and Orbs: The Medieval Cosmos, 1200–1687* (Cambridge: Cambridge University Press, 1994); and Stephen C. McCluskey, *Astronomies and Cultures in Early Medieval Europe* (Cambridge: Cambridge University Press, 1998).

2 Ornella Faracovi, "The Return to Ptolemy," in *A Companion to Astrology in the Renaissance*, ed. Brendan Dooley (Leiden: Brill, 2014), 87–98, esp. 96. On the connection between "the reform of astrology" and "Luther's revival of the gospel," see Barnes, *Astrology*, 133. On astrology and the English Reformation, see Phebe Jensen, "Astrology in the Long Reformation: 'Doctor *Faustus* in Swadling Clouts'," *Reformation* 24, no. 2 (2019), 92–106.

3 On Copernicus and the reform of astrology, see Capp, *Astrology*, 192–193; Faracovi, "The Return to Ptolemy," 94–95; Robert S. Westman, "The Melanchthon Circle, Rheticus, and the Wittenberg Interpretation of the Copernican Theory," *Isis* 66, no. 2 (1975): 164–193; Westman, *The Copernican Question*.

4 See this definition in Ptolemy, *Tetrabiblos*, 3–5. As Robbins notes, "in Ptolemy's time the two words ἀστρολογία and ἀστρονομία meant much the same thing, astronomy": Robbins, ed., *Tetrobiblos*, xi. See John D. North's discussion of the relative ease of distinguishing the two in actual practice, "Astrology and Astronomy," in *The Cambridge History of Science, Volume 2*, eds. David C. Lindberg and Michael H. Shank (Cambridge: Cambridge University Press, 2013), 456–484, esp. 458.

5 For a full overview of the state of cosmological learning in the sixteenth century, see Francis R. Johnson, *Astronomical Thought in Renaissance England: A Study of the English Scientific Writings from 1500 to 1645* (Baltimore, MD: The Johns Hopkins Press, 1937).

6 John D. North, "Celestial Influence: The Major Premise of Astrology," in *Astrological Hallucinati: Stars and the End of the World in Luther's Time*, ed. Paolo Zambelli (Berlin: De Gruyter, 1986), 45–100; see also John D. North, "Medieval Concepts of Celestial Influence: A Survey," in *Astrology, Science, and Society: Historical Essays*, ed. Patrick Curry (Woodbridge: Boydell and Brewer, 1987).

7 More technical descriptions of horoscope casting can be found in John D. North, *Horoscopes and History* (London: University of London, 1986), and

32   *Backgrounds*

Giuseppe Bezza, "Representation of the Skies and the Astrological Chart," in *A Companion to Astrology*, Dooley, ed., 59–86.
8 Hilary M. Carey, "Astrological Medicine and the Medieval Folded Almanac," *Social History of Medicine* 16 (2004), 345–363, esp. 352. On astrological medicine, see also Laurel Braswell, "The Moon and Medicine in Chaucer's Time," *Studies in the Age of Chaucer* 8 (1986), 145–156; Cornelius O'Boyle, "Astrology and Medicine in Later Medieval England: The Calendars of John Somer and Nicholas of Lynn," *Sudhoffs Archiv* 89, no. 1 (2005), 1–22. On its later practice, see Alan Chapman, "Astrological Medicine," in *Health, Medicine, and Mortality in the Sixteenth Century*, ed. Charles Webster (Cambridge: Cambridge University Press, 1979), 275–300.
9 Harry Bober, "The Zodiacal Miniature of the Tres Riches Heures of the Duke of Berry: Its Sources and Meaning," *Journal of the Warburg and Courtauld Institutes* 11 (1948), 1–34, esp. 3.
10 John Eisner, ed., *The Kalendarium of Nicholas of Lynn* (Athens: The University of Georgia Press, 1979), 206. The *Centriloquum* is almost certainly not by Ptolemy, but it was widely attributed to him into the seventeenth century. On Cardano's close reading of Ptolemy's *Tetrabiblos* and his conclusion that the *Centriloquium* "was a later forgery" (137), see Grafton, *Cardano's Cosmos*, 134–144.
11 For the medieval history of the equal and unequal hours, see Jacques Le Goff, *Time, Work and Culture in the Middle Ages*, trans. Arthur Goldhammer (Chicago: University of Chicago Press, 1980), 29–42; Dohrn-van Rossum, *History of the Hour*, 29–118; and Richards, *Mapping Time*, 44–46.
12 On the doctrine of critical days, whereby the progress of the illness was studied in relationship to changing astrological aspects, see Chapman, "Astrological Medicine," 287–289; O'Boyle, "Astrology," 12; Nancy G. Siraisi, *Medieval & Early Renaissance Medicine: An Introduction to Knowledge and Practice* (Chicago: University of Chicago Press, 1990), 135; and Pearl Kibre, "'Astronomia' or 'Astrologia' Ypocratis," in Kibre, *Studies in Medieval Science, Alchemy, Astrology, Mathematics, and Medicine* (Trowbridge, Wilshire: The Hambledon Press, 1984), 133–156.
13 Eisner, ed., *Kalendarium*, Canon 12, "Canon for giving and receiving medicine," 208–222.
14 On lunaries, see Irma Taavitsainen, *Middle English Lunaries: A Study of the Genre* (Helsinki: Memoires de la Societe Neophilologique de Helsink, 1988); and Laurel Braswell Means, *Medieval Lunar Astrology: A Collection of Representative Middle English Texts* (Lewiston, NY: Edwin Mellen Press, 1993).
15 Linne R. Mooney, "A Middle English Verse Compendium of Astrological Medicine," *Medical History* 28, no. 4 (1984): 406–419, esp. 415, line 128. These dates appear to be Egyptian dates in that they are anchored in the calendar; they are unusual in referring only to bloodletting.
16 David Juste and Hilbert Chiu, "The 'De Tonitruis' Attributed to Bede: An Early Medieval Treatise on Divination by Thunder Translated from Irish," *Traditio* 68 (2013), 97–124, esp. 105.
17 Ibid., 97. Juste and Chiu track extant versions of this text, establishing that it was translated from the Irish, and providing both a Latin edition and an English translation.
18 John Metham, *The Works of John Metham*, ed. Hardin Craig (London: Kegan Paul, Trench, Trubner, & Co., for The Early English Text Society, 1916), xxxii–xxxvii.
19 MS Ogden 24. I am grateful to Heather Wolfe for sharing photographs of this manuscript. See Heather Wolfe, "A Third Manuscript by Thomas Trevelyon/

Trevilian," *The Collation: Research and Exploration at the Folger* (December 7, 2012, https://collation.folger.edu/2012/12/a-third-manuscript-by-thomas-trevelyontrevelian/).

20 On Trevelyon, see Heather Wolfe, ed., *The Trevelyon Miscellany: A Facsimile Edition of Folger Shakespeare Library MS V.b.232* (Washington, DC: Folger Shakespeare Library, 2007). Nicholas Barker, ed., *The Great Book of Thomas Trevilian* (London: The Roxburghe Club, 2000), reproduces in facsimile some of the dominical letter prognostications (Plates XVII, XVIII, and XXIII).

1.2 Calendars

The Julian calendar

The calendar that provided the basis for medieval and early modern calendars was the Julian calendar, established by decree by Julius Caesar in 44 BCE and subsequently adapted to suit the religious needs of the church in the first centuries of the Christian era. Though many of the details of the pre-Julian calendar have been lost to history, it is known that the previous Roman calendars were lunar calendars, structured (like Jewish and early Islamic calendars) around twelve months that marked twelve lunations (complete cycles of the Moon). The basic problem concerning all calendar makers interested in tracking the cycles of both the Sun and the Moon is that the two are fundamentally incommensurate. The Moon takes approximately 29.53 days to circle the earth; the original Roman months were originally either 29 or 30 days long. A twelve-month lunar calendar, then, is approximately 354 days—eleven days short of the 365.25 days of the solar year. In a lunar calendar, there is no easy way to keep track of the dates of such important solar events as the solstices and equinoxes, and the seasons they mark. Unanchored in a lunar calendar, without correction these migrate back eleven or twelve days every year. To solve this problem, the pre-Julian Roman lunar calendar—as in its Jewish counterpart—added a month every few years to keep the solstices, equinoxes, and seasons in the same place relative to the seasons.

The Julian calendar replaced the earlier Roman lunar calendars with a solar calendar. To account for the fact that the Sun's (apparent) orbit is not a whole number, but 365.25 days, this new calendar added an extra or intercalary day to February every fourth year, with the goal of keeping the calendar in line with astronomical fact, and keeping the Spring Equinox on the day decreed by Caesar, March 25th. But the actual length of a sidereal year—the length of time it takes for the earth to return to an original point in its orbit—is not 365.25, but closer to 365.256 days (with additional fluctuations). That fractional difference was more than enough to throw the Julian calendar off over the centuries, so that by the early sixteenth century, the Spring equinox had moved backwards to March 11th. This discrepancy was corrected by the Gregorian Reforms of 1582, described below.

The Julian calendar did not track the lunations or cycles of the Moon. But the twelve original Roman months, established for exactly that purpose, were retained by being partially adapted for the new solar calendar. The reason for this retention was apparently a desire to keep intact the festival year that marked holidays by their position in the month-by-month calendar. To turn the lunar twelve-month calendar into a solar one, eleven days were added to the twelve months. This raised the number of days in a year from 354 (twelve lunar cycles) to 365 (the approximate length of a solar year). Exactly where those dates were added depended on particular festival days. February, which had been originally twenty-nine days, lost a day, making it a twenty-eight day month, though it would regain its lost day every four years in leap years. Other months gained one or two days. In this way, the basic form of the calendar that the medieval, early modern, and modern worlds were to inherit was formed: eleven months with thirty or thirty-one days, and February with twenty-eight days—twenty-nine in leap years. The months that define our calendar, then, are vestigial: they once marked the cycles of the Moon, but ceased to perform that function in 44 BC, and were retained for social (rather than astronomical) reasons.[1]

The Julian calendar did not number the days of the month, but rather, kept track of them with a system of three named days: *kalends*, *ides*, and *nones*. This comprised the dominant form of counting the days throughout the middle age, and this system continues to appear in printed prayer books, calendars, and almanacs into the sixteenth century.[2] In this way, the Julian calendar retained a system of labeling days of the month that originally tracked the phases of the Moon. The *kalends*, or first day of a month, had marked the date of a new Moon. *Ides*, which fell on either the thirteenth or fifteenth day of the month (depending on the length of the lunar cycle that month), had marked the full Moon. *Nones* was nine days before *ides*. (To us, *nones* appears to be eight days before *ides*, but the Romans counted inclusively.) In the new Julian solar calendar, the placement of those three named days was determined not by the phase of the Moon, but by the length of each month. In the months of March, May, July, and October, *ides* falls on the fifteenth and *nones* on the 7th. In January, April, June, August, September, November, and December, *ides* falls on the thirteenth and *nones* on the 5th. All the other days in the Roman calendar were identified by their position relative to one of those four named dates, counting backwards. For example, for the month of January, the first day of the month is *kalends*, the second day *IV nones*, and the third day *III nones*. Since the day just before a named date was always called *pridie*, the fourth of January was *pridie nones*. The fifth of the month was *nones* itself, and the sixth, *VIII Ides*, with that series continuing to *pridie ides* on the 12th, and *ides* itself on the thirteenth. The dates for the days between *ides* and the next *kalends* were given the name of the next month; these varied, depending on the number of days in the month. So in January, the day after *ides* is *XIX kalends February*; in April, June, September, and November, the day after *ides* is *XVIII kalends*, and in February, the day after *ides* is *XVI kalends*. In longer months, the day after ides was *XVII ides*. In the intercalated or leap years, *VI kalends March*—what we would identify as February 23rd—was repeated to add the extra day. It is for this reason that later calendars and early modern almanacs refer to leap years as the bissextile: *VI kalends* occurs twice.

One final, substantive change to the Western calendar that appeared around the time of Constantine was the insertion of the seven days of the week to the 365-day year. That innovation had no connection to astronomical information of any kind, but rather reflected the establishment of Christianity as the official religion of the Roman Empire. The details of the earlier origins of the seven-day week are unclear, but the system appears to have arisen from the merging of the Jewish calendar and traditions of Babylonian astronomy. In the Jewish calendar, the seven-day week reflected the seven-day creation described in Genesis; it was for this reason ready for adoption in the West with the advance of Christianity. The traditional names for the weeks, however, came from the Babylonians, who may have devised a seven-day week to honor the seven planets. The names of the days in the Roman world reflected this attachment: *dies Solis, dies Lunae, dies Martis, dies Mercurii, dies Jovis, dies Veneri, dies Saturni*. By the time the names of the days of the week begin to appear in Anglo-Saxon texts, they had undergone changes that reflect their translation into Germanic culture. Four of the Latin planetary names were switched out in favor of Norse deities: Tiw for Mars (Tuesday), Woden for Mercury (Wednesday), Thor for Jupiter (Thursday), and Freya or Frigg for Venus (Friday). With the insertion of the seven-day week in the 365-day solar year and the translation of some of the Greek gods into their Germanic counterparts, the basic English calendar was complete.

The *compotus*

The central issue in calendar construction for medieval Christianity was the need to reconcile solar and lunar cycles in order to determine the correct date for the celebration of the most important Christian feast of the year, Easter. That date of course also determined many other holy days in the season from January to June—from Septuagesima Sunday (the ninth Sunday before Easter) through Trinity Sunday (the Sunday after Pentecost). It can be difficult for a modern reader to grasp the urgency, intensity, and indeed passion that existed over the correct computation of Easter. These calculations generated heated theological disputes. As a side effect, they initiated clerics, students, and academics into the mathematical and astronomical mysteries of God's created universe.[3] The *compotus* was a practice that served a real need—determining the date of Easter—but also became a vehicle for religious worship, education, and discovery. Its problems had been all but solved by the sixteenth century, but the *compotus* continued to be practiced; it remained in the University curriculum at Oxford and Cambridge, and at least one manual to its protocols was printed in England in the early sixteenth century, the anonymous *Compotus Manualis ad usum Oxoniensium* (Oxford, 1519).

Easter is a movable feast because it attempts to fix in a solar calendar events that were recorded in a lunar calendar. The Last Supper was the feast of the first night of Passover, which begins on the fifteenth day of the Jewish month of Nisan. In the Jewish calendar, the first day of each month marks a new Moon; Nisan was (and is) the first month in a new solar year, measured from the Spring Equinox. Early Patristic writers believed, not quite accurately, that Passover was always held on the first full Moon after the Spring Equinox. The first two parameters for determining the date of Easter are that it must occur after the Spring Equinox, but also after the first full Moon of the new solar year, called the Paschal Moon. The third parameter—contested by some early *compotists*, but soon adopted as orthodoxy by the Roman Church—was that Easter must fall on a Sunday, as this was conventionally thought to be the day of Christ's resurrection, and was also the Sabbath.

Faith Wallis's work on the *compotus* provides a lucid and accessible analysis of the many mathematical problems and theological controversies that shaped *compotus* calculations, as well as a succinct definition of the *compotus* as "[t]he science of calculating time and the art of constructing calendars."[4] Though the more arcane aspects of *compotus* calculations are beyond the scope of the present study, that history did introduce some key terms that appear in early modern calendars. Many solutions were proposed to the central problems in *compotus* calculations: reconciling the essentially incommensurate lunar and solar calendars, and then factoring in the day of the week to correctly place Easter on a Sunday. The most influential was the nineteen-year Metonic cycle, credited in modern times to the fifth century BCE Greek astronomer Meton. This was the discovery that every nineteen years the solar and lunar calendars reconcile, at least within a few minutes; that is, every nineteen years, the 29.53-day lunations of a 365.24 solar year fall on the same solar calendar day, as long as some minor corrections are implemented. So, if the Moon is new on January 2, 1500, it will next be new on January 2, 1519. The dates of full and new Moons will correspond all year in the years that are nineteen years apart, such as 1500 and 1519. To keep track of the date of lunations, each year in the Metonic cycle is assigned a golden number from one to nineteen. With that number, which was included in almost all medieval Latin prayer books, English primers, and in the Book of Common Prayer, it is theoretically possible at a glance to find not only the date of the Paschal Moon that determines Easter, but the phase of the Moon for any date of any given year. In actual fact, as a result of inevitable mathematical inaccuracies that magnified over the centuries, the Metonic cycle had fallen behind the date of the golden number by the early fifteenth century, though not in any easily predictable way. This meant that one of the purposes of a fifteenth-century calendar was to reconcile the actual phases of the Moon with the golden numbers in perpetual almanacs.

The Metonic cycle and the golden number are no help in factoring in the third parameter in *compotus* calculations, the day of the week, which must be done in order to ensure that Easter falls on a Sunday. To do this, compotists used a twenty-eight year cycle that reconciled the day of the week to the solar calendar. This was called (somewhat counter-intuitively, given it has little to do with the Sun), the "circle of the Sun". The circle of the Sun is simply derived by multiplying seven (the number of the days of the week) with four (the number of years in the leap-year cycle). Some *compotus* manuscripts produced 532-year tables, which multiply the Metonic cycle (nineteen), with the circle of the Sun (twenty-eight). The 532-year cycle was not accurate, however. Time revealed that the most accurate and useful of all the proposed cycles was in fact the nineteen-year Metonic cycle, with regular corrections.

Other, even more complex formulae, terms, and mnemonic practices were generated by the calculation of the *compotus*. Most were obsolete by the sixteenth century. One that survived in University curricula was the practice of calculating time on one's hands and fingers, called the *manualis compotus*. One of the many ways the fingers and hands could be used to keep track of the cycles necessary to compute the time of Easter involved counting both the digits of the hand and the tips.[5] The number arrived at in this way is nineteen—the number of the Metonic cycle and the golden number. Those practices, which necessitated both a mastery of Latin and initiation into especially arcane computational mysteries, rarely appeared in vernacular publications, and did not make the transition to the printed almanac.

Another way in which *compotus* calculations are important for the later history of the calendar is that they helped shape calendars as capacious miscellanies including various tables, documents, and ancillary material. The *compotus* calculations described above are preserved in *compotus* manuscripts centered around the two central tables involved in their calculations—the Julian tables (the twelve Julian calendar months) and the Paschal table. The Julian tables became the basis for later month-by-month calendars; the Paschal tables were the basis for the multi-year charts, usually named almanacs, that provided the dates for Easter and other movable feasts for a range of dates. As Wallis has shown, these two tables "attracted into their respective orbits other materials not strictly calendrical in nature, but associated with the calendar by analogy, or for paedagogical reasons." The Paschal table in *compotus* manuscripts "tended to travel with a baggage of apologetic texts that defended its accuracy and orthodoxy, as well as supplementary materials such as notes on astronomy and mathematics."[6]

Other material that often appeared in calendar manuscripts included calendar poetry, medical advice on diet and hygiene, lunar prognostics that provided medical and meteorological prognostications based on the age of the Moon, and lists of good and evil days known as the Egyptian Days—all elements that would linger into later centuries.[7] These manuscripts established a somewhat fluid yet also enduring sense of what a calendar was: an anthology of related tables, treatises, and poems, comprising not only religious and astronomical material but also medical, meteorological, and horticultural advice and prognostications.

Late medieval calendars and the folded almanac

Medieval calendars in the *compotus* manuscripts of the early middle ages included basic astronomical information concerning the cycles of the Sun and the Moon. The next important development in the Western calendar began in the wake of the European encounter with Islam in the tenth and eleventh centuries, when knowledge of Greek, Roman, and Arabic astronomy began to enter the learned Latin tradition. Those developments introduced astronomy and astrology to the West over several centuries. In this sense, the story of calendars in the Latin West is one part of the larger history of the transformation of science in the high middle ages.[8]

The adoption of this rich and scientifically rigorous discourse into Western Europe was initiated, in part, by the translation of key Arabic texts and Arabic translations of Greek texts into Latin. These included Ptolemy's *Almagest* and *Tetrabiblos*. Calendars in later medieval England took new shapes partly because of the spread of astrological literacy that accompanied—that was indeed inextricable from—the increase of knowledge concerning classical, Ptolemaic, and Arabic astronomy in the West. By the middle of the fourteenth century, astrology had become "a standard part of the curriculum of most European universities" with particularly renowned programs in Italian and Spanish Universities.[9] In England, key figures in this history include Robert Grosseteste (c. 1175–1253) and Roger Bacon (c. 1219–c. 1292) in the thirteenth century, and Richard of Wallingford (1292–1336) in the fourteenth, who produced *compotus* calendars with astrological information for English latitudes.[10] These and other later calendars mingled religious, medical, astronomical, and astrological information.

An important moment in the history of the calendar occurred in the fourteenth century, when a calendar calculated by Walter Odington for the years 1282–1367 was about to expire.[11] In the 1380s, two English Friars associated with Oxford—the Carmelite Nicholas of Lynn (fl. 1386) and the Franciscan John Somer (fl. 1386)—wrote separate calendars for England for the four Metonic cycles that covered the years from 1386 to 1462.[12] The *kalendaria* of John Somer and Nicholas of Lynn marked, as Linne Mooney has noted, "the beginning of the calendar boom…in manuscript," and they also provided a model followed by many English calendars into the sixteenth century.[13] These calendars were on the one hand aimed for users with high status and educational achievement: clerics, physicians, and the educated elite. The calendars' patrons were educated lay royalty: Joan, Princess of Wales, commissioned Somer's calendar, and John of Gaunt was the patron for the calendar of Nicholas of Lynn.[14] It was perhaps the royal encouragement of astrology, and its association with glamorous court culture, that spurred increased interest among the aristocracy and "literate middle classes" in calendars and astrology.[15]

The Somer and Lynn *kalendaria* survive in various manuscripts, but it is their frequent appearance in one particular format that is of the greatest interest for the later history of the almanac: the folding medical almanacs that first appear in the late fourteenth century. J. Gumbert's catalog of these artifacts lists sixty-six survivals; almost half of these (twenty-nine) were created for England.[16] These books have been variously named girdle books, "physician's *vade mecum*," "physician's folding almanacs," and "bat books," the latter Gumbert's whimsical nod to the way they unfold, like bat wings.[17] Hilary Carey's more neutral and descriptive term, folded almanacs, distinguishes these manuscripts from other girdle books and registers the probability that they were used by a range of professionals and medical practitioners, not only physicians.[18] Like later almanacs and writing tables, these calendars are designed for portability. Not only do they fold ingeniously to a pleasingly small size, but many surviving examples include leather cases and loops for attaching to belts; Bodleian Ms. Ashmole 6 is a representative example.[19] The densely written, intricately folded pages of these almanacs include a wealth of information designed to support medical, astrological, and religious needs. Most importantly for the later history of the calendar, as Carey has written, "The folded almanac can be seen as the progenitor of all later compact-form diaries, calendars, and electronic organizers."[20]

Calendars in print: pre-Reformation primers

Compotus manuscripts, medical calendar anthologies, and folding medical almanacs were all important repositories for calendars in the medieval period. Another category of manuscripts in which elite members of the laity would have most often encountered calendars were books of hours, also known in England as primers. In the late middle ages, even lower end manuscript primers were accessible only to the most privileged. But the advent of print soon made the printed primer the most popular printed book in England, as Eamon Duffy has shown.[21] In the early decades of the sixteenth century, the calendar began its transformation from an elite document accessible (and probably legible) to the few, to a practical guide available to the many. The main vehicle for this evolution, as Anne Lawrence-Mathers has argued, was the calendars in printed primers, which can be seen as the "missing link" between elite late medieval calendar traditions and the calendars in the popular printed almanac of the sixteenth and seventeenth centuries.[22]

As Duffy has shown, the mass production of primers in the early sixteenth century "made possible inexpensive Books of Hours which were incomparably more sophisticated than all but the most lavish manuscript books."[23] That sophistication extended to the calendars, which included a wealth of astrological, astronomical, and medical information, coupled with visual images and poetry linked specifically to calendars. These calendars were often illustrated and rubricated, as had been the case in the late medieval manuscript books of hours they mimicked. The calendars in primers were especially accessible because they were often in the vernacular, unlike the main content of these prayer books, which were almost entirely in Latin before the 1530s.[24]

The standard material included in printed primer calendars can be seen in an example from the high end of the market: the December calendar from a 1520 primer made for English consumers by Simon Vostre of Paris (Figure 1.2.1).

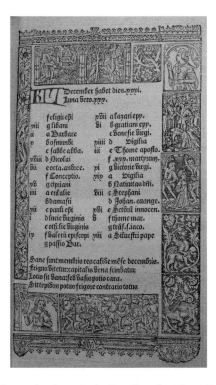

Figure 1.2.1 December calendar, Catholic Church, *Hore Beate Virginis Marie* (Paris, 1520, STC 15926), A7v-A8r. Photograph by Phebe Jensen, from the collection of the Folger Shakespeare Library, STC 15926.

42 *Backgrounds*

Like all prayer book calendars, this is a perpetual calendar. It includes two keys that enable it to be useful in any given year. The first of these is the golden number, which theoretically identified the phase of the Moon each day (though as discussed above, in actual practice those numbers were no longer accurate by the fifteenth century). The second is the dominical letter, which can be used to identify the day of the week in each year. At the bottom of the calendar is a traditional Latin calendar poem with health and diet advice for the month. Other calendar poetry often found in primers includes mnemonics for remembering the saints in a particular month, as well as a popular longer calendar poem, "The dayes of the weke moralized."[25] Of course the main information in this calendar is the full list—not a single day is left blank—of saints recognized in England. Like all lists of saints, this list was not stable, but there is relative consistency in the primers produced for the English market before the Reformation.

The beautiful engravings in the margins of this elegant calendar brought the tradition of sumptuously illustrated manuscript illustrations to the printed books of hours, while registering a variety of religious and secular material associated with calendars. At the head is the Zodiac sign for December, Capricorn, along with a traditional labor of the month for December, slaughtering livestock; the man slits a hog's throat, while a woman carries the dish to catch the blood. In other primers, the "many prayers / and goodly pictures in the kalender" sometimes advertised on title pages track the scheme of the twelve ages of man, whereby each month is imagined to represent six years of human life in a series of twelve verses.[26] At the foot of the Vostre calendar is the image of a game with balls—probably a reference to the festive pastimes of the Christmas season. In the right border are two December Saints: St. Barbara (December 4th), shown at the moment of her beheading, and St. Thomas à Becket (December 29th), shown at the moment of his assassination in Canterbury Cathedral. This calendar page, then, includes information from a variety of categories: religious (the lists of saints), astronomical (the golden number and days of the Moon), medical (the dietary poem), astrological (the Zodiac sign), secular (the labor of the month), and festive (pastimes for December). The twelve-month calendars (including lists of the Sarum saints) were the most prominent characteristic of the primer perpetual calendars. In addition, most (if not all) primers included an almanac. The word almanac in this context refers to the single table, that is, essentially, the Paschal tables familiar from medieval manuscript calendars. These almanacs listed the movable feasts for multiple years along with the dominical letter and the leap year. Figure 1.2.2 shows an example from a 16° primer printed by Yolande Bonnhomme, widow of Thomas Kerver, in Paris in 1532.

All perpetual calendars need an almanac such as this one for the reader to determine the dates for Easter and its related holidays for a particular year, as well as the day of the week and the phase of the Moon. There is no need for such multi-year charts in annual almanacs, but they do feature in most prayer books that include perpetual calendars, including the later Book of Common Prayer.

In addition to the dates for the Sarum saints and the multi-year almanacs, the primer calendars also often provided more detailed astronomical information or basic guides to lunar astrological medicine.[27] For example, the Bonnehomme almanac in Figure 1.2.2 tells its readers how to adjust the golden number in the face of its inaccuracy: "the newe mone is comynly every moneth in the fyft day before the golden nombre that renneth for the yere" (A8r). The same primer provides almanacs for 1533–1538; these indicate the precise time and location (by degree) within the Zodiac for both the full and new Moons, and the date for relevant eclipses, in a format that will recur later in multi-year almanacs (Figure 1.2.3).

In addition to providing data about the location of the Moon in the Zodiac, many primers included the image that guided the use of that data: Zodiac Man, described in more detail in Chapter 1.1. The example in Plate 1.2, from a Regnault primer of 1530, provides the customary textual reiteration of the diagram: the *"Aspectus duodecim signorum,"* a didactic that appears in many primers including (without the diagram itself) the Bonnhomme primer in Figure 1.2.2. The version of Zodiac Man in Plate 1.2 includes additional information that assigns the major organs to the seven planets as explained in the text: Saturn rules the spleen, Jupiter the liver, etc. Other diagrams in early printed primers show Zodiac or Planetary Man surrounded by personified figures for the four temperaments: the choleric with a lion, the melancholic a pig, the sanguine an ape, and the phlegmatic a lamb.[28]

In conclusion, the primer calendars were clearly serving the market for almanacs and calendars in the first four decades of the sixteenth century by providing a wealth of practical material and (in the poems) calendar lore. Primers served the calendar needs of ordinary English people before that role was fully taken over by other formats, especially the annual book form almanacs and prognostications that developed in the second half of the century.

Calendars in print: prayer book calendars, the Reformation, and the saints

Most English primers up through the 1530s continued to include full lists of saints for almost every day of the year. In English primers, these were the traditional English saints from the Sarum Rite, and that basic (though fluid) roster would later be replicated in the printed almanacs.[29]

There are a few early exceptions, as in a 1508 primer printed by Wynkyn de Worde which deleted some saints and replaced the standard list with a narrative poem that situates each saint in a prayer. Despite such occasional

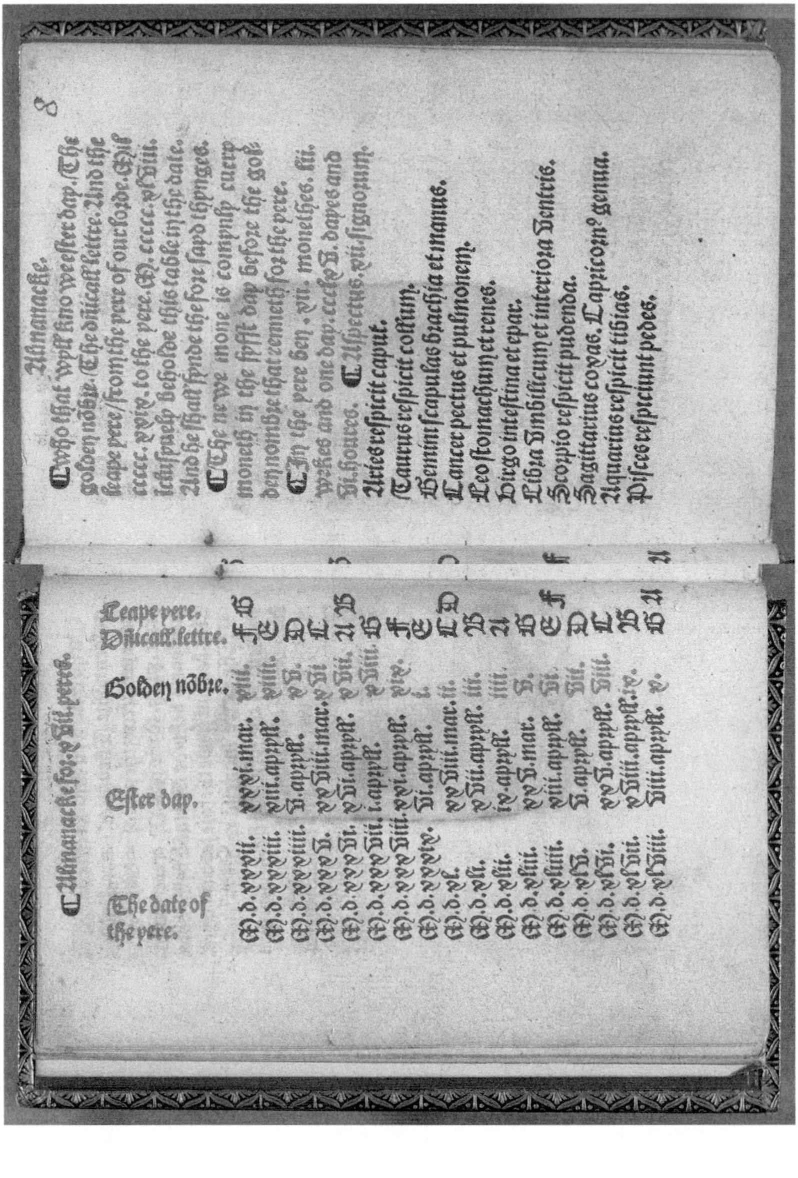

Figure 1.2.2 Almanac for seventeen years, Catholic Church, *This Prymer of Salysbury Use* (Paris, 1532, STC 15978), A7v-A8r. The Huntington Library, San Marino, California, RB 438000:579.

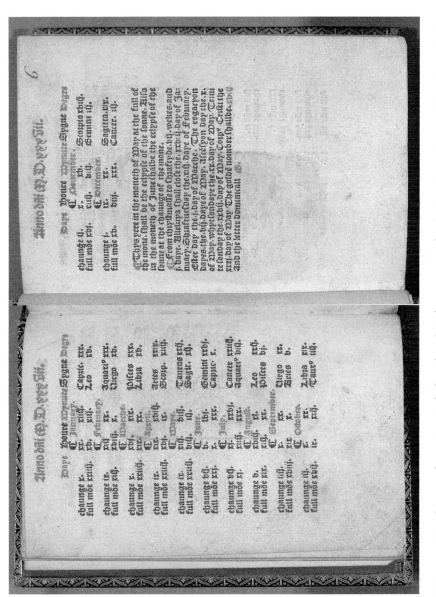

Figure 1.2.3 Almanac for 1537, Catholic Church, *This Prymer of Salysbury Use* (Paris, 1532, STC 15978), A5v–A6r. The Huntington Library, San Marino, California, RB 438000.579.

variations, almost all early printed English primers up until 1545 include the full complement of Sarum saints, though after Henry VIIIth's 1538 proclamation de-sanctifying Saint Thomas à Becket that saint summarily disappeared from primer calendars (and is often crossed out from surviving earlier calendars).

In the 1530s, there were a few intermittent post-Reformation signs of discomfort with the full roster of saints. The first impulse to reform in this vein appears in one of the early "reforming primers," the first of a series of primers printed in London by John Byddell for William Marshall, printed in 1534 (STC 15986).[30] The calendar in this primer omits most of the Sarum saints and includes only those holy days recognized by reformers: those that commemorated incidents in the life of Jesus and the Holy Family (the Circumcision, the Purification, the Nativity, etc.) and the life and death of the twelve apostles and the four evangelists. However, in the next two editions of the Marshall/Byddell primer in 1535 (STC 15988) and 1538 (STC 15998), that more radical Reformist calendar disappears, and the standard Sarum-based list returns. Similarly, in the 1539 primer created by Bishop John Hilsey at the direction of Thomas Cromwell, *The Manual of Prayers* (STC 16009), the traditional calendar has been transformed to reflect the Reformation effort to swerve devotional practices from saints to the Bible. In a "Prolog to the Calender." Hilsey explains that Catholic calendars "had a great number of sayntes wythout profyte to the unlearned"; they have been replaced with "certayne places of the scripture whych the church doth use to reade at Matens, that the reader may knowe what scripture the church do use thorow out the yeare, and to study and use the same" (A2r). This calendar is, in a sense, a compressed and somewhat visually incoherent precursor to the more orderly schedule of readings that will be affixed to the calendars in the Book of Common Prayer beginning in 1549. But whether for ideological or simply practical reasons, this calendar is not reproduced in the 1540 edition of the *Manuall of Prayers* (STC 16017); instead, as was the case with the Marshall/Byddell primer, the full Sarum roster is once again restored, and the more radical calendar deleted. As the subsequent perseverance of the saints in later Tudor and Stuart almanacs suggests, readers expected calendars to include the Sarum saints, which were necessary for a variety of secular purposes, and deemed inoffensive by all but the most passionate reformers.[31]

The saints were at last decisively excised from official and quasi-official English prayer books in a primer first printed by Richard Grafton in May 1545: *The Primer, Set Foorth by the Kynges Maiestie and his Clergie*.[32] The calendar in this work lists the official holy days along with a handful of calendrically useful and/or specifically English saints (St. Hilary, St. Valentine's, St. Edward King and Martyr). Unlike earlier, temporary reforms of the calendar in the 1535 Marshall primer and the first edition of Hilsey's 1539 *Manual of Prayers*, these changes stuck, and all subsequent editions of this particular primer until 1552 included the same, denuded calendar.

The next important development in prayer book perpetual calendars was the publication of the first Book of Common Prayer in 1549. The calendar in the first 1549 version of this prayer book (STC 16267) included only those saints and holy days for which there were appointed special readings and collects in the liturgy. The calendar here (and in subsequent editions) had been reconfigured so that its purpose was to associate each day with the appropriate reading for morning and evening prayer from both the Old and New Testaments. Other Edwardian Books of Common Prayer issued in 1552 (STC 16288) and 1553 (STC 16290.5) added back to the official Church of England calendar a number of Saints now distinguished as appropriate for commemoration—so called black-letter Saints, not represented in the liturgy but noted in the calendar. This list included saints such as St. Hilary, St. Valentine, Saint George, St. John of Beverly, St. Margaret, and St. Mary Magdalene.

The Book of Common Prayer was in a sense a Protestant replacement for the primer, yet as Helen White has argued, there was still a need perceived for Protestant books to guide private devotion.[33] The official Henrician primer first printed by Richard Grafton in 1545, with its minimal calendar, continued to be issued until 1552. The first Edwardian book of private prayer, *A Primmer or Boke of Private Prayer,* was printed several times in 1553 by William Seres, who that year was granted a patent "for the sole printing of Primers containing the Psalter."[34] In the calendars in these prayer books, some Sarum saints of national, legal, or festive significance are restored, though the saints included differ between the editions (see STC 20373 and STC 20374) and they also differ from those in the calendars in the 1552 and 1553 editions of the Book of Common Prayer.[35]

Inevitably, these reformed prayer books and the calendars they contained were outlawed following the accession of Mary Tudor. In 1555 the new regime authorized *An uniforme and Catholyke Prymer in Latin and Englishe* (STC 16060), first printed by John Wayland, "set forth by certayne of the cleargye with the assente of the moste reverende father in god the Lord Cardinall Pole hys grace" (title page). Despite Wayland's patent, other domestic and foreign printers rose to the challenge of resupplying English readers with Catholic prayer books: thirty-five editions of the Sarum primer (and four of the York primer) were produced in the Marian reign, eleven by the Rouen operation of Robert and Florent Valentin, ten by John Wayland or under his assigns, and the rest by enterprising English printers such as Thomas Petyt, Robert Caly, John Kingston, Henry Sutton, John King, and John Day.[36] Of course the calendar was only a small part of the revisions made in these prayer books, but through those primers the full roster of Sarum saints were once again widely reproduced in religious calendars, as well as (as discussed below) in the secular calendars of the almanacs, which by then were growing in popularity and number.

With the death of Mary in 1558, the religious pendulum swung again, and the prayer book calendars followed suit. In 1559, the first editions of the Book of Common Prayer (STC 16291, STC 16292) included the severely curtailed calendar of the 1549 prayer book. Almost immediately, in an edition of the prayer book printed in either 1559 or 1561 (STC 16292a), more saints were added back as black-letter commemorations, as in the Edwardian prayer books. That edition of the Book of Common Prayer (STC 16292a) also clarified the official calendar with a narrative of the days "to be observed for holy dayes, and none other" (A4v). In keeping with Protestant doctrine, the holy days included "al Sundayes in the yere," the Monday and Tuesday in Easter week, the Monday and Tuesday following Whitsun Sunday, and twenty-three additional holy days" (A4v): commemorations for the Circumcision, the Epiphany, the Purification, the Annunciation, the Ascension and Nativity of Christ, Holy Innocents, St. Michael the Archangel, and the twelve apostles and four evangelists. From 1559 on, the official prayer book calendar stabilized with this list of red-letter holy days, as well as the black-letter commemorations listed in the month-by-month calendars (illustrated for each month in Part III).

Yet, the larger roster of Sarum saints never completely left prayer books, even in the Elizabethan reign. They remain in the Latin version of the Book of Common Prayer—the *Liber Precum Publicarum*, first published in 1560 (STC 16424); perhaps they were thought to pose less religious danger to the academic audience for this scholarly version of the official prayer book.[37] The saints were also restored to the Elizabethan versions of the Edwardian prayer books printed by William Seres and later, under his assign, by Thomas Purfoote, such as the 1560 *Primer or Boke of Private Praier Nedeful to be used of All Faythfull Christians* (STC 20375) and the 1570 *A Primer and a Cathechisme* (STC 20377.3). The full Sarum list also appears in many of the Seres' editions of *The Psalter or Psalmes of David* (STC 2384.5) from 1563 onward.[38]

The persistence of the saints in many English prayer book calendars should be considered against a different approach taken in a work that helped shape English Protestant religious culture, John Foxe's *Actes and Monuments*, first published in 1563. As part of its larger agenda to replace Catholic saints with Protestant martyrs, Foxe's work provides a radically revised calendar which includes the official Book of Common Prayer holy day saints—only those with official liturgical commemoration—yet replaces traditional Sarum saints with Protestant martyrs. But as Alison Chapman has argued, Foxe's calendar even more radically challenges the very ideological structure of the commemorative saint calendar. The calendar does this by detaching the newly identified true martyrs from specific days of the month and rearranging the saints within each month, based on the year of martyrdom (Figure 1.2.4).[39]

The calendar in this way profoundly reduces the temporal grounding that allows for the sacralization of certain dates and times. Though not widely repeated, Foxe's radical restructuring of the calendar does resurface in seventeenth century almanacs and calendars, including an almanac compiled by William Beale for 1631 (Figure 3.4.7).

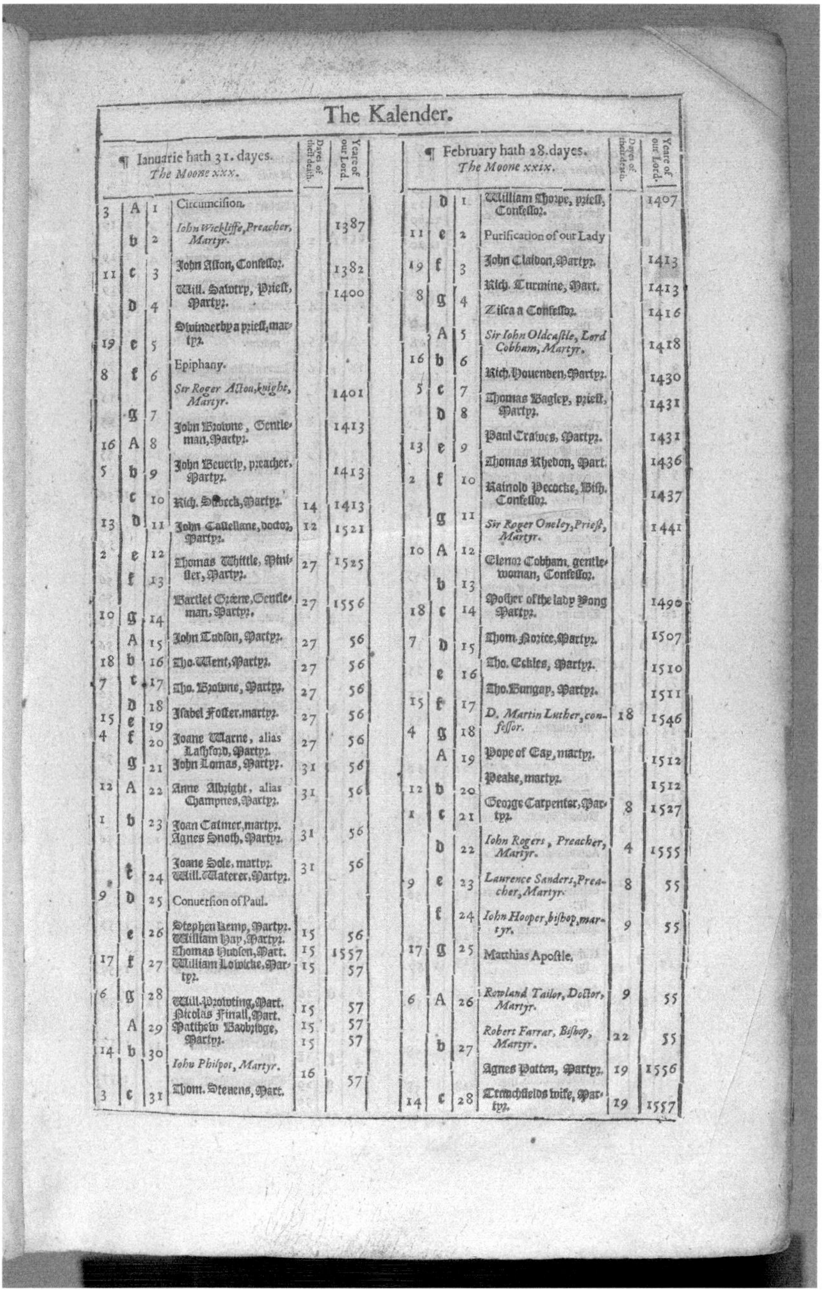

The Kalender.

¶ Ianuarie hath 31. dayes.
The Moone xxx.

				Dayes of their death.	Yeare of our Lord.
3	A	1	Circumcision.		
	b	2	*Iohn Wickliffe, Preacher, Martyr.*		1387
11	c	3	John Aston, Confessor.		1382
	d	4	Will. Sawtry, Priest, Martyr.		1400
19	e	5	Swinderby a priest, martyr.		
8	f	6	Epiphany.		
	g	7	*Sir Roger Acton, knight, Martyr.*		1401
16	A	8	John Browne, Gentleman, Martyr.		1413
5	b	9	John Beuerly, preacher, Martyr.		1413
	c	10	Rich. S[illegible]beck, Martyr.	14	1413
13	d	11	John Castellane, doctor, Martyr.	12	1521
2	e	12	Thomas Whittle, Minister, Martyr.	27	1525
	f	13	Bartlet Greene, Gentleman, Martyr.	27	1556
10	g	14			
	A	15	John Tudson, Martyr.	27	56
18	b	16	Tho. Went, Martyr.	27	56
7	c	17	Tho. Browne, Martyr.	27	56
	d	18	Isabel Foster, martyr.	27	56
15	e	19			
4	f	20	Joane Warne, alias Lashford, Martyr.	27	56
	g	21	John Lomas, Martyr.	31	56
12	A	22	Anne Albright, alias Champnes, Martyr.	31	56
1	b	23	Joan Catmer, martyr. Agnes Snoth, Martyr.	31	56
	c	24	Joane Sole, martyr. Will. Waterer, Martyr.	31	56
9	d	25	Conuersion of Paul.		
	e	26	Stephen Kemp, Martyr. William Hay, Martyr.	15	56
17	f	27	Thomas Hudson, Mart. William Lowicke, Martyr.	15 15	1557 57
6	g	28	Will. Prowting, Mart. Nicolas Finall, Mart.	15 15	57 57
	A	29	Matthew Bradbridge, Martyr.	15	57
14	b	30	*Iohn Philpot, Martyr.*	16	57
3	c	31	Thom. Steuens, Mart.		

¶ February hath 28. dayes.
The Moone xxix.

				Dayes of their death.	Yeare of our Lord.
	d	1	William Thorpe, priest, Confessor.		1407
11	e	2	Purification of our Lady		
19	f	3	John Claidon, Martyr.		1413
8	g	4	Rich. Turmine, Mart. Zisca a Confessor.		1413 1416
	A	5	*Sir Iohn Oldcastle, Lord Cobham, Martyr.*		1418
16	b	6	Rich. Houenden, Martyr.		1430
5	c	7	Thomas Bagley, priest, Martyr.		1431
	d	8			
13	e	9	Paul Crawes, Martyr.		1431
			Thomas Rhedon, Mart.		1436
2	f	10	Rainold Pecocke, Bish. Confessor.		1437
	g	11	*Sir Roger Onely, Priest, Martyr.*		1441
10	A	12	Elenor Cobham, gentlewoman, Confessor.		
	b	13			
18	c	14	Mother of the lady Yong Martyr.		1490
7	d	15	Thom. Norice, Martyr.		1507
	e	16	Tho. Eckles, Martyr. Tho. Bungay, Martyr.		1510 1511
15	f	17	*D. Martin Luther, confessor.*	18	1546
4	g	18			
	A	19	Pope of Cay, martyr.		1512
12	b	20	Peake, martyr.		1512
1	c	21	George Carpenter, Martyr.	8	1527
	d	22	*Iohn Rogers, Preacher, Martyr.*	4	1555
9	e	23	*Laurence Sanders, Preacher, Martyr.*	8	55
	f	24	*Iohn Hooper, bishop, martyr.*	9	55
17	g	25	Matthias Apostle.		
6	A	26	*Rowland Tailor, Doctor, Martyr.*	9	55
	b	27	*Robert Farrar, Bishop, Martyr.* Agnes Potten, Martyr.	22 19	55 1556
14	c	28	Trunchfields wife, Martyr.	19	1557

Figure 1.2.4 January Calendar, John Foxe, *Acts and Monuments of Matters most Speciall and Memorable* (1632), v.1, A2r. The Huntington Library, San Marino, California, RB 2049.

50 Backgrounds

The Gregorian reforms

As noted above, the imprecision of the Julian calendar meant that the date of the Spring Equinox drifted forward from its original date of March 25th. For centuries. natural philosophers had been coping with this discrepancy, which by the sixteenth century meant that the Spring Equinox actually fell around March 11th, with all the other solstices and equinoxes similarly positioned on the tenth, eleventh, or twelfth days of the month (they migrate as the four-year leap year cycle progresses). In the sixteenth century, the Summer Solstice, for example, fell near St. Barnabas' day, June 11th, as commemorated in Edmund Spenser's *Epithalamium*. Astrologers and astronomers had long complained about the discrepancy, but the final impetus for change came from the Church. Since Easter was calculated as the Sunday following the full Moon after the Spring Equinox, the concern was that Easter and all the movable feasts surrounding it were being regularly miscalculated.

The longer story of how the Gregorian reforms were instituted in Rome has been thoroughly told, and Robert Poole has provided a detailed account of how England almost adopted those changes in 1582.[40] The adjustment to the Roman calendar took place in March, 1582, when March 11th became March 22nd in European Catholic countries. In England, the Queen had previously gathered a committee of some of the foremost mathematicians, astronomers, and academics in the country, including John Dee, Thomas Digges, and Henry Savile. Their recommendation that the realm adopt the new Gregorian calendar passed unanimously through various committees, including in Parliament, but Elizabeth's bishops blocked it, primarily because of an ideological unwillingness to approve a Papal decree. A few other Protestant countries were also slow to adopt the new calendar, but none were as slow as England, which switched to the Gregorian calendar only in 1752. That means that throughout the early modern period England used a calendar (the Julian) which was eleven days behind the calendar used by much of Europe (the Gregorian).

This discrepancy offered a commercial opportunity which was quickly seized by almanac compilers. The eleven-day difference meant that Sundays were marked on different dates through any given year. It also meant that there were often two different dates for Easter and all its associated holy days. Given the number of holy days attendant on Easter, the discrepancy was profound, and anyone doing business outside England would need to know both calendars. The earliest surviving English almanac that includes both calendars is a 1587 William Farmer quarto almanac computed for Dublin. This provides a "new Kalender of the Romans" that is "diarily compared" to the English calendar, as is "necessarie for all estates, whosoever that have cause to travel, trade, or traffique into any Nation which hath alreadie receyved this new Kalender" (title page). In 1591, J.D. (probably John Dade) went Farmer one better in his *A triple almanacke for the yeere of our Lorde 1591*, which provided columns for the Julian calendar, the Roman calendar, and a third calendar calculated by J.D. himself (Figure 3.3.6). This third option was, J.D. claimed, "The true and exact" calendar (Alm A2v), calculated after discussions with a "company of divers, as well Worshipfull as Learned men" as a result of "sundry argumentes about the true keeping of Easter" (Prog A2v). (This eccentric third calendar was never adopted.) In later years, once everyone was used to the existence of dual calendars, almanac compilers almost always listed the alternative dominical letters and movable feasts of Easter in the opening portion of almanacs—known as the declaration, or common or vulgar notes—and often quietly included columns in their Julian calendars that tracked these discrepancies.[41]

Clog almanacs and xylographic calendars

In *A Restitution of Decayed Intelligence* (1605), Richard Verstegan provides the earliest surviving reference in England to the medieval practice of keeping track of the time with marks carved into sticks. According to Verstegen, the Saxons

> ...used to engrave upon certaine squared sticks about a foot in length, or shorter or longer as they pleased, the courses of the Moones of the whole yeare whereby they could always certainly tell when the new Moons, full Moons, and changes should happen, as also their festival daies; and such a carved stick they called an Al-mon-aght that is to say, Al-mon heed, to wit, the regard or observation of all the moones, and here hence is derived the name of Almanac.[42]

The credibility of this claim is perhaps undercut by the dubious etymological reasoning: this is an entirely made-up origin for the word "Almanac." Aside from Verstegen, there is one other extant reference to clog almanacs in print in the early modern period, in Robert Plot's 1686 *Natural History of Stafford-shire*, which provides an image of one of these instruments. Given the dearth of evidence, it is difficult to trace the actual origin, extent of use, and provenance of the clog almanacs that survive in England.[43]

As in Verstegen's account, clog almanacs are sometimes thought to represent a popular calendrical form, devised and used by the poor and illiterate. But in fact, the information on most surviving clog almanacs demands relatively high-level knowledge concerning the Metonic cycle, as well as a familiarity with runes and arcane Christian iconography. An example of the complexity of the information can be seen in a clog almanac now at Chetham's Library in Manchester (Plate 2.1). The bottom edge in this image presents a perpetual calendar for April and the first few weeks of May. The dominical letter is indicated by the notches on the edges; the largest notch is for Sundays. The golden number is given in runes. That information is only useful if the almanac's owner has another source from which to determine each year's dominical letter and golden number; the almanac in this sense is not usable without outside information (such as can be found in an almanac). Above the notches for the dominical letters are carved symbols for the fixed saint's days. In April, for example, St. Richard of Chichester is represented by an arrow (for April 3rd), St. George by a spear (April 23rd), and St. Mark by a traditional symbol of a square containing a polyhedron. Moving to the right, the tree represents the first of May (the feast of Philip and Jacob) and the cross the Invention of the Cross on May 3rd. Though this almanac does not demand alphabetical literacy, it does require numeracy, the ability to read runes, and knowledge of esoteric symbols, though perhaps those were not as obscure in their time.[44] It seems possible, though, that the more sophisticated surviving examples of such clog almanacs were not produced by or for the poor and uneducated.

The format of the clog almanacs—linear perpetual calendars with golden numbers and dominical letters, accompanied with images or symbols to indicate holy days—aligns with other similarly organized manuscript and later print calendars, including a unique sixteenth century English xylographic almanac—printed from woodblocks rather than with movable type. This calendar, which survives in five or six copies and fragments, was produced on vellum and hand colored. Though primarily pictorial, there is a modest amount of printed text and numbers in black-letter—the names of saints, dominical letters, and Roman numerals indicating the golden number—and handwritten text in red. Of the three copies of this perpetual calendar in the British Library, two fold into small squares making a compact, portable package (similar to the medieval folded almanacs), and the third is rolled into a scroll.[45] This printed perpetual almanac includes images for the twelve labors of the month next to diagrams indicating the hours of daylight for each month, and crude chronologies indicating the years since key biblical events (creation, expulsion from the garden, the Crucifixion). It also includes a calendar in linear form that provides images for holy days, written labels for some of the saints (either printed in black-letter or written by hand in red ink), the dominical letter, and two columns of golden numbers, one (in black) representing the golden number printed in prayer books, and the other (in red) correcting that number to provide the actual dates for the new Moon in the early sixteenth century.

The exact same format reappears in a later nautical xylographic almanac printed in Normandy in the 1540s, also on vellum, and also hand-colored (Plate 2.2). This almanac belonged to Samuel Pepys, who claimed it had been previously been owned by Sir Francis Drake.[46] The calendars in this almanac mimic the format and content of the earlier printed xylographic calendar. The labors of the month and day and nighttime hours are provided in small symbols by each calendar; in Plate 2.2, for example, the labor of the month for September is a "flail for winnowing" in threshing season, and for October, the symbol is perhaps a mattock (for trimming trees?), or a stick for knocking down acorns to fatten up livestock for slaughter in November (a month represented in this calendar with a knife).[47] A later, equally unusual calendar that echoes this format is a clog almanac with a Reformist bent once owned by Archbishop Laud and now in the History of Science Museum in Oxford (Plate 2.3). In that almanac, each month's information is carved on a thin piece of wood. The number of daylight hours is indicated to the left, followed by a symbol linked to the labor of the month (in this image, grapes for the winemaking of October) and the Zodiac symbol for the month (here Scorpio, the Scorpion). The days of the week are represented by black triangles, with Sundays marked with red diamonds; the phases of the Moon are marked at the full (a red circle), half (red and black circles), and new (black circle). Since the calendar gives the day of the week and the phase of the Moon, it is not a perpetual but an annual calendar; it is in fact the calendar for 1633, the year it was presented to Archbishop Laud. The saints and holy days represented here include St. Francis (October 4th), St. Dennis (October 9th), and St. Luke the Evangelist (October 18th).

It has sometimes been suggested that xylographic calendars represent a transitional form between the clog almanacs of the illiterate and the printed calendars of the literate.[48] As suggested above, clog almanacs themselves were probably not entirely the work of the uneducated, nor did they probably serve the truly illiterate. Further, later printed xylographic calendars, like the elegant earlier examples in medieval manuscripts, were almost certainly not marketed to the poor, given that the survivals are hand-colored calendars printed on vellum. It seems probable that these unusual calendars were actually luxury items—calendrical novelties designed as collectables for the elite.

Notes

1 On the names of the months see Richards, *Mapping Time*, 211–212.
2 This account of the Roman calendar is derived from Richards, *Mapping Time*, 210–219.
3 This account of the *compotus* is derived from Faith Wallis, ed., *The Reckoning of Time, by The Venerable Bede* (Liverpool: University of Liverpool Press, 1999); Wallis, "Medicine," 105–109; McCluskey, *Astronomies and Cultures*, 77–96 and 149–157; and Richards, *Mapping Time*, 354–378.
4 Wallis, "Medicine," 105.
5 Anon, *Compotus Manualis*, A2r-A4v.
6 Wallis, "Medicine," 106–107.
7 Ibid., 112–122. For a fifteenth century example, see Faith Wallis, "Michael of Rhodes and Time Reckoning: Calendar, Almanac, Prognostication," in *The Book of Michael of Rhodes: A Fifteenth Century Maritime Manuscript, Volume 3, Studies*, ed. Pamela Long (Cambridge, MA: MIT Press, 2009), 281–319.
8 On this history see McCluskey, *Astronomies and Cultures*, 188–208; North, "Astronomy and Astrology" and "Medieval Concepts of Celestial Influence";

and Charles Burnett, "The Twelfth-Century Renaissance," in *The Cambridge History of Science, Volume 2*, 365–384.

9 William Eamon, "Astrology and Society," in *A Companion to Astrology*, ed. Dooley, 141–191; Eamon identifies programs at Ferrara, Bologna, Salamanca, Valencia, and Alcala de Henares, 147–148. See also Laura Ackerman Smoller, *History, Prophecy, and the Stars: The Christian Astrology of Pierre d'Ailly* (Princeton, NJ: Princeton University Press, 1994); and Hilary M. Carey, *Courting Disaster: Astrology at the English Court and University in the Later Middle Ages* (New York: St. Martin's Press, 1992). On medieval debates concerning astrology see Theodore Otto Wedel, *The Medieval Attitude toward Astrology, Particularly in England* (New Haven, CT: Yale University Press, 1920), especially 60–89.

10 See Jennifer Moreton, "Robert Grosseteste and the Calendar," in *Robert Grosseteste: New Perspectives on his Thought and Scholarship*, ed. James McEvoy (Turnhout, Belgium: Brepols, 1996), 77–88; Jennifer Moreton, "John of Sacrobosco and the Calendar," *Viator* 25 (1994): 229–244; Linne Mooney, ed., *The Kalendarium of John Somer* (Athens: The University of Georgia Press, 1999), 8–12; and Eisner, ed., *Kalendarium*, 5–8.

11 Mooney, ed., *Kalendarium*, 9. Odington (fl. C 1280–1301), was also known as Walter of Evesham, fl. c. 1280–1301. There was a nineteen-year gap before the end of Odington's calendar and the creation of the calendars composed by Somer and Nicholas of Lynn.

12 On Somer see Mooney, *Kalendarium*, 1–8; on Nicholas of Lynn, see Eisner, *Kalendarium*, 1–10.

13 Linne R. Mooney, "English Almanacs from Script to Print," in *Texts and their Contexts: Papers from the Early Text Society*, eds. John Scattergood and Julia Boffey (Dublin: Four Courts Press, 1997), 11–25, esp. 12. See the discussion of *kalendaria* and folded almanacs in Peter Murray Jones, "Medicine and Science," in *The Cambridge History of the Book in Britain, Volume III: 1400–1557*, eds. Lotte Hellinga and J. B. Trapp (Cambridge: Cambridge University Press, 1999), 433–448, esp. 438–440.

14 Mooney, *Kalendarium*, 34; Eisner, *Kalendarium*, 10.

15 Carey, *Courting Disaster*, esp. 23.

16 J.P. Gumbert, *Bat Books: A Catalogue of Folded Manuscripts Containing Almanacs or Other Texts* (Turnhout: Brepols, 2016). The British Library owns fifteen of these manuscripts, all of digitized and viewable online; see (for example) Addl. MS 17358, http://www.bl.uk/manuscripts/Viewer.aspx?ref=add_ms_17358_f001r.

17 On these works, and especially the question of terminology, see Hilary M. Carey, "What Is the Folded Almanac?," *Social History of Medicine* 16, no. 3 (2003): 481–509, esp. 485–488, and Carey, "Astrological Medicine"; C.H. Talbot, "A Mediaeval Physician's *Vade Mecum*," *Journal of the History of Medicine and Allied Sciences* 16, no. 3 (1961), 213–233; John B. Friedman, "Harry the Hawarde and Talbat His Dog: An Illustrated Girdlebook from Worcestershire," in *Art Into Life: Collected Papers from the Kresge Art Museum Medieval Symposia*, eds. Carol Garrett Fisher, Scott Fisher, and Kathleen L. Scott (East Lansing: Michigan State University Press, 1995), 115–153; and Gumbert, *Bat Books*.

18 Carey, "What Is the Folded Almanac," 485–488.

19 Viewable on digital.bodleian.ox.ac.uk.

20 Carey, "Astrological Medicine," 345.

21 Eamon Duffy, *Marking the Hours: English People & Their Prayers, 1240–1570* (New Haven: Yale University Press, 2006). See also on printed primers Charles C. Butterworth, *The English Primers, 1529–1545* (Philadelphia: University of Pennsylvania Press, 1953); Helen White, *The Tudor Books of Private Devotion* (Madison: University of Wisconsin Press, 1951); Edgar Hoskins, *Horae Beatae*

Mariae Virginis or Sarum and York Primers with Kindred Books (London: Longmans, Green, and Co., 1901); and Pollard and Redgrave, *Short-Title Catalogue*, 73–80.
22. Anne Lawrence-Mathers, "Domesticating the Calendar," in *Women and Writing, c. 1340–c. 1650*, eds. Anne Lawrence-Mathers and Phillipa Hardman (York: York Medieval Press, 2010), 34–61, esp. 44.
23. Duffy, *Marking the Hours*, 30.
24. On the incremental translation of the primer into English see White, *Tudor Books*, 67–86; Mary Erler, "The *maner to live well* and the coming of English in Francois Regnault's Primers of the 1520s and 1530s," *The Library*, 1984, 229–243; and Edwyn Birchenough, "The Primer in English," *The Library*, Series 4, 18 (1938): 177–194.
25. Catholic Church, *This Prymer of Salisbury Use* (Paris, 1529), C4v.
26. *This Prymer* (1532), title page.
27. Lawrence-Mathers, "Domesticating the Calendar," 45–46 and *passim*.
28. See, for example, *Hore presentes ad usum Sarum*, STC 15887 (Paris, 1498), A2r; *Hore beatissime Virginis Marie* (London, 1523), STC 15934, A1r. Versions of this image also appear in manuscript sources, such as Cambridge Fitzwilliam 167, fol. 102r, a fifteenth century *Calendrier des Bergeres* accessible via The MacKinney Collection of Medieval Medical Illustrations hosted by the University of North Carolina at Chapel Hill, https://dc.lib.unc.edu/cdm/landingpage/collection/mackinney.
29. There are some differences between the saints in the York and Sarum calendars, but these are not consistent or significant, and the York Rite was rarely represented in the primer trade. See the list of York primers (1510–1555) Pollard and Redgrave, *STC*, 80.
30. On the Marshall/Byddell primers see White, *Tudor Books*, 89–91; Birchenough, "The Primer in English," 182–183; and Butterworth, *The English Primer*, 59–69.
31. See, for example, Richard Grafton's defense in his Elizabethan guide to calendars, where he includes all the "olde Saynctes days, not of superstition" but because "it hath bene a custome of auncient tyme to use their names, in signifying and making certayne" the dates for "Deeedes, Evidences, and Recordes," including law terms. *A Briefe Treatise Conteinyng many Proper Tables and Easie Rules* (1573), A7r.
32. On this primer see Birchenough, "The Primer," 191–192; White, *Tudor Books*, 124–131; Butterworth, *The English Primer*, 256–275.
33. White, *Tudor Books*, 119.
34. Cyprian Blagden, "The English Stock of the Stationers' Company," *The Library*, 5th Series, 10 (1955): 163–185. Though this patent was dissolved with the death of King Edward, Seres had it renewed for life in June 1559 (164).
35. I have been unable to consult the third 1553 version of this prayer book, which survives in a unique copy at the Bodleian Library, STC 20373.5.
36. Peter Blayney, *The Stationers' Company and the Printers of London, 1501–1577* (Cambridge: Cambridge University Press, 2013), 2.776–2.778.
37. On this prayer book, and its use in Latin services in the universities, see Norman L. Jones, "Elizabeth, Edification, and the Latin Prayer Book of 1560," *Church History* 53, no. 2 (1984): 174–186.
38. The complete Sarum saint calendar is reproduced in some of subsequent editions of this work in 1567, 1571, 1579, and 1599.
39. Chapman, "Now and Then:" 91–123, especially 93–101.
40. G. V. Coyne, S.J., M.A. Hoskin, and O. Pedersen, eds., *Gregorian Reform of the Calendar* (Rome: Pontificia Academia Scientiarum, 1983); Robert Poole, *Time's Alteration: Calendar Reform in Early Modern England* (London: UCL Press Limited, 1998).

56 Backgrounds

41 For a typical example of later almanac calendars that note both Julian and Gregorian dates, see Figure 3.3.10, a Thomas Bretnor calendar for 1616.
42 Richard Verstegen, *A Restitution of Decayed Intelligence: In Antiquities* (Antwerp, 1605), 58.
43 Clog almanacs are said by Plot and others to have originated in Scandinavia, where they are known as *primstaver* or runic calendars, and survive in greater numbers. There is little scholarly work on clog almanacs in English.
44 The symbols are decoded in *The Calendar of the Prayer-Book Illustrated, with an Appendix of the Chief Christian Emblems* (Oxford and London: James Parker and Co, 1866), xi–xvi.
45 In Pollard and Redgrave this xylographic calendar is STC 388; some library catalogues retain an additional STC (392), but this is the same edition. The copies in the British Library are C.36.aa.5, C.41.a.28 (reproduced on EEBO), and C.29.c.6. The Bodleian copy, Douce A632, is described in Alan Edward Coates, Nigel F. Palmer, and Silke Schaeper, *A Catalogue of Books Printed in the Fifteenth Century Now in the Bodleian Library* (Oxford: Oxford University Press, 2005). See also Bosanquet, *English Printed Almanacks*, 77–78.
46 The almanac is reproduced in facsimile, with an introduction and notes, in Guillaume Brouscon, *Sir Francis Drake's Nautical Almanack, 1546* (London: Nottingham Court Press in association with Magdalene College, 1980).
47 Brouscon, *Sir Francis*, 21.
48 Capp, *Astrology*, 26.

1.3 Almanacs and prognostications

Calendars, Latin almanacs and ephemerides were among the first books to emerge from continental presses at the beginning of the age of print. Gutenberg printed an almanac in 1457, and the famous astronomer Regiomontanus produced multiple calendars, almanacs, and ephemerides in Nuremberg in the 1450s and 1460s. By the early decades of the sixteenth century, popular almanacs in the vernacular were among the best-selling books in Germany, and gaining popularity in France and the Netherlands. In England, however, annual almanacs and prognostications were slower to catch on. This was certainly a function of the delayed development of the printing industry in England, and possibly also of lower demand due to lower levels of astrological literacy.[1] Before the 1540s, a majority of almanacs and prognostications—as well as primers—were printed abroad for the English market; most were also written by foreign compilers, including the Antwerp-based Laet family who produced English almanacs for multiple generations. Only in the 1540s did English printers and compilers begin to dominate the production of English almanacs.[2]

This chapter begins with a description of three kinds of almanacs and prognostications that, together with the primer calendars discussed in Chapter 2, served English calendar needs before the 1540s: multi-year almanacs, single sheet almanacs, and single-year prognostications. It then traces the development of the combined annual book form almanac and prognostication in the middle of the sixteenth century, recounts the sudden increased popularity of the almanac following the incorporation of the Company of Stationers in 1557, describes the impact of licensing and monopolies on the almanac's fortunes in the Elizabethan era, and concludes with an overview of the history of the almanac from 1603 to 1640, when almanacs were part of the English Stock.

Multi-year almanacs

Because they were perpetual, the calendars in the printed primers did not by themselves provide all the information needed to navigate time and ascertain basic astronomical data (such as the conjunctions and oppositions of the Sun and Moon) for particular years. For that, additional annual information was needed that provided the date of Easter, the golden number, and the dominical letter for a particular number of years. This was usually given in the single-page tables included in many primers titled "Almanacs," that were in fact early modern versions of medieval Paschal tables (see Figure 1.2.3). From the first decade of the sixteenth century enterprising printers also produced separate multi-year almanac tables, applicable for a range of years. These could be used in conjunction with the perpetual calendars in primers to transform the latter into annual calendars.

The oldest surviving example of a multi-year almanac is the anonymous *Almanack for Twelve Years*, printed by Wynkyn de Worde in 1508 (STC 387).[3] This tiny book (32°), printed in English, targets a literate but unlearned audience. The preface provides instructions on how to use the charts in the almanac, explaining basic terminology such as the fact that the conjunctions and oppositions are the same thing as the new and full Moons. For the next thirty years, multi-year almanacs (all with anonymous compilers) in this format were produced by the same printers who were also in the primer trade. Two years after De Worde's almanac ran out in 1519, he printed another one covering 1522–1527 (STC 389). Richard Faques' *Almanacke for, xv, yeres* (STC 390) covered 1525–1540, Robert Wyer's 1539 *Almanacke for xiiii years* (STC 392.3) covered 1539–1552, and Richard Grafton's *An Almanacke Moste Exactly Sette Foorth for the Terme of xiiii Yeres* (STC 393) covered 1544–1557. At that point, the annual combined almanac and prognostication obviated the need for these multi-year almanacs.

The primer calendars and the multi-year almanacs were complementary. The multi-year almanacs provided the movable feasts and phases of the Moon, the dominical letter and the dates of Easter. The perpetual calendars in the primers supplied permanent information such as the fixed holy days, general rules for astrological physic, and in some cases, the light calendrical poetry and images traditionally attached to calendars. The almanacs printed by de Worde and Faques would be useful for the owners of older primers for which the calendar had fallen out of date, or for the owners of primers that did not list conjunctions, oppositions, and movable feasts. But even when used together, the primer and multi-year almanacs provided only a small percentage of the calendar information that would later be gathered together in the annual combined book form almanac and prognostication.

Single sheet imported almanacs

In addition to the calendars in the imported printed primers and the multi-year almanacs printed domestically, single-year almanacs were imported, perhaps in significant numbers, in the first decades of the sixteenth century. Not much survives of this material apart from a few ambiguous allusions and scattered fragments of the almanacs themselves; because they were imported in barrels and not liable to custom fees, and because their low price kept them off lists of purchases with credit, there are almost no financial or regulatory records of the trade.[4] Suggestive evidence of their existence appears in the records kept by the Oxford bookseller John Dorne who in 1520 sold (by Peter Murray Jones' calculation) a total of thirty-two almanacs in a twelve-month period. Aside from two expensive almanacs for thirty years which sold at 4s 8d, each of these almanacs and prognostications sold for 1d or 2d, which suggests they were broadsides.[5] Dorne's list makes it possible to imagine that the single sheet almanac was a popular form of calendar long before that popularity began to register in the records and almanac survivals after 1540.

A few survivals can suggest the format for these early single sheet or broadside almanacs. The earliest extant example is a 1510 almanac by Gaspar (or Jasper) Laet the Elder, the patriarch of a family of physicians native to Belgium but based in Antwerp, who dominated English almanac production into the 1540s.[6] In addition to providing the dominical letter, golden number, and movable feasts, this almanac identifies conjunctions and oppositions for the year, along with good and bad days for phlebotomy and administering medicine.[7] Fragments also survive from a 1523 broadside almanac, but the earliest full survival of a single-sheet almanac is one compiled by Gaspar Laet the Younger for 1530, printed in Antwerp by Christofe of Ruremunde.[8] By this time, the single sheet almanac had achieved the format that, with minor variations, would continue into the seventeenth century. The information here includes a full list of English saints and holy days, the location of the Moon in the Zodiac every day, the phases of the Moon, dates for eclipses, a didactic to remember which signs rule which parts of the body (similar to the example in Figure 1.2.2 and Plate 1.2) and a key to elections for phlebotomy, taking medicine, bathing, and sowing.[9] Thomas Hill's 1572 single sheet almanac (Plate 3) provides similar information in a somewhat different format, adding woodcuts of the twelve labors of the month, an eclipse diagram with a prognostication based on the eclipse, and the diagram of Zodiac Man. Jacobean examples of the single sheet almanac include Thomas Johnson's almanac for 1604, and Jeffrey Neve's for 1609.

Annual prognostications

Annual prognostications are associated with calendars because they provide information for a single calendar year that has been ascertained through the practice of judicial astrology described in Chapter 1. Prognostications were even more popular than almanacs in the Oxford bookshop of John Dorne, who in the twelve months of 1520 sold a total of eighty-five copies, ranging in price from 1d to 3s 12 d. At the lower end of the price spectrum, these were probably single sheets or very short pamphlets.[10] Prognostications were usually produced in narrative form, without tables, charts, or diagrams.

The prognostications for the English market that survive from the period before the 1540s were mostly (if not entirely) authored by foreigners or resident aliens in England, including William Parron, the French astrologer resident at the court of Henry VII, Gaspar Laet the Elder, Gaspar Laet the Younger, and Jean Thibault, an Antwerp printer and physician who described himself on the title page of a 1530 *Pronosticacyon* as "Astrologyer to the Emperoures Majesty."[11] Initially published in Antwerp, Laet prognostications were subsequently printed in London by Richard Pynson, Richard Bankes, and Robert Wyer. Though they range in size from quarto to single sheets, these prognostications follow a standard format that was to endure into the later book form annual almanacs and prognostications. The author identifies the grounds for the prediction—usually the revolution of the year and relevant eclipses—then provides prognostications for weather and other events for the four seasons, the twelve months, and for standard categories such as "Of peas and warre," "Of plenty & scarcite of this yere," and "Of sickenesses that shall reygne this yere" (Laet 1517, [A2v]). Political predictions might also be specified by country; Laet provided predictions for "Louayne," "Antwarpe," "Bruxelles," "Flauders," "Gaunte" (1533, [A4r]). The prognostications in these early works are generally more specific than later in the sixteenth century. For 1517, for example, Laet made predictions concerning "the moste noble & mightey emperour of Rome Marimylian," "the moste cristen kynge of france Fraunceys," and "the moste mighty & faithful kingee of Englonde Henry" (1517, ([A5v]). Yet, despite these political references, there is little evidence that these early prognostications were censored or otherwise controlled.[12] Stand-alone annual prognostications continued to be printed in the 1540s, as in the lengthy *Pronostication for the yere of our LORD GOD M.CCCCC.xliiii* by "the right expert Doctour in Astronomy and phisycke Maister Cornelys Scute resydent in Bridges in the Wolfe strete" (1544, title page).[13] A few survive from the 1550s, including a prose prognostication by the Brussels physician Arnould Bogaert in 1553, and Antonius de Montulmo's *A Ryghte Excellente Treatise of Astronomie*, which is in fact an extended prognostication for 1554. Prognostications were rarely published separately after the 1550s, however, as by that time they had fully merged with the annual almanac.

Annual book form almanacs and prognostications, 1540–1571

The earliest extant annual English book form almanac and prognostication is an anonymous sextodecimo almanac printed in London for the year 1539 (STC 392.3), surviving in fragments in the Huntington Library. This almanac represents the merging of the extended astrological information in the annual prognostications (based on judicial astrology) with the calendars and lunar astrological content of the single sheet almanacs. Like the latter, these almanacs include calendars with the Sarum saints, rules for elections (bathing, purging, taking medicine, sowing and pruning), Zodiac Man, and notations of significant eclipses. Some of the surviving book form fragments from the 1540s include greater detail; in the unfolded sheets of a Laet sextodecimo almanac for 1545, for example, each month is headed with a Zodiac image and description of the qualities of that sign, information not usually provided in the broadsheets. It appears that the basic format and content for these publications—described in more detail in Part II—was established by the early 1550s.

This new format slowly became the most popular one for almanacs and prognostications. The story of the period from 1540 to 1571 is of increasing numbers and the slow domination of English compilers and printers. Among compilers, the Laet family ceased production in the late 1540s (with almanacs authored by Alphonse Laet, the brother of Gaspar the Younger). Foreign compilers still occasionally produced English almanacs; one of the earliest complete survivals is a 1551 almanac by the German physician and almanac maker Simon Heuring.[14] But the 1540s also sees the first named English compilers: the physician and erstwhile Carthusian monk Andrew Boorde, and Anthony Askham, also a physician and the brother of Roger Askham. Soon most English almanac compilers were English. In the 1550s, compilers included Henry Low and William Cuningham (both physicians) and the mysterious Lewes Vaughan. Two other prolific compilers begin producing almanacs in the 1560s: Thomas Buckminster, a minister and physician active until 1599, and the Salisbury physician John Securis, active into the 1580s. Other English compilers active in the period before 1571 include Alexander Mounslowe, and the physician Francis Coxe; the latter issued almanacs for 1566 and 1567 even though he had previously renounced "Curiouse Astrologie" after being pilloried for practicing forbidden arts in 1560 and 1561.[15] The exception to the general trend towards English compilers, however, was the work of the notorious French astrologer and almanac compiler Michel de Nostradamus, whose first printed work in English was *An Almanacke for the Yeare of Oure Lorde God, 1559*.

Just as English compilers become dominant in almanac production in these mid-century decades, so did English printers. In the 1530s, at least half of the annual almanacs and prognostications were printed abroad. In the 1540s, however, English printers began to take a greater role, with Robert Wyer, John Redman, John Walley, Richard Grafton, Richard Lant, John Mayler, Nicholas Hill, and Robert Jugge all producing almanacs and/or prognostications. This larger participation is probably a corollary of the growth in the printing trade in England, as the "number of new printers introduced in each decade continued to climb, with twenty-four joining the trade in 1541–50."[16] As that trend continued, so did the number of printers involved in printing almanacs. In the next decade, other printers who produced almanacs include John Day, William Seres, J. Turke, William Powell, J. Kingston, Henry Sutton, and Thomas Marsh.

A most significant year in the history of English printing in general and the almanac in particular is 1557, when the Company of Stationers was incorporated and granted the right to license books. From that point until 1571, all almanacs were licensed by the Company and listed in the Stationers' Register, which means the records improved significantly, and it is possible to identify editions of almanacs and prognostications for which no copies survive. Each year's almanac, even if written by the same compiler as in the previous year, was treated as a new edition by the Company, and separately licensed and assessed; Thomas Marsh, for example, records a license to print a Henry Low almanac and a Henry Low prognostication (4d each, for a total of 8d) for 1558, then pays for subsequent licenses to print combined Low almanacs and prognostications (8d each) for 1563, 1564, 1566, 1567, and 1569.[17]

Almanacs were also regulated by the stipulations of the Royal Injunctions of 1559, which required all books, pamphlets, and ballads to be seen and allowed by ecclesiastical authorities.[18] The Stationers' Register entries for almanacs in these years often include the notation that prognostications have also been authorized by the terms of the injunction. Almanacs, like other books, were in this way doubly controlled by the Company of Stationers' licensing process and by the ecclesiastical review process. Yet until 1571, there was no monopoly that prevented printers from becoming involved in this lucrative trade. The lack of a monopoly explains the extensive participation of so many printers in the production of almanacs in the mid-sixteenth century. In the 1560s, roughly twenty-five different printers issued almanacs and/or prognostications. The total number of almanacs mentioned in the records and/or surviving for this decade is close to one hundred—far above the number for the 1550s or, as we will see, for the 1570s, 1580s, and 1590s. Though the more extensive records of almanacs in these years might exaggerate the actual numbers, even allowing for this possibility it is clear that in the 1560s, with the English printing industry operating robustly and English printers able to participate without restraint, the almanac reached an early high-water mark for popularity.

Despite the oversight of ecclesiastical authorities, almanacs continued to report on the social and political topics thrown up by the practice of judicial astrology, albeit usually in generalized terms.[19] That content generated anxiety among government authorities and, eventually, greater control. Among the most important almanacs in this history are the English almanacs and prognostications of Nostradamus. Now better known for the long-term prophecies in *Les Propheties*, Nostradamus was the attributed author for English almanacs from 1559 until 1568 (though he died in 1566). The earliest of these has no surviving prognostication, though there is extant a separate Nostradamus prognostication for the same year printed in Antwerp. But even the almanac section of this work, unusually, includes plenty of ominous prognostications, as can be seen in the February calendar in Figure 3.2.2. Each date has a short prognosticatory phrase or sentence, made all the more menacing (and at times comic) by incoherence. The topics range from mundane weather predictions—"colde, drye," and "snow, yce" (A2v)—to pointed warnings of calamities, including political ones: "Popular sedition (A2r), "Sedition by a preacher" (A3r), *Morbus popularis*," "Victory of ye gaules," "Enemyes of the church destroyed" (A4r). As Capp notes, the prognostications that head each month are even more elliptical and obscure, as in this verse for August: "The earthen potte founde, the citie tributary, / Fieldes divided, newe begylynges, / The Spanyard hurt, hunger, warly pestilence / Obstinate mockery, confusednes, evyll, ravyng" (A5v). The Nostradamus prognostication for the same year printed in Antwerp is, at nearly a hundred octavo pages, considerably longer than most annual prognostications. It provides predictions for each of the twelve months, covering all manner of meteorological, agricultural, epidemiological, social, and political topics with the same combination of inflammatory, banal, and confusing rhetoric seen in Nostradamus' almanacs.

But Nostradamus' almanacs and prognostications, though unusual in tone and degree of gnomic illegibility, were not at heart all that different from the standard prognostications made in the annual almanacs in the 1550s and 1560s. For example, for the same year, 1559, Lewes Vaughan predicts "great mischiefe, discorde, manslaughter, hatred and wrath, aswel betwene great princes and ecclesyasticall persons, as the common people: aswel private as publike, with deceite, treason, theft, burnynge, adulterye, robberie, and fynally all kind of wickedness" (Prog. B3v). Vaughan also warns against excessive taxation: "great princes whiche are under Jupiter shal levey great charges upon the poore people, and with great vexation and damage" (Prog. A3v). Ecclesiastical oversight did little to dampen the prognostications in the 1560s. Buckminster for 1567, for example, predicts that "False Prophetes, and workers of false miracles shalbee heard of, and Coniurers," and that "Castelles, Cities, Tounes, and buildynges neare or upon the Seas, shall be troubled and brought in feare, by meanes of rumours and brutes, spred and noysed abrode" (Prog. A5v). In the 1567 edition of his unusual multi-year almanacs, Philip Moore presages "craftie counsailes, and treasons," children conspiring against their parents, and "the furour of the people, shalbe kindled against their magistrates" (1567, E7r). On the one hand these predictions are as vague and void of political traction as the prophecies of Nostradamus, but they also clearly delve into potentially sensitive issues.

These prognostications were a source of alarm; they provoked the earliest Tudor pamphlet against astrology by William Fulke, discussed in Chapter 1.4. Yet, they were not suppressed—at least not immediately. The great popularity of Nostradamus' almanacs and prognostications spawned competition and piracy among printers and booksellers; three different printers were fined for producing unauthorized editions (licensed to other printers) of Nostradamus almanacs in 1562 and 1563, and twenty booksellers were fined for selling them.[20] But these were efforts to protect the economic interests of the printer who had duly registered the work, not political censorship. Nostradamus almanacs, like the other pointed works of Vaughan and later Buckminster, appear to have been licensed with little fanfare: to Thomas Hackett for 1560 and 1561, John Walley for 1562, Henry Denham for 1566, Henry Bynneman for 1567, and to Walley again for 1568. From surviving fragments of these works, it appears that Nostradamus never curbed his penchant for commenting obliquely on regime change, religious upheaval, and the fortunes of great rulers. In sum, there is little evidence that the almanac was subject to serious censorship in the 1560s by the ecclesiastical authorities who were charged with overseeing them.[21]

The Watkins and Roberts monopoly, 1571–1603

On May 12, 1571, Richard Watkins (or Watkyns) and James Roberts were granted a monopoly to print almanacs and prognostications. The patent was renewed in 1578 for ten years and in 1588 for an additional twenty-one years. Watkins was already prominent in the Company of Stationers by the early 1570s, and he continued to rise within the ranks, becoming Under Warden in 1578 and serving as licenser in the 1580s and 1590s. The younger Roberts, a printer specializing in ballads, printed little aside from almanacs after 1571, until in the 1590s he married Alice Charlewood, the widow of John Charlewood, and took over the profitable literary list of that printing house.[22] Roberts became the sole holder of the monopoly on almanacs and prognostications between the death of Watkins in 1599 and the dissolution of the Elizabethan patents in 1603.

The patent was extremely lucrative for Watkins and Roberts and the Crown, which shared "one moiety" of the profits.[23] One of several monopolies about which other printers complained with great bitterness, it is mentioned specifically in the manuscript petition of c. 1577, *The Griefes of the printers glasse sellers and Cutlers sustained by reason of privileges granted to privatt persons,* where Roberts and Watkins are singled out for their patent for "all Almanackes and Pronosticacons the which was the onelie releif of the most porest of ye printers."[24]

Since their monopoly released Watkins and Roberts from the requirement that they apply for licenses and pay fees for printing annual almanacs and prognostications, almanacs now disappear from the Stationers' Register, though works falling slightly out of that category are still listed. For this reason, from 1571 to 1603, we know of almanacs only if a copy (or reference in another text) survives. Even allowing for that deficiency in the records, it is clear that annual almanac production decreased during the period of the Watkins and Roberts monopoly in the 1570s and 1580s, before beginning to rise back to the levels of the 1560s (and eventually beyond) in the 1590s.[25] There is no evidence this decline was market-driven. Rather, it appears that the Elizabethan regime took the opportunity of the

Watkins and Roberts monopoly to control the publication of potentially disruptive prognostications more carefully.[26] It seems probable that the regime was particularly skittish concerning political prophecies in the years following the rebellion of the North in 1568. All almanacs were still subject to the review outlined in the Royal Injunctions of 1559; the 1571 patent explicitly required that they be "allowed by the Commissioners for causes ecclesiasticall."[27]

Clearly the Crown was pleased with Watkins' and Roberts' efforts in controlling content; the renewal of the patent, granted in 1578, notes that "by the diligent foresight of Watkins and Robertes many fantastical and fond prophesyings which have been accustomed to be sent forth in former times in almanacks and prognostications are now left unprinted."[28] In the few surviving almanacs from the 1570s, the compilers seem slightly more restrained than they had been in the previous decade when reporting the data from horoscope charts for eclipses and revolutions. Securis, for example, in considering the revolution of the year for 1574, discusses every topic covered by the twelve houses except politics, refusing to analyze the significance of the placement of the Sun in the tenth house: "what he signifieth, they that have but a small taste or smacke in Astronomie, can judge" (B5r). But this restraint was short lived, and the compilers soon returned to generalized yet still provocative predictions about politics, religion, and social disharmony. Mounslowe, for example, notes in 1579 that the ascendency of Saturn in the chart for August might "betokeneth privie grudges and mutterynge among the people, and some secrete hate and conspiracy" (C4v) and prophesies that a 1581 eclipse presages "the sicknesse of a great King, or the death of some famous and mightie honourable Man" (B4r). Walter Gray warns in 1591 of the "brabbles and brawles of foreign Regions" (C3v). For 1593, Gabriel Frende foresees "many reportes of Warre and bloodshed," as well as "Much discention, strife, sedition, and sundry hurliburlies amongst many.... also contempt of laws, and neglect of Christian pietie and brotherile charitie one towards another" (C4r), and two years later the same compiler predicts "contentions, envyinges, quarrels, and trouble" which he says he will "omit to write"—even as he mentions them (Frende 1595, C2v).

Throughout the Elizabethan period and into the seventeenth century, compilers were careful in how they phrased their predictions, often drawing attention to the fact that they were omitting from their work some calamities they saw presaged in the horoscope charts. For example, after describing a 1591 lunar eclipse that was ruled by "the malignant planet *Saturne*," J.D. (possibly John Dade) demurs from further comment: "what it may presage, I leave it to others to judge" (A4r). Buckminster (in 1571) explains that in reporting on weather, diseases, and dearth, and famine, he has avoided more dangerous topics: "I coulde have combred thee with many mo matters: but because they are nothing profitable for thee, I ceasse from troubling thee" (A2r). In his prognostication for the Winter quarter of

66 *Backgrounds*

1588, based on the horoscope for the entry of the Sun into Capricorn, Walter Gray writes that there "might be noted…many strange eventes to happen, which purposely are omitted in good consideration" (B2r). Another way that compilers evade the direct reporting of politically sensitive predictions is by slipping into Latin at opportune moments. Arthur Hopton, for example, reports in English on the weather for Spring 1606, but puts the prognostication concerning famine, sedition, and the death of kings into Latin: "*Magni regis morten seditiones et famen portendit*" (B8r).

The records include only a few isolated incidents involving the direct censorship of an annual almanac. One concerns a 1600 William Woodhouse almanac called in when it was interpreted as predicting the Earl of Essex's rebellion, as described in a 16 February 1601 letter by Vincent Hussey:

> A foolish prognostication of one Woodhouse considers this tumult the effect of an eclipse last year. He set down that its influence would begin 20 January 1601, and continue slight until 18 Nov. following, when it would be most felt, and last till 14 Sept. 1602, and then gradually decrease till 12 July 1603. This eclipse, he says, shows the unfortunate state of sundry great persons, great destruction of many mean ones, and threatens death to ecclesiastical persons, lawyers, rulers, &C, the middle aged and lusty especially threatened. This book is called in, though it be but a toy.[29]

No copies of Woodhouse almanacs for 1600 or 1601 have survived, so we do not know the specific language that got this compiler in trouble. But Woodhouse himself was apparently undeterred: his 1602 almanac, for example, prophecizes "cruell & unheard-of murders, warres, seditions, tumults, roberies, violent & sodaine death, & the unfortunate fall of sundry people" (B4v). The evidence of Hussey's letter is ambivalent. On the one hand it offers clear proof that prognostications could be considered dangerous. On the other hand, Woodhouse's almanacs presumably made it past the ecclesiastical authorities. His chastisement did not significantly change his behavior, and in his account of this incident, Hussey clearly feels that the suppression of this "foolish prognostication" was an overreaction for what was nothing more than a "toy."

In conclusion, Elizabethan almanacs were controlled in three overlapping ways. From 1557 to 1571, they were licensed by the Company of Stationers, which protected printers from piracy. From 1559, they also fell under the Royal Injunctions, and so were subject to ecclesiastical oversight that checked their politically dangerous content. From 1571 to 1603, the monopoly of Watkins and Roberts precluded other printers from printing almanacs unless they were granted assigns. The amount and specificity of political prognostications in Elizabethan almanacs fluctuated at least partially (if not wholly) due to the threat of censorship, though political predictions never entirely disappear.

The English Stock, 1603–1640

In October 1603, King James 1 issued a new grant to the Stationers' Company for primers, psalters, almanacs, and prognostications, thereby resolving decades of complaints about the printing monopolies that had long benefited a few rich printers, and marking a new chapter in the Company's history. The portion of the grant concerning almanacs specifically provided the company "full proviledge and aucthoritie" to

> prynte and cause to be prynted all manner of *Almanackes and Pronosticacons* whatsoever in the Englishe tonge and all manner of bookes and Pamphlettes tending to the same purpose and which are not to be taken or construed other than *Almanackes* or *Pronostycacons* being allowed by the Archbushop of CANTERBURY and Bishup of LONDON or one of them.[30]

This grant marks the creation of what became known as the English Stock—so named to distinguish it from monopolies covering books in other languages (such as the Latin and the Irish Stock).[31] From this date forward, the Stationers' Company sold shares in the almanac monopoly for a fee, with slots available for printers at different ranks on the company: fifteen for Assistants, thirty for Livery members, and sixty for printers in the Yeomanry. This meant that a hundred and five printers owned the right to print books in these categories, including almanacs. Unfortunately, these printers are not usually named in the records, until the accounting system changed in 1644.[32]

Clearly, the transfer of the monopoly to the Company, and the greater number of printers thereby authorized to participate, enabled the steady and swift rise in the number of almanacs. Because almanacs were still not individually licensed, they do not appear in the Stationers' Register, and so it is difficult to arrive at accurate (or even credible) figures for production in the first decades of the century. It is equally if not more difficult to determine the print run for each edition in the period before the 1650s, when the records yield more data.[33] But the number of surviving copies can provide a rough sense of the increase in almanac production. Counting only single sheet or booklet form almanacs and prognostications, there are approximately twenty to twenty-five almanacs and prognostications surviving in separate editions from the period from 1594 to 1603. In the next decade, from 1604 to 1613, that number jumps up to approximately 100. Meanwhile, the number of compilers similarly escalates. A dozen or so compilers were active in the 1590s; twice that many were producing almanacs by 1620. It is only really after 1603, then, that the almanac can truly be said to have become one of the most popular publications of early modern England. When the records improve in the second half of the century, the volume they reveal is truly astonishing: Capp estimates that "sales averaged about 400,000 copies annually" in the 1660s.[34]

There had been a slight but perceptible increase in pointed political prognostications in almanacs of the late 1590s, and that trend continued in the first years of the new reign. In these years compilers did not fear to mention in their prognostications matters concerning rulers, civil government, and religion, though as always, those statements were vague. Perhaps this temporary shift simply reflects the transition to a new system of oversight, as the Stationers' Company took full charge of the almanac. Certainly, the mechanisms for oversight were not efficient. On October 27, 1634, the Court of the Company of Stationers noted that "the Companies Almanacks which have byn heretofore printed are now questioned in the high Comission Cort. for not being Licensed according to Order." As a result, the court ordered "That noe Almanacks shall be hereafter printe without Lawfull License."[35] That of course had been the rule since 1559, reiterated in all the monopoly grants; the 1634 order may suggest just how inconsistently it had been enforced. The same order also requires that almanacs "be entered [in] the Register booke of Copies," though as William A. Jackson notes, that order "does not seem to have been obeyed."[36]

The greater pointedness of political prognostications in the early Jacobean years was perhaps a result of shoddy oversight, but whatever the reason, that shift in tone was short-lived. By the end of the first decade of the seventeenth century, and continuing into the 1640s, prognostications became increasingly "vague and in decline," as Capp notes, with the exception of those by John Booker in the 1630s. Eclipse predictions in this period mostly provide the time, duration, and extent of each eclipse—with mathematical precision, but little or no interpretation. The quarterly and monthly prognostications stick to the crops and the weather. The visual format of the almanac becomes increasingly standardized in these years, while more information begins to stuff the almanac in ancillary tables: rules on mensuration, detailed information on planetary aspects, information on calculating planetary hours (not unheard of before 1603, but more frequently seen afterwards), and itineraries for travel. These changes are described in more detail in Part II, "How to Read an Early Modern Almanac."

Another change in the almanac in the Jacobean period concerned the profile of almanac compilers. In the seventeenth century, the ranks included fewer physicians and more self-taught astrologers such as Booker and, after 1640, William Lilly.[37] This development may reflect the rise of the professional astrologer in London in the last decades of the Elizabethan reign.[38] It might also suggest a general increase in astrological literacy, fueled partly by the almanacs themselves. Increasingly, anyone with a modicum of mathematical knowledge might consider compiling an almanac. That possibility is suggested by a unique manuscript in the Huntington Library: a how-to on almanac compilation, titled "Instructions For the making of an Almanacke."[39] The anonymous author of this unpublished manuscript uses as a template a George Gilden almanac for 1620. Bound with a "Meteorologicall Dyary" by Sir Christopher Heydon, the author of *A Defence of Judicial*

Astrology and the posthumously published scientific work, *Astrological judgments*, this primer on almanac construction stops before the trickier part of the enterprise, the prognostication. Its existence demonstrates the extent to which the business of almanac compilation was now open to an increasing number of men—not only the physicians who dominated the trade in the mid-sixteenth century.

The career of John Booker, a London astrologer whose first almanac appeared in 1631, suggests the increasing opportunities for auto-didacts in the field, the continuing appeal of more pointed social and political prognostications, the dangers of dabbling in sensitive areas, and the sudden shift in the nature of prognostications that would occur in the 1640s.[40] Originally bound to a haberdasher in London, Booker proved himself to be a talented self-taught astrologer. He also chafed against the need to limit his prognostications to anodyne generalizations. He did take some steps towards self-protection, using the old trick of putting positive or banal prophecies in English, and slipping into Latin for more ominous predictions. Booker took to writing brief, original calendar poetry for each month that described and interpreted the major planetary aspects, as in a poem for September, 1632, which (according to Capp) was later seen to predict the fall of Gustavus Adolphus:

> How many changes sees the Sun on earth?
> Kings, Kingdomes, States their buriall and their birth,
> And if wee may believe th'Astrologer,
> Who saith at th'AEquinox bright *Jupiter*
> by *Saturne* is oppos'd: This great aspect
> Will amongst mortals, worke some strange effect.

(B6r)

This particular almanac was not suppressed; it was Booker's prediction of a "wonderful change in the church" (1633, C5v) in his next year's almanac that got him arrested, jailed, and fined 500 pounds. Yet he resumed almanac compilation in 1636, and ultimately had his revenge when in 1643, he was made a licenser of mathematical books—including almanacs. Looking back on the 1630s from the more liberal vantage point of the 1640s, Booker wrote that he had been

> almost discouraged in prosecuting the Writing of my Annuall Prognostick, when as in Licensing the same, half my Astrology or what was most pertinent to the present times was most maliciously expunged, so that I ever appeared a lame & deficient Person, ambiguous, and not easily to be apprehended: the fault not being mine.... but those peevish Episcopall Chaplaines who had sole Licence either to permit, or disanull my Writings.[41]

70 Backgrounds

According to Booker, the ecclesiastical authorities (and the Company of Stationers') took their job seriously and "expunged" prognostications that were too specific. That enforcement rings true, as it helps explain why the almanacs of the period from 1610 to 1640 are so general and dull compared to earlier—and certainly later—years.

John Booker is useful for closing out the present account of the almanac in England before 1640. Though his almanacs generally conform to the standards of the day, they also pushed against the boundaries created by the ecclesiastical licensing system—boundaries that were to be "shattered by the revolution."[42] As Capp, Patrick Curry, and Ann Geneva have shown, after the hostilities of the 1640s began and astrologers were no longer muzzled by official licensers, astrology was to play a key role in public political debates, with Parliamentarian astrologers such as Booker and William Lilly pitted against Royalist astrologers, notably George Wharton. This was the era of the celebrity astrologer, a category that included Booker and Lilly as well as John Gadbury, and of renewed debates over astrology's legitimacy, including Lilly's defense in *Christian Astrology* (1659), which he wrote in the face of multiple attacks on the art.[43] What could not have been predicted in 1640 was the degree to which the astrology bubble, still growing in the 1630s, would so quickly burst in the decades after the English Civil War, discrediting the art and presaging the decline in the astrological almanac.

The university press almanacs

The almanac monopoly was extraordinarily valuable both for the 105 or so printers with shares in the English Stock, and the Company of Stationers itself, which collected a dividend in addition to the fees for licenses. It is hardly surprisingly that the Company was zealous in pursuing violators in London and elsewhere. The Company was, however, unable to prevent the successful effort by the University Press at Cambridge to participate in the trade, which was allowed by a grant from the Privy Council in 1623. The printing rights allowed by that grant were modified and reduced in 1631, and then in 1639 the Press agreed to curtail its production of almanacs still further in exchange for an annual fee of 200 pounds from the Company. The University Press at Oxford, perhaps hoping to strike the same deal, printed almanacs only briefly in the late 1630s, before settling separately with the Company for the same fee of 200 pounds per year.[44]

In accordance with these arrangements, the University Press at Cambridge printed annual almanacs and prognostications starting in 1623, though at a relatively low volume until the second half of the seventeenth century. The dispensation from the Privy Council allowed the University to publish only almanacs offered to them directly by compilers. But it seems clear that the press maneuvered around this rule by "sponsoring editions rather than waiting for them to be offered."[45] These were usually printed under fictitious names. Perhaps playing off the name of the real Edward Pond (a London compiler active for almost thirty years beginning in 1601), or the already popular mock almanacs featuring birds (such as Thomas Dekker's *The Ravens Almanac* of 1609 and Thomas Middleton's *The Owls Almanac* of 1618), the Cambridge press bestowed on their almanacs fictional names of birds or bodies of water, including Jonathan Dove, William Rivers, Thomas Swallow, Fr[igid] Waters, and Peregrine Rivers (whose name usefully covered both categories).[46] A variation on these fictional names was Frig[id] Winter, the supposed compiler of several Cambridge almanacs in the 1630s. These almanacs did not differ appreciably from those printed in London, though as a group they perhaps contain a slightly greater proportion of mathematical information, especially concerning planetary aspects and planetary hours.

Notes

1 Capp, *Astrology*, 23–30; 17–22; Barnes, *Astrology*, 25–47.
2 See the account of the early sixteenth century development of the English printed almanac and prognostication in Bosanquet, *English Printed Almanacks*, 1–10; Capp, *Astrology*, 23–30; and Jones, "Medicine and Science," 441–442.
3 A multi-year almanac is also attached to a 1507 Latin *Almanach Ephemerides* by William Rede, the Merton School astronomer and Bishop of Chichester, printed by Robert Pynson (STC 504).
4 Jones, "Medicine and Science," 441–442.
5 Ibid., 445–447.
6 On the Laets see Bosanquet, *English Printed Almanacks*, 18–19, and Capp, *Astrology*, 317. Printed in Borchloen (modern Borgloon) by the Dutch printer W. Vosterman, the almanac is not listed in the STC, but it is reproduced in Bosanquet, Plate XXII.
7 As Bosanquet notes, there "is nothing to show that this Almanack was issued for England," yet as three copies survive in the British Library, it was probably imported (*English Printed Almanacks*, 146).
8 Bosanquet, *English Printed Almanacks*, 147. The 1523 *Almanack* is Bosanquet, Plate CXXX; the 1530 almanac, STC 471, is Bosanquet, Plate CXXXI.
9 The symbols are invisible in the EEBO scan of this almanac; they can be seen in Bosanquet, *English Almanacks*, Plate XXIV.
10 Jones, "Medicine and Science," 444.
11 On William Parron see Hilary Carey, "Henry VII's Book of Astrology and the Tudor Renaissance," *Renaissance Quarterly* 65, no. 3 (2012): 661–770. On Parron, the Laets, Thibault and other continental authors of annual prognostications, see Capp's capsule biographies (arranged by name) in *Astrology*, 293–340, and Bosanquet, *English Printed Almanacks*, 17–24.
12 As Capp notes, there is "nothing really offensive" in the prognostications (*Astrology*, 68), and no evidence to support Bosanquet's assertion that the 1541 Act against Sorcery was used to control them (*English Printed Almanacks*, 5).
13 Given these mid-century prognostications often survive in fragments, it is possible some of them were originally printed as the second half of a combined almanac and prognostication. Before the 1570s, the two halves of the combined almanac and prognostication were often printed on separately signed sheets, with the prognostication beginning with a new sheet A.

72 Backgrounds

14 This book form 1551 almanac was printed in Worcester (STC 464.3); a single sheet almanac by Heuring for the same year was printed in London (STC 464).
15 On Coxe's renunciation of astrology see Chapter 1.4.
16 Blayney, *The Stationer's Company*, 2.931.
17 Edward Arber, ed., *A Transcript of the Registers of the Company of Stationers 1554–1640 A.D.* (London and Birmingham: privately printed, 1875–1894); "The Stationers' Register Online," accessed January-July, 2019, https://stationersregister.online/.
18 Capp, *Astrology*, 29. See the fuller account of these controls in Blayney, *Stationers' Company*, 1.482–1.487, and Cyndia Susan Clegg, *Press Censorship in Elizabethan England* (Cambridge: Cambridge University Press, 1997).
19 On astrological prognostications in the first years of Elizabeth's reign see Sanford V. Larkey, "Astrology and Politics in the First Years of Elizabeth's Reign," *Bulletin of the Institute of the History of Medicine* 3, no. 3 (1935): 171–186.
20 See Arber, I.101, I.184, I.216–I.218, and the notes in Pollard & Redgrave for STC 492.2, STC 492.7, and 492.9.
21 Capp, *Astrology*, 29.
22 On Watkins see Cyprian Blagden, *The Stationers' Company: A History, 1403–1959* (Cambridge, MA: Harvard University Press, 1960), 41, 50–51. Roberts is now the better known of the two because he became involved in printing Shakespeare quartos; see David Kathman, "Roberts, James (b. in or before 1540, d. 1618?), Bookseller and Printer," *Oxford Dictionary of National Biography*, 23 Sep. 2004, accessed 20 Nov. 2019, and John Jowett, "The Writing Tables of James Roberts," *The Library* 20, no. 1 (2019): 64–88.
23 This is the language of the second patent, granted in 1578 to begin in 1581. *Calendar of Patent Rolls, Preserved in the Public Record Office. Elizabeth I, 1558–1603* (London: H.M. Stationary Office, 1939, rpt. Nendeln/Liechtenstein: Kraus Reprint, 1976), 7: 440, entry 2891.
24 Arber, *Transcript*, 1.111. On complaints against the printing patents—including the "guerilla warfare against the patentees" (167) which ended only with the establishment of the English Stock in 1603—see Blagden, "The English Stock."
25 Capp, *Astrology*, 29.
26 Ibid., 29.
27 Great Britain, *Calendar of Patent Rolls Preserved in the Public Record Office* (Nendein, Lichtenstein: Kraus Reprints, 1976), 5:240, entry 1952.
28 Ibid., 7: 440, entry 2891.
29 Letter from Vincent Hussey, February 18th 1601, in *Calendar of State Papers, Domestic Series, of the Reign of Elizabeth, 1598–1601*, ed. Mary Anne Everett Green (London: Longmans, Green, and Co., 1869), 585.
30 Arber, *Transcript*, III.43.
31 On the English Stock and the Company of Stationers in the Jacobean reign see William A. Jackson, *Records of the Court of the Stationers' Company 1602 to 1640* (London: The Bibliographical Society, 1957), viii–xiii; Cyprian Blagden, "The English Stock of the Stationers' Company in the Time of the Stuarts," *Library: The Transactions of the Bibliographical Society* 12, 5th series (1955): 167–186; Cyndia Susan Clegg, *Press Censorship in Jacobean England* (Cambridge: Cambridge University Press, 2001); and Arnold Hunt, "Book Trade Patents, 1603–1640," in *The Book Trade and Its Customers 1450–1900: Historical Essays for Robin Myers*, eds. Arnold Hunt, Giles Mandelbrote, and Alison Shell (Winchester: St. Paul's Bibliographies, 1997), 27–54.
32 Blagden, "English Stock...Stuarts," 168.

33 For that later period see Cyprian Blagden, "The Distribution of Almanacks in the Second Half of the Seventeenth Century," *Studies in Bibliography* 11 (1958): 107–116. See also Thomas A. Horrocks, *Popular Print and Popular Medicine: Almanacs and Health Advice in Early America* (Amherst: University of Massachusetts Press, 2008).
34 Capp, *Astrology*, 23; Blagden, "Distribution," 115–118.
35 Jackson, *Records*, 260.
36 Ibid., 260n.
37 Capp, *Astrology*, 51.
38 On that rise, see Keith Thomas, *Religion and the Decline of Magic*, 356–362.
39 *A Meteorological Dyary and Prognostication for This Present Yeare of Our Lord*, 1609–1620, MSS HM 80396, 28.
40 On Booker see Capp, *Astrology*, 71–77, and Capp, "Booker, John (1602–1667), Astrologer," *Oxford Dictionary of National Biography*. 23 Sep. 2004; Accessed 19 Nov. 2019.
41 John Booker, *A Bloody Irish Almanack* (London, 1646), A3r.
42 Capp, *Astrology*, 72.
43 On astrology in England after 1640 see Geneva, *Astrology*, and Patrick Curry, *Prophecy and Power: Astrology in Early Modern England* (Princeton, NJ: Princeton University Press, 1989), 6–8 and *passim*.
44 This account is taken from Capp, *Astrology*, 37–38.
45 Ibid, 37.
46 See biographical notes on these compilers in Capp, *Astrology*, 293–340.

1.4 Related publications and controversies

The increasing popularity of the astrological almanac in England in the late sixteenth and early seventeenth centuries suggests a parallel increase in popular astrological literacy. That rising knowledge is also indicated by the publication of related works, including perpetual almanacs, vernacular guides to astrology, books and pamphlets that translated Ptolemaic astronomy and astrology to a general audience, and books of secrets. This chapter seeks to place early modern almanacs, and the calendars they contained, into the context of those widely accessible related works. The goal here is to understand the early modern almanac as one dimension of popular science in Elizabethan and Jacobean England, and in doing so, to contribute to the broader scholarly effort—led by scholars such as Deborah Harkness and Lauren Kassell—to reconstruct the nature of popular scientific knowledge in post-Reformation England. That lower-level knowledge was more utilitarian and practical than the academic astrology of higher-level astrological practitioners such as Girolamo Cardano and John Dee, which to date has been more fully studied.[1]

A second goal of this chapter is to trace the defenses and attacks on astrology that were provoked by the rising popularity of the art, reviewing attacks on astrology and the astrological almanac in English from William Fulke's 1560 *Antiprognosticon* through 1640, including the satirical attacks in mock almanacs. This review reveals the relatively wide acceptance of judicial astrology in this period. Yes, some of its practices were seen as suspect, including the practice of horary questions that formed the basis for the work of professional astrologers in London. And yes, those who attacked the art had louder voices than those who defended it. There was in addition a powerful (though as opponents noted, deeply uninformed) aversion to astrology exhibited by some English Calvinist divines. But as the review of the vernacular literature on the subject suggests, the attacks do not represent a coherent, sustained attack on judicial astrology, and certainly not on the reformed Ptolemaic judicial astrology practiced by almanac compilers. Rather, the critiques were mostly isolated instances, reacting to particular events such as the Nostradamus prognostications of the late 1550s. Though sometimes squarely lodged at almanacs, these attacks did little to slow the popularity of those works, or the spread of astrological knowledge in early modern England.

Perpetual almanacs

The mother of all almanacs in early modern England was the *Kalender of Shepherds*, the earliest, most often reprinted, and most influential English perpetual almanac. The *Kalender* brought into early modern culture an important set of motifs, images, and concepts that conveyed medieval calendar traditions into early modern England. Like many perpetual almanacs, it also provided a straight-forward primer for Ptolemaic astrology—the first and most extensive overview of this material printed in English before the 1550s.

The complex story of the translation and printing of English editions of the *Kalender* has often been told.[2] First published in Paris in 1502, it was reprinted at least a dozen times in England before 1656, though H. Oskar Sommer speculates that copies have survived from only two-thirds of actual editions.[3] As Martha W. Driver notes, the images in the *Kalender* "were particularly influential on English book illustration and were copied and recopied in a variety of contexts."[4] That influence is especially clear in the history of the early modern calendar.

Driver has rightly emphasized the *Kalender's* "didactic and salvational" content, and indeed, the *Kalender* is a compact guide to Christian living that presents copious religious instruction.[5] But its astrological, astronomical, medical, and calendrical content is equally rich. All versions of the *Kalender* include twelve-month perpetual Julian calendars. As can be seen in the January calendar from the c. 1518 Julian Notary *Kalender* (Figure 3.2.1), the monthly calendar repeats motifs from the primers (such as the December calendar from Vostre's 1508 primer, Figure 1.1.4.). The *Kalender* supplies the reader with extensive tables that can be used to convert these perpetual monthly calendars to annual calendars in order to calculate for any given year the date of Easter and other movable holidays, the phases of the Moon, and the location of the Moon in the Zodiac. The *Kalender* therefore provides the reader with all the data needed for the practice of astrological medicine described elsewhere in its pages. It also includes a wealth of other calendrical material: calendar poetry (including the long poem, "The Days of the Week Moralized"), mnemonic verses for remembering the saints, poems concerning the character of each month, and eclipse tables, which were updated as the century progressed.

In addition, approximately one third of the *Kalender* is an explication of sixteenth century thought concerning cosmology, astrology, and astrological medicine—a readable, almost conversational digest of the *Almagest* and *Tetrabiblos,* which describes the celestial and sublunar spheres, defines terms such as ecliptic and meridian, and teaches readers how to plot celestial objects in the sky and tell the time at night with homemade instruments. The book includes images of Zodiac Man, Vein Man, and Planetary Man, rules for phlebotomy, and descriptions of Galenic and Hippocratic humoral medicine, including the four temperaments, the characters of the planets, and the nature of people born under the seven planetary rulers. The appeal of this material is strongly suggested by the fact that the printer Robert Wyer later excerpted the astrological and astronomical portions of the *Kalender* and published this material as *The Compost of Ptolemy* (Anonymous), first printed in octavo in c.1530 and reprinted in 1540 in quarto, then again in octavo in 1550, 1552, 1562, and 1638.[6] The *Kalender* translated Ptolemaic astrology downwards to a literate reading public; the usually smaller and presumably cheaper *Compost* pushes this material into even lower markets.

The second important perpetual calendar of the sixteenth century was the learned Leonard Digges' *A Prognostication of Right Good Effect*, first published in 1555 and reissued the next year in a revised edition, *A Prognostication Everlasting of Right Good Effect*.[7] One of the most noteworthy mathematicians of the Tudor era next to his son, Thomas Digges, and his friend John Dee—later Thomas Digges' tutor and guardian—Leonard Digges wrote multiple works of practical mathematics, including an oft-reprinted work on surveying, *A Boke named Tectonicon* (first published in 1561), *A Geometrical Practice, named Pantometria* (1571), and *An Arithmeticall Militare Treatise, named Stratioticos* (1571). Leonard Digges also produced a single-sheet almanac for 1556. The *Prognostication Everlasting* proved to be an enduring and influential book, reprinted over a dozen times into the early seventeenth century. Its material overlaps in significant ways with the contents of annual almanacs, though that information is augmented with scientific rationales and diagrams of scientific instruments such as the wind rose and the quadrant, which could be cut out and used to make paper instruments. Editions from 1556 on have Zodiac Man on the title page (Figure 1.4.1).

The *Prognostication* includes tables for finding the location of the Moon, dates for movable feasts and the dominical letter, rules for medical and husbandry elections, lists of evil days, aspects of the Moon with the other planets, tide tables, and the length of dawn, daylight, twilight, and nighttime (necessary for calculating the planetary hours). Digges' work appears to have been a resource for other calendar makers; its images of the relative size of the planets, for example, are copied into the manuscript miscellanies of Thomas Trevilian or Trevelyon.[8] Always printed in quarto, the first two editions of this book were published by the talented Thomas Gemini, an immigrant instrument maker in London. Famously, it was to the 1576 edition of *A Prognostication Everlasting* that Thomas Digges appended a treatise that endorsed the cosmological theories of Copernicus and included the first diagram of the Copernican heliocentric model printed in England.[9]

Related publications and controversies 77

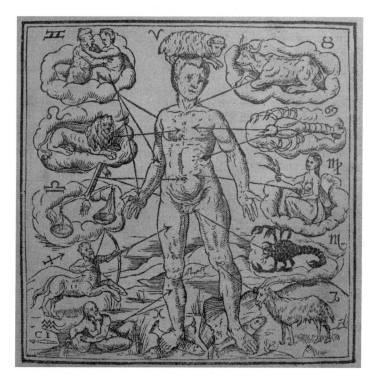

Figure 1.4.1 Zodiac Man, Leonard Digges, *A Prognostication Everlasting of Ryght Good Effecte* (1556), Title Page. Photograph by Phebe Jensen, from the collection of the Folger Shakespeare Library, STC 435.39.

Another work that loosely falls into the category of the perpetual almanac is *A Litle Treatise, Conteyning many Proper Tables and Rules Very Necessary for the Use of All Men* (1571), written by the powerful printer and chronicler Richard Grafton, who for many years had been publishing calendars in almanacs, primers, and chronicles. Like the *Kalender* and Digges' *Prognostication Everlasting*, this work would become a key resource for later almanac compilers. It was published (with slightly revised titles) an astonishing fifteen times between 1571 and 1611. Grafton's *Treatise* includes a perpetual calendar with all the Sarum saints, as well as many of the tables that appear in almanacs: a historical chronology, dates for law terms, principal fairs, tide tables, rules for bloodletting, a sixty-year almanac to find the date of Easter and, if sixty years proved too short, the rule for calculating the date of Easter in perpetuity. Printed in octavo like the almanacs, though much longer (the 1571 edition is seven sheets and over a hundred pages), this book was a standard source of calendar information for over forty years.

Grafton's treatise would received its final printing in 1611. The next year it was replaced by a similar book that updated the calendar information for the new century and provided an extensive primer on the Ptolemaic astrology needed to understand, or indeed, to write almanacs: Arthur Hopton's *A Concordancy of Years*. The *Concordancy* describes (among other things) the Ptolemaic universe, the planetary and astral spheres, the solar, Julian, and Gregorian years, the planetary hours, the qualities of planets and signs, and how to find the phase of the Moon and its location in the Zodiac forever. It includes both a perpetual calendar (with complete Sarum saints) and other mensuration tables that often appear in seventeenth century almanacs, such as instructions for reckoning expenses, tables for currency exchange, and a historical chronology. Hopton's *Concordancy* was reprinted in 1615, 1616, and 1635. Like Digges' *Prognostication*, Hopton's work both communicates the contemporary science of Ptolemaic astrology, and scoffs at some traditional calendar lore.

In addition to these perpetual almanacs a few multi-year almanacs appear after the 1550s. The first is Philip Moore's unusual work, *A fourtie yeres Almanacke, with a Prognostication*, initially printed in 1567 in octavo by John Kyngston for H. Saunderson. At over one hundred pages, this work bears little resemblance to the modest multi-year almanacs designed for use with perpetual primers and printed in earlier years by de Worde, Wyer, and Grafton. Like the *Kalender*, it includes explanations about basic Ptolemaic cosmology, as well as information on how to predict the weather by the appearance and quality of air, fire, and water—lore that will reappear in the annual almanacs of the seventeenth century. Like the annual almanacs, it includes Zodiac Man, rules for medical elections, a chronology, a list of principle fairs, tables for finding the location of the Moon every year, and general husbandry guides by month. It also presents prognostications based on eclipses and revolutions for each year between 1567 to 1606, covering the usual topics of dearth and plenty, war and peace, sickness, and political and social events. Moore's work would be reissued in 1570, 1571 (this edition adds itineraries), and 1573, though the annual prognostications were never extended beyond 1606. The only other author of multi-year almanacs in the Elizabethan period is William Bourne, who compiles one three-year almanac for the years 1571 to 1573 that, unusually, includes extensive rules for navigation that reflect his expertise; Bourne is also the author of the much reprinted *A Regiment for the Sea*.[10]

Astrological guides

Almanacs depend on a certain level of knowledge of Ptolemaic astronomy and astrology, and during the time they gained in popularity, many vernacular works, of various degrees of scientific or medical credibility, were also published to explain that science. These guides sometimes included calendars, or more often, general seasonal or monthly guides to physic.

Putting almanacs into the context of this material allows us to see them as part of a body of work that both reflected and enhanced growing popular literacy concerning astrology and astrological medicine in later Tudor and early Stuart England.

An early work in this vein is Thomas Moulton's *This is the Myrour or Glasse of Helthe*, first published before 1531 by Robert Wyer. Moulton's book reviews aspects of astrological medicine such as the qualities of men born under each of the twelve signs and the timing of medical interventions depending on planetary ruler (C4r-E1r); it was published at least a dozen times by ten separate printers before 1550.[11] In the 1540s and 1550s, two almanac compilers wrote brief but accurate guides to astrology, perhaps attempting to increase the market for their annual productions: Andrew Boorde in *The Pryncyples of Astronamye* (c. 1547) and Anthony Askham in *Litell Treatyse of Astronomy, very necessary for Physyke and Surgerye* (1550). Another book that served a similar purpose, though at a higher academic level, was the English translation of the French astrologer Oronce Fine's *Righte Ample Documentes, Touchinge the Use and Practise of the Common Almanackes*, printed twice in 1558 and again in 1570. Over one hundred pages in octavo, Fine's work not only provides descriptions of astral and planetary qualities and astrological medicine; it is also a high-level how-to guide for practicing judicial astrology. A similar book is Claude Dariot's *A Breefe and Most Easie Introduction to the Astrologicall Judgement of the Starres*, printed in 1583, 1598, and (in a revised edition) 1653. Another astrological guide less directly connected to the astrology of the almanacs was John Maplet's *The Dial of Destiny*, a treatise on the planets and their influence published in 1581 and 1592.[12] Much later, George Simotta's *A Theater of the Planetary Houres for All Dayes of the Yeare*(1632, STC 22561) explained the use in astrological medicine of the planetary hours that by then were a standard part of the annual almanacs.

The works listed above are directly focused on either the almanacs or the Ptolemaic astrological practices of lunar and judicial astrology they communicated. Astrology also received explication in longer works of mathematics and natural philosophy. Robert Record's *The Castle of Knowledge* (1556), a learned work on the sphere primarily aimed at mathematical practitioners, also provided basic astrological information in the vernacular.[13] *The Cosmographical Glasse* (1559), by the almanac compiler William Cuningham, was a scholarly and ambitious work that includes basic information on astrological principles and calculations. The late medieval encyclopedia *De Proprietatibus Rerum*, with its extensive overview of Ptolemaic astrology and Galenic medicine, was reissued in 1582 under Stephen Batman's name, as *Batman upon Bartholome*. Brief discussions of astrology are included in John Blagrave's *The Mathematical Jewel* (1585) and Robert Tanner's *A Mirror for Mathematiques* (1587), which provides instructions for constructing a horoscope and calculating the location of astral bodies with an astrolabe and other instruments. Finally, the polymath Thomas Blundeville's *M. Blundeville His Exercises*, with its handy "plaine Treatise of the first principles of Cosmographie," was first printed in 1594 and reprinted six times up until 1638.[14]

Another category of publications related to almanacs are ephemerides, the charts delineating the relative position of the stars necessary for writing an almanac. Almanac compilers must have mostly obtained their ephemerides from foreign sources, as only a few printed in England survive for the century from 1540 to 1640. The earliest printed in England are by John Field; his ephemerides (one for 1557, another for 1558–1560) adapt the tables of Copernicus and Erasmus Rheinhold. Another ephemerides by an English compiler is the *Calendaria* by the minister and almanac compiler George Hartgill, published in two editions (English and Latin) in 1594, a work that also included a significant defense of astrology on Christian and indeed explicitly Protestant grounds. In the next century John Searle's *An Ephemeris for Nine Yeeres* (1609) provided both the astral charts needed for almanac compilation and related tables, at least one of which subsequently found its way into an almanac (Figure 2.7).

All the works described above represent concepts that were mainstream and widely accepted as part of mathematics and natural philosophy, though translated from high academic language into ordinary, more accessible terms. But these works flourished amidst more dubious guides to astrology and prognostications. In lower level publications, standard astrological belief mingled with what is more clearly lore and superstition, though the line was drawn differently for early moderns than it is for us today. The most popular of the lower level publications was *The pronostycacyon for ever, of mayster Erra Pater*, first published in c. 1540 by Robert Wyer and reprinted thirteen times before 1639. Erra Pater became a symbol of astrological ineptitude; in the seventeenth century, John Booker and William Lilly "labelled each other 'Erra Pater' as a term of abuse."[15] The book certainly contains dubious calendar lore: the brontologies, the Esdras or dominical letter prophecies, and the good and evil Egyptian days are all included (even though presumably they must conflict in any given year). Yet, the various editions of *Erra Pater* also provide a basic yet accurate overview of Ptolemaic cosmology along the lines of *The Compost of Ptolemy*. *Erra Pater* reveals its kinship to almanacs and prognostications by accumulating in later editions some of the tables typical in almanacs; for example, the 1605 edition includes a list of principal fairs, and the 1609 edition includes a chronology and the rules for determining law terms. In 1622, Gervase Markham attempted to salvage the book by producing a new version, *Verus Pater*, clearly meant to capitalize on the original's popularity and raise its academic credibility. Yet the spurious original continued to be reprinted, while Markham's revision was not.

Another popular astrological guide at the lower end was the *Briefe introductions, bothe naturall, pleasaunte, and also delectable, unto the Art of*

Chiromancy, attributed to the fifteenth century French priest John Indagine and first published in England in 1558. The third of three sections in this volume is a perfectly adequate account of Ptolemaic astrology, titled "A compendious description of Naturall Astrologye, never so briefely handeled before" (L2v), which lays out the basic qualities of the planets, signs, and houses, the section on chiromancy having earlier explained how the signs and planets manifest in the human face. Indagine's work was printed twice in 1558, four more times by 1633, and in five additional editions before the end of the seventeenth century. A similar work, first printed in English in the early 1560s and published fifteen times before 1679, is *The Most Excellent, Profitable, and Pleasant Booke of the Famous Doctor and Expert Astrologien Arcandam or Aleandrin*, popularly known as *Arcandam*, and attributed to Richard Roussat. This is an enduringly popular astrological treatise of seriously doubtful credibility that, among other things, encourages the use of the Sphere of Apuleius for assessing individual destiny, and (like Indagine) explores the connection between the stars and human physiognomy. *Arcandam* is focused on astrological nativities rather than the revolutions, eclipses, and elections of the almanacs and prognostications, but in addition to its more questionable elements it also contains standard descriptions of the qualities of the Zodiac signs.

Finally, at the farthest reach from the academic astrology of a Digges or a Cuningham was the material that appears in books of secrets and other miscellaneous prognostications. Books of secrets attributed to Aristotle in the sixteenth century usually have little astrological content except for a general description of the four seasons, but as mentioned in Chapter 1.1, two books ascribed to the philosopher repeat the days of the Moon prognostications, Esdras prophecies, and brontologies: these are the *De Cursione Luna* (1528), and *Here Begynneth the Nature, and Dysposycyon of the Days in the Weke* (1554). The most popular book in this category was the *Boke of Knowledge* attributed to Godfridus (first published c. 1554), which includes plenty of calendar lore (the Esdras prophecies, Egyptian days, days of the Moon, etc.) and almost no true astrological material. Published twice in the 1550s and once in 1585, when it was reprinted in 1619 it also included an excerpt from Proclus' eminently respectable *Treatise on the Sphere*, as well as *The Husbandmans Practise*, first published separately in 1585, another hodgepodge that included the Esdras prognostications.[16] The Godfridus *Boke of Knowledge* enjoyed quite astonishing popularity in the seventeenth century, with a total of seventeen separate editions between 1619 and 1700. Another publication in this category, I.A.'s *A Perfyte Prognostication Perpetuall* (c. 1556), includes an almanac for the date of Easter from 1556 to 1570, followed by the Esdras prognostications based on the day of the week of New Year's Day. These are given not only in text, but in emblems that prefigure the later Trevelyon dominical letter prognostications; the predictions are sometimes (but not always) consistent between these two versions. The anonymous author's stated goal for the book is to communicate these important prophecies concerning plenty and dearth, the abundance of fruit and wine, and the likelihood of war, to "the Ignoraunt people, that is not skylled on the Booke" (A2v), but in truth, the emblems are quite indecipherable without the text.[17] *The Boke of Secretes of Albertus Magnus,* printed in English in 1560 and approximately seven more times before 1684, includes a description of the planetary hours, and the 1599 edition adds a mainstream description of the qualities of the seven planets.

Controversies

As the eight volumes of Lynn Thorndike's *History of Magic and Experimental Science* attest, astrology was the subject of a vast literature from the classical period into the seventeenth century. Natural philosophers, physicians, academics, and in the Christian era, ecclesiasts of all stripes attacked, defended, refined, qualified, augmented, and attempted to curtail the art from the classical period through the early Christian era and into the middle ages, both before the reintroduction of Ptolemaic astronomy and its Arabic accretions into the West, and after. In the sixteenth century, astrology was generally accepted as academic practice; it was also, as Robin B. Barnes has shown, embraced by Lutheran Reformers as perfectly compatible with the Gospel.[18] The mild paradox here is that, while intermittent religious objections to the art arose in England in the hundred years spanning the mid-sixteenth and mid-seventeenth centuries, they did nothing to hamper the spread of astrological literacy and interest. That paradox can be partially illuminated by considering the attacks on astrology in the more precise cultural and scientific contexts in which they were produced.

As Don Cameron Allen has shown, the arguments of both attacks and defenses of astrology invariably draw on a long tradition. The most important source for attacks on the art was Pico della Mirandola's massive late fifteenth century *Disputationes adversus astrologiam divinatricem,* portions of which was published posthumously in 1495.[19] This *magnum opus* gathered together centuries of objections to astrology, and added new ones. It was a central resource for all later astrological critiques, and most English attacks borrow heavily from it. But the critique of astrology in England is also connected to the rise of the astrological almanac and prognostication, and in the Elizabethan period, more specifically to the almanacs of Notradamus (in the late 1550s and 1560s), and the hullabaloo surrounding the great conjunction of Saturn and Jupiter in 1583.

The first dedicated anti-astrology work printed in English in the Tudor period was William Fulke's 1560 *Antiprognosticon...an Invective against the Vayne and Unprofitable Predictions of Nostradame, etc.* The Latin version of this work (published the same year) adds to the title page the English compilers who were deemed to offend almost as much as Nostradamus: William Cuningham, Henry Low, Thomas Hill, and Lewes Vaughan.

Fulke's work, perhaps the most extreme criticism of astrology printed in the Tudor period, attacks astrology mainly on scientific grounds. He repeats the argument, also found in Pico's *Disputationes*, that astrology cannot be called a science because its precepts cannot be proven; in this, it differs from other true sciences, such as geometry. He reiterates the assertion that astrological rules are arbitrary: the qualities of planets and signs depend entirely on fanciful and fictional stories, made up by men. There is no objective reason to believe that Jupiter is benevolent, or Saturn earthy, or that a triune aspect means anything different than an opposition or a quadrature. Fulke takes aim at Nostradamus for his "darke wrynkles of obscuritie, that no man could pyke out of them, either sence or understanding certain" (A8r-v). Cuningham he acknowledges to be "a man... bothe lerned and honest," before attacking him as incompetent (B1r). Fulke grants, following Aristotle, that the stars influence the sublunar world, but denies that influence can be specifically applied to individuals (also a point made by Pico).

Although Fulke would later become known as a passionate Godly reformer, the grounds on which he attacks astrology are not those of other religious writers such as Miles Coverdale and Roger Hutchinson.[20] Those writers echo St. Augustine's claim that astrology abrogates Christian free will—a claim that, as Chapter 1 has shown, does not reflect the actual practice of Ptolemaic astrology in the Christian West.[21] Fulke, however, acknowledges that astral influence does not compel the will; the stars only create "a certaine inclination" that may "by divers meanes be averted or tourned to some other effect" (B8v). Moral arguments in the *Antiprognosticon* mostly concern the irresponsible effects of prognostications, as with farmers who store grain against a prophesied dearth. And though Fulke's attack is severe, it is not clear that he was a lifelong opponent to astrology, or even how fully serious he was in 1560. The title page of the Latin edition of the *Antiprognosticon* carries the same motto found on almanacs, *Sapiens dominabitur Astris* and Richard Bauckam posits that the *Antiprognosticon* might have been more a youthful rhetorical exercise than a serious attack.[22] Fulke's later works—including an astrological game designed to teach its players the very principles of the art he attacks as contrived in the *Antiprognosticon*—suggest a "less unambiguous attitude to astrology than that expressed" in this 1560 pamphlet.[23]

The next year, 1561, Francis Coxe was involved in two attacks on astrology. The first appeared in a broadside, *The unfained retraction of Fraunces Cox*, in which Coxe renounced necromancy, the conjuring of spirits, and "that curious part of Astrologie, wherein is contayned the Calculatying of Nativities." In the second, *A Short Treatise Declaring the Detestable Wickednesse of Magicall Sciences,* Coxe more extensively denounced the art, insisting that even academic astrology was dangerous because "Never was there any that coulde yet holde hym selfe content with the simple knowledge of Astrologie: but wolde wade furder in those sciences of prediction" (A7v).

But Cox evidently found a way to practice true astrology without veering into necromancy, as he later compiled two almanacs (for 1567 and 1568).

The other attack on astrology printed in English in 1561 was John Calvin's *An Admonicion against Astrology Judiciall*, earlier published in Geneva in French in 1549. Though written over a decade earlier, the publication of this tract in English may have been provoked, as Fulke's pamphlet was, by the notoriety of Nostradamus' almanacs.[24] Calvin's position in this work is more nuanced than has sometimes been assumed, for the pamphlet defends "true astrologie" (A7v) as a subset of the "humaine sciences" (A5v). In addition to endorsing the basic principle that there is "a link or as it were a knott and tying together of the things which ear above with the things that are beneth," Calvin provides a qualified endorsement of nativities, acknowledging that "the starres may empryinte certain qualities in the persones," though he stresses that they "can not cause that this thing or yt shuld fall upon them aftrwarde of other occassions" (B5r). That position is in fact in line with the stance of most Christian astrologers from St. Aquinas onwards. As did Fulke, Calvin objects to the art on the grounds of its inaccuracies, but the most significant attack is made (unsurprisingly) on religious grounds. The root problem with astrology for Calvin is that it distracts its adherents from a focus in the divine and undermines the faith that accepts the future without trying to predict it. Like all human learning the study of astrology can encourage "wicked curiositie" (E2r) that provokes meddling into secrets God has purposely hidden. Astrology's focus on the physical influence of the stars also fails to give precedence to the spiritual; indeed, one of Calvin's possibly original points in this pamphlet is that, if God calls men to be reborn in Christ, then their true spiritual nativity would cancel out the influence of the physical nativity.

Calvin's rejection of astrology—though not always his precise arguments—are repeated in works by other English Protestant reformers, including Philip Stubbes and Reginald Scot.[25] Yet, despite this opposition, it does not seem to be the case that most Elizabethan Protestants were opposed to astrology. As Capp has shown, a significant minority of almanac compilers were ministers, and the great and rising popularity of the astrological almanac suggested its mainstream appeal. On an ideological level, English astrologers and at least some divines were well aware that astrology had a powerful Protestant advocate in the Lutheran disciple, Philip Melanchthon, by whose influence the study of astrology at the University of Wittenberg was flourishing in the mid-sixteenth century.

Calvin's *Admonicion* was the last direct criticism on astrology until the 1580s, though there was one other significant attack on almanac compilers: *The Astronomers Game* by Nicholas Allen (1569). This work is partially a parody of an almanac, which it visually echoes with charts, rubrication, and calendars formatted in the ordinary way. Like Fulke, Allen goes after specific compilers, targeting Buckminster, Securis, and Low, whose inadequacies are exposed when Allen lists their variable predictions for 1569 against each day. Allen's letter "To the Reader" mocks the compilers directly, claiming their calculations "jarre as much as any three clockes in Englande, how dronken so ever the Sextons be" (*1r). But though *The Astronomers Game* attacks English almanacs, it spares astrology itself; the errors he discovers are "in the artificer, not in the Arte within hir boundes" (*4r).

The next significant flurry of works attacking astrology and almanacs appears to have been in part a response to the publicity surrounding the great conjunction of Saturn and Jupiter in 1583. As Margaret Aston and Carroll Camden have shown, this was no ordinary astrological event; though Saturn and Jupiter meet in conjunction approximately every twenty years, only once every 960 years does that conjunction occur at an especially significant moment in the astrological year, at the "end of the watery trigon or triplicity of the signs of Cancer, Scorpio, and Pisces, and at the beginning of the fiery trigon or triplicity of the signs of Aries, Leo, and Sagittarius."[26] The conjunction's importance was magnified by the fact that it was to occur only five years before 1588, a year that Regiomontanus and other astrologers (and some divines) had long predicted would mark the end of the world. Small wonder it excited alarm and intense interest from academics, ecclesiastical officials, and ordinary Elizabethans.

Though astronomers working in academic circles had long anticipated the great conjunction of 1583, it entered into English popular print only in January 1583 when Richard Harvey, a younger brother of Gabriel, first published *An Astrological Discourse upon the Great and Notable Conjunction of the Two Superior Planets, Saturne & Jupiter*. Richard Harvey's work includes a long preface dedicated to John Aylmer, the Bishop of London, that is essentially an extended defense of astrology in academic terms—the first in the English vernacular outside the more limited defenses offered in almanac letters to the reader. Like other Christian defenders of astrology Harvey cites biblical passages, classical authorities, and divines, including Philip Melanchthon. The preface is followed by an extended prognostication in which Harvey walks his readers through his analysis of the charts for the conjunction itself, as well as charts for significant subsequent astronomical events, including several eclipses in the 1580s. This prognostication represents a greatly extended example of what one finds in the contemporary annual almanacs, though its tone is especially dire. Its connection with the annual prognostications is suggested in the title, which advertises that its goal is partly "to supplie that is wanting in comon Prognostications."

The most important aspect of Harvey's *Astrological Discourse* was its extraordinary popularity: it was printed five separate times in 1583. Perhaps to ride this tide of interest, another astrologer, Robert Tanner, almost immediately (also in 1583) released a different assessment of the great conjunction's impact, in *A Prognosticall judgement of the great conjunction.*

Yet it was the response to Harvey by Thomas Heth (or Heath), published in March 1583, that created the greatest controversy. In *A manifest and apparent confutation* Heth attacked Harvey for having identified the wrong date and time for the conjunction—a fundamental error that (of course) would completely undermine the prognostication. Soon John Harvey—the youngest of the three Harvey brothers—supported his brother in print with *An Astrologicall Addition* (also 1583), which provides detail to shore up Richard Harvey's original prognostication.

In the context of this controversy two important attacks on astrology appeared: Henry Howard, Earl of Northampton's *A Defensative against the Poyson of Supposed Prophecies.* (1583, reprinted 1622) and William Perkins' *Foure Great Lyers* (1584). Howard's book—over three hundred pages in quarto—was (as Allen notes) "little more than an English summary" of Pico's *Disputationes*.[27] Among other things, Howard' repeats Pico by denying that astrology can qualify as a science, and notes the arbitrary assignation of qualities and properties to the Zodiac signs and planets. Howard's *Defensative* goes after "blinde almanacks" (1622, 11r), though these were only one small part of a larger attack on all astrological divination. Perkins' *Foure Great Lyers*, however, takes direct aim at the annual almanacs by repeating the strategy of *The Astronomers Game*. He humiliates compilers by listing the weather forecasts as they were predicted for every day in the year (probably for 1585) by "B.," "F.," and "T.," possibly Buckminster, Frende, and Thomas Twyne, a Cambridge academic who published a single sheet almanac in 1579 and an octavo almanac for 1585 (neither extant except in a few fragments). The second half of Perkins' pamphlet articulated its goal in its title: "A resolution to the Countrye-man, provyng it unlawfull for him to bye or use our yearly Prognostications" (B1r). The problems concerning astrology for Perkins were the ineptitude of practitioners, the impossibility of charting the stars with accuracy (a point wholly supported by the Harvey-Heth disagreement), and the familiar argument that astrology bore no resemblance to other verifiable sciences. The moral and religious arguments are in the same vein as Calvin's *Admonicion:* an obsession with the stars distracts from the contemplation of the maker of those stars. Like most of astrology's detractors, Perkins has no quarrel with basic Ptolemaic astrology; he endorses the idea that the stars influence the material sublunar world, and so can be useful in husbandry, physic, and forecasting the weather.

It has sometimes been suggested that the failure of the 1583 predictions to materialize, coupled by Heth's attack on Harvey's calculations and the appearance of the Howard and Perkins tracts, damaged the credibility of the astrologers and contemporary confidence in astrology. This may be true to a certain extent, but it also seems that the animosity was mostly *ad hominem*, damning the Harveys but not necessarily damaging the reputation of astrology itself. Heth thinks little of Richard Harvey's skill—he calls him an "unskilfull Astronomer"—but he also pleads with readers not to let Richard Harvey's inaccuracies discredit astrology itself, asking "that no indifferent person will thinke the worse of so excellent a science, for that the students in the same profession, seeme to write the one directly contrary to the other" (A2v). Similarly, the account of the fracas in Holinshed attacks Richard Harvey when it describes the foolish credulity of the "common sort of people" who believed the predictions of "a certeine astrologicall discourse" (1587, 3.1356), but it also does not seek to undermine astrology. The popular writer Robert Greene joined the fray to attack the Harveys in print in support of his friend Thomas Nashe, in a pamphlet war that was to extend into the 1590s. But in 1585, Greene also published *Planetomachia*, a work that both implicitly endorses astrology and explicitly defends it, inserting a Latin excerpt of Giovanni Pontano's defense of astrology against Pico—a text that, in this context, might be seen as a swipe against the Pico arguments plagiarized in Howard's *Defensative*.[28] In conclusion, although the 1583 predictions may have discredited the Harveys, and they certainly put wind in the sails of anti-astrology writers, they simultaneously showcased the art of the prognostication, casting it in a scholarly light in Richard Harvey's preface and indeed in the other 1583 prognostications authored by Tanner, Heth, and John Harvey. As Aston notes, "[a]s the result of all this publicity, perhaps many people who would not normally have bothered much with such things were made conversant with astrological terminology."[29] Certainly, if one tracks the publication of almanacs, it seems that in the 1580s, their numbers begin to rise, *en route* to the explosion in the genre that would occur in the first decade of the seventeenth century.

Most defenses of astrology in the Elizabethan period appear in the almanacs themselves; these are reviewed in Part II. Yet, the Tudor era ends with both a significant attack and an extensive academic defense of astrology which, together, usefully encapsulate many of the major arguments for and against the art. The attack came from John Chamber, an Oxford fellow, in *A Treatise against Judical Astrologie* (1601). Succinct, witty, and rhetorically lively, the *Treatise* rehashes many of the previous arguments mounted against astrology from St. Augustine to Pico della Mirandola to Calvin, covering the art's imprecision, its prohibition by the Bible, the moral and religious problems raised by telling the fortunes of Christian men, and the dubious scientific credibility of an art which had no way of validating its claims. Unlike Calvin, however, Chamber is well versed in astrology; his book is all the more devastating, as he limits his attack to issues that were undeniably reflected in the contemporary practice of Ptolemaic astrology. Yet, this argument was answered, point by point, and with three or four times the number of authorities marshalled at each laborious stage in Sir Christopher Heydon's *A Defence of Judiciall Astrologie* (1603). As Allen has noted, the concise and direct Chamber was met with his rhetorical opposite in the methodical, detailed, ponderous Heydon, who in responding to *A Treatise* produced a book four times the length of its target. Chamber wrote a manuscript rejoinder to Heydon which was never published, but the Chamber position was championed by the ecclesiast George Carleton, published twenty years later (in 1624) as *Astrologomania*. Carleton's work takes a radical position against astrology. Reiterating one of Augustine's claims, he insists that astrology is magic, not science, and goes further than Fulke, Calvin, Perkins, and Chambers himself in order to deny that the stars are natural causes in the sublunar world—a claim that goes to the bedrock assumptions of the art. Carleton's extreme position may well have found favor in religious circles, and some of his arguments reappear in the 1650s.

The Chamber-Heydon print debate usefully articulates the most academic claims for and against astrology at the end of the Elizabethan reign. Though to a modern reader the position of Chamber (and later Carleton) seems the reasonable one, in fact, Chamber's attack was printed on the cusp of an explosion of the art that Heydon's *Defence* supported, as the astrological almanac was poised to become one of the most popular books of the seventeenth century.

John Melton's *Astrologaster, or The Figure-Caster* (1620) is usually categorized with anti-astrology works such as Carleton's *Astrolomania*. It does indeed attack astrologers, but it does so with a tone, literary panache, and satirical verve that associates it equally with the genre of the mock almanac (considered below). As with Thomas Middleton's *The Owles Almanac, Astrologaster* could be classified as a work of urban comedy, as suggested by a satirical "Table Made by the Learned Astronomer *Erra Pater*" that lines up the London trades with planets and the stars: Scriveners, for example, are Children of Mars and so ruled by Sagittarius, while "Tobacco men" are children of Venus, under the sway of Taurus (11–12). Melton's target is primarily astrological practitioners; he provides lively scenes of crowds consulting the astrologers who by this time were a regular feature of London life, directing his spleen especially against "the ever-moving tongues" of women (4). He is particularly disturbed by the use of horary questions in elections—the central practice of professional astrologers, not almanac compilers. *Astrologaster*, which is not a particularly serious or scholarly attack on the art, is also the last surviving work dedicated specifically to undermining astrology printed in English until the 1650s.

Mock almanacs

The first English mock prognostication, *A Mery Pronostication* of 1544, closely follows the standard format for its satirical target, presenting humorous verse prognostications for eclipses, the four quarters of the year, and the twelve months, as well as a verse "Of diseases and syckenesses," "Of kynges," and others on the children of some of the planets. The satire operates partly through the ponderous elucidation of the obvious or ridiculous: "But I saye yf the nynth daye of Novembre / Had fallen upon tenth daye of Decembre / It had bene a mervaylous hote yere for bees / For then had the Moone ben lyke a grene chese" (A2r).

There are no surviving contributions to the mock almanac genre until 1591 and the publication of Adam Foulweather's *A Wonderfull Strange and Miraculous Astrologicall Prognostication*. This work partially repeats the rhetorical maneuvers of its predecessor in grandiose statements of the factual or banal. Eclipses, for example, which happen every year, are predicted to happen this year "in one of the 12 monethes, & some of the foure quarters of the year" (A3r-A3v). Primarily, however, Foulweather uses the format of the annual prognostication in order to attack human sinfulness, rather than astrology itself. For example, Foulweather predicts that

> Cancer being the sole house of the Moone, doth presage that this yeere fruits shalbe greatly eaten with Catterpillers: as Brokers, Farmers, and Flatterers, which feeding on the sweate of other mens browes, shall greatly hinder the beautye of the spring, and disparage the growth of all hottest hearbes, unless some northerly winde of Gods vengance cleere the trees of such Catterpillers, with a hotte plague and the pestilence.
>
> (A3r-A3v)

Many of the elements here are familiar from annual prognostications: predictions on the year's "fruits," "hearbes," and other crops, prognostications for the four quarters (here, the Spring), and a prophecy for plagues and pestilence, which can be understood as God's punishment for wicked behavior. But they have been metaphorically twisted so that the passage becomes a critique of the rapacious behavior of men—"Brokers, Farmers, and Flatterers." The work is not centrally focused on astrology, and so—like other mock almanacs—should perhaps not be seen in the same category as direct attacks on the art.[30]

In the Jacobean period, literary writers got into the business of satirizing almanacs. Thomas Dekker's *The Ravens Almanacke* (1609) is in part a witty riff on calendars; for example, he personifies the months which he imagines to each "have his followers, some of them being thirtie in number, some 31, onely one (by falling into decay, or else because he keeps but a colde house[)], keeping but 28" (A2v). Mostly *The Ravens Almanacke*, like Foulweather's *Prognostication*, uses the structure of the astrological prognostication as vehicle to deliver social satire. For this year, for example, the author predicts "certaine diseases that are likely to raigne amongst trades-men—as the lazie evill, the Lethargie...dizines of the head, (caused by the fumes of good drinke) and such like" (B2v). But most of *The Ravens Almanacke* has little connection to astrology or almanacs, digressing instead into stories and jests unrelated to the calendar, such as one concerning

"An excellent diet for an Usurer" (E8V), and another relating "How in a household of civill warre, a woman may be safe from a cruell husband," (F8v). Mock almanacs which continue the use of the genre for social satire include two published in 1623: W.W.'s *A New, and Merrie Prognostication,* and (continuing the bird theme) Jack Daw's *Vox Graculi, or Jacke Dawes Prognostication.*

Middleton's *The Owles Almanac* (1619), as Neil Rhodes has noted, is without question "the most elaborate and also the cleverest parody of the early printed almanac."[31] Middleton was apparently intimately familiar with almanacs, which he also mocked in *No Wit No Help Like a Woman's*. As David George has shown, Middleton clearly had Bretnor's 1611 almanac in front of him while concocting Weatherwise's comic obsession with almanacs in that play.[32] *The Owles Almanac* shows the same detailed familiarity with both the genre as a whole and the Jacobean almanacs of Edmund Pond and Thomas Bretnor, as it "stitches together a ludicrous sampler" of the standard offerings of almanacs—the law terms, chronologies, tide tables, Zodiac Man, elections, lists of fairs, etc.[33] This mock almanac is a true parody, and it participates in some of the same rhetorical gestures of the earlier mock almanacs when it bombastically states the obvious and turns the standard elements of almanacs to social parody. But *The Owles Almanac* is also much more: an exuberant comic "performance," as Rhodes has suggested, that is firmly embedded in the urban and economic world of Jacobean London. Like the earlier mock almanacs, though much more extensively and effectively, *The Owles Almanac* makes fun of astrological belief without obviously or directly attacking the art's underlying principles.[34]

Notes

1 Deborah Harkness, *The Jewel House: Elizabethan London and the Scientific Revolution* (New Haven, CT: Yale University Press, 2008); Kassell, *Medicine and Magic*; Schaffer, "Science"; Jones, "Medicine and Science." On Cardano see Grafton, *Cardano's Cosmos*; on Dee, see Parry, *The Arch-Conjuror of England*, and William H. Sherman, *John Dee: The Politics of Reading and Writing in the English Renaissance* (Amherst: University of Massachusetts Press, 1995). Some higher-level astrological practitioners were influenced by the works attributed to the mythical Hermes Trismegistus, transmitted by Marsilio Ficino; this strand of astrology played little or no part in the popular vernacular material, including almanacs. On Hermeticism, see Frances A. Yates, *Giordano Bruno and the Hermetic Tradition* (London: Routledge and Kegan Paul, 1964). See also skepticism towards Yates' thesis in Kassell, *Medicine and Magic*, 9, and Brian P. Copenhaver, "Natural Magic, Hermeticism, and Occultism in Early Modern Science," in *Reappraisals of the Scientific Revolution*, eds. David C. Lindberg and Robert S. Westman (Cambridge: Cambridge University Press, 1990), 261–302. For useful overviews of astrology that differentiate the various areas of astrological thought and practice in the period and outline the porous lines between astrology and magic, see also Copenhaver, "Astrology and Magic," and Rutkin, "Astrology."

2 The most comprehensive overview of the *Kalender* is the introduction in H. Oskar Sommer, ed., *The Kalender of Shepherdes; The Edition of Paris 1503 in Photographic Facsimile* (London: Kegan, Paul, Trench, Trubner & Co., 1891). See also Driver, "When is a Miscellany." On Edmund Spenser's rewriting of the *Kalender* in *The Shepheardes Calender* see Alison Chapman, "The Politics of Time," and Abigail Shinn, "'Extraordinary Discourses of Unnecessarie matter': Spenser's *Shepheardes Calender* and the Almanac Tradition," in *Literature and Popular Culture in Early Modern England*, eds. Andrew Hadfield and Matthew Dimmock (Farnham, Surrey: Ashgate, 2009), 137–150.
3 Sommer, *The Kalender*, 11–26.
4 Driver, "When is a Miscellany," 214.
5 Ibid., 211.
6 Thomas describes the *Kalender* as one of several "crude works of prognostication, vaguely astrological in character, but lacking the rigour of the astrological almanac proper" (*Religion*, 390), but the Ptolemaic material in this work and its offshoot, *The Compost of Ptolemy* is in fact an accurate popularization of contemporary astrological theory and practice.
7 On Leonard and Thomas Digges see Stephen Johnston, "Digges, Leonard (c. 1515–c. 1559), Mathematician," and "Digges, Thomas (c.1546–1595), Mathematician and Member of Parliament." *Oxford Dictionary of National Biography*. 23 Sep. 2004; Accessed 20 November 2019. Leonard Digges (1588–1635), the London poet and translator, was Thomas Digges' son.
8 Heather Wolfe, ed. *The Trevelyon Miscellany: A Facsimile Edition of Folger Shakespeare Library MS V.b.232* (Washington, DC: Folger Shakespeare Library, 2007), "Introduction" 16, and 21r.
9 On Gemini and Digges, see Gerard L'Estrange Turner, *Elizabethan Instrument Makers: The Origins of the London Trade in Precision Instrument Making* (Oxford: Clarendon, 2000), 12–16, and Harkness, *The Jewel House*, 107–108.
10 Bourne, *Regiment for the Sea*, first printed in ca. 1574 and in multiple editions until 1631.
11 On Moulton's popularity see the useful overview of early modern printed medical guides in the vernacular in Paul Slack, "Mirrors of Health and Treasures of Poor Men," in *Health, Medicine, and Mortality in the Sixteenth Century*, ed. Charles Webster (Cambridge: Cambridge University Press, 1979), 237–273.
12 On Maplet see Lauren Kassel, "Maplet, John (d. 1592), Writer on Natural Philosophy," *Oxford Dictionary of National Biography*, 23 September 2004, Accessed 19 June 2019.
13 On Record, see E.G.R. Taylor, *The Mathematical Practitioners of Tudor & Stuart England* (Cambridge: Cambridge University Press, 1967), 167 and 317–318.
14 For a description of the mathematical culture of Elizabethan London within which many of these works were produced, see Harkness, *The Jewel House*, 97–141.
15 Capp, *Astrology*, 31; Thomas, *Religion*, 350. On Erra Pater and the Esdras prophecies see also Jonathan B. Friedman, "Harry the Hawarde and Talbot his Dog," 128, and on Erra Pater in the seventeenth century, Mary Fissell, "Readers, Texts, and Contexts: Vernacular Medical Works in Early Modern England," in *The Popularization of Medicine, 1650–1850*, ed. Roy Porter (London: Routledge, 1992), 72–96.
16 There are similar guidelines in later English almanacs of the 1530s, though it is unclear whether these are the same set of instructions. See below, Part II.
17 The *Prognostycacion, and Almanacke of Two Shepher[ds]* (London, 1556) is a series of home-spun moral admonishments that has little or nothing to do with almanacs or prognostications.

18 Barnes, *Astrology*, 130–171.
19 On Pico and the *Disputationes* see, from a large literature, Garin, *Astrology in the Renaissance*, 77–112; Anthony Grafton, *Commerce with the Classics* (Ann Arbor: University of Michigan Press, 1997), Chapter 3, "Giovanni Pico della Mirandola: Trials and Triumphs of an Omnivore," 93–134; Sheila J. Rabin, "Pico and the Historiography of Renaissance Astrology," *Explorations in Renaissance Culture* 36, no. 2 (2010): 170–180; Willam G. Craven, *Giovanni Pico della Mirandola: Symbol of His Age* (Geneva: Librarie Droz, 1981), 131–155; and H. Darrel Rutkin, "Mysteries of Attraction: Giovanni Pico della Mirandola, Astrology and Desire," *Studies in History and Philosophy of Biological and Biomedical Sciences* 41, no. 2 (2010): 117–124. For a summary of the *Disputationes* and its importance for later English debates, see Allen, *Star-Crossed*, 19–35 and *passim*.
20 Miles Coverdale's critique is implicit throughout *A Faythful and True Pronostication* ([1547]), also described on the title page as "*A Spirituall Almanacke*" compiled "*not after the lernynge of Ptolemy or other heythen Astronomers.*" See also Roger Hutchinson, *The Image of God, or Laie Mans Booke* (1550), fol. 62r.
21 For a longer discussion of these writers and the role of Augustine's work in Reformation anti-astrology literature, see Phebe Jensen, "Astrology and the Long Reformation: 'Doctor *Faustus* in Swadling Clouts," *Reformation* 24, no. 2 (2019): 92–106.
22 Richard Bauckman, "Science and Religion in the Writings of Dr. William Fulke," *British Journal for the History of Science* 8, no. 1 (1975): 17–31, esp. 19–27.
23 Ibid., 26.
24 The translator was the young Goddard Gilby, the son of a Marian exile partially raised in Geneva; see Claire Cross, "Gilby, Anthony (c. 1510–1585), Religious Writer and Church of England clergyman," *Oxford Dictionary of National Biography*, 23 September 2004, Accessed 3 March 2019.
25 Philip Stubbes repeats Calvin's objections (without citing Calvin) while noting that he himself does not "condemn astronomie nor astrologie, nor yet the makers of prognostications, or almanacks for the yeere" (J8r), in *The Second Part of the Anatomie of Abuses* (1583), H5v-J9r. Reginald Scot takes a more extreme anti-astrology position in *The Discoverie of Witchcraft* (London, 1584), 210–213. King James 6th of Scotland takes a mildly negative position against astrology in *Daemonologie in Forme of a Dialogue* (Edinburgh, 1597), 11–14.
26 Margaret Aston, "The Fiery Trigon Conjunction: An Elizabethan Astrological Prediction," *Isis* 61.2, no. 207 (1970): 159–187, esp. 160; Carroll Camden, "The Wonderful Year," in *Studies in Honor of Dewitt T. Starnes*, eds. Thomas P. Harrison, Archibald A. Hill, Ernest C. Mossner, and James Sledd (Austin: The University of Texas Press, 1967), 163–179.
27 Allen, *The Star-Crossed Renaissance*, 116.
28 On this dispute see Aston, "Fiery Trigon," 180–183. Nashe claimed that Bishop Aylmer preached against Harvey in St. Paul's, Richard Tarlton mocked the Harveys on the stage, and William Elderton wrote ballads against them. On Greene see Nandini Das, ed., *Planetomachia* (Aldershot: Ashgate, 2007), xxvii–xxxiii.
29 Aston, "Fiery Trigon," 183.
30 See a different perspective on Foulweather in Walker, "'Daring to Pry,'" 141–144.
31 Neil Rhodes, introduction to *The Owl's Almanac*, in *The Collected Works of Thomas Middleton*, eds. Gary Taylor and John Lavagnino (Oxford: Oxford University Press, 2007), 1271–1302, esp. 1271.

32 Ibid., 1271; David George, "Weather-Wise's Almanac and the Date of Middleton's 'No Wit No Help Like a Woman's,'" *Notes and Queries* 211, no. 13 (1966): 297–301. See also Donna Murphy, *The Mysterious Connection Between Thomas Nashe, Thomas Dekker, and T.M.: An English Renaissance Deception?* (Cambridge: Cambridge Scholars Publishing, 2013), 80–90. On *No Wit No Help Like a Woman*, which had the alternate title, *The Almanac*, see John Jowett's edition of the play in *Collected Works*, eds. Taylor and Lavagnino, 779–882.
33 Rhodes, ed., *The Owl's Almanac*, 1271.
34 Through see Walker's argument in "Daring to Pry" that the pamphlet "speaks directly to the question of astronomical determinism" 151.

Plate 1.1 Brontology, Manuscript Almanac, British Library BL Addl. MS 17,367, 16th century. © The British Library Board.

Plate 1.2 Zodiac Man, Catholic Church, *Hore Beatissime Virginis Marie* (Paris, 1530, STC 15968), ✱9v. Photograph by Phebe Jensen, from the collection of the Folger Shakespeare Library, STC 15968.

Plate 2.1 April and May, Clog Almanac, Chetham's Library, Manchester. Photograph by Phebe Jensen.

Plate 2.2 September and October, Guilaume Brouscon, Xylographic Nautical Almanac on Vellum ([Brittany, 1546?]), F11r. By permission of the Pepys Library, Magdalene College Cambridge.

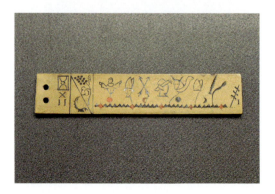

Plate 2.3 October, Clog Almanac owned by Archbishop William Laud (1636), History of Science Museum, University of Oxford. © History of Science Museum, University of Oxford, Inv. # 33963.

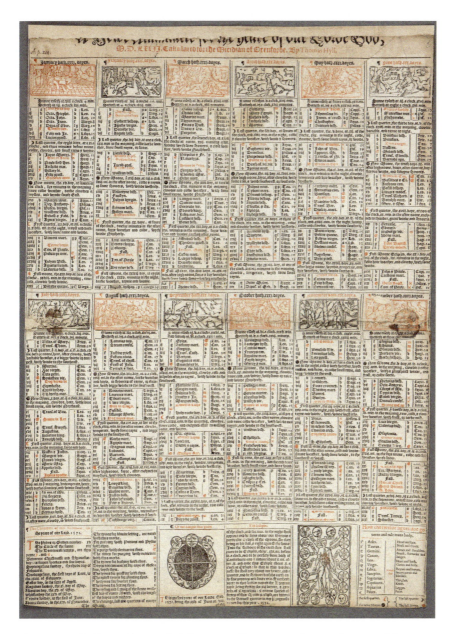

Plate 3 Single Sheet Almanack, Thomas Hill, *A New Almanack* (1572). The Huntington Library, San Marino, California, RB 18308.

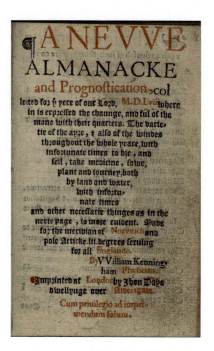

Plate 4.1 Title Page, Cuningham, William, *A Newe Almanacke and Prognostication* (1558), A1r. University of Illinois at Champaign-Urbana, Rare Book and Manuscript Library, 529.5 H484a.

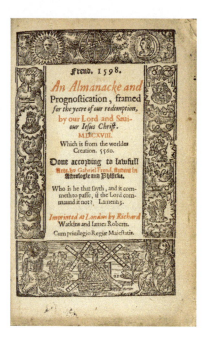

Plate 4.2 Title Page, Gabriel Frende, *Frend. 1598. An Almanacke and Prognostication*, A1r. The Huntington Library, San Marino, California, RB 30068.

Plate 5.1 Almanac Title Page, Richard Allestree, *Allestree. 1626. A New Almanacke and Prognostication*, A1r. The Huntington Library, San Marino, California, RB 28229.

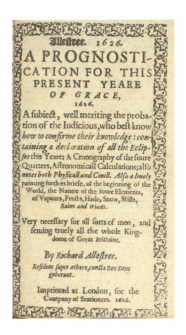

Plate 5.2 Prognostication Title Page, Richard Allestree, *Allestree. 1626. A New Almanacke and Prognostication*, C1r. The Huntington Library, San Marino, California, RB 28229.

Plate 6.1 Almanac Title Page, Arthur Sofford, *Sofford. 1633. A New Almanacke and Prognostication*, A1r. Photograph by Phebe Jensen, from the collection of the Folger Shakespeare Library, STC 515.16.

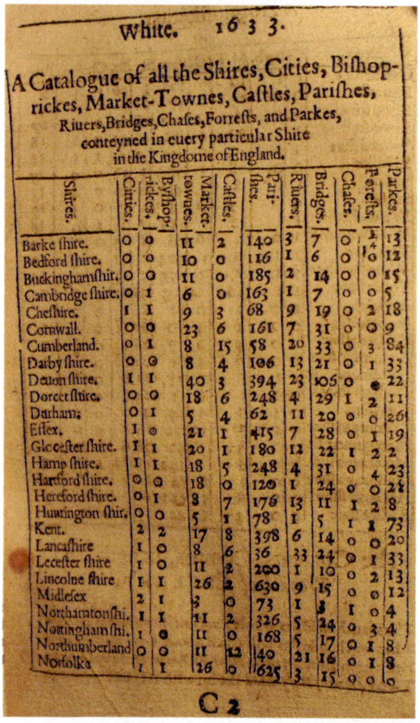

Plate 6.2 A Catalogue of all the Shires, John White, *White. 1633. A New Almanacke and Prognostication*, C2r. Photograph by Phebe Jensen, from the collection of the Folger Shakespeare Library, STC 527.23, bound with STC 419.2.

The Contents of this double Kalender for the yeare of our Lord God. 1621. which is the first yeare after the Bissextile or Leape yeare, according to the Accompt and Computation of the Church of England.

The Prime or Golden Number,		7.
The Circle of the Sunne		6.
The Epact is,		17.
The Dominicall Letter,		G
The Roman Indiction,		4.
The space betweene Christmas and Shrouesunday, is sixe weekes and 6. dayes.		
Shrouesunday,	February	11.
Easter day,	Aprill	1.
Ascention day,	May	10.
Whitsunday,	May	20.
Aduent sunday,	December	2.
Betweene Trinity and Aduent, are Sundayes.		26.
Betweene Easter and Ascention, is 5. weekes, & 3. dayes.		
Between Whitsunday & Midsummer, is fiue weekes.		
Between Midsummer & Barthol: are 8. weeks & 4. dayes.		
Between Barthol: & All Saints, are 9. week. & 3. dayes.		

The Forraine Computation.

The Golden number		7.
The Circle of the Sunne,		6.
The Epact,		7.
The Dominicall Letter,		C
The Roman Indiction,		4.
Shrouesunday,	February	21.
Easter day,	Aprill	11.
Ascention day,	May	20.
Whitsunday,	May	30.
Aduent Sunday,	Nouember,	28.
The space betweene Christmas and Shrouesunday, is 8. weekes and 2. dayes.		

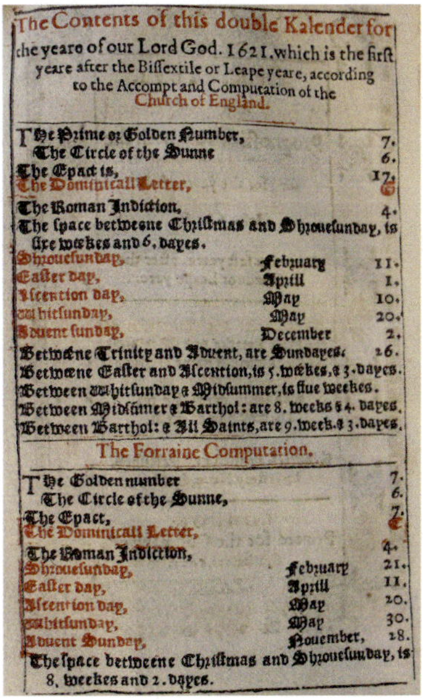

Plate 7.1 Declaration, Jeffrey Neve, *Neve. 1621. A New Almanack, and Prognostication*, A1v. Photograph by Phebe Jensen, Houghton Library, Harvard University, STC 407.4 (no. 3).

A briefe and necessary Computation of Yeares.

From the Creation of the world, untill this present yeare of our Lord God. 1621.	5591
From the Creation untill the Floud.	1656
From the Floud to Christ.	2306
From Moses to Christ.	1514
Since the promised seede of Abraham.	3934
Since the Israelites departed out of Egypt.	3137
Since the destruction of Troy.	2804
Since Brute entered this Iland.	2728
Since the building of the Temple of Salomon.	2657
Since the building of the Citty of Rome.	2372
Since Nabuchadonozer the King.	2369
Since Alexander the great dyed.	1945
Since Julius Cesar slaine with bodkins.	1670
Since the happy birth of our Sauiour Christ.	1621
Since Jerusalem destroyed by Titus.	1548
Since England receiued the Christian Faith.	1441
Since the Danes entered England.	603
Since the Conquest of England.	554
Since the Science of Printing was inuented.	161
Since King Henry the 8. wonne Bulloigne.	77
Since Ketts Rebellion at Norwich.	72
Since the infectious sweating sicknes.	64
Since St. Pauls steeple fiered by Lightning.	60
Since the great Plague at New hauen.	58
Since the Earles rebellion in the North.	52
Since the blazing Starre and Frosty winter.	49
Since the fierie Apparition in the Heauens.	47
Since the Deepe snowe.	42
Since the generall Earthquake in England.	41
Since the Campe at Tilbury in Essex.	33
Since the last Earthquake in England.	19
Our Kings Maiesties Raigne, whome the King of Heauen graunt long and prosperously to Raigne ouer us. Amen.	19

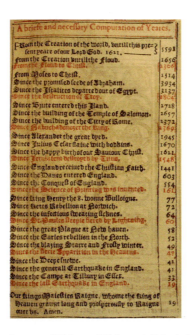

Plate 7.2 Chronology, George Gilden, *Gilden, 1621 A New Almanacke, and Prognostication*, A2r. Photograph by Phebe Jensen, Houghton Library, Harvard University, STC 407.4 (no. 3).

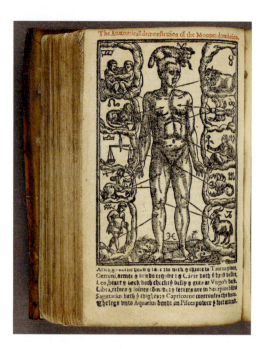

Plate 8.1 Zodiac Man, Arthur Hopton, *Hopton. 1608. An Almanacke for this Present Yeare of Our Redemption*, A2v. The Huntington Library, San Marino, California, RB 447931.

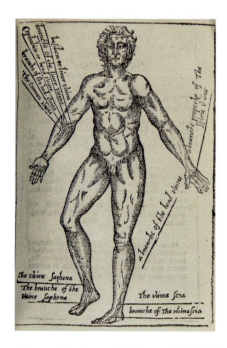

Plate 8.2 Vein Man, Thomas Rudston, *Rudston. 1607. A New Almanacke and Prognostication*, A2r. Lambeth Palace Library, YY751.27.

Part II
How to read an early modern almanac

Part II of *Astrology, Almanacs, and the Early Modern English Calendar* provides a primer on the annual printed English almanac and prognostication in the period from 1540 to 1640. Moving sequentially through the standard elements of these ubiquitous pamphlets, this section of the book considers the almanac as a material object that renders early modern scientific knowledge into textual, visual, and graphic form, for use by a wide audience. Almanacs were on the one hand predictable in their formats, even uniform. But the almanac's layout and contents varied depending on the expertise and interests of the compiler, and the genre also evolved over the early modern period. Accordingly, the goal of this part of *Astrology, Almanacs, and the Early Modern Calendar* is to show modern readers how to decipher these intriguing yet puzzling publications, to demonstrate the variety beneath the apparent uniformity of the genre, and to suggest the worthiness of the almanac for further study within the context of the history of the book.

Part 3

How to read an early modern almanac

2.1 The almanac

Physical format

In the first three decades of the sixteenth century, most annual almanacs printed in England appear to have been produced as single-sheet broadsheets. Annual prognostications, on the other hand, were produced in a range of sizes: quarto, octavo, 12°, and single sheets. Multi-year almanacs might be as small as 32°, or as large as octavo. When the single-year combined almanacs and prognostications first appeared in the late 1530s, they were produced in various sizes. The earliest surviving single-year book form almanac was printed in 16°; that is the format for several extant Gaspar Laet almanacs from the early 1540s. In the 1570s, when other aspects of the genre were also becoming more standardized, this 16° or even 32° format began to disappear. By the end of the 1560s, the standard format was octavo, and almost all annual book form almanacs and prognostications published after 1571 are in this format. Meanwhile, single sheet almanacs such as Thomas Hill's 1572 broadside (Plate 3, Figure 3.4.4) continued to be printed into the seventeenth century.

Though the size of the book form almanac and prognostication became standardized in the 1570s, related publications continued to be produced in various sizes. Ephemerides, stand-alone prognostications, and unusual almanacs such as T. H.'s *An Almanack Published at Large, in Forme of a Booke of Memorie* were often printed in quarto. A smaller format was used for a series of perpetual almanacs, *Wryting Tables, With a Necessarie Calender* (1577), initially "made at London by Franke Adams, bookebinder," and later produced by Robert Triplet.[1] These books, designed for portability, were printed in 16°s; many surviving examples include traveling cases. Though the content differs among extant copies, these writing tables often include a perpetual calendar, a multi-year almanac with lists of movable feasts and dominical letters, directions for travelers, currency conversion charts, and images of foreign currency. Their most notable and well-studied feature is the erasable writing tables advertised in their titles.[2]

The book-form annual almanac and prognostication was most often printed in three sheets, A^8-C^8, for a total of forty-eight pages, though shorter and longer examples are extant. Before the 1570s, the prognostication usually began with a new set of signatures, at A1. This separate pagination perhaps reflected licensing practices before the Watkins and Roberts monopoly of 1571, when almanacs were individually registered with the Company of Stationers, and each part assessed a licensing fee. The fee was usually 4d per pamphlet, and the almanacs were usually assessed at 8d, so they appear to have been counted as two separate pamphlets.[3] Whether for this or other reasons, after 1571, when the monopoly exempted Watkins and Roberts from the individual licensing fees, almanacs and prognostications are usually continuously signed.

Rubrication

Like their predecessors in medieval calendars and early printed primers, annual printed almanacs were almost always rubricated. Red ink was usually used on the first title page, as can be seen (for example) in the title pages in Plates 4–6. The calendars in almanacs were also rubricated, with official holy days and other information deemed significant by the printer or compiler, such as the date of the sun's entry into a new Zodiac sign, printed in red. Declarations (Plate 7.2) and chronologies (Plate 8.1) were also frequently rubricated. However, aside from the red-letter holy days, it is difficult to discern any consistent pattern or rationale for rubrication in early modern almanacs.[4]

Title pages

Most annual almanac and prognostications had two title pages. The first announced the entire "Almanacke and Prognostication"; this was followed by (at a minimum) the declaration, Zodiac Man and accompanying instructions on lunar medicine, and a twelve-month calendar. A second title page, discussed below, announced the Prognostication. These second title pages became less common in the 1620s and 1630s.

The first almanac title pages visually articulated the scope, purpose, and ambitions of these small pamphlets, as Martha Driver has written of early printed title pages more generally.[5] Both the text and the graphic elements—rubrication, borders, and other decoration—communicated a great deal of information to readers; they also provide useful clues about the period's understanding of calendars and time-reckoning, as well as about the almanacs themselves.

Images and borders

Before the 1570s, the title page designs on prognostications, multi-year almanacs, and combined book-form almanac prognostications were not standardized. In the first decades of the sixteenth century, these were often little more than what Margaret M. Smith has termed "label-titles," as in the title page for Wynkyn de Worde's anonymous multi-year almanac first printed in 1508.[6] As Driver has noted, "visual continuity, which can occur within one book or across collections of books, creat[ed] networks of meaning for fledgling readers."[7] Woodcuts or other decorations, when they did appear on almanac title pages, associated early almanacs with other books of vernacular science by using motifs such as armillary spheres, astrologers gazing at the stars, and astronomical diagrams. Such visual themes can be seen, for example, in the man measuring the stars with a giant quadrant on the title page of Gaspar Laet the Younger's 1533 prognostication, and the image of Ptolemy with his armillary sphere on the title page of Jean Thibault's prognostication for the same year. Some of the woodcut blocks for these images may have come from continental presses; certainly—as was the case with woodcuts generally—they were shared between printers, or passed on.[8]

After the development of the combined almanac and prognostication in the early 1540s, title pages followed the general trend towards greater decoration and more information, much of it geared towards advertising the book.[9] From the 1540s to the 1570s, astronomical diagrams often appeared on title pages. These images were sometimes reprinted from perpetual almanacs or related works. For example, the image in Figure 1.2 of an armillary sphere held by the hand of God from a 1528 de Worde *Kalender of Shepherds* had earlier appeared in a Latin cosmological treatise by Hieronymous de Sancto Marco, *De Sancto Marco* (1505, fol. 2r), and it would later grace the title page of a 1545 Laet prognostication.[10]

Most almanacs before the 1560s did not have title page borders, but instead, long titles (with quixotic rubrications) as in William Cuningham's 1558 almanac title page (Plate 4.1). After the Watkins and Roberts monopoly of 1571, almost all almanacs have title page borders. A rare exception is the title page on John Harvey's 1589 almanac, on which appears the horoscope chart for the Spring Equinox—a chart usually tucked inside prognostications (Figure 1.1.3). It seems possible that Watkins and Roberts made the conscious decision to brand the products of their valuable monopoly with the visual cue of title page borders. The title page was in this sense a leading element in the larger move towards standardization of content.

Among the almanacs and prognostications that survive from the 1570s and early 1580s the title pages usually have borders of a relatively simple floral design, coupled with inset images with astronomical or astrological themes. For example, a small rectangular cut featuring the Moon and stars, an armillary sphere, and the Sun appears on the title page of William Bourne's multi-year almanac published for 1571, on Securis almanacs for 1574 and 1581 (Figure 2.1), and on George Hartgill's almanac for 1581.

100 *How to read an early modern printed almanac*

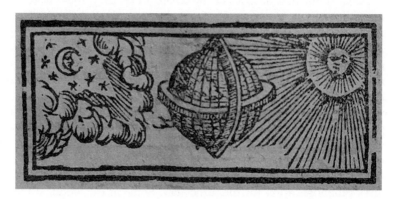

Figure 2.1 Sun, Moon, and Armillary Sphere, John Securis, *1581. An Almanacke and Prognostication*, C1r. Photograph by Phebe Jensen, from the collection of the Folger Shakespeare Library, STC 512.11.

Beginning in the 1580s, inset images mostly disappeared from almanac title pages, but the title page borders remain. From this point until the 1640s, these borders often contained generic designs of geometric or floral patterns, pillars, and other classical elements.[11] But a substantial number of title page borders incorporated some of the motifs previously presented as separate, inset images, such as images of astronomers and astrologers armed with Jacob Staffs or dividers, portraits of Ptolemy, armillary spheres, the twelve signs of the Zodiac, and the seven planets.

The motif of the planets was especially popular. An early example appears on the title page of John Harvey's treatise on the great conjunction of Saturn and Jupiter, *An Astrological Addition* (1583), as well as his almanac and prognostication for 1584. The same woodcut then did duty from 1593 to 1607 on almanacs by Gray, Dade, Watson, Westhawe, Johnson, and Gresham.[12] A second, more simplified version of the seven planets motif first appeared in a Ponde almanac of 1601.[13] A third common planetary border survives on the title page to a Gabriel Frende almanac for 1588; it was used for subsequent Frende almanacs as well as almanacs by Watson, Dade, Pond, and Buckminster, up until 1601 (Plate 4.2).[14] The border contains the personified seven planets with identifying attributes (the *cadaecus* for Mercury, the helmet for Mars, the scythe for Saturn, etc.). Zodiac symbols float in stylized clouds, and at the foot, there is an astrolabe, two Jacob's Staffs, and astronomers using a quadrant and a pair of dividers to assess celestial positions.

Such astronomical and astrological imagery often filled the borders of annual almanacs and prognostications. Some Allestree almanacs of the 1620s and 1630s sported a rubricated title page border representing the twelve signs of the Zodiac, with the Royal Arms at the head, and the Stationers' Company arms at the foot (Plate 5.1).[15] Armillary spheres were a common motif; an especially popular title page border, seen in Plate 6.1

from a Sofford almanac for 1633, included four. That composition, which survives in at least two different versions, was in print from 1582 to 1631, by which time it had graced at least fifty different almanacs by dozens of different compilers.[16]

The images in almanac title page borders of planets, the Zodiac, and the armillary spheres identified the astronomical and astrological content of the almanacs, but they perhaps also implicitly endorsed the credibility of the scientific knowledge contained in the almanac. The scholarly chops of the compiler were even more directly indicated by a popular title page border sporting the seven liberal arts, topped with a pile of books and two cornucopia-bearing putti, which appears on a Dade almanac for 1607, a John White 1633 almanac (Plate 6.1), and on John Donne's *An Anatomie of the World* (1625).[17]

In sum, the images on the title pages of almanacs, including thematic borders, defined the genre by associating it with scientific instruments, images of planets and the Zodiac, and humanistic learning. The title page borders used by Watkins and Roberts apparently transferred to other printers in 1603, as there was no interruption in their use. As Louise Curth has noted, such decorative borders continued until the middle of the seventeenth century, when they shrunk or disappeared altogether in favor of other "types of text."[18] Until they disappeared, these title page images helped to brand the almanac—not entirely convincingly, as the proliferation of mock-almanacs and derisive commentary suggests—as reputable carriers of mainstream, early modern scientific knowledge.

Title and year

Almanac titles were entirely descriptive. They varied within limited parameters that in most cases are insignificant, and not usually recorded in Pollard and Redgrave's *Short Title Catalog*.[19] As with other aspects of these publications, titles became standardized during the Watkins and Roberts monopoly and even more consistent after 1603. Standard formulations before 1590 were along the lines of Evans Lloyd's *An Almanacke and Prognostication for the Yeere of Our Lord M.D. LXXXII* [1582] and Buckminster's *A New Almanacke and Prognostication, for the Yeere of Christes Incarnation. 1589*. Some almanac titles led with the date, as did Alexander Mounslowe's *1581. An Almanacke and Prognostication, made for the Yeere of Our Lord God M.D.LXXXI*. In 1590, Watkins and Roberts appear to have decided to standardize the titles by beginning with the last name of the compiler and the date: that year Buckminster's almanac became *Buckmynster. 1590. A New Almanacke and Prognostication*, and Frende's almanac became *Frende 1590. An Almanacke and Prognostication*. From that point on, this is the most common form of the titles. As this shift emphasizes the compilers, it is perhaps a subtle sign of their importance to consumer choice. There were always slight variations, however, especially in atypical almanacs such as J. D.'s *A triple almanacke*, printed in quarto for 1591.

Like many almanacs, Gabriel Frende's title page for 1598 (Plate 4.2) gives the date in two separate forms: as the *anno domino* 1598, and the years since creation, 5565. Together, these numbers express a central understanding of time in the early modern period: that it was finite, its parameters defined by the period between Creation and the Day of Judgment. The two forms of dating position any given year in that cosmic Christian span: both dates are anniversaries, one since creation, the other since the birth of Jesus. The number of years since creation might, alternatively, be found inside the almanacs in the declaration or chronology.

Compilers

Almanac title pages almost always list the compiler's name, and often a brief credential. In the sixteenth century, most almanac compilers were physicians (as discussed in more detail in Chapter 1.3). Non-physician compilers were becoming more frequent the end of the Elizabethan period; for example, William Woodhouse was a customs clerk, and Thomas Johnson a member of the Company of Salters and possibly a surveyor.[20] In the seventeenth century, the number of compilers who were teachers, surveyors, instrument makers, and eventually astrologers "expanded at the expense of the physicians," who were still represented, but no longer dominant.[21]

Compilers used various rhetorical flourishes to identify themselves with the mathematical arts on almanac title pages. Arthur Sofford styled himself a "Philomathist" (1633); and so did Thomas Rudston, G Gilden, and Richard Allestree, translating the term into Greek to reinforce the evidence of their learning. Being a "well willer to the Mathematickes" (Browne 1620) was a popular qualification; the phrase appears on almanacs by Daniel Browne, Samuel Perkins, and John White. Some teachers advertised their pedagogical services in their almanacs, or at least noted them on the title page: Bretnor, for example, described himself as a "teacher of Arithmetik and Geometrie in the famous City of London" (1607), and later, as a "Physitian, and teacher of the Mathematicks" (1619). Joseph Chamberlaine and Richard Lighterfoote both identified themselves as "Student in the Mathematicks Gent" (Chamberlaine 1631). Compilers often touted their expertise in astronomy and astrology, with Allestree calling himself rather grandly a "Practitioner in Sidera Scientia" (1620).[22] Many later compilers are known almost entirely from their self-description, such as it is, on the almanac title pages.

Leap year, meridian, and pole arctic

Almanac title pages often indicate the year's position in the four-year cycle of leap years, usually using the term bissextile (discussed in Chapter 1.2).

Early modern printed almanacs emphasize a fact that modern time zones tend to obscure: that the astronomical time differs significantly even over relatively short distances. The small difference between Oxford and

London matters for astrological calculations. Noon, or the point when the sun reaches its highest position in the sky, of course varies according to longitude, while the number of hours of daylight—important information in all almanacs—varies according to latitude. The positions of all the planets and stars vis-a-vis the earth, so central to horoscopes, varied depending on an observer's geographical location on the globe.[23]

All almanac compilers, then, had to make their calculations for a particular location, whether or not they publicized that fact in their almanacs. As Alison Chapman has shown, compilers increasingly broadcasted this information.[24] Locations were not usually given in multiple year almanacs, perpetual almanacs, stand-alone prognostications, or very early book form annual almanacs. But beginning in the late 1550s, annual almanacs by English compilers began to specify location more regularly, a trend that continued and intensified in the seventeenth century. An early example can be seen on William Cuningham's 1558 almanac, which notes on the title page that it was "Made for the meridian of Norwich and pole articke lii degrees serving for all Englande" (Plate 4.1). Meridian is a contemporary term for longitude, though it was not often given as a number—indicated in degrees and minutes—but as here, indicated with a town (on Cuningham's almanac, Norwich). Greenwich would not be set as the prime meridian until 1851, and it is rare, though not unheard of, to find English compilers using the prime meridian proposed by Regiomontanus (Budapest). The pole arctic is an early modern term for latitude; it is expressed (for northern locations) in degrees above the equator, so that any position on the earth north of the equator is called an elevation (or sometimes sublimity) of the pole artic. By identifying the meridian of Norwich with its pole arctic of fifty-two degrees, Cuningham is indicating longitude and latitude. Almanacs practiced what Chapman has termed a significant "spatial pinpointing" that has profound implications for our understanding of early modern ideas about time and space.[25]

London is the most cited location for calculation in English almanacs. But many compilers calculated for their own cities (or even villages), and some calculated for more than one site over their careers. The almanacs of John Securis and Henry Low were calculated for Salisbury, Cuningham cast for London as well as Norwich, and Lewes Vaughan calculated for Gloucester. Alexander Mounslowe cast one almanac for Oxford in 1561 (perhaps when he was a student), and a second batch for Chester in 1576–1581. William Farmer wrote almanacs cast for Dublin, while Walter Gray calculated almanacs for Dorchester. Compilers whose names had been invented by the printers, or real people whose names were posthumously appropriated, could become unmoored from particular locales. While alive, Gabriel Frende calculated almanacs for Canterbury, but after his death at the turn of the century, someone put his name to another series for 1614–1623, calculated for London. Edward Pond, a prolific compiler who wrote almanacs for London, Chelmsford, Stanford, and Peterborough, died in 1629, but his name was subsequently appropriated for almanacs published for the rest of the century, calculated ultimately for Saffron-Walden, Essex.[26]

Most (though not all) surviving book form Elizabethan almanacs specify—on the title page—the particular location for which the almanac was cast. Over time, that information became even more precise. For example, Alleyn's almanack for 1608 was "calculated speciallye for the Latitude and Meridian of the ancient towne of Petworth in Sussex, which may verie fitly serve for the Cittie of Chichester, the Borowes & townes of Arundel, Horsham, Midhurst Haselmore, & generally for all England." Earlier almanacs, such as Cuningham's of 1558, indicate the pole arctic by degree, but some almanacs add minutes, such as Johnson's almanac for 1624, which was "Calculated for the Meridian of the most Honorable City of London, where the Pole Articke is elevated 51 grad. [degree] 32 min" (title page).

In almost every case throughout the period, however, the almanac compiler (or the printer) was also careful to balance the precision of the location with the assurance that the almanac could be used anywhere in England, as is the case in Cuningham's 1558 almanac. Precision was valued, in other words, but so was expanding the market for a particular almanac. The degree of precision needed probably depended on the uses to which the almanac would be put. For example, the series of almanacs now in the Huntington Library, bound together for the years 1616–1620 and annotated by a single hand (by a relative of Sir Henry Montague), includes almanacs compiled for London, Derby, and Chester.[27] The owner might have had little choice among available almanacs, or perhaps they took to heart the assurance that the almanac for Derby "may serve generally, for the most part of Great Britaine" (Allestree 1620, title page).

Epigraphs

Many almanac title pages include epigraphs, with some adding additional sayings to the second title page (for the prognostication). Some epigraphs present generalized morality that does not seem particularly germane to the almanac genre, as in Gray's 1588 *Ocium sive litteris mors est, et viui homiis sepultura* (leisure without literature is death and burial for a living man, from Seneca), or George Hartgill's quotation from Jonah 3.8, "Let man and beast put on sackcloth, and cry mightily unto God: yea let every man turne from his evil way, and from the wickedness that is in their hands" (1581).

More often, though, the quotations connect thematically to the cosmological or astrological preoccupations of the almanac, by praising the glory of God as expressed in the cosmos, repeating astronomical or astrological proverbial sayings, or implicitly defending the almanac-compiler in the ongoing debates about astrological prognostication. The most cited source for almanac epigraphs is probably the Bible. Among favored quotations are Genesis 1.14, as on the title pages of John White's almanacs: "God said, let there be lights in the firmament of the heaven, to separate the day from the night, and let them be for signes, & for seasons, and for dayes, & yeares" (1619). John Vaux cites Ecclesiastes: "Behold, how that I have not laboured for my selfe onely: but for all of them that seeke knowledge" (1622). Allestree quotes Deuteronomy: "The secret things belong to the Lord our God, but the things revealed belong unto us, and to our children for ever" (1620). As with Allestree's quotation, Gabriel Frende's epigraph from Lamentations on the title page of a 1598 almanac can also be seen as a subtle defense of the almanac-maker's profession: "Who is he that sayth, and it cometh to passe, if the Lord commaund it not?".

Epigraphs were taken from the usual classical suspects: Cicero (Vaux, 1624); Horace (Frende for multiple years); Ovid (Sofford, 1639), and Seneca (Gray, 1588). Virgil's *Georgics* is often cited (Frende 1591 and Frende 1620, Langley 1639), no doubt because of its association with the agricultural year. Epigraphs were also taken from Galen (Frende 1593, Westhawe 1594). Astrology is implicitly defended in some epigraphs with the popular astrological aphorism *Sapiens dominabitur Astris*, a wise man rules the stars, quoted on (for example) title pages for Hopton 1607 and Dove 1639. Another common astrological aphorism that defends the astrologer from charges of idolatry is *Astra regunt homines, & regit astra Deus* (Browne 1624): the stars rule man, and God rules the stars. In sum, almanac epigraphs are a rich source for future study, as they present, in condensed form, defenses of astrology based on the biblical and classical texts that also often appear in more extended arguments for and against the art.

Printers and privileges

Up through 1571, almanacs usually indicated the printer on the title page; that information might appear instead (or be repeated) at the end of the pamphlet, as was typical in early printed books. Between 1572 and the end of century, almanacs were almost exclusively printed by Watkins and Roberts, who usually indicated their monopoly on the title page with *cum priviligio*, or *cum priviligio Regiae Maiestatis* (as in, for example, Buckminster, 1590). Though Watkins and Roberts were also required to clear the almanacs with the ecclesiastical authorities, *cum privilegio* almost certainly refers to the monopoly, not clearance by the censors.[28] There are almost no examples of a printer's name other than Watkins or Roberts appearing on any annual almanac from 1572 until the death of Watkins in 1601. After Watkins' death, Edward White began printing almanacs at the assigns of Roberts; indeed, White printed all the extant almanacs for 1602: those compiled by John Dade, Thomas Johnson, William Matthew, Edward Pond, Robert Watson, and William Woodhouse.

Once the Company of Stationers took over the monopoly in 1603, almanac title pages usually indicated that they were "Printed for the Company of Stationers," as in the Allestree title page for 1626 (Plate 5.1) and the Sofford almanac for 1633 (Plate 6.1). From then until the 1620s, it is rare to be able to attach a particular printer to a specific almanac. However, on January 18, 1630, it was ordered in the Court of Stationers "yt ye Printers yt use to print the Almanackes shall sett their names or 2 letters of it whereby ye Company may knowe by whom they are printed." This was possibly part of a larger concern over accountability and quality; for the next month, the court designated "Mr. Warden Kingston Mr. Islip Mr. Semthwicke Mr. Aspley to take care of the workmanshipp of the Almanacke."[29] For almanacs published after this year it is more usual (but by no means certain) to find the printer's name or initials on almanacs. If the name or initials do appear, it is sometimes possible to see that the almanacs and the prognostications were printed by different printers. For example, the first title page of a 1633 White almanac indicates it was "Printed by W.S. for the Companie of Stationers," but the prognostication title page lists the printer as "A. Math" (B1r), though the entire book is consecutively signed.[30]

Declarations

The declaration is the first element in most early modern printed English almanacs. Sofford's 1621 almanac (Plate 7.1) provides a typical example.

This portion of the almanac is sometimes alternatively titled the common notes, vulgar notes, or contents. The Declaration includes basic calendar data for that particular year, typically including the following:

a The golden number, which gives the year in the nineteen-year Metonic cycle, used to identify the phases of the Moon in the Julian solar calendar.
b The circle of the Sun, a number from one to twenty-eight that tracks the cycle of leap years by multiplying seven (the number of days of the week) with four (the four years of each intercalcary cycle).
c The epact: the age of the Moon on January 1st. In the late middle ages, the epact had sometimes been alternatively calculated for the Spring Equinox.
d The Roman Indiction: The fifteen-year cycle used to date papal documents from the time of Constantine.
e The dominical letter. This letter, from A to G, indicates the day of the month on which Sunday falls. In annual calendars, the dominical letter is usually rubricated. In leap years, the dominical letter changes after the intercalated day in February.
f The dates for the movable feasts of Easter and Advent. Almanacs often give the elapsed time between those holidays, as in Sofford's example.

After 1583, this information was usually provided, as in Sofford, for both the Julian and Roman calendars, called here the "Church of England" and "Forraine Computation."

Law terms

The date for the law terms for the particular year covered by each almanac was almost always listed in a chart near the declaration, and often indicated for particular dates in the twelve-month calendar as well.

Figure 2.2, from a 1615 Bretnor almanac, is an especially detailed example. This chart lists not only the start and end date for law terms, but also the exact return days within each term, as well as the dates for Star Chamber.

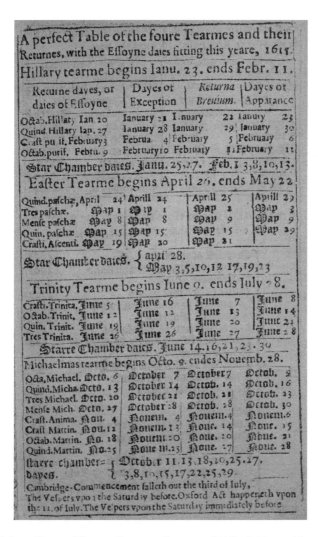

Figure 2.2 Law Terms, Thomas Bretnor, *Bretnor. 1615. A Newe Almanacke and Prognostication*, A3r. Photograph by Phebe Jensen, from the collection of the Folger Shakespeare Library, STC 420.8.

Chronologies

Beginning in the seventeenth century, almanacs often included chronologies (usually single pages) that presented key events in the history of the world from the creation to the present year. As with the dating of the *anno mundi* and the *anno domino*, these chronologies represent time elapsed from the dates, rather than fixed historical dates. As in the example from George Gilden's 1621 almanac (Plate 7.2), the chronologies were often rubricated, though as always with rubrication, the scheme governing its use is difficult to discover.

Almanac chronologies provide compressed histories of the world. As Capp has shown, the most frequently noted events in the chronologies are biblical; as is typical, the first entries in Gilden's chronology list Old Testament events, beginning with Creation.[31] Like other compilers, Gilden also calculates elapsed time between some of these events: the years "From the Creation untill the Floud," "from the Floud to Christ," and "From Moses to Christ." The years "Since the happy birth of our Saviour Christ" (which is also the *anno domino*) is always, as here, provided.

Events from English history comprise the second category of information most frequently included in almanac chronologies. This information was often derived (indirectly) from the mythical history of England of Geoffrey of Monmouth, represented in Gilden's notation of the elapsed time from "the destruction of Troy" and since "Brute entered this Iland."[32] The invasion of the Danes and Normans and military and political dates in Tudor history were also a regular feature; Gilden lists the time elapsed "Since king henry the 8 wonne Bulloigne," since "the Earles rebellion in the North," and since "the Campe at Tilbury in Essex." That historical information is interspersed with medical, astrological, or meteorological events. In Gilden's chronology, that miscellaneous quality is suggested by the notation for the destruction of St. Paul's steeple by lightning (1561), the "great Plague at New Haven" (1563), the "frosty winter" and "blazing star (the Nova) of 1572, the "Deepe snowe" of 1579, and "the fierie Apparition in the heavens" of 1574. Gilden's chronology also provides (as was typical) a date for the invention of the printing press (1460); other almanacs acknowledge technological developments such as the invention of the gun. Over time, the nature of the information included in chronologies varied; as Capp notes, they "became far more partisan in tone" during the civil wars.[33]

Zodiac Man

Zodiac Man, the staple diagram in late medieval medical almanacs, made the transition into sixteenth century calendars in early printed primers, then to printed almanacs of every size and format: broadside, 32°, 16°, 12°, quarto, and octavo. Ruth Samson Luborsky and Elizabeth Morley Ingram identify Zodiac Man as the most often reproduced secular image produced in print from 1536 to 1603. The majority of these images appear in annual printed almanacs.[34] As described in more detail in Chapter 1.1, the information in the Zodiac Man diagram was essential for the practice of lunar astrology. The diagram of Zodiac Man provided a visual reminder—often with accompanying didactic verse—of which Zodiac sign ruled which part of the body, information necessary for using the data concerning the phases of the Moon, and its location in the Zodiac, found in the calendar. Less frequently, almanacs included images of Vein Man, which provided further guidance for phlebotomy by indicating the principle veins for bleeding (Plates 8.1, Plate 8.2).

The mock almanacs often singled out Zodiac Man for ridicule; yet, as discussed in Chapter 1, this figure—and the principles it articulated—had the weight of tradition. Zodiac Man was central to astrological humoral medicine, and the diagram had long been standard in almanacs, in manuscripts, and in print. Despite the mockery, the figure of Zodiac Man remained central to almanacs until after the fall of astrology from intellectual respectability in the late seventeenth century.

Elections

The "Elections" portions of early modern almanacs provided, in digested form, the basic rules for the practice of astrological medicine. Most almanacs also included "Rules for Husbandry," which added advice on the best time to plant, graft, sow, cut timber, geld cattle, etc. Additional elections sometimes added guidance on the best time to cut hair or travel.

Information concerning elections varied in level of detail and placement in the almanac. In mid-sixteenth century almanacs, elections usually appeared in the first pages of the almanac, near Zodiac Man and the declaration. By the 1590s, they had migrated to the prognostication portion of the almanac, and the amount of information included in them had generally expanded.

Osborne's 1622 almanac provides the typical information included in the elections section of early modern almanacs in a common graphic format (Figure 2.3).

The table begins with the standard advice to avoid physic in the Dog Days (the "Canicular Daies"), as well as in the extreme temperatures of either Winter and Summer, "but upon great necessitie," advice repeated in the monthly calendar poems. The table then lists the most auspicious times to "prepare humours" (or prepare the body for purgation, often with medicine), to vomit, sneeze, apply glisters, gargle, stop rheums and fluxes, and purge with "electuaries," potions, or pills. Purging is always recommended "in the wane of the moon." The planets that govern the four "virtues"—attractive, retentive, digestive, and expulsive—are listed, along with the lunar location that strengthens those virtues. This information is quite standard across almanacs. The most detailed medical information

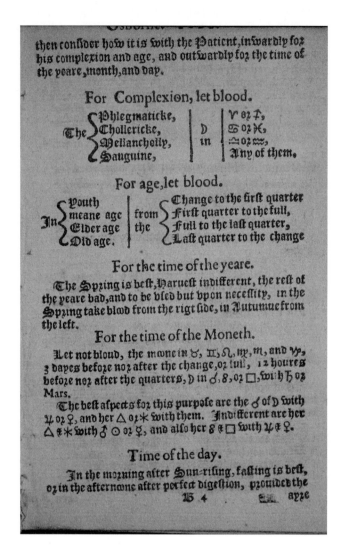

Figure 2.3 Elections for Physic and Phlebotomy, George Osborne, *Osborne 1622. A New Almanacke and Prognostication*, B3v-B4r. Photograph by Phebe Jensen, from the collection of the Folger Shakespeare Library, STC 494.

concerns phlebotomy: for that potentially hazardous intervention, it is necessary to consider the patient's complexion and age, the time of year, the location of the Moon in the Zodiac, and the time of day, though the best medical practice would factor in these variables for all elections. Osborne's astrologically sophisticated example also provides more detailed advice about the "best aspects" for this purpose, such as the conjunction, triune, or quadrature between Jupiter and Venus. Similar charts in Sofford and other almanacs provide guidance on the best time for bathing and for agricultural tasks. These "Husbandicall Elections" (Figure 2.4) indicate the best time to set or sow, plant or graft, geld cattle, manure, shear sheep, trim hedges, prune or cut trees, cut hair, kill swine, harvest fruit, and trim vines.

Additional guidelines for husbandry sometimes also appeared in the twelve-month sections of the prognostications, discussed below.

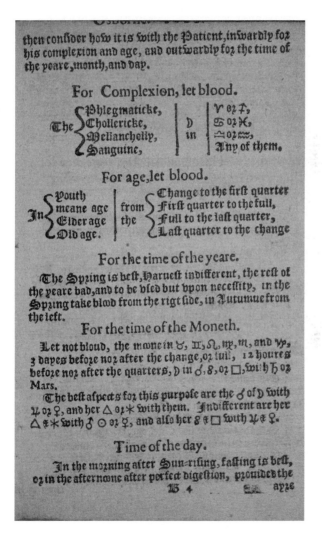

Figure 2.4 Elections for Husbandry, George Osborne, *1622. A New Almanacke and Prognostication*, B4r. Photograph by Phebe Jensen, from the collection of the Folger Shakespeare Library, STC 494.

The calendar

As with almanac title pages, the layout for the monthly calendars became increasingly standardized from the mid-sixteenth to the mid-seventeenth centuries. More detail about that evolution can be seen in the graphic variations of calendar examples from 1518 to 1640 in Chapter 3.4.

The January calendar from Cuningham's 1558 almanac (Figure 2.5) can provide a guide to the basic information a consumer would have found in an almanac calendar throughout the period.

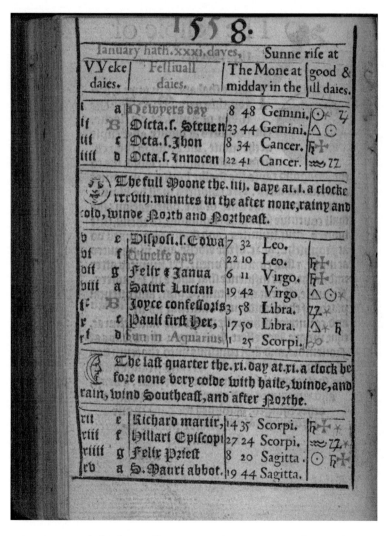

Figure 2.5 January Calendar, William Cuningham, *A Newe Almanacke and Prognostication* (1558), Alm.A3v-A4r. University of Illinois at Champaign-Urbana, Rare Book and Manuscript Library, 529.5 H484a.

General format. The Cuningham calendar (Figure 2.5) is in a format often seen before the 1580s, in which vertical columns are broken up with horizontal panes with the phases of the Moon and other information (see also the Buckminister calendar for 1568, Figure 3.2.3). In the later Elizabethan decades, vertical columns win the day as part of the general trend towards standardization; examples can be seen in Figures 3.4.10 and 3.4.12.

Sunrise and sunset. As was standard, Cuningham's calendar for January notes the number of days in the month and the time for sunrise and sunset on the first day of the month. Many later almanacs provide more precise

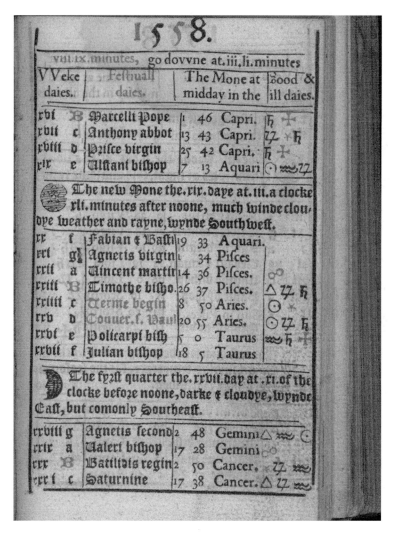

Figure 2.5 (Continued).

114   *How to read an early modern printed almanac*

data, including the exact time for sunrise—in some cases for every day of the year.

Weekdays. The day of the month (*dies mense*) is presented here in Roman numerals, though by the 1580s, this was usually indicated in Arabic numbers. Next to the day is the dominical letter, which indicates the day of the week in the calendar for that particular year: 1558 was a "B" year, with the first Sunday of January falling on the sixth. In annual almanacs, the dominical letter for the year was often rubricated, as here.

Festival days. The third column in the calendar lists the saint's or festival day. The holy days in the Book of Common Prayer are shown in red; for January, those days include the Circumcision or New Year's Day, Epiphany or Twelfth Day, and the Conversion of Paul on January 25th. Other saints are listed in black letter. The entry of the Sun into a new Zodiac sign is also provided in this column; Cuningham has calculated that the Sun entered Aquarius on January 11th this year. That information is sometimes provided with greater detail in later calendars; Booker's 1640 calendar, for example, indicates the degree of the sun within each sign on each day of the year. Finally, like many other almanacs, Cuningham's calendar reiterates the information about the law terms: Hilary term begins this year on January 24th (which is always the case unless the 24th falls on a Sunday).

Exactly what was included in the column for the "festival days" varied. Most almanac calendars provided the full complement of late medieval English saints from the Sarum Rite, with the justification that they were necessary for legal reasons, particularly the dating of contracts. Some religious writers resisted that list, such as W. Prid in *The Glasse of Vaine-Glorie* (Figure 3.4.7) and William Beale (Figure 3.4.11). Occasionally, later almanac compilers also included information from chronologies in this column; Edward Pond, for example, provided the days elapsed since the start of the reign of English kings (and also the length of their reigns) from the Norman Conquest on. This would aid consumers in identifying regnal years, information needed for ascertaining dates for long-term leases and contracts, though generally almanacs do not provide enough detail for legal dating.[35]

The Moon's location. The next column in Cuningham's calendar indicates the location of the Moon in the Zodiac, which is essential for timing elections. Here, the location of the Moon in each sign, given for noon, is provided in both degrees and minutes. Other calendars might include more astrological information in calendars; both Bretnor and Booker typically provide information on planetary aspects (see Figures 3.4.10 and 3.4.12).

Lunar phase and weather. In four separate horizontal sections that interrupt the vertical calendar grid, Cuningham provides information about the phases of the Moon, giving the time of the new and full Moon to the minute, and the first and last quarters to the hour. In this calendar, brief weather prognostications are also provided with notations about the Moon's phases. Other calendars might provide more or less detail about the weather in the calendars; usually, extensive weather forecasts were part of the month-by-month prognostications in the second half of the almanac.

Good and evil days. Cuningham's calendar brings the advice included under "Elections" into the twelve-month Julian tables with symbols that indicate "good & ill daies." These are not the Egyptian days, but rather, the good and evil days astrologically calculated for each year. The declaration of this almanac includes a key to these symbols. The red cross indicates good days to sow, the symbol for Jupiter good days to take medicine, the symbol for Saturn good days to plant or graft, the waves good days to travel by water, and the circle with a dot good days to travel by land. The system of using symbols for the good and evil days is usually used on single sheet almanacs; see, for example, Hill 1572 (Plate 3). It is not always clear how compilers calculated good and evil days, which vary between almanacs. In the seventeenth century, Thomas Bretnor took to listing good and evil days in the monthly prognostications (rather than the calendar) by providing short, cryptic prognosticatory phrases worthy of Nostradamus by each date: "All for thy love," "At better leisure," "It will not fadge," "All blankes" (Figure 2.6).[36]

Gregorian dates. In 1558, only one calendar governed the year in Western Europe, but after 1583, almanacs often included both the Julian and Gregorian holy days in the declaration. Most almanacs also put that information into the calendars. Examples can be seen in Figure 3.4.6 (J.D.'s *Triple Almanack* of 1591), Figure 3.4.10 (Bretnor 1616), and Figure 3.4.12 (Booker 1640).

Blanks. The Cuningham calendar does not include blanks—blank areas opposite the dates which invite consumers to annotate the pages. These first appear in the 1560s, with the earliest example in a perpetual rather than annual almanac: the anonymous *A Blancke and Perpetuall Almanack* (1566, STC 401), printed by Thomas Purfoote. This work's title fully indicates the usefulness its producers envisioned:

> A blancke and perpetuall almanack, serving as a memoriall, not only for al marchautes and occupiers, to note what debtes they haue to paie or receiue, in any moneth or daie of the yeare: but also for any other that will make & keepe notes of any actes, deedes, or things that passeth from time to time (worthy of memory, to be registred) which may be written in this almanack, or the like that may be made to serue for any yeere that you will, noting on the same, the same date of the yeere of our Lorde, that you would haue that almanack to serue for.

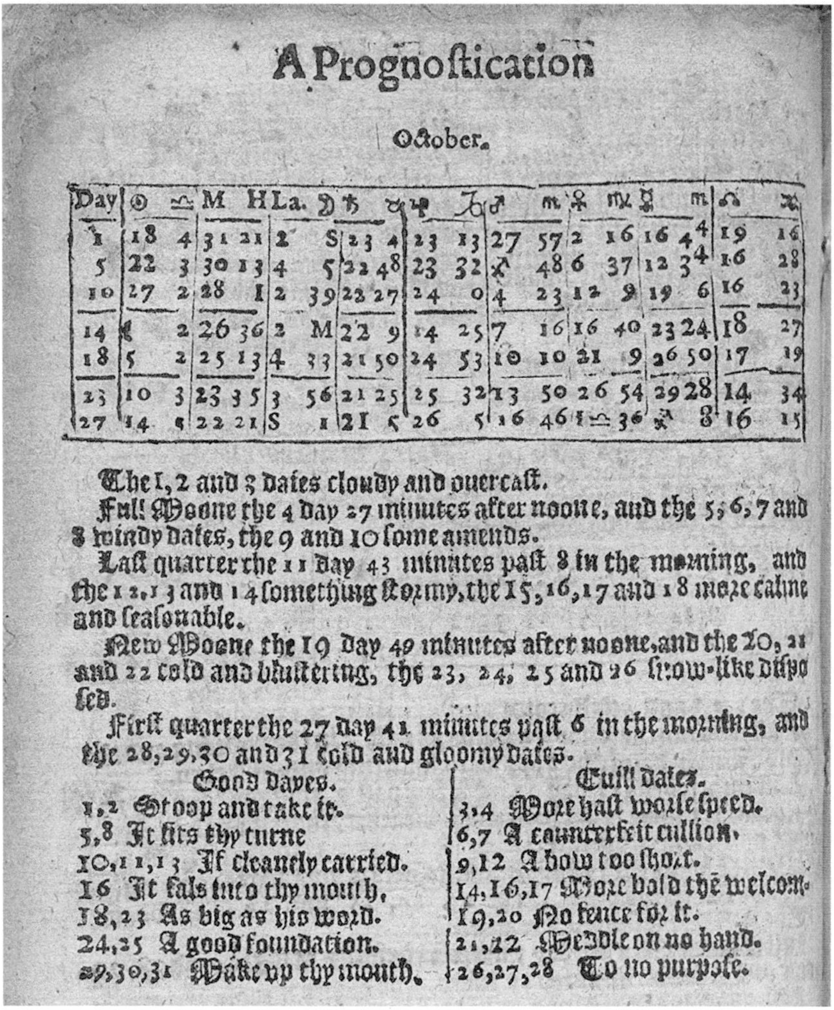

A Prognostication

October.

Day	☉	♎	M	HLa.	☽	♄	♃	♂	♏	♀	♍	☿	m	☊	♌
1	18	4	31 21	2	8 23 4	23	13	27	57	2	16 16	4 4	19	16
5	22	3	30 13	4	5 32 48	23	32	✶	48	6	37 12	3 4	16	28
10	27	2	28	1	2 39 23 27	24	0	4	23	12	9	19	6	16	23
14	☾		2 26 36	2	M 22 9	14	25	7	16 16	40	23 24	18	27
18	5		2 25 13	4	33 21 50	24	53	10	10 21	9	26 50	17	19
23	10	3	23 3	5	3 56 21 25	25	32	13	50 26	54	29 28	14	34
27	14	5	22 21	S	1 21 5 26	5	16	46	1 ♎	36	♐	8	16	15

The 1, 2 and 3 daies cloudy and ouercast.

Full Moone the 4 day 27 minutes after noone, and the 5, 6, 7 and 8 windy daies, the 9 and 10 some amends.

Last quarter the 11 day 43 minutes past 8 in the morning, and the 12, 13 and 14 something stormy, the 15, 16, 17 and 18 more calme and seasonable.

New Moone the 19 day 49 minutes after noone, and the 20, 21 and 22 cold and blustering, the 23, 24, 25 and 26 snow-like disposed.

First quarter the 27 day 41 minutes past 6 in the morning, and the 28, 29, 30 and 31 cold and gloomy daies.

Good Dayes.	Euill Daies.
1, 2 Stoop and take it.	3, 4 More hast worse speed.
5, 8 It fits thy turne	6, 7 A counterfeit cullion.
10, 11, 13 If cleanely carried.	9, 12 A bow too short.
16 It fals into thy mouth,	14, 16, 17 More bold then welcom.
18, 23 As big as his word.	19, 20 No fence for it.
24, 25 A good foundation.	21, 22 Meddle on no hand.
29, 30, 31 Make vp thy mouth.	26, 27, 28 To no purpose.

Figure 2.6 Good and Evil Days, Thomas Bretnor, *Bretnor 1617. A Newe Almanacke and Prognostication*, C7v. The Huntington Library, San Marino, California, RB 20495.

Purfoote's almanac has more in common with the portable writing tables first produced in 1577 under the title *Wryting Tables, With a Necessarie Calender*, than with annual almanacs. Indeed, those perpetual calendars, with their ingenious reusable writing tables, caught on where the perpetual almanac marketed by Purfoote did not. Instead, blanks soon became a prominent feature of the annual almanacs. An early surviving example is a

Joachim Hubrigh almanac for 1568, which includes a *recto* page following each month's *verso* calendar that is left mostly blank, with only the day of the month repeated from the left-hand side of the page, and a notation for the length of the day and night at the top of the *recto* page. Another early, unusual example of blanks is in *An Almanack published at large, in forme of a Booke of Memorie*, by T. H. (probably Thomas Hill), which is printed in quarto: the larger format, coupled with the shrinking of the calendar to a small box on the left hand side of each verso page, allows plenty of room for annotations.[37] In the Watkins and Roberts years, and even more frequently after 1603, almanacs were often printed with blanks; a typical example can be seen in Figure 3.4.10, the Bretnor calendar for October 1617. For almanacs without blanks, consumers were sometimes encouraged to create blanks themselves by paying a binder to insert blank pages by each month's calendar.[38]

2.2 The Prognostication

Title page

The prognostication half of the annual almanac and prognostication usually began with a separate title page. Though sometimes the title border of the initial title page was repeated—that was the case for most of the Frende almanacs of the 1590s—usually the second title page was less elaborately decorated, with a simpler border and no rubrication. A comparison between the first title page in Allestree's 1626 almanac (Plate 5.1) and the second title page (Plate 5.2) illustrates the difference. As here, second title pages frequently added new text describing the scope of the prognostication, along with new epigraphs or quotations.

To the reader

Brief dedicatory letters, usually no more than three pages, were included in many early modern printed annual almanacs from the 1550s until the end of the seventeenth century. Sometimes, these letters appear at the very front of the almanac section, before the declaration; more frequently, they begin the prognostication, appearing just after the second title page. Occasionally they are slipped into the prognostication later, or as an epilogue. The address to the reader is usually in prose, but a number of compilers make their case in verse. Not all almanacs include such letters, and they never appear in almanacs with fictional compilers, or those published under the posthumously appropriated names of real men such as Gabriel Frende, William Dade, and Edward Pond.

Though most prefatory letters were addressed to the reader, a minority—a dozen or so before 1640—named patrons. For example, Evans Lloyd dedicated almanacs to the Lord Chancellor, Sir Thomas Bromley (1582) and William Fleetwood, the Recorder of London (1585); John Harvey to Thomas Meade of Saffron Walden (1584); and Gervase Dauncy to his tutor, a Fellow of Trinity College, Cambridge.[39] The practice of naming dedicatees in annual almanacs continued until the end of the seventeenth century.

Almanacs and astrology were the subjects that dominated prefatory letters. Compilers quite often defended themselves against detractors of their art and profession. Some described their goals in writing the almanac, usually to serve the state, the people, and God; others attempted to educate the reader on astrology; still others explained the compatibility of astrology with religion. For example, in one of the earliest surviving letters to the reader in an English almanac (1544), the Bruges physician Cornelys Scute attacks a previous compiler for claiming that "the scyence of Astronomye is nothynge worth / but evyll" (A2r). Scute then defends astrology and astrological medicine in an unusually long prefatory letter that cites Hippocrates, Galen, Ptolemy, Aristotle, and Johanus Pontano, among others, in order to show "that the science of Astronomy is a godly connynge & nedefull for Phisitions to know" (B1r). William Cuningham differentiates his own work from the "danable practice of *Necromancie, Socerie, & witchcraft*" (1558, Pro. A2v). Lewes Vaughan identifies his audience in 1559 as "the ingenious whiche desyere knowledge, havynge a dexteritie in natural thynges, thirstinge after infallible pleasaunt conclusions, lovynge wysdome, hating the contrary," and not for the haters, those "wylye wether watchers, for inverters, scoffers and scorners" (A1v). Such defenses against "scoffers and scorners" continued. John Securis, a target for Nicholas Allen's *The Astronomers Game* (1569), noted in 1568 that men "do so taunt, dispise, and laughe to scorne" the almanac compiler that "it wer better for us...not to write any thing at al." But like his colleagues, Securis perseveres, certain that what he does is to the glory of God and "comodity" of the "comon wealth" (Pro.A2r).

The defense of astrology also appears in almanacs by Thomas Buckminster, Robert Westhawe, Edward Pond, Jeffrey Neve, Arthur Hopton, Thomas Bretnor, Daniel Browne, and John Johnson. Buckminster makes his case in a verse titled "Thus sayth Buckmynster's Booke, to all those that therein looke" (1589, C8r). Edward Pond, who has a special fondness for doggerel even by almanac standards, also defends his work in verse (1609, A1v), as does Arthur Hopton, who ends a 1606 almanac with a verse "Apothegmaticall Apologie for Prognosticators: OR, The Authors Epilogue" (C7v-C8v). Although an ephemerides rather than an annual almanac, the preface to the English edition of George Hartgill's 1594 *Generall Calendars* articulates a particularly significant defense of astrological practice.[40] A minister (as well as an almanac compiler), Hartgill defends astrology as "no unworthie exercises for a professed divine," and attacks the "dapper confuters" of astrology for failing to acknowledge the credible defense of astrology by centuries of Christian natural philosophers and theologians. Most notably, Hartgill's attack on the "loathsome" attackers of astrology does not spare Calvin and his inheritors. "*Calvine, Gualter, Zegedine,* & a few other," who have "in other respects...deserved exceeding well of the Church," have "against Astrologie...shaken theyr weapons," Hartgill notes, but "by good hap," these weapons were "but blunt pointed." Hartgill excuses these writers on the not entirely complimentary ground of ignorance: "because they knew nothing in this facultie," they "may be disallowed for indifferent judges" (A4r).

As Capp has shown, almanac compilers also used letters to the reader to express their position on the new astronomy. In the early seventeenth century, Thomas Bretnor and Edward Gresham endorsed Copernicanism, but before the 1640s, it was not Copernicus but Tycho Brahe whose theories were most often supported by the annual compilers; the latter's theories were endorsed in almanacs by John Booker, Philip Ranger, William Rivers, John Rudston, Arthur Sofford, and Jonathan Dove.[41] Other compilers presented their readers with various theories without committing to one: as Capp notes, Arthur Hopton "wavered between Ptolemy and Tycho," and Abraham Grammar presented Tychonic and Copernican systems without articulating a preference for either.[42] Many compilers—especially in the Elizabethan period—listed the astrologers and astronomers whose work had been consulted in the calculation of prognostications. Lewes Vaughan, for example, explains in his almanac for 1559 that he has taken for his authorities "Ptholomeus, Albumazar, Abraham, Judaeus, Avenezra, Messahala, Alchindus, Haly, Bonatus, Leapaldus, and divers other" (A2r); Cuningham notes (in almanacs compiled from 1558 to 1566) that he is using the reformed astrological tables of Copernicus and Erasmus Rheinhold.

The commentary in almanacs, usually presented in letters to the reader in the prognostications, remains a rich source for evidence about the slow and fitful advance of the new astronomy in England in the early seventeenth century, as well as for contemporary defenses of astrology. As the place in the annual almanacs where the individual compiler's voice is most directly heard, the prefatory letters also mitigate against the assumption that all almanacs are alike.

Calculating prognostications

In the prognostication portion of English annual almanacs, compilers analyzed key astrological charts, or horoscopes, in order to make predictions for the upcoming year about a wide range of human and natural occurrences, including storms, floods, high seas, earthquakes, the plague, infestations, dearth or abundance, economic prosperity or hardship, and political and religious upheavals. These prognostications were the product of the judicial astrology outlined in Chapter 1.1. The charts usually consulted included the horoscope of the year: the Sun's entry into the first point of Aries at the Spring Equinox which, by the Julian calendar, fell on the 11th or 12th of March. Also factored into prognostications were charts for lunar and solar eclipses still in effect, and sometimes charts for the Summer Solstice, Autumn Equinox, and Winter Solstice. For weather predictions, the age and the location of the Moon in the Zodiac would be considered, along with the planetary aspects throughout the year.

The prognostication portions of annual almanacs, then, represented the end result of a complex set of calculations and interpretations that used data from multiple sources. That process is helpfully visible in some early Elizabethan prognostications where compilers show their work. William Cuningham, in particular, explains his process in useful detail, as in the chart in Figure 2.7 from Cuningham's 1558 almanac, which maps the heavens at the moment of the sun's entry into Capricorn the previous December, 1557.

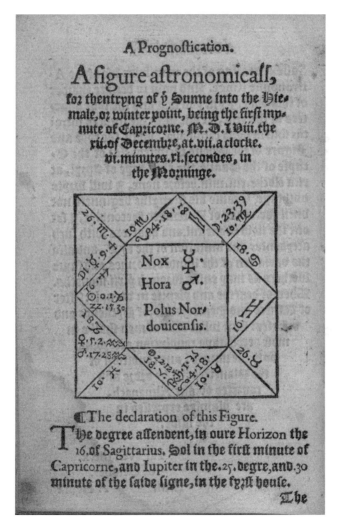

Figure 2.7 Winter Solstice Horoscope, William Cuningham, *A Newe Almanacke and Prognostication* (1558), Pro.A3v-A4r. University of Illinois at Champaign-Urbana, Rare Book and Manuscript Library, 529.5 H484a.

122 *How to read an early modern printed almanac*

An error has the year, incorrectly, as 1558; this chart would have been cast for the previous December, in 1557. Despite that error, Cuningham, like most astrologers, is elsewhere punctilious about time, giving the moment of the Winter Equinox to the second.

Cuningham puts into narrative form the mathematical information in this chart in the accompanying "declaration of this Figure" (Pro.A3v) and metes out that information in seven later brief "chapters" (each the length of a paragraph) on the Winter, Spring, Summer, and Autumn quarters, and on "Plentie and dearthe in victualles," "warre and Peace," and "Sickenesse and infirmities" (Pro.B5v-B6r). In the "declaration," Cuningham identifies the position of the Zodiac signs and planets in each of the twelve houses. He begins with the most important position on the chart, the ascendant, which is also the first astrological house (at 9:00 on the diagram). In this particular chart, half of Sagittarius and half of Capricorn are situated in the first house, along with the Sun and Jupiter. Moving counter-clockwise, he then indicates the Zodiac sign, planet, and location of the dragon's tail and dragon's head (the points at which the Moon traverses the Sun's orbit, twice a year) for each of the ensuing twelve houses. The chart also provides the aspects of the planets: whether they are in the same house (conjunction), in opposite houses (opposition), or in trine, quartile, or sextile relationships.

As discussed in Chapter 1.1, horoscope charts provide data on the twelve loosely defined aspects of human life suggested by the signification of the houses, and Cuningham's interpretation for this chart shows how political topics appeared alongside benign predictions about the natural world. For example, Cuningham determines that "the Wynter is like to be verye colde, and muche weete, and vehement flawes of winde, hurtfull to Oxen, horsse and shepe, and to trees, and sedes sowne," but also that "there is like to be murmuring amog the people" (Pro.A8r-A8v). Thankfully, due to a positive aspect, Mercury "by his eloquence...shal throughe wisdome & wise government, kepe al thinges in a laudable estate" (Pro.A8v). That characteristic mingling of political, agricultural, medical, and meteorological topics in the annual prognostications is especially clear in Cuningham's later prediction for Summer:

> Also *Saturne* Lord of this quarter in *nona* wyth *Venus*, & the Mone, having their sextile beames unto *Mercury*, Lord of the fyrst house, declare that the Magistrates and such as rule shal travel in altering lawes, ordenauncs, and statutes: frutes on the earth shall have indifferente good successe, except the great windes, or sharp driving shoures, do indamage them, men shal be troubled with Ulceres and biles, proceding of color, also apostemes, cardiacis, & trimbling of hart, burning fevers, and such like.
>
> (B1v)

Like his fellow compilers in these years, Cuningham does not shy away from reporting on religious and political topics. Generally, as outlined in more detail in Chapter 1.4, prognostications were bolder when it came to sensitive political and social topics before 1571, became more vague after the start of the Watkins and Roberts monopoly, then more pointed in the 1580s, 1590s, and early 1600. Predictions on dangerous topics all but disappear from almanac prognostications from approximately 1610 until the 1640s. What is important to recognize is that across these years, compilers were using the same protocols of judicial astrology to make their prognostications—just not necessarily reporting all the results. Horoscope charts were also a source for the weather predictions in prognostications—especially the eclipse charts, which were believed to provide warnings of extreme weather. Quotidian weather, though, appears to have been mostly forecast by assessing planetary aspects for every day of the year. The principles of astral weather prognostication derive originally from Ptolemy's *Tetrabiblos*. They are explicated in several early modern sources, such as Leonard Digges' perpetual almanac, *A Prognostication Everlasting*.[43] In "A declaration of weather by aspectes of the Moone with Planets," for example, Digges identifies the planetary aspects that predict certain meteors, including rain, winds, clouds, or thunder (fol. 8r). If on a given day the Moon and Mars are in "Conjunction, Quadrature or Opposition… in watrye Signes," for example, one would expect rain; the same planetary configuration in "hoate Signes" will result in "divers coloured clouds" (fol. 8v). "[G]reat windes" can be expected when Jupiter is in conjunction, quadrature, or opposition with Mercury, whereas that same configuration between Saturn and the Sun will "shew darke weather, haile, rayne, thunder, and colde dayes" (fol. 9r). Other crucial information for weather forecasting concerned the orientation of the planet *vis a vis* the sun: whether it was "combust" (behind the Sun), "Orientall" (to the East), or "Occidental" (to the West) (fol. 10r).

When it came to predicting the weather, a compiler's skill lay partly in their ability to assess and synthesize a large amount of data. The predictions from planetary aspects and Zodiac location for a particular day, for example, might be trumped by the information in eclipse and revolution charts. Some compilers also predicted weather based on the visual appearance of the atmosphere and the behavior of birds, fish, and beasts, described in more detail below. The complexity of the process partially explains why the predictions differed so markedly, an aspect of the annual almanacs that was roundly mocked. But however wrong the conclusions of these compilers, the weather reports were not arbitrary or contrived, but based on complex calculations that were governed by widely accepted scientific beliefs of the time.

Formatting prognostications

The data and analysis described above was packaged, formatted, and written up in a variety of ways in the early modern almanacs. What follows below is a description of those typical formats and the range of information that usually included.

Revolutions and the four seasons

Most early modern almanacs organized prognostications into predictions for each of the four seasons of the year, based on the charts for the revolutions, that is, for the two equinoxes and two solstices. Exactly how much information was included in these prognostications varied greatly. At one end of the spectrum compilers might simply note, banally, the general characteristics of the season: Winter is cold, and respiratory illnesses abound; Summer is hot, and tempers run high. At the other end, some compilers slipped judicial forecasts into the four quarters, using this section of the almanac to prognosticate the death of great ones, sedition among the people, dissension between husbands and wives, etc. Before 1610, most almanacs fell somewhere in the middle of these two extremes.

Eclipses

As in Cuningham's 1558 almanac, in the Elizabethan and early Jacobean years, almanacs often printed the horoscope charts for eclipses as well as revolutions, providing detailed prognostications on all the categories covered by the interpretive framework of the twelve houses. In almanacs up through the first decade of the seventeenth century, eclipse predictions included prognostications concerning diseases, crops, and livestock, as well as—to different extents—predictions on political and religious social topics. In later almanacs, eclipse charts are less frequently included, and instead of interpreting them, compilers simply note their mathematical characteristics: the exact time, the duration, the degree to which the Sun or Moon was eclipsed, the geographical area in which the eclipse is visible, the geographical area which would feel the eclipse's effects, and the period of that influence. This data followed Ptolemaic guidelines. For example, according to Jeffrey Neve, the effects of the lunar eclipse of March 24, 1605 would "both beginne and end this year," but the effects of the September 17th lunar eclipse "shall not beginne until the next yeere." The effects of the October 2nd eclipse of the Sun would be felt beginning in 1606, and then "continue aboute the space of two yeeres" (C3r).

Though the general trend is for political and socially sensitive topics to drop out of eclipse predictions in the early seventeenth century, there were always exceptions. Some Elizabethan almanac compilers, such as Westhawe, never ventured into areas more sensitive than the weather, whereas some Jacobean compilers, such as Thomas Bretnor, continued—against the general trend—to include detailed analysis of eclipse charts, and to hint darkly at the calamitous events they presaged.

Monthly prognostications

Most annual English almanacs also included month by month predictions; these primarily focused on weather and elections for husbandry. The monthly predictions appear to be based on the planetary meteorology outlined by Digges' perpetual almanac, discussed above. Watson's 1598 almanac provides a typical daily weather and lunar phase report: in May, "Full Moone the x being Wednesday, a wet day; the xi & xii better weather; the xiii and xiiii dry coole daies; the xv & xvi sometime raine falls" (B6r). In the seventeenth century some almanacs began providing the raw data used to calculate the weather. Thomas Bretnor's almanacs often give the location of all the planets in the Zodiac for each day and brief weather predictions, along with notations of good and evil days (Figure 2.7). A number of compilers in the seventeenth century (including John Kinde, Arthur Sofford, and Edward Pond) include some version of the table in Figure 2.8,

Figure 2.8 Weather and Planetary Aspects, George Gilden, *Gilden. 1621. A New Almanacke, and Prognostication*, B7r. Houghton Library, Harvard University, STC 407.4. Photograph by Phebe Jensen.

from George Gilden's 1621 almanac: a chart that can be used to predict the weather according to planetary aspects.[44]

Other almanacs listed non-astrological signs useful for assessing the weather. These may have derived from Virgil's *Georgics* and Pliny's *Natural History*.[45] In the seventeenth century, some compilers listed such portents, presumably to prepare their readers for assembling do-it-yourself weather predictions. N. Einer, for example, includes in his almanac for 1626 an eighteen-page overview of the "Divers signes, whereby to know what weather will follow" (B3v). These include the visual characteristics of the Sun, the Moon, other planets and stars, thunder, lightning, clouds, rainbows, sea-water, flickering trees and grasses, fire, and feathers (B3v-C4v), as well as the behavior of fish, beasts, and "flying Creatures" (B8v). Some of this material also appears in Godfridus' *Boke of Knowledge* and similar sources. Other seventeenth century compilers, such as Allestree, John Kinde, and John Evans, routinely (though not always) included versions of these more extensive signs useful in weather prognostication in their almanacs.

In their month-by-month prognostications compilers sometimes provided further guidelines for sowing, setting plants, harvesting, mowing, and slaughtering livestock, adding to the general guidelines presented under elections. This advice mostly matches the information in Tusser's *Five Hundred Points of Husbandry*; in fact, Henry Alleyn's 1607 almanac simply quotes excerpts from Tusser's monthly "Abstracts," without attribution. In 1633, John Woodhouse inserts "Notes of husbandry…in every Moneth of the Yeare" (B6v). His advice for November, for example, typically merges guidelines for crops, trees, livestock, the kitchen garden, and a healthy diet:

> In the beginning of this Month, sow Wheat, and Rye, in hot ground. Cut downe Ashes for Plow timber; Make Malt. Kill hogs. Trench gardens with dung. Set Crabtree stocks. Use wholesome meates, and drinks, with good exercise to preserve health.
>
> (B8r)

A source for this material may be Arthur Hopton's *Concordancy*, which included almost identical advice to that provided by Woodhouse, in "abstracts" for each month (101). Other almanac compilers that were especially generous with husbandry advice include Philip Moore (in his Elizabethan almanac for forty years), Thomas Bretnor, Augustine Upcote, Gregory Burton, and the seventeenth century almanacs of the by then long-dead Gabriel Frende.

Additional astronomical and astrological content

Almanacs frequently included basic or advanced instruction on astrological principles. In this, they complemented other popular printed guides to astrology aimed at the literate layman and described in Chapter 1.4, such as Boorde's *The Pryncyples of Astronamye* and Dariot's *Breefe and most Easie Introduction*. Some compilers, including William Bourne, Thomas Hill, John Dade, and John Booker, included in their almanacs printed descriptions of the "nature, disposition, and qualities of the seaven planets" (Hill, *Almanack Published at Large*, E3r). In his 1614 almanac, Gervase Dauncy presented in florid verse the qualities of the planets as they follow the seven ages of man (B1v-C4v). George Gossene organized his overview of planetary qualities by the seven days of the week, "which raigne and govern the influences...unto the dayes" (1571, B1r-C3r). Patrick True's brief cosmological overview in a 1636 almanac is described as "A short view of Astronomy, to give satisfaction to the Vulgar" (C5v). If readers already knew the Lord of their nativity horoscope, they might have benefited from Cuningham's assessment of the outlook for those governed by each planet for 1558; for example, the "gentle Jovist shalbe in good estate the Winter season," but "subject to syckness" in the Spring (B7r).

Other almanacs included miscellaneous astronomical and astrological information such as that provided by Digge's *Prognostication*. That might describe "how farre each Planet is distant from the Earth" (Carre 1593, B7v), explain the reasons for lunar and solar eclipses, sometimes with diagrams, or describe the relative size of the planets (Hewlett 1627, B7r). The annual almanacs varied considerably in the amount of additional astronomical and astrological information they included; some of the most frequent additional categories are listed below.

Planet and star tables

In addition to the standard information about planetary aspects and locations of the Sun and Moon in the Zodiac, some compilers added more elaborate astronomical or astrological tables. One example is a table provided by Abraham Grammar in a 1628 almanac: "A Table of the Houre and Minute of the Moones coming to the South every day this year" (B8v). Other compilers provided instructions on how to tell the time at night by the Moon; Thomas Kidman's almanacs of the 1630s supply "A table to finde the coming to the South of the Moon, Planets, and fixt Starres" (1631, B3r), information replicated in Jonathan Dove's Cambridge almanacs of the 1620s. Arthur Hopton, that master of mensuration, included in his 1613 almanac "A Table of the Semidiurnall arke of the 12.Signes" (1613, C3r). In the 1630s, John White included single-page calendars suitable for cutting out and putting on a wall, which gave the location of the moon in the Zodiac for every day of the year (Figure 2.9).

Such tables (and their variants) suggest the ingenuity and thoroughness with which compilers attempted to package the astronomical information that appears to have been of increasing interest to their readers.

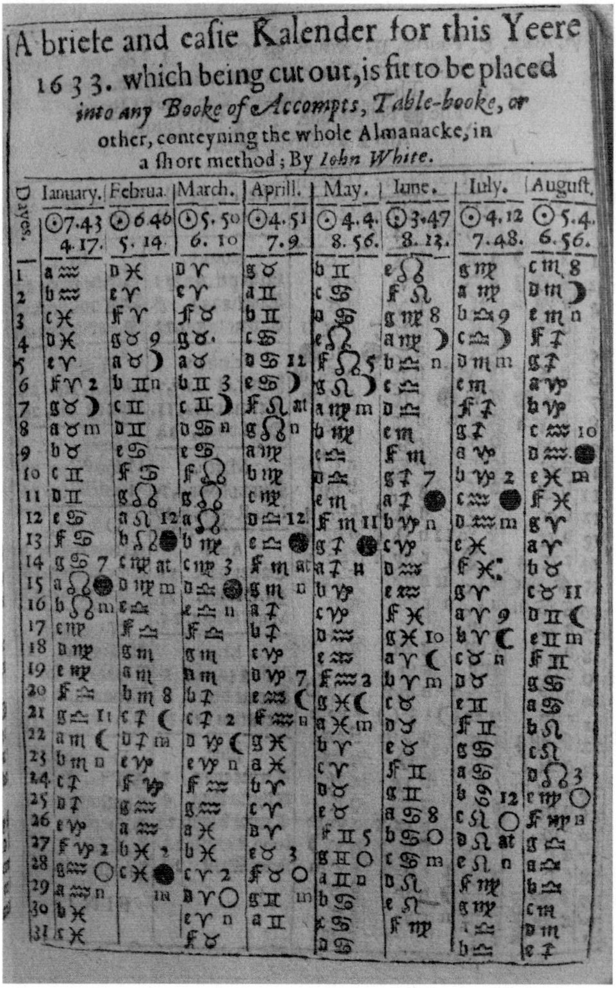

128 *How to read an early modern printed almanac*

Figure 2.9 Calendar for the Year, John White, *White 1633: A New Almanack and Prognostication*, C4r. Photograph by Phebe Jensen, from the collection of the Folger Shakespeare Library, STC 527.23.

Planetary hours

Another category of astrological information that appeared in almanacs more frequently as the seventeenth century progressed concerns the calculation of the planetary or unequal hours. Such instructions can be found in the 1591 *Triple Almanac* compiled by J.D and in almanacs compiled by William Mathew (1602–1614), George Gilden (1616–1632), and William Hewlett (1627–1629), as well as in standard guides to popular astrology such as those by Boorde, Askham, Dariot, and Fine, and in an anonymous 1598 broadsheet, *A Table Declaring What Planet Dooth Raigne Every Day and Houre Enduring for Ever.*

George Simotta's 1631 *Theater of the Planetary Houres* provided an extensive guide to using this information in physic. The principle itself, discussed in more detail in Chapter 1.1 above, was a simple one, with each planet assigned an hour beginning with the Sun on the first hour of Sunday, moving inward in the Ptolemaic scheme (Venus, Mercury, the Moon), then jumping outward to end the cycle (Saturn, Jupiter, Mars). The trickiest part of the calculation involved discovering the length of the hour for every day, since the planetary hours were dependent on the unequal hours that fluctuated in length throughout the year. The increasing appearance of instructions for the planetary hours in seventeenth century almanacs appears to be yet another index to an increase in astrological literacy.

Additional miscellaneous content

The printed almanac in early modern England was increasingly standardized, especially after the 1603 monopoly made it part of the English stock, but the anthology format also allowed for the continued addition of new categories of information. That additional information depended upon the interests, background, or profession of the compiler, and perhaps on the printers' assessment of consumer interest and need. The list provided below strives to be representative, though it is not exhaustive, as there were always eccentric outliers among the compilers.

Given this ancillary information, a word should be said about the claim that almanacs became increasingly specialized as their numbers increased.[46] That is true after the middle of the seventeenth century with, for example, almanacs targeting women by Sarah Jinner (1659) and Mary Holden (1688), and *The City and Countery Chapmans Almanacke*, first published in 1684. Before then, there are no truly specialized almanacs, with the arguable exception of William Bourne's three-year almanac for 1571–1573, to which Bourne appends "Rulles of Navigation" that obviously target seamen (title page). It is true that some almanac title pages advertise their usefulness for particular groups—especially merchants and lawyers—but the content is not particularly tailored to those consumers. The regional particularity on the title page, as explained above, was a function of the fact that all almanacs had to be calculated for a particular location; they were also always explicitly designed to serve for all England.[47] The point is important because, if anything, the almanacs in the first four decades of the seventeenth century seem to have moved in the opposite direction from specialization. By including an ever-increasing amount of information, they seek to become all things to all people.

Principal fairs

One category of information invariably included in the almanacs was the list of principal fairs. These seem to have been relatively consistent throughout the period; the list may have been copied from almanac to almanac, or deduced from perpetual almanacs and other sources such as Holinshed's *Chronicle*, Richard Grafton's *A Litle Treatise*, and Hopton's *A Concordancy of Years*. The approximate number of fairs for each month, and the days most popular for fairs, are described before each of the month-by-month calendars in Part III.

Calendar history

The annual almanac and prognostication included a wealth of calendar information, but some compilers went further, providing commentary on the history and structure of calendars themselves. For example, William Farmer begins the prognostication portion of his 1587 almanac for Dublin with a lengthy disquisition on the calendar, no doubt provoked by the newly instituted Gregorian Reforms (C2r-D1r). J.D.'s *Triple Almanacke* was the result of extensive ruminations on the calendar to which he alludes in the letter "To the Reader" (A2v). Beginning in 1606, Edward Pond often used the space usually reserved for monthly calendar poetry to explain to his readers the cross-cultural history of the calendar. John Vaux, compiling for 1628, provided rules on how to find the golden number, the Roman Interdiction, the epact, and the circle of the sun, even though such instructions are rendered unnecessary by the tables this work also includes, which provide those numbers for 1627 until 1654 (B7r-C2r). Clark in 1633 related historical information on calendars concerning the names of the days, the origins of the seven-day week, and the different kinds of months: solar, lunar, and "usual" (B6r). This material perhaps provides insight into the minds of compilers who became obsessed with calendars, by virtue of their vocations.

Travel and geography

Almanac compilers had long identified those who traveled for a living as a prime market for almanacs. Indeed, the practice of including both the Gregorian and Julian calendar calculations after the 1582 calendar split was often directly identified as a useful feature for "merchants, and those who travel across the seas" (Carre 1593, title page). The almanac's small size made it ideal for this purpose. Useful information for travel, including tide tables and lists of fairs, appeared from an early stage, but other travel information was intermittently added to the annual almanac.

Tide tables

From the mid-sixteenth century on, annual almanacs usually included tide tables, either for London and other English ports, or in rarer cases, for all of Europe. These became more frequent and extensive in the seventeenth century. Thomas Bretnor, for example, listed the time for "Full sea at London Bridge" by each day in the monthly calendar (1612, A3r); in the Prognostication, he included tables for using that data to calculate high tide for principle ports in England, Scotland, Ireland, Wales, and a few key sites on the continent, such as the Bay of Biscay and Cadiz (B5r-B5v). Bretnor's tables demand the user calculate, but for the ignorant or lazy, Daniel Browne provided "An easie table, for such as know not how to adde or subtract, to finde the houre and minute of the ebbing, and flowing, in most of the principle Ports about this Empire" (1620, C3v). Other Jacobean compilers who included tide tables in their annual almanacs, in addition to Pond and Bretnor, were George Osborne, M. Adkin, Thomas Rudston, Arthur Hopton, Reinold Smith, and William Barham.

Itineraries, rhombs, and latitude

Almanacs frequently included itineraries for travel by land in England. These may originally derive from the short list in John Stow's *Summarie of the English Chronicles* (London, 1566), titled "Howe a man may journey from any notable towne in England, to the Citie of London" (A5r).[48] An expanded set of itineraries—including more towns, as well as directions between provincial towns, and between regional towns and London—appears in Grafton's *Treatise* (1573 C6r-D2v), and an almost identical version is printed in *Holinshed's Chronicle* as part of William Harrison's *Description of England*.[49] The origin of this material, and line of descent between the different versions, is difficult to determine. But almanac compilers were clearly adopting and adapting the itineraries, perhaps to appeal to consumers in specific regions. For example, the almanacs published for Cambridge in the late 1620s under the pseudonym Peregrine Rivers include detailed, Cambridge-centered "Description of the High-wayes in England and Wales" (1627, B4v). Pond, Robert Butler (1629 to 1632), and Thomas Balles (1631) incorporated tables of directions similar if not identical to the lists in Grafton and Holinshed, "The Geographicall description of wayes from one notable Towne to another, over all *England*" (Perkins 1633, C1r). Other compilers who incorporated itineraries in their almanacs include Henry Alleyn, Edward Pond, N. Einer, and Joseph Chamberlaine.

Less frequently, compilers included information about the rhomb—compass direction—and distance to farther flung destinations, as well as those cities' latitude and longitude. Starting in 1607, Thomas Bretnor's almanacs sometimes include a "Table of the Rhombe and Distaunce, &c, of some of the most famous Cities of the World, from the Honorable Citie of London" (1610, B5r). That list, which does not include itineraries, is relatively rare. The cities in such lists varied, but they might include the major cities of Europe—Paris, Antwerp, Copenhagen, Geneva, Athens, Rome, etc.—as well as select destinations in Africa, Asia, and North and South America.

Catalogues of shires and choreographies

Some almanac compilers added additional geographical or choreographic information about England to their almanacs. John White's almanacs of the late 1620s and early 1630s, for example, usually include a "Catalogue of al the Shires, Cities, Bishopricks, Market-Townes, Castles, Parishes, Rivers, Bridges, Chases, Forrests, and Parkes, contayned in every particular shire in the Kingdome of England" (1633, C2r). George Hawkins replicates a list from the "Description of England" in Holinshed, of "The names of the Counties, Cities, Boroughs and Ports, that sendeth Knights, Burgesses and Barons, to the house of Parliament in England" (1627, B4v-B5r). The trend toward stuffing almanacs with more and more choreographical information appears to have increased as the seventeenth century progressed.

Measurement

As we have seen, in the prognostication portions of these compilers' almanacs, and especially in the letters to the readers, new astronomical and astrological theories were proposed and debated, with a clear preference for Tycho Brahe until several decades into the seventeenth century.[50] But in addition to that higher-level academic discourse, almanacs also provided more utilitarian guidance for the practical uses of mathematics, including not only the measurement of time and distance (discussed above) but also of goods and currency, and directions for bookkeeping. For example, the "Rules of Mensuration" in Arthur Hopton's 1606 almanac indicates not only the circumference and diameter of the Earth and the speed and distance traveled by the Sun ("7,884,0000 Myles in a yeere"), but also more prosaic measurements: "Three Barly Cornes make an Inch, 12 Inches a Foote, 3 Foote a Yard, 5 Yardes and a halfe a Pearch, 40 Pearches a Furlong, 320 Pearches a Mile, 8 Furlong a Myle," etc. (B4r-v). Hopton also refers readers who wish more of such useful information to "a Booke I intende to publish (God willing) shortly: entituled, The Flowers of the Mathematickes," which is not extant (B5v). Almanacs routinely included conversion tables for these kinds of measurements, as in Thomas Turner's almanac for 1633 (B8v) and Allestree's almanacs beginning in 1617. Allestree's 1639 almanac included the prototype for an instrument that could be used both to "get the houre of the day throughout the yeare forever" and to measure "all heights accessible standing straight up" (C7r-v). M. Adkin's single almanac (for 1640) included not only the equivalences common in almanacs such as Hopton's, but useful tips for calculating square inches in board, glass, or timber, as well as tables and other guides for their correct measurement (C2r-C4r). Adkin, possibly a pseudonym for the Thomas Kidman who wrote almanacs for Saffron Walden, includes an unusual mathematical key: "How by these 2 numbers 338 and 371, being kept in memory, to find the weight of the penie white loaf according to the true assize by Troy weights" (C1v).

A final category of mensuration involved rules for calculating expenses, bookkeeping, and the value of coins. Sofford's almanac for 1621, for example, includes "A necessarie Table for expences" that shows how to calculate expenses by the week, month or year; three pence a day, for example, would add up to twenty-one pennies a week, seven shillings a month, and four pound, eleven shillings, three pence for the year. Similar tables—for bookkeeping, calculating interest, and managing expenses—appear increasingly in almanacs, such as in those by Robert Butler in the early 1630s, and William Barham's almanac of 1639.

Advertisements

In his multi-year almanac for 1581, William Bourne included a list of "such bookes as have been written by the Authour...that are extant in Print," including his *A Regiment for the Sea*, *The Treasure for Traveilers*, and *The Art of Shooting in Great Ordenaunce* (A6v). Though such self-advertisements were rare in Elizabethan almanacs, it was the shape of things to come. Starting in the seventeenth century, compilers and printers began to include advertisements for books, services, mathematical instruments, and medicine. In 1612, Edward Pond used a letter to the reader to pen an extensive advertisement for the instruction he provided in arithmetic, geometry, cosmography, astronomy, the "Art of Dyalling," and navigation, as well as the "practice, making, and Demonstration" of mathematical instruments and clocks and watches, which he also sold "at my Shop at the Globe, a litle without Temple bar, betweene the Bull head, and the Mermaide Taverns" (A2r). Pond also put in a plug for "The Geodeticall Staffe, and Topographicall Glasse," described in books by Arthur Hopton, and "solde by Mayster Waterson, at the Crowne in Paules Church-Yard" (A2r). In 1615, Thomas Bretnor similarly advertised the instruction he offered in languages, arithmetic, geometry, navigation, astronomy, and astrology, and notes the availability of "all Instruments fitting the Mathematickes," made in either brass or wood from Bretnor's "loving friend, Mr. Elias Allen," and his "kind neighbor, Mai. John Thompson" (1615, A2r). Advertisements for books, services, and instruments become more frequent as the seventeenth century progressed; as Louise Curth's quantitative analysis of extant almanacs has shown, by 1640–1644, approximately one in three almanacs included at least one advertisement, while by the end of the century, the average was eleven advertisements per almanac. That phenomenal rise reflected the later advertising of proprietary medicines in the last two decades of the seventeenth century.[51]

Notes

1. On this series and the history of its publication, which may have initially been outside the Watkins and Roberts monopoly but in which they subsequently became involved, see Jowett, "Writing Tables," 65–77, including a list of editions with STC numbers and variants, 67.
2. See Peter Stallybrass, Roger Chartier, J. Franklin Mowery, and Heather Wolfe, "Hamlet's Tables and the Technologies of Writing in Renaissance England," *Shakespeare Quarterly* 55, no. 4 (2004), 379–419.
3. On fees and their variants, see W. A. Jackson, "Variant Entry Fees of the Stationers' Company," *The Papers of the Bibliographical Society of America* 51, no. 2 (1957): 103–110.
4. On rubrication see Margaret M. Smith, "Red as a Textual Element during the Transition from Manuscript to Print," in *Textual Cultures: Cultural Texts*, eds. Orietta da Rold and Elaine Treharne (Cambridge, D.S. Brewer, 2010), 187–200.
5. Martha W. Driver, "Ideas of Order: Wynkyn de Worde and the Title Page," in *Texts and their Contexts: Papers from the Early Book Society*, eds. Julia Boffey and V. J. Scattergood (Dublin: Four Courts, 1997), 87–149.
6. Margaret M. Smith, *The Title-Page: Its Early Development, 1460–1510* (London: The British Library & Oak Knoll Press, 2000), especially 59.
7. Martha M. Driver, "Woodcuts and Decorative Techniques," in *A Companion to the Early Printed Book in Britain, 1476–1558*, eds. Vincent Gillespie and Susan Powell (Woodbridge: Brewer, 2014), 95–123, especially 95.
8. On early woodcuts see Martha W. Driver, "The Illustrated de Worde: An Overview," *Studies in Iconography* 17 (1996): 349–403, as well as *The Image in Print: Book Illustration in Late Medieval England and its Sources* (London: British Library, 2004). On the woodcuts in the *Kalender of Shephards*, see Driver, "When is a Miscellany," 206–210.
9. See the discussion of the "role of mass production" and the use of title page as a "marketing tool" (12) in Smith, *The Title Page*, 11–23 and *passim*, and Driver, "Ideas of Order." See also the discussion of longer-term developments in A.F. Johnson, "Title-pages: Their Forms and Development," in *Selected Essays on Books and Printing*, ed. Percy M. Muir (Amsterdam: Van Gendt & Co, 1970), 288–297.
10. Edward Hodnett, *English Woodcuts 1480–1535* (Oxford: Oxford University Press, 1973), #1590, Figure 166. See Driver's discussion of the "peregrinations" (207) of woodcuts from the *Kalender*, "When is a Miscellany," 206–210.
11. On almanac title pages, see Curth, *English Almanacs*, 40–42.
12. Ronald Brunlee McKerrow and F. S. Ferguson. *Title Page Borders used in England & Scotland, 1485–1640* (London: Printed for the Bibliographical Society at the Oxford University Press, 1932), 160–161 and no. 197.
13. Ibid., 186–189 and no. 228.
14. Ibid., 167–168 and no. 209.
15. Ibid., 210 and no. 285, copied in no. 298.
16. Ibid., 159–160 and 186–189, nos. 196 and 238. The blocks were apparently split and repaired at some point after 1607. The composition was later copied again for almanacs printed in the 1630s; see 214, no. 299.
17. Ibid., 163, 190–191, 212, nos. 202, 240, 241, and 293.
18. Curth, *English Almanacs*, 40–42.
19. The print edition of Pollard and Redgrave only gives titles for almanacs by named compilers "where the title differs considerably from the standard 'An almanack…' or 'A new almanack…'" (1.15). Actual titles, though with discrepancies in capitalization, are provided in the English Short Title Catalogue online (ESTC), and EEBO.

20 Capp, *Astrology*, 340, 315.
21 Ibid., 51.
22 Ibid., 63. The sheer number of compilers from 1603 to 1640 makes generalizations difficult, but see Capp's invaluable biographical listings in *Astrology*, 293–340.
23 Chapman, "Marking Time," 1262–1263, 1265.
24 Ibid., 1259–1260, 1263–1264.
25 Ibid., 1259.
26 Joad Raymond, "Pond, Edward (d. 1629), almanac maker," *Oxford Dictionary of National Biography*, 23 September 2004, Accessed 7 December 2018.
27 The bound almanacs are Bretnor 1616, Bretnor 1617, Bretnor 1618, Allestree 1619, and Brown 1620, Huntington Library RB 46191, RB 46192, RB 46193, RB 46194, and RB 46195.
28 On this term and its meaning in early printed books see Blayney, *Stationers' Company*, 1: 482–485.
29 Jackson, *Records*, 221, W224.
30 Curth suggests that "prognostications were attributed to a printer different from the one used for the first section" (*English Almanacs*, 44). This was the case in the 1630s, but it is not confirmable for earlier decades.
31 Capp, *Astrology*, 214–224; Anthony Grafton and Daniel Rosenberg, *Cartographies of Time: A History of the Timeline* (Princeton, NJ: Princeton Architectural Press, 2010). On chronologies in almanacs in the later seventeenth century, see Ryan J. Stark, "The Decline of Astrology in the Jonathan Dove Almanac Series," *Renaissance and Reformation / Renaissance et Reformation* 30, no. 2 (2006), 43–66.
32 Capp, *Astrology*, 216.
33 Ibid., 218.
34 Ruth Samson Luborsky and Elizabeth Morley Ingram, *A Guide to English Illustrated Books, 1536–1603* (Tempe, Arizona: Medieval & Renaissance Texts & Studies, 1998), 2.114. See their extensive guide to Zodiac Man diagrams in "Appendix 4, Zodiac Man," 2.114-[134].
35 On regnal dating see C. R. Cheney, ed., *Handbook of Dates for Students of English History* (Cambridge: Cambridge University Press, 1995), 12–31.
36 Thomas Trevelyon did not understand that Bretnor's good and evil days change every year when he copied the list from an annual Bretnor almanac into the perpetual calendar of his 1609 miscellany, probably from a lost 1608 almanac. See Heather Wolfe, ed., *The Trevelyon Miscellany*, 16.
37 See the copy of T.H.'s *An Almanack Published at Large* in the Huntington Library, RB 60628, on which an early owner has covered almost every available bit of white space with writing.
38 On annotations to early modern almanacs see Smyth, *Autobiography*, 15–56; Kassell, "Almanacs," 436–437; and Anne Lake Prescott, "Getting a Record: Stubbs, Singleton, and a 1579 Almanac," *Sidney Journal* 22, nos. 1–2 (2004): 131–137.
39 See Appendix II, "Index of Dedications," in Capp, *Astrology*, 341–346.
40 On Hartgill see Paul Morgan, "George Hartgill: An Elizabethan Parson-Astronomer and his Library," *Annals of Science* 24, no. 4 (1968): 295–311; and Joseph Gross, "Hartgill, George (b. in or before 1555, d. in or Before 1597), Astronomer and Astrologer," *Oxford Dictionary of National Biography*, 23 September 2004, Accessed 19 December 2018.
41 Capp, *Astrology*, 192. See also Noriss S. Hetherington, "Almanacs and the Extent of Knowledge of the New Astronomy in Seventeenth Century England." *Proceedings of the American Philosophical Society* 119, no. 4 (1975): 275–279; and Marjorie Nicholson, "English Almanacs and the 'New Astronomy,'" *Annals of Science* 4, no. 1 (1939): 1–33.

42 Ibid., 192.
43 S.K. Heninger, *A Handbook of Renaissance Meteorology* (Durham: Duke University Press, 1960), 217.
44 Gilden's version of this table reproduces the chart in John Searle's 1609 *An Ephemeris for Nine Yeeres* (171).
45 Heninger, *A Handbook*, 217–224.
46 Kassell, "Almanacs and Prognostications, 437; Smyth, "Almanacs and Ideas of Popularity," 129. Simmons more accurately notes specialization was a feature of the "latter seventeenth century, "ABCs," 512.
47 Two anonymous works sometimes used to support the claim for specialization—*The Money Monger. Or, The Usurers Almanacke* (first published in 1626), and *The Treasurers Almanacke* (1627)—are not actually almanacs, despite their titles; they simply appropriate the term almanac to describe tables of interest and other data useful to money managers. John Tapp's *The Sea-mans Kalender* (first published in 1602) is also not an almanac, but an ephemerides and guide to the use of navigational instruments.
48 On the travel material in almanacs see Laura Williamson Ambrose, "Travel in Time: Local Travel Writing and Seventeenth-Century English Almanacs," *Journal of Medieval and Early Modern Studies* 43, no. 2 (2013): 419–443, and Andrew McRae, *Literature and Domestic Travel in Early Modern England* (Cambridge: Cambridge University Press, 2009), especially 76–77.
49 William Harrison, *The Description of England*, ed. Georges Edelen (Ithaca, NY: Cornell University Press, 1968), 247–249.
50 Capp, *Astrology*, 191–193.
51 Louise Curth, "The Commercialisation of Medicine in the Popular Press: English Almanacs 1640–1700," *The Seventeenth Century* 17, no. 1 (2002): 48–69, esp. 49.

Part III
Early modern calendars

3.1 The four seasons

Introduction

Ancient astronomers divided the solar year into four seasons, each beginning with a significant point on the Sun's annual journey. Spring starts when the Sun crosses the equator at the Spring (or Vernal) Equinox, Summer when it reaches the Tropic of Cancer, Autumn when it recrosses the equator at the Autumn Equinox, and Winter when it arrives at the Tropic of Cancer. The Vernal Equinox is also called the first point of Aries; it marks the start of the 360-degree imaginary band, stretching over the earth along the elliptic, that is divided evenly by astrologers to create the twelve signs of the Zodiac. Because of the precession of the equinoxes, the Sun does not actually cross into the constellation of Aries on that date, nor has it for millennia. But the failure of the signs and constellations to align is (and always has been) irrelevant for astrology.

Astrologically, then, each season is initiated by the Sun's entry into the four cardinal signs: Aries (Spring), Cancer (Summer), Libra (Autumn), and Capricorn (Winter). In the Julian calendar in the sixteenth century, those entries occurred on the tenth, eleventh, or twelfth days of March, June, September, and December. The date and time vary from year to year depending (in part) on each year's position in the leap-year cycle. Not only the exact annual date, but the exact time for the start of each season—often to the second—was noted in annual almanacs, and sometimes astrological charts for that moment were printed (most frequently for the Spring Equinox).

Though the seasons are primarily defined by astronomical dates connected to the annual journey of the Sun between the Tropics of Cancer and Capricorn, they have also over the centuries accrued a rich set of iconographical associations that permeate the mythological, literary, medical, scientific, folk and religious discourses of early modern England (as today).[1] Biblically, the seasons were said to have been established on the fourth day of creation when (in the words of the 1599 Geneva Bible) "God said, Let there be lights in the firmament of the heaven, to separate the day from the night, and let them be for signs, and for seasons, and for days, and years" (Genesis 1:14). Another key Genesis passage was God's promise to Noah that "Hereafter seed time and harvest, and cold and heat, and Summer and Winter, and day and night shall not cease, so long as the earth remaineth" (Genesis 8.21).

At the same time, classical literature provided the early modern period with multiple iconographical traditions concerning the seasons, traditions that have been traced through medieval and early modern art and culture by scholars such as Rosamond Tuve, Erwin Panofsky, Raymond Klibansky, and Fritz Saul.[2] Though it is impossible to identify all the sources for this tradition, or disentangle its various strands, a few key classical texts were especially foundational for the iconography concerning the seasons in early modern English calendars. Ovid looms large. *Metamorphoses* provided an influential (though brief) description of the pageant of the four seasons in the creation myths of Book II, but Book XV is the major *locus classicus* for a motif that would become especially popular in the sixteenth century in continental engravings: the identification of the four seasons with the Four Ages of Man, described in the *Metamorphoses* by Pythagoras.[3] Ovid's *Fasti*, though taken up more directly in the twelve labors of the months, also influenced seasonal representations. Aside from Ovid, the other Roman author especially important to later imagery of the seasons was Virgil. The *Georgics* provided practical agricultural guidelines alongside a philosophical exploration of the relationship between nature and man, and the *Eclogues* was especially important in literary motifs concerning Spring, as the text that established the idealized landscapes of pastoral.[4] Another classical iconographic tradition associated each season with a Greek and Roman deity: Spring with Venus or Flora, Summer with Ceres, Autumn with Bacchus, and Winter with Neptune or Aeolus. Representations of the seasons in popular print sources—almanacs, books on vernacular science, agricultural guides, books of secrets—sometimes diverged from, but at other times reflected, the classical literary traditions which, as Tuve has demonstrated, were reiterated and transformed in late medieval English popular and literary culture.

From an early stage, the classical and English literary traditions of the four seasons merged with medical and agricultural information of a more practical bent. For example, the Four Ages of Man trope appears as early as Bede's *On Time*, which emphasizes the scheme's usefulness in disease prognosis and medical interventions. Medical precepts about the seasons, including the identification of particular diseases incident to each of the four quarters of the year, appear in popular medical guides, perpetual almanacs, and sixteenth and seventeenth century annual almanacs. As Faith Wallis has shown, seasonal medical guidelines had early on become attached to the calendars of *compotus* manuscripts.[5] Galen was often identified as the source of the association of each of the seasons with temperaments and qualities, though Hippocrates gets his share of the credit too. Another important medieval text in this vein was the pseudo-Aristotelian *Secretum Secretorum*, which circulated widely in manuscript and was printed in an

English translation by Robert Copland in 1528. This material also undergirds many of the descriptions of the seasons in popular medical works, such as the *Regimen Sanitatis* (attributed to Joannes de Mediolano, and first printed in England in 1528), Andrew Boorde's *Breviary of Healthe* (1552), Thomas Cogan's *The Haven of Health* (1584), and Sir Thomas Elyot's *The Castel of Helth* (1539). As this material attests, most medical practitioners operating according to the precepts of humoral medicine would have considered the seasons when prescribing diet, giving advice on the maintenance of health, and treating disease. From the time of the early *compotus* calendars on, that seasonal advice was also carved up and assigned to the three months that comprised each season, so there is significant overlap between medical prescriptions for months and seasons.[6]

In the popular medical literature, seasonal advice about physic overlaps with other, miscellaneous discourses about the four quarters of the year. As noted in the *Kalender*, wise shepherds "governe them[selves] as the seasons requyreth to their myndes, & the better it is for them," for "as the season chaungeth, so chaunge they theyr maner of lyvinge & doyng" (1570, J1r). This material often concerns medical perils associated with certain times of the year.

The prognostication sections of annual almanacs varied when it came to the specificity of their seasonal prognostications. On the one hand, some compilers simply repeated banal descriptions of the weather to be expected in Spring, Summer, Autumn, and Winter, information of dubious practical use. On the other hand, astrologically sophisticated compilers such as William Cuningham, John Securis, Thomas Bretnor, and John Booker provided detailed prognostications based on their readings of the horoscope for the start of each quarter, predicting anomalous patterns—hot Springs, cold Summers, mild Winters, and meteorologically calm Autumns—that diverged from general expectations.

The goal of the seasons section of *Astrology, Almanacs, and the Early Modern English Calendar* is to identify standard motifs of seasonal imagery in order to provide a resource for exploring the more complex reimaginings of this material in the aesthetically ambitious literature of the period, particularly in the genre of pastoral, seventeenth century Georgic (including great house poems) and the metaphorical language of writers such as Spenser, Marlowe, Shakespeare, and Milton.[7] The description of each season summarizes astronomical, astrological, iconographical, and medical material (including advice on diet) that appears in a wide range of early modern popular English texts, including calendars. Representative visual examples of seasonal imagery are provided, most from Northern European engravings popular in the English market. As Ilja M. Veldman has shown, in the sixteenth century the Four Ages of Man became a standard motif in northern European engravings.[8] These engravings were sometimes used for domestic decoration in Elizabethan and Jacobean England, as scholars including Anthony Wells-Cole and Tara Hamling have demonstrated.[9] For example, four seasons make their way from the engravings in a series by Adriaen Collaert after Maerten de Vos (1570–1618), to the Four Seasons tapestries from Hatfield House (Plates 11–14), as well as a ceiling decoration of Venus as Spring at Hardwick Hall in Derbyshire. In more modest houses, the engravings themselves might have been tacked on the walls. The visual iconography of the seasons, which frequently include pastimes and labors for the relevant months, are suggested by selected engravings for each season.

Spring

Astronomy and astrology

Spring begins at the Vernal Equinox, the moment the Sun crosses the equator on its annual northward journey and enters into the Zodiac sign of Aries. Given the importance of this moment—which marked the start of the astrological year, provided the earliest possible date for Easter, and produced the horoscope of the year central to prognostications—the day, hour, minute, and sometimes second of this moment is often included in annual almanacs.

The three Zodiac signs for the Spring months are Aries the Ram for March, Taurus the Bull for April, and Gemini the Twins for May. The fixed stars most closely associated with Spring are the Pleiades or Seven Sisters: the cluster of stars in Taurus which in mid-April are on the Eastern horizon at dawn (at the key position of the ascendant). The bright star Arcturus in the constellation Bootes is also sometimes said to mark the start of Spring, when it rises at sunset: "at the vespertine rising of this starre, Swallowes be seene, and the Spring Commeth" (Hopton, *Concordancy*, 103).

Allegory

> What? Seest thou not how that the yeere as representing playne
> The age of man, departes itself in quarters fowre: first bayne
> And tender in the spring it is, even like a sucking babe.
> Then greene, and voyd of strength, and lush, and foggye, is the blade,
> And cheeres the husbandman with hope. Then all things florish gay.
> The earth with flowres of sundry hew then seemeth for too play,
> And vertue small or none too herbes there dooth as yet belong.
> (Ovid, *Metamorphosis, fol.* 189r)

In the Four Ages of Man scheme in Ovid's *Metamorphosis*, Spring represents childhood; the season is "like a sucking babe," the vulnerability of infancy reflected in the tenderness of early plant life, which is "greene, and voyd of strength." Children, like young buds, lack potency ("virtue").

In allegorical representations of the seasons as the Four Ages of Man, however, Spring is more often represented as a strapping adolescent youth, as in the Philips Galle engraving after Maarten van Heemskerck (Figure 3.1.1). Garlanded (perhaps for athletic honors), the central figure carries the tools of the hunt: he has a bow in one hand, a falcon perches on the other, and a quiver of arrows can be seen at his back. As the Latin poem below the image notes of the central figure, "Vigor of mind and physical effort are in full bloom."[10]

In a second allegorized tradition that represented each season as a classical deity, Spring is Venus, accompanied by Cupid, as in the Four Seasons tapestry for Spring (Plate 11).[11] Here, as in the original composition in the Adriaen Collaert engraving after Maerten de Vos, Venus wears an enormous flowered headdress; her doves perch on her left thigh, where they touch their beaks together affectionately. In one hand Venus holds more flowers, while the other grabs the wrist of a rambunctious Cupid. Whereas the central figure in the Phillips Galle engraving emphasizes the athleticism of youth, Venus in the Hatfield tapestry invokes two other elements

Figure 3.1.1 Lente (Spring), Engraving, Philips Galle, after Maarten van Heemskerck, 1563. Rijksmuseum, Amsterdam.

associated with April and May in the tradition of the labors of the months: flowers and love.

Another classical figure associated with Spring was Flora, the goddess of flowers. That identification, prominent in Ovid's *Fasti*, survives in a range of cultural material from the early modern period, including sumptuous French and northern European tapestries, pastoral poems, and the modest calendar poetry of the early modern printed almanac.[12]

Pastimes, activities, and labors

Spring is perhaps the most described and celebrated season in classical, medieval, and early modern literature, associated with the golden age, the tradition of the *locus amoenus*, the eternal Spring of pastoral, and the busy bucolic fields of Virgil's *Georgic*s and its literary heirs. Its idealization in literature is reflected by the more prosaic, but similarly joyful, representation of Spring in almanacs, medical guides, and agricultural handbooks. Annual as well as perpetual almanacs describe Spring in glowing terms: Hopton calls it "the most comfortablest quarter in all of the yeare" (Hopton, *Concordancy*, 96) and Frende identifies it as "the most pleasant and temperate time of the yeere," the one season "not subject to such inconveniences as other times doe bring, nor annoying living creatures with any great distemperatures" (Frende 1597, C2v). The positive human mood is reflected in nature, for in this season "[b]oth byrdes and Beasts, for joy doth skip and syng" (Frende 1597 C2v).

The allegorical representations of Spring in the Philips Galle engraving after Heemskerck (Figure 3.1.1) and the Hatfield tapestry (Plate 11) include pastimes and chores typically associated with the season. The attributes of the engraving's central allegorical figure recall the hunting activities that were traditional in April and May: birding (represented by the falcon) and game hunting, perhaps for deer or hares (represented by the bow and quiver of arrows). To the left of the central figure two men in the middle ground move into the background, enjoying the rural walk recommended for both health and pleasure in the calendar poetry for April. Behind them, a group of nymphs bathe in a fountain as a servant approaches with a tray of food, near two water-bearers with jugs on their heads: this grouping alludes to the elaborate outdoor picnics also associated with May. The labors of Spring are represented to the right of the central figure. There, a group of workmen stake grapevines in the background, while two others tend and milk cattle closer to the foreground. As is usual for allegorical representations of Spring, the Zodiac signs for March (the Ram), April (the Bull), and Gemini (the Twins) float in spaces framed by clouds.

The Spring scene in the Hatfield tapestry (Plate 11) includes a similar mixture of work and play, though pleasure—especially the pleasure of aristocratic pastimes—is emphasized. On the right, a richly dressed man and woman fish in a river; above them, three servants with canes beat the bushes and sound a hunting horn, following a group of hounds who have trapped a large hare. In a further association of Spring with returning fertility, the artist has made it clear that one of these hounds is a new mother. In the distance ride hunters, armed with spears, following another type of hunting dog (courser) as they chase deer. Another figure, almost obscured behind a tree, fires a gun that erupts with a decorative flourish. Birds abound: nestling in the flowers, perching in the trees, and flying through the air. To the left a man, woman, several children, and a servant engage in a standard April pastime, picking flowers, and indeed, as in the *millefleurs* tapestry tradition, the flowers associated with both April and May cover almost every inch of the ground. Labor in this idyllic scene is represented by the milkmaid in the lower left foreground, though her bovine charges appear to be gazing at each other with an amorous delight that seems entirely appropriate for the season of love.

These and other traditional spring labors are also seen in *Ver*, an engraving by Pieter van de Heyden after a drawing by Pieter Brueghel the Elder (Figure 3.1.2).

Figure 3.1.2 Lente (*Spring*), Engraving, Pieter van der Heyden, after Pieter Bruegel, 1601–1652. Rijksmuseum, Amsterdam.

Here Spring is represented through a motif that, as Bridget Ann Henisch has shown, became popular in Book of Hours calendars in the fifteenth century: the enclosed formal garden.[13] Though not much evident in English almanacs, the enclosed pleasure garden motif was important in later printed prayer book calendars as well as literary representations of the season. The central focus of this image is the laborers perfecting the geometrically precise beds: raking, sowing, setting plants, digging, smoothing, and watering.[14] The work is being directed by the wealthy householder, a middle aged woman who is framed by a grape arbor and attended by a younger woman (perhaps her daughter) with a small dog. The standard pleasures of Spring represented included feasting—the aristocratic group enjoying a meal *al fresco* in the grounds of the castle in the upper left hand corner—and love—three couples, two sprawled on the ground, a third escaping to the privacy of a wooded island in a boat. The group is entertained by music, here a cello, as was common in almanac labor images for May. Elsewhere, however, the print emphasizes work rather than pleasure. To the right of the central garden, two laborers trim and train vines, a typical labor for March. Sheep-shearing—associated with the Summer month of June in the English calendars—is underway behind the garden, and in the center distance, a farmyard includes a neat row of beehives, as well as a small group of swarming bees and other livestock (perhaps calves). There are more workers laboring in a distant field. Beneath the image, Latin inscriptions allude to other attributes of Spring: the Ovidian Four Ages in the phrase, *Pueritie comper* (Spring is like childhood), and the focus on love and flowers in *Ver Venus gaudet florentibus aurea sertis:* truly golden Venus rejoices in blossoming garlands.

Complexion, qualities, and disease

All early modern medical treatises agree that the dominant complexion of the Springtime is sanguine, identified with the element of air and the humor of blood. In defining the season's manifest qualities, there were differences of opinion about whether the season was hot and moist, as Hippocrates' work claimed, or temperate, following Galen. For example, Thomas Cogan in *The Haven of Health* insists that Springtime is "not hoat and moyst after the old opinion, but in a meane without all excesse, as Galen proveth, and the equal mixture of the foure qualities in it, to wit, of heate and colde, moyst, and dryth" (178).

All medical authorities also stressed, however, that Spring is the season of increasing humors, and particularly of blood. In Spring, as suggested in the *Secretum Secretorum*, "ye blode moeveth and spredeth to all the membres of the body, and the body is parfyte in temperate complexion" (Aristotle, *Here begynneth*, C3v). But it was also the case that the coursing of the blood could engender "fevers, and swete humours, which doo shortely putrifye" (Elyot, *Castel of Helth*, 70). As "the most temperate and healthfull tyme of all the yeare," Spring is a "very comfortable tyme...to whole and sound bodies, which are not stuffed or fylled with foule and hurtfull humours," but it is potentially hazardous to weaker or "uncleane" bodies, and the potential disorders are legion (Buckminster 1571, C1r-v). Sometimes the illnesses in Spring are the result of nefarious humors lingering from previous seasons: "If syckenesse happen in prymetyme it is not of his nature, but procedeth of the humours gathered in the winter passed" (*Kalender* 1570, J1v). John Dade reiterates this principle in a 1602 almanac: Spring "sheweth foorth many sicknesses, not ingendring them by excesse, but discovering them which were inwardly bred, by the distemperance of other times" (B2v).

Illnesses particular to Spring, then, were thought to be caused by overactive blood or the manifestation of humors previously deranged in Winter or Autumn. Disorders of the Spring include "leprosies, red spots, tooth-ach, fevers of bloud, pushes or wheales in the face, small pox, ring-wormes, falling-sickenesse, paines in the throate and necke, the kings evill, wens, griefes in the shoulders and armes caused by bloud" (Hopton, *Concordancy*, 97–98). The throat troubles endemic to the season can include "coughs" and "Squinsies" (tonsillitis) (Frende 1597, C3r).

The medical advice associated with both the curing of disease and the maintenance of health in Spring was complicated by the season's unpredictable nature. Rather than prescribe a single regimen, popular medical writers noted that the start of the season "doth participate with Winter, and the end with summer" (Cogan, *Haven of Health*, 103). Consequently, recommendations for diet, purging, phlebotomy, or sexual activity might vary, depending on whether it was early, middle, or late Spring. More specifically, perpetual almanacs sometimes proposed different regimens depending on different climatological scenarios; Arthur Hopton's *Concordancy,* for example, describes the dangers attendant on a moist, hot, dry, or cold Spring.

Despite these variables, and the more precise medical prescriptions suggested in the monthly recommendations, the general advice for Spring is consistent. Spring is the very best time for medical interventions: "the best lettynge of blode of any time," and also good "to be laxatyfe," to bathe, and "to eate such thynges as wyll purge the bely" (Aristotle, *Here begynneth*, C3v). It is also a good time to "take medicines," "to eat light meats which doe refresh, as Chickens, Kids with verjuice, Borage, Beets, yolkes of egges, egges in moone-shine [poached in rose-water], Roches, Perches, Pickerels, and all skaled fish" (*Kalender* 1631, L5r).

Summer

Astronomy and astrology

Summer begins at the Summer Solstice as the Sun reaches the Tropic of Cancer—the apogee of its annual northward journey—and enters the sign of Cancer. In the Julian calendar, that event usually occurs between

June 10th and 12th; the red-letter holy day commemorating the Apostle St. Barnabas, on June 11th, was often identified as the longest day of the year (as in Spenser's *Epithalamion*). The Sun enters Leo approximately a month later, in August, and Virgo in early September.

The most notable astrological phenomena of the Summer were the dangerous, choleric Dog Days, thought to be caused by the ascendancy of the Great and Little Dog Stars: Sirius (in the constellation Canis Major) and Procyon (in the constellation Canis Minor). The actual start and duration of the Dog Days varied depending on the method of calculation, but generally they were thought to begin in the second or third week of July and run until late August or early September. The effects of the Dog Days are described in greater detail in the overview of July below (3.3). In addition to Sirius and Procyon, the star Arcturus (in the constellation Bootes) and the constellation Orion were believed to influence the weather and sublunar organic matter during the Summer quarter.

Allegory

> The yeere from springtyde passing foorth to summer, wexeth strong,
> Becommeth lyke a lusty youth. For in our lyfe through out
> There is no time more plentifull, more lusty whote and stout.
> (Ovid, *Metamorphosis*, fol. 189v)

Though the passage on the Four Ages of Man from Ovid represents Summer as "a lusty youth," most of the literary and visual allegorical figures representing Summer show the figure as a man in his prime, as in the Summer engraving in the series by Philips Galle after Maarten van Heemskerck of 1563 (Figure 3.1.3). There the central figure is notably more mature than the youth representing Spring in the same series (Figure 3.1.1). The pose suggests the commanding power of the season he represents, which is associated with wealth, plenty, and vigor, represented in the human form at maximum strength. Summer holds a sheaf of wheat, material which also comprises his crown—appropriate for the season in which the corn is reaped.

Summer was alternatively identified with the Roman goddess of agriculture, Ceres, who often appears as the central figure in allegorical representations of this season, usually surrounded by the bounty which she symbolizes. For example, in both the Summer print from the Collaert after Maerten de Vos series (Figure 3.1.4) and the Hatfield House version of this composition (Plate 12), Ceres sits on a bale of wheat with a wheaten crown, under a fruit tree laden with ripe fruit, holding a sickle in her hand. Alternatively, Ceres is sometimes identified not with Summer but with Autumn, the period when the harvest is fully in, as in George Whitney's *A Choice of Emblemes* where "CERES doth in all her pompe appeare" as "autumne ripes" (1586, 23).

The seasons: introduction 149

Figure 3.1.3 Zomer (*Summer*), Engraving, Philips Galle, after Maarten van Heemskerck, 1563. Rijksmuseum, Amsterdam.

Pastimes, activities, and labors

Whereas Spring is primarily associated with pleasure, Summer is a time for work, and images of the season emphasize the intense agricultural tasks also represented in the labors for the three months of June, July, and August: sheep-shearing, mowing, and harvesting the corn.

In the Philips Galle engraving of Summer (3.1.3), mowing takes place to the left of the central figure, with workers brandishing long-handled sickles and gathering the hay into hayricks; reaping (using short-handled scythes) occurs in the right background, and sheep-shearing in the right foreground. These three tasks are also represented in the Collaert engraving of Summer (Figure 3.1.4), and the Hatfield tapestry (Plate 12). Despite the hard work associated with Summer, this season, like Spring, is often idealized, as in Nicholas Breton's description of a Summer landscape in which the "Hony-dewes perfume the Ayre," the "Sunny-showers are earths comfort," Flora brings forth her full "wardrobe," and animals such as the bull, the hare, and the greyhound both cavort and work together in harmonious bliss (*Fantasticks*, B2r-B2v).

150 *Early modern calendars*

Figure 3.1.4 Zomer (Summer), Engraving, Adriaen Collaert, after Maerten de Vos, 1570–1618. Rjksmuseum, Amsterdam.

Complexion, qualities, and disease

> Bright Soll having got his highest grade,
>   lookes downe on earth with hot aspect:
> Parching the ground and Corny blade,
>   ripening all things with good effect.   (Frende 1622, B3v)

Summer is not only the hottest season but also the most productive, as its heat brings "all fruits to their ripenesse, cattell to their fatnesse, and men to their wealth" (Hopton, *Concordancy*, 99). In Summer, as noted in a 1555 version of the pseudo-Aristotleian *Secretum Secretorum*, "The myghtes of mannes body be fortyfyed. And all ye worlde is full of welth, as the fayre bryde that is goodly stature and in perfyte age" (Aristotle, *Here begynneth*, C4r).

But representations of the season in almanacs also stress the dangers attendant on Summer's heat. The dominant humor is choler, hot and dry, which ripens fruit but also causes illness and disease. These perils are exacerbated by the influence of the Dog Star. Stomachs are delicate in these conditions: "Mans stomacke now more weaker is," Frende reports, "than earst it was before: / To gormandize it is not good, / take heed, twill make thee poore" (1622, B3v). Digestive troubles predominate in Summer because, as Thomas Cogan puts it in *The Haven of Health*,

> the poares of the bodie are more open, whereby the spirites and natural heat are the more resolved and wasted, and by that meanes the vertue digestive is infeebled, so that the stomacke and inner parts are not then so well able to digest as at other times.
>
> (1584, 179)

Medical advice is unanimous on the best preventative behavior: "therefore eate and drinke moderately, least that you surfet and bring your selves into desperate and dangerous diseases" (Frende 1622, B4r). Other diseases and disorders prevalent in the Summer, many associated with heat and compromised digestion, include

> hot burning feavers, giddines in the head, Laskes [loose bowels], Plurisies, Jaundis, hot Impostumes, Inflammations of the liver, scalding of the Urine, vomitings, head ach, purse [scrotum] ach, which is like to breed the hart ach or consu[m]ption, with other infirmities proceeding of hot and chollericke humors.
>
> (Frende 1622, B4r)

Medical interventions should be avoided in Summer—guidance reiterated in the more specific proscriptions for the months—with all bleeding, bathing, purging, or taking medicine put off until September. Sexual activity, spicy food, and wine-drinking are also not recommended.

The weather in the Summer is, of course, hot, and thought to be primarily dry (in keeping with the dominant humor of choler.) As John Dade notes, sometimes Summer will "vary from his kinde, and be mixed with sweet and pleasant shewers" (1602, B3r). Hopton provides an astrological explanation of such variations, noting that in June and early July, the heat is mitigated by the effect of the moist star Asellus in Cancer, but the later ascendancy of Syrius and Procyon in Leo causes the heat to "groweth most vehement" (*Concordancy*, 98).

Autumn

Astronomy and astrology

Autumn begins in the English Julian calendar on the 10th, 11th, or 12th of September at the Autumn Equinox, when the hours of day and night are equal as the Sun crosses the equator on its way south to the Tropic of Capricorn. The three Zodiac signs of the season are Libra, which the Sun enters with at the Autumn Equinox, Scorpio which begins in October, and Sagittarius which begins in November. Hopton attributes the season's meteorological variability to the influence of the three Zodiac signs of the

152 Early modern calendars

season: under airy Libra, there is "heat with temperate moysture", in watery Scorpio, "the aire is made more cold and moist", and after entering fiery Sagittarius, "there is made a restraint of the extremitie of wet and cold, for the good of such as sow and plow" (*Concordancy*, 99).

Allegory

> Then followeth Harvest when the heate of youth growes sumwhat cold,
> Rype, meeld, disposed meane betwixt a young man and an old,
> And sumwhat sprent with grayish heare.
>
> (Ovid, *Metamorphosis*, fol. 189v)

In keeping with the Ovidian scheme of the four seasons, the allegorical figure for Autumn is an aging man, as in the engraving by Philips Galle after Maarten van Heemskerck of 1563 (Figure 3.1.5). In this image Autumn, adorned by a crown of grapes, carries a cornucopia filled with the plenty of the harvest (including what appears to be two miniature boar's heads). But the figure's agedness is also indicated by his lined face and anxious

Figure 3.1.5 Herfst (*Autumn*), Engraving, Philips Galle after Maarten van Heemskerck, 1563. Rijksmuseum, Amsterdam.

mien, the off-kilter, tentative pose, the scrawny knee visible beneath his robes, and the thick coverings protecting his aging body from both the season's intemperate weather and the cold of encroaching age.

The Roman deity associated with Autumn is Bacchus, appropriate for a season in which grapes are harvested and wine made. In Plate 13, the Hatfield tapestry for Autumn, Bacchus (as in the original in the Adriaen Collaert series) strikes a typically festive pose: he is crowned with grapes, raises a grape-filled glass, and is surrounded by more grapes and other fruits of the harvest, some in a cornucopia and others in the basket on which he sits. Those fruits include melons, squash, turnips or carrots, apples, cucumbers, and onions. Bacchus is the god who most often personifies Autumn in northern engravings of the sixteenth and seventeenth centuries. A four seasons series by Jan Saenradam after Hendrick Goltzius merges that iconography with domestic scenes of ordinary people completing seasonal tasks (Figure 3.1.6).[15]

Figure 3.1.6 Herfst (Autumn), Engraving, Jan Saenredam, after Hendrick Goltzius, 1590–1600. Rijksmuseum, Amsterdam.

154 *Early modern calendars*

In this engraving a woman—the wife of the man in the ruff, as is clear from the rest of the series—grasps a basket of fruit that represents the bounty of the season, also suggested by the cabbages and squash strewn on the ground. Her husband, in his elegant hat and a large ruff, enjoys a glass of wine with the mythological figure of Bacchus.

Pastimes, activities, and labors

> For good husbands paine, harvest yeilds gaine,
> whatsoever now on earth doth grow:
> Each tree, plant, shrub, all for mans good,
> shewes them their duty God unto. (Frende 1622, B4r)

Like Summer, Autumn is the time for work, not play; in this season "The Ant and the Bee worke for their winter provision" (Breton, *Fantastickes*, B2v), as do human laborers. Corn harvesting is usually all but over by September, though the aftermath continues as the grain is threshed and stored for the Winter. In allegorical representations of the season, the standard labors for Autumn are harvesting grapes, picking, storing, and processing fruit, sowing, including preparing the ground with a plow, and knocking down acorns with which to fatten the livestock that will be slaughtered in December. These tasks—also the labors for October, September, and November—are all represented in the Philips Galle engraving for the season (Figure 3.1.5), along with slaughtering livestock, a labor more frequently identified with Winter (and December) in English sources. The Hatfield Autumn tapestry (Plate 13) includes scenes of grape and fruit harvesting, wine making, and acorn gathering, but omits plowing and sowing, adding instead livestock and wild animals: fighting rams, lions, pards, a doe, and a smug-looking, thirteen-point buck.

Complexion, qualities, and disease

> Crooked old age, humor, Melancholly,
> doth Autumnes nature truely verify. (Frende 1622, B4r)

Autumn is the melancholic season; descriptions often stress sadness, loss and decay. For example, the 1555 version of *Secretum Secretorum* describes the earth in Autumn as "an olde naked woman that goeth from youth to age" (Aristotle, *Here Begynneth*, D1r). For Gabriel Frende, Autumn is the "mad shaver or barber of the year" and also the "kind hearted Prodigall, that gives all away and leaves himselfe nothing, no not so much as a bare coate to put on his backe, to cover himselfe against the fury of that old frost bitten churle, Winter" (Frende 1622, B4v).

All medical authorities agree that cold, dry Autumn poses serious health threats. Autumn is "as Hipocrate sayth, the Mother or Nurse of dangerous sycknesses" (Buckminster 1589, B7r), and "the most contagyous tyme of the yeare, in the which perillous infirmities happeneth and commethe" (*Kalender*, J2r). Galen, the "prince of Phisitions," confirms the danger: Autumn is "the most perilous tyme of all the yeere: for what hath been evyl in the seasons before, or through the condition of the ayre in Sommer, shall now give great force unto syckness, and breede pestilent fevers," as well as Botches [goiters, ulcers, or boils), mangines [angina], and such like, both lothsome & greevouss" (Buckminster 1589, B7r-B7v). One reason for the spread of disease is the variability of the weather: pores open during the warm days, but the diseases such warmth lets into the body can breed during the cold nights. But September marks the first time since late Spring in which medical interventions are once again recommended: "now it is a fit time againe to take Phisicke, not onely such as feele diseases in their bodies to begin & grow, but also such as have had long and old diseases" (Frende 1622, B4v). Purging, bleeding, and vomiting are part of the physician's arsenal in the Autumn, though as usual, the medical literature advises against "mountebanks, and such quack-salving knaves, or women Doctors (unskilfull) who kill more than they cure" (Frende 1622, B4v). Bathing, however, is not recommended past November, a month where warnings against "venery" also begin anew. The seasonal dietary guidelines for Autumn repeat the advice also provided for the three months of the season: be careful eating cold, raw fruit, which can cause corruption, introduce spice, heat, and wine back to the diet, and eat up—welcome advice, no doubt, after the abstinence recommended for July and August.

Given the health dangers of the season, it is no surprise that the list of potential diseases for Autumn is long. These include "bastard Plurisies, obstructions in the Liver, straightnes in the breast, stitches in the sides, Inflamation in the Lungs, hardnes of the Splene, quartaine Agues, blacke Jaundies, windines about the Midriffe, Crampes, Pyles, Goute, with other sicknesses very grievous" (Dade 1602, B3v) To this list, other medical guides add painful coughs, dropsies, consumptions, strangury (urinary disease), lameness in the limbs, melancholy passions, angina, fistulas, fluxes of blood, cankers, botches (boils or goiters), vision problems, pains in the back and genitalia, infirmities in the face, hemorrhoids, and gallstones.

Winter

Astronomy and astrology

Winter begins at the Winter Solstice on December 10th–12th, when the Sun enters the sign of Capricorn as it reaches the Tropic of Capricorn; St. Lucy's Day (December 12th) is often identified as the shortest day of the year. In January the Sun enters Aquarius, and in February, Pisces, to end the astronomical and astrological year. Among the most prominent constellations in the night sky in Winter in England are Orion, Canis Minor, and Canis Major, including the Great and Little Dog Stars (Sirius and Procyon), who cause such havoc in the Dog Days of Summer.

156 *Early modern calendars*

Allegory

> Then ugly winter last
> Like age steales on with trembling steppes, all bald, or overcast
> With shirle thinne heare as whyght as snowe.
>
> (Ovid, *Metamorphosis*, fol. 189v)

The final season of the year brings man to age, decrepitude, and death in the Ovidian scheme of the four seasons. In the Winter engraving from the series by Philips Galle after Maarten van Heemskerck of 1563 (Figure 3.1.8), an old man with thick boots, a fur-lined robe and hat, a warm cloak, and a grizzled beard, bends over a steaming pot that warms up his thin, aged hands.

In the Winter engraving from another series by the English engraver Martin Droeshout (Figure 3.1.7), a jolly white-bearded central figure also

Figure 3.1.7 The Four Seasons: Winter, Engraving, Martin Droeshout, 1620–1630. The Trustees of the British Museum.

warms his wrinkled hands at a fire, this time at a small but blazing brazier. Another classical deity who sometimes represents Winter is Aeolus, the Greek god of winds, who can be seen in the Hatfield tapestry for Winter (Plate 14).

Pastimes, activities, and labors

The traditional labors for Winter include slaughtering livestock in December, feasting (often by a fire) in January, and gathering wood or sitting by the fire in February. Allegorical representations of Winter often also gesture towards the importance of a good harvest to survive the coldest months of the year. In the Droeshout engraving (Figure 3.1.7), the figure's headdress—carrots, turnips, fruits, nuts, etc.—represent the importance of the harvest for the feasts of December and January, a motif replicated in the pile of fruits and vegetables at the feet of Aeolus in the Hatfield Tapestry. Gabriel Frende expresses this idea negatively, describing Winter as "the sworne enemy to Summer, Brother to old Age, the eater and devourer of that which summer (like the Ante) hath provided" (Frende 1622, B2r). Feasting is the central activity in the engraving of Winter by Jan Saenradam after Hendrick Goltzius, with a roaring fire partially obscured by the allegorical figure in a wheaten crown presenting the bounty of the harvest (Figure 3.1.9). Another scene of indoor dining by a fire appears to the left of the central figure in the Philips Galle engraving (Figure 3.1.8); in the landscape depicted in the Winter Hatfield Tapestry, the usual hearth is replaced by an outdoor bonfire (Plate 14).

In Netherlandish prints, another common Winter pastime is skating, seen in the right side of the engraving for the season by Philips Galle (Figure 3.1.8). That activity may not have held much interest for an English market. In the Hatfield tapestry rendition of the Collaert image for Winter (Plate 14), for example, the skating in the original engraving is replaced with additional scenes of animal slaughtering, the standard labor for December, as well as gathering wood, the labor for February.

Complexion, qualities, Weather and disease

> Instead of flowers and grasse so greene,
> The earth hath got another hew:
> Frosts, Snow, and durty dales are seene:
> where pleasant plants most fruitfull grew.   (Frende 1622, B2r)

Winter is the phlegmatic season, cold and moist, and the almanacs and medical literature are filled with ominous imagery of decay, decrepitude, and starvation. In Winter, earth is like "an olde decrepyte persone, that by great age is naked and nyghe to the death" (Aristotle, *Here Begynneth*, D2r). In Winter men should "spendeth that which he had hath gathered and kept

158 Early modern calendars

Figure 3.1.8 Winter, Engraving, Philips Galle, after Maarten van Heemskerck, 1563. Rijksmuseum, Amsterdam.

in the tyme passed, and if he have spared nothing, he abydeth poore and naked as the earth and Trees" (*Kalender* 1570, J1v). To Gabriel Frende, the season itself is a "frostbitten churle" (B2r); Nicholas Breton describes it as "a wofull Season, the punishment of Nature's pride, and the play of misery" (*Fantasticks*, B7v). The season is "unpleasaunt and dangerous for the most part to Travellers, eyther by Lande or by Sea" (Buckminster 1589, B5v), largely because of the wind: as Breton notes, in this season "*Boreas*," the North Wind, "beginnes to fill his cheeks with breath, shaketh the tops of the high Cedars, and hayleth the waves of the Sea, to the danger of the Saylers comfort" (*Fantasticks*, B3r). Those particular dangers are also represented in the Hatfield tapestry for Winter, both by the central allegorical figure—Aeolus, the Greek god of winds—and by the tempests that threaten sea-faring vessels in the top right corner, to the dismay of onlookers (Plate 14).

The elderly and infirm suffer most from the cold moistness of Winter, a season that is "not hurtfull unto healthfull people, but very greevous

Figure 3.1.9 Winter, Engraving, Jan Saenredam, after Hendrick Goltzius, 1590–1600. Rijksmuseum, Amsterdam.

to them that are sicke" (Buckminster 1589, B5v). Those in greatest medical danger this season are "aged persons" for whom the moist cold weather is "very comberous and noysome, causyng…[an] abundaunce of moystnes to overflowe theyr bodyes, to their great trouble and unquietnes" (Buckminster 1589, B5v). Other writers concur that the medical perils of the season are the result of the "greater aboundance of colde crudities, and superfluous moysture in mans body" (Dade 1602, B2r). The wetter the Winter, the more perilous for both people and plants: "A warme, and moist Winter is unwholesome," Hopton notes, "and an enemy to husbandmen, but reasonable store of snow doth ranken [fertilize] the fields, and preserve corne" (*Concordancy*, 96).

160   Early modern calendars

Yet Winter is in many respects a healthy time of year—especially a dry Winter. The greatest health benefit is increased digestive power, "for the coldnesse of the air without, environing our bodies about, must needs keep in, and unite and fortifie the inward heat" (Cogan, *Haven*, 206). Because the "virtue digestive" is stronger, "one may eate as much as he will, that is to say, more than in other seasons, and not onely more but also meats of grosser substance" (Cogan, *Haven*, 206). Medical guides and almanacs stress the salutary effects of warm meats, spices, and wine in Winter. The extensive list of healthy foods for Winter in the *Kalender* also identifies the digestive benefits and wholesomeness of the season. In Winter,

> Shephardes do eate befe, porke, and brawne, of hartes, handes, and all maner of venyson, pertryches, fesauntes, hares, fowles of the ryver, and other meates that they love best. For that is the season of the yeare that nature suffreth moste great plentye of vittayle for the naturall heate that is drawen within the bodye. In this tyme also they drynke ofte stronge wynes, after theyr complexion, bastard wyne, or Osey [Portugeuse wine]. Two or three tymes in the weke they use good spyces in theyr meates. For this is the most holsome tyme of all the yere, in the which cometh no syckenesse but by greate excesse & outrages done to nature, or by evyll governement.
>
> (*Kalender* 1570, J2v)

Notes

1 On medieval traditions concerning the seasons see Derek Pearsall and Elizabeth Salter, *Landscapes and Seasons of the Medieval World* (Toronto: University of Toronto Press, 1973), and Paul S. Langeslag, *Seasons in the Literatures of the Medieval North* (Woodbridge, Suffolk: D.S. Brewer, 2015).
2 Rosamond Tuve, *Seasons and Months: Studies in a Tradition of Middle English Poetry* (Totowa, NJ: D.S. Brewer Ltd, 1933); Erwin Panofsky, *Studies in Iconology: Humanistic Themes in the Art of the Renaissance* (New York: Harper & Row, 1972); Erwin Panofsky, Raymond Klibansky, and Fritz Saxl, *Saturn and Melancholy: Studies in the History of Natural Philosophy, Religion and Art* (London: Thomas Nelson and Sons, LTD, 1964).
3 The most complete overview of this tradition is J.A. Burrow, *The Ages of Man: A Study in Medieval Writing and Thought* (Oxford: Oxford University Press, 1988).
4 Other classical writers whose work influenced seasonal descriptions include Pliny, *Natural History*, printed in an English translation in 1601; Hesiod, *Works and Days*, printed in an English translation by George Chapman in 1618; and Lucretius, *De Rerum Natura*, not widely available until late in the seventeenth century. The *Georgics* found its way into representations of the seasons through learned calendars and Edmund Spenser's *The Shepheardes Calendar*. See Helen Cooper, "Pastoral and Georgic," in *The Oxford History of Classical Reception in English Literature, Volume 2*, eds. Norman Vance and Jennifer Wallace (Oxford: Oxford University Press, 2015), 201–224.
5 Wallis, "Medicine," 112–115.
6 Ibid., 113.

7 Recent work on the seasons in Shakespeare includes Dympna Callaghan, "Confounded by Winter: Speeding Time in Shakespeare's Sonnets," in *A Companion to Shakespeare's Sonnets*, ed. Michael Schoenfeldt (Oxford: Blackwell Publishing, 2007), 104–118, esp. 104; Frederick Kiefer, *Shakespeare's Visual Theatre: Staging the Personified Characters* (Cambridge: Cambridge University Press, 2003), 25–41; and Maurice Hunt, "Climacteric Ages and the Three Seasons of *The Winter's Tale*," *Renascence* 69, no.2 (2017): 69–80.
8 Ilja Veldman, "Seasons, Planets and Temperaments in the Work of Maarten van Heemskerck: Cosmo-Astrological Allegory in Sixteenth-Century Netherlandish Prints," *Simiolus* 11, nos. 3/4 (1980), 149–176.
9 Hamling, *Decorating the Godly Household*, 9; Wells-Cole, *Art and Decoration*, passim. See also Sara Trevisan, "The Impact of the Netherlandish Landscape Tradition on Poetry and Painting in Early Modern England," *Renaissance Quarterly* 66, no. 3 (2013), 866–903.
10 The verses were apparently "composed by the philologist and town physician of Haarlem, Hadrianus Junius"; they are translated in Veldman, "Seasons," 150.
11 Peter M. Daly, "The Sheldon 'Four Seasons' Tapestries at Hatfield House: A Seventeenth-Century Instance of Significant Emblematic Decoration in the English Decorative Arts," *Emblematica* 14 (2005): 251–296; A.F. Kendrick, "The Hatfield Tapestries of the Seasons," *The Annual Volume of the Walpole Society* 2 (1912–1913): 89–95.
12 Botticelli's *Primavera*, which includes both Flora and Venus as avatars of Spring, is perhaps the most famous, as well as the most enigmatic; see Charles Dempsey, *The Portrayal of Love: Botticelli's Primavera and Humanist Culture at the Time of Lorenzo the Magnificent* (Princeton, NJ: Princeton University Press, 1992). For examples of the identification of Flora with spring or "prime" in pastoral poetry, see, for example, the excerpts from poems "Of the Spring" in Robert Allott's popular *Englands Parnassus* (London, 1600), 364–370, and Barnabe Barnfield, *Cynthia with Certaine Sonnets* (London, 1595), B1v.
13 Bridget Ann Henisch, *The Medieval Calendar Year* (University Park: The Pennsylvania University Press, 1999), 135–165.
14 See the discussion of this image in H. Arthur Klein, *Graphic Worlds of Peter Bruegel the Elder* (New York, Dover Publications, 1963), 52. The original Bruegel drawing for this engraving is in the Albertina Museum, Vienna.
15 See on this series Veldman, "Seasons," 162.

3.2 The planets and seven days of the week

Introduction

The seven-day week was fully merged with the 365-day Julian calendar in the early Christian era. The Latin names for the weekdays, which honored the seven planets, were initially inherited from Babylonian astrology, though in the early medieval period these were changed in English to honor certain Norse gods (Woden to replace Mercury on Wednesday, Thor to replace Jupiter on Thursday, and Freya or Frigg to replace Venus on Friday). Following the reintroduction of Ptolemaic astrology into the West after the tenth century CE, the planetary hours—the idea that each planet ruled a particular day, and also certain hours in each day—became an important part of astrological understandings of planetary influence, as described in more detail in Chapter 1.1 and Part II, above.

This section of *Astrology, Almanacs, and the Early Modern English Calendar* briefly outlines the characteristics of the seven planets which, by the tenets of early modern astrology, were thought to govern certain increments of time. Those characteristics were produced at the intersection of the scientific and the mythological. Five of the seven planets—Saturn, Jupiter, Mars, Venus, and Mercury—took their names from Roman gods. The Sun and Moon were more tenuously associated with the Roman gods Apollo and Diana. That mythology informed the qualities and characteristics of those planets, and therefore of the days and hours they were thought to rule. Each overview, below, identifies the planets' mythological backstory, as well as their qualities: melancholic, sanguine, phlegmatic, or choleric, hot, cold, wet, or dry, masculine, feminine, or changeable (in the case of Mercury). The physical, psychological, and vocational profiles of those born under the influence of each planet are also provided. This information was quite consistent across almanacs, astrological primers, books of secrets, guides to astrological medicine, and other popular works concerning astrology in the early modern period.

The planetary hours had long been central to the practice of alchemy and horary astrology of higher-level astrologers and natural magicians. They were a key part of the creation of sigils, and guidelines for planetary influence can be found throughout contemporary books of magic, including

The planets and seven days of the week 163

Figure 3.2.1 Planetary Rulers, Book of Magic, Manuscript, Folger Shakespeare Library V.b.26 (1), ca. 1577–1583, 63. Photograph by Phebe Jensen, from the collection of the Folger Shakespeare Library.

the grimoire in the Folger Shakespeare Library, V.b.26 (Figure 3.2.1). It is unclear how fully ordinary early modern men and women in England identified planets with particular days of the week, but it is certainly the case that instructions for calculating the planetary hours became more frequent in almanacs in the seventeenth century. That development presumably reflects the larger rise in astrological interest and literacy in this period, and it suggests planetary hours were again (or perhaps still) being used to track the progress of diseases and guide elections for physic and husbandry.

Sunday: The Sun

> [The] *Sun* is moderately hot and dry, Masculine of the day, fortunate by aspect, infortunate by corporall conjunction.
>
> (Dariot, 16)

The Sun is the "king of al the planets": he "norisheth every age" and "comforteth both man and beast, fishe, and all foules that flyeth in the ayre" (*Kalender*, L3r). Hot and dry, the Sun is the antithesis of cold, wet Saturn. Unlike the equally hot but usually evil Mars, the Sun is beneficient, and his children are blessed with "long life, and a healthful body" (Hopton, *Concordancy*, 83). The Sun is "the princypall workeman of God, and the planetes are instrumentes and toles wherewith the Sonne worketh" (Askham, *Treatyse*, A3v). The single Zodiac sign governed by the Sun is Leo.

As the ruler of the planets, the Sun's iconography overlaps with imagery associated with Jupiter, though he is primarily identified with the Greek and

164   Early modern calendars

Roman god of the Sun, Phoebus Apollo. The Sun signifies "kings, Princes," and "Potentates" (Hopton, *Concordancy*, 83); images of this planet and his children are often illustrated with rituals concerning secular or religious authority. For example, the engraving of the Sun by Johann Sadeler after Maerten de Vos (Figure 3.2.2) shows the crowning of bishops and kings, the conferring of a knighthood, and an elaborate royal processional (complete with kneeling spectators). The allegorized Sun in this image holds a scepter indicating kingship, and he drives a chariot pulled by the four mythical horses of the Sun, named in Ovid's recounting of the myth of Apollo and his rash son, Phaeton: "Aeous, Aethon, Phlegon, and the firie Pyrois" (17). The connection with Apollo may explain the frequent images of music-making among the children of the Sun. Above all, however, the Sun is known as "the most universall cause, and the very beginning & fountayne of light and influence, & also of vitall heat" (Maplet, 23).

Figure 3.2.2 The Sun, *De Zone en Zijn Invloed op to Wereld*, Engraving, Johan Sadeler (I), after Maerten de Vos, 1585. Rijksmuseum, Amsterdam.

Children of the Sun benefit from the qualities that make strong leaders: they are "magnanimous, industrious, provident, ambitious," as well as "valiant, secret, honest, [and] quiet" (Hopton, *Concordancy*, 83). They are "very desirious of glory and renowne" and "studious of difficult and hard matters"; as a consequence, they are "advanced often to great honours and dignities" (Maplet, 23). The children of the Sun enjoy "long life, and a healthfull body" (Hopton, *Concordancy*, 83), even tempers, attractive faces with white or very pale skin (*Kalender*, L3r), and "sincere and very good minde[s]" (Dariot, 22). In some calendar material, children of the Sun are said to be particularly attached to hawking and hunting, as well as to music (*Kalender*, L3r). The relatively mild character flaws of people born under the Sun's influence include vanity, excessive ambition, and arrogance.

The period when the Sun reigns in the calendar is almost always auspicious. Agriculturally. the Sun "giveth al thinges lyfe, and makethe all herbes to growe, tyl they come to their perfection" (Askham, *Treatyse*, A4v). Medically, the Sun rules "the Brayne, the herte, the thyghes, the mary [marrow], ... the handes, feete, and synewes" (Askham, *Treatyse*, B4r). He rules the right eye of men, but the left eye of women (Dariot, 22). The Sun oversees the "spiritual life" and rules the "vertue fantasticall" (Askham, *Treatyse*, B4r). The days and hours in which the Sun governs are almost always positive for medical interventions, except in dangerously hot periods, such as the Dog Days.

Monday: The Moon

> The *Moone* is...cold and moyst...Feminine, of the night, and Phlegmatick, and sendeth unto us the vertue and impression of all the other Planets: for all the influences of the superiour bodies, passing through her Circle, are by her proximity to the earth derived unto us.
>
> (Dariot, 16)

Next to the Sun, the Moon is the most influential of the seven planets, her proximity to the earth affording her an especially powerful influence over sublunar life. Not only does the Moon govern the waxing and waning of all fluids on earth, including the humors of the human body, but she serves as the "mediatrix" and "conveyre of the vertues and properyes of al the other planets" (*Kalender*, L5r). Phlegmatic, feminine, governing the sign of Cancer, the Moon is primarily associated with the element of water, and she of course "ruleth the sea by ebbe and fludde" (*Kalender*, L5r). As discussed in more detail in Chapter 1.1, though casting horoscopes was well beyond the skill set of most ordinary people in early modern England, anyone with a calendar—and even enterprising people without one—could know the location of the Moon in the Zodiac and follow the basic guidelines for maintaining health and treating disease by the well-known tenets of lunar medicine.

The gentle children of the Moon are drawn to water; they "will have great desire to be masters & mistresses over great streames, ryvers, and flyddes"

(*Kalender*, L5r). Water figures prominently in most allegorical representations of the Moon, such as the Jansz Muller engraving after Maarten van Heemskerck in Figure 3.2.3, which shows men and women fishing with spears, nets, and by hand, and swimming and cavorting in the waves. The Moon in this image is pulled by the two maidens that link to her classical association with Diana or Artemis, goddesses of the Moon who are particularly associated with chastity. Indeed, children of the Moon are usually characterized—sometimes paradoxically—with both chastity and changeability. On the one hand, the children of the Moon are "honest, true, steadfast," despising all "harlots and brothels, and unable to hold a grudge (*Kalender*, 5r). On the other hand, they can be "fearfull, faynt-harted," vagabonds, unstable, and prodigal, as well as "naturally mutable & movable, without fidelity and constancy, given to provoke much anger & discord betweene friends" (Maplet, 13v). On the negative end of this character spectrum, those under the Moon's influence are naturally envious, prone to feeling "agreed with the prosperity and good fortune of others: they bee also ful of hatred, and in their conversation and manner of lyfe they be very childish" (Maplet, 13v).

Figure 3.2.3 The Moon, *Luna, de Maan, En Haar Kinderen*, Engraving, Harmen Jansz Muller, after Maarten van Heemskerck, 1566–1570. Rijksmuseum, Amsterdam.

The Children of the Moon are attractive, "well fourmed of body," with "mery lokes" (*Kalender*, L5r). Agriculturally, the Moon "geveth the leaves, and watry humour" to growing plants (Askham, *Treatyse*, A3v). Medically, the parts of the body governed by the Moon include the "brayne, longes, backebone, the... stomake, and all the excrementes of the body" (Askham, *Treatyse*, B6v); she also rules the left eyes of men, and the right eyes of women (Dariot, 26). Generally, however, the Moon rules "all the hole bodye" given her proximity to earth, power over sublunar fluids (including humors), and role as transmitter of the influence of higher planets and stars to the earth (Askham, *Treatyse*, B6v). The Moon is certainly the most important planet when it comes to the practice of astrological medicine.

Tuesday: Mars

Mars is immoderately hot and dry, Cholerick, Masculine...of the night, evill, and the lesse[r] misfortune.

(Dariot, 16)

Mars is the angry planet, hot and dry, associated with fire and the choleric complexion; he rules the Zodiac signs of Aries and Scorpio. Next to Saturn, Mars is the most dangerous planet for human health. As the planet representing the Roman "God of battell" (Batman, 130), Mars "stiyrreth up mens myndes to debate and stryfe, and letteth the league of Tranquillity & peace" (Maplet, 43v). On the positive side, when aspected with good planets, those under the sway of Mars can be "generous, fit for government and rule, valiant, [and] strong," as well as fearless, noble, and unconcerned with material wealth (Hopton *Concordancy*, 83).

Mars governs "All Souldiers from the Generall to the common man[,] Brawlers, contumelious and seditious persons, Conjurers, Quarrellers, Thieves, [and] Drunkards," and all those whose professions involve "fiery works," such as gun-makers, cutlers, and alchemists (Dariot, 20–32). The children of Mars make good physicians and surgeons, because of their affinity with blood. Those under this planet's influence are known for being "full of malice, and ever doing wrong" and for being great "walker[s]; "under Mars is borne all theves and robbers that kepeth highe ways, and hurteth true men" (*Kalender*, L3r). With hardy, stalwart bodies, they are adventurous, and disposed "by a certaine naturall inclination to aptness and dexterity to the quicke and expedite obtayning of such artes and crafts as be manual or don by hand" (Maplet, 45r). Physically, the children of Mars are characterized by a "lively, high colour like Sun-burnt, or like raw tanned leather, fiere countenance," with "eyes sparkling or sharp," and reddish hair (Dariot, 21).

Figure 3.2.4, attributed to the German printermaker Georg Pencz, shows the typical kind of strife associated with the reign of Mars. Fire, the element of choleric Mars, is emphasized by the town that burns in the far background, as well as the farmhouse in flames to the right. In the middle ground, a small army appears to be pillaging—attacking a herd of cattle

Figure 3.2.4 Mars, *Mars En Zijn Planeetkinderen*, Engraving, Anonymous, after Hans Sebald Beham, after Georg Pencz, 1531. Rijksmuseum, Amsterdam.

with their spears. To the left, violent men (perhaps the highway robbers who are often children of Mars) accost and rob travelers, two of whom have been stripped naked and tied together. The even more alarming mayhem in the foreground depicts two small children fleeing while their mother is brutalized by a group of armed men; behind them, another man is about to be thrust through with a spear. Such scenes are typical for representations of the children of Mars, who "stirreth a man to be very wylfull and hastye at once" (*Kalender*, L2v). Above this scene, Mars himself, riding in a chariot pulled by two greyhounds, is shown in full armor, with a shield in one hand and a sword in the other: the two Zodiac signs ruled by this planet, Aries and Scorpio, are emblazoned on the wheels.

"[L]et every man beware of the days of Mars," the *Kalender* warns (L3v). During the day (Tuesday) and hours ruled by Mars, one is much more likely to run into thieves, or to be murdered. The day or hour ruled by Mars is not auspicious for entering into matrimony. Like Saturn, Mars is medically perilous, especially to those who are already choleric. Mars increases the danger of all burning sicknesses: fevers, the plague, "Aposthumes, Yellow Jaundies, Ulcers, red Choler...Madnesse, foul tetters in the face...Carbuncles, swellings, [and] sharp diseases in the skin," and he increases the likelihood of injury or death from "4 footed beasts" or "torments by Sword, Iron, or fire" (Dariot, 21). The virtue of this planet in medicine is his "property...to bind, dry up and staunche" (Maplet, 50r). Mars rules particularly over the "Gall, Reins [kidneys], Veins, & their diseases" (Dariot, 20). In husbandry, Mars is the force that "hardeneth and gyveth the wooddy stalkes...strength" (Askham, *Treatyse*, A3v).

Wednesday: Mercury

Mercurie in all things is common and variable, he is good with the good, and evil with evil, with the Masculine he is Masculine, with the Feminine feminine, hot with hot, moist with moist, &c.

(Dariot, 16)

Though of his own nature cold and dry, Mercury is the tricky, shape-shifting planet, "now male, now female: for he tourneth himselfe soone to the Planet that hee is joyned with" (Batman, 131). For this reason, he is not identified with a single humor or temperament. Mercury rules the Zodiac signs of Virgo and Gemini.

Mercury is the "lorde of spech, in likewise as the Sunne is lorde of light" (*Kalender*, L4r). As "the father, workeman, or procurer of eloquence and good wit" (Maplet, 16r), Mercury rules over intellectual and artistic pursuits: mathematics, rhetoric, philosophy, theology, geometry, poetry, and as well as mechanical arts associated with learning and the arts, such as print-making, engraving, sculpting, and painting. The anonymous engraving after Hans Sebald Beham and Georg Pencz (Figure 3.2.5) shows

170 *Early modern calendars*

Figure 3.2.5 Mercury, *Mercurius en Zin Planeetkinderen*, Engraving, Anonymous, after Hans Sebald Beham, after Georg Pencz, 1531. Rijksmuseum, Amsterdam.

a typical range of such endeavors: male scribes at work, another man collating finished sheets of printed paper, a female sculptor, an artist at his easel, astronomers calculating planetary aspects, a doctor examining a vial of urine, and in the background, tradesmen selling to customers. Mercury is the "called God of Merchants," because the planet endows its children with skill at accounts, which are "most needfull to Merchants" (Batman, 131). In the Beham/Pencz engraving, as was conventional, Mercury wields the *cadaecus*, the symbol for medicine, on a chariot pulled by two roosters.

The clever children of Mercury enjoy both intellectual and physical dexterity, but they are also given to the instability that characterizes this planet more generally. They are at once "wise, ingenious, wayward, wavering, violent," as well as "not seldome mournfull, inconstant…crafty, instable," and subject to "all melancholy diseases" (Dariot, 25). Mercury is the planet most closely identified with madness—even more so than the lunatic Moon. Medically, Mercury rules the "memory, tongue, Phantasie, brain, [and] spirits," as well as the "hands, fingers, gall, bones, thighs, sinews of the brain"; this planet can cause "sicknesses of too much abundance of good bloud infecting the brain, deprivation of common sense, Lethargie, doting[,] Stammering, impediment of the tongue, the falling sicknes, Coughs, abundance of spittle, stopping of the gall, vomit, Cathars," and "abundance of humours in the head" (Dariot, 25). The children of Mercury tend to be "valiant of body," despite their "slippery and chaungeable mindes" (Maplet, 16). In husbandry, Mercury infuses "the barke and sede" with its secret and occult qualities (Askham, *Treatyse*, A3v).

Thursday: Jupiter

> *Jupiter* is hot and moist, sanguine, a friend and preserver of the life and nature of Mankind[,] masculine of the day, and is termed the greatest fortune.
>
> (Dariot, 16)

The noble planet Jupiter, which is good in all aspects, is also the crucial planet for tempering his evil outer neighbor, Saturn. Warm and moist, sanguine, and associated with the element of air, Jupiter is dominant in the "two noble signs of love," Pisces and Sagittarius (*Kalender*, L2r). Negative commentary about Jupiter and his children is rare, though Hopton notes that "being evilly affected," Jupiter can create adherents who are "prodigall and proud" (*Concordancy*, 83).

Images of Jupiter often include representations of the legal, religious, or political authority for which he is known. In the Harmen Jansz Muller engraving after Maarten van Heemskerck (Figure 3.2.6), Jupiter's chariot is pulled by peacocks—the standard attribute for this god and planet. Jupiter strokes an eagle, a symbol of rulership and military prowess. As in other contemporary engravings, Jupiter here bestows coins (in a bowl) on

Figure 3.2.6 Jupiter, *De Planeet Jupiter en zijn Kinderen*, Engraving, Harmen Jansz Muller, after Maarten van Heemskerck, 1638–1646. Rijksmuseum, Amsterdam.

a kneeling attendant, a gesture that represents the monetary fortune associated with this beneficent planet. Other images in the engraving concern religious and secular authority: to the right a Pope crowns a King, while to the left, a judge passes a sentence on a petitioner. Another activity often associated with Jupiter, the hunt, is represented here by the mounted hunters and dogs chasing a large hart in the background.

The children of Jupiter are "honest, religious, just, doers of good turnes, magnanimous, faithfull, verecundious, benevolent, manly, famous governours, of great diligence, grave, and modest" (Hopton, *Concordancy*, 82–83). They are "very pure and clear of nature," as well as physically attractive; they live clean and upright lives voide of "rybawdry" (*Kalender*, L2r). Fair and judicious rulers, they can be lawyers, judges, magistrates, noblemen, and ecclesiastical officials. Children of Jupiter are loyal, "lovers of their owne, and of their friends, liberall, and without fraud (Hopton, *Concordancy*, 83). They "love to singe and to be honestly merry"

(*Kalender*, L2r) and are fortunate in worldly affairs—especially in piling up gold and silver, minerals which are also ruled by this planet. Jupiter advances his children "to great Prosperity, good successe, much Riches, high Honoure, and getteth them Favour and friendship in the Worlde"; the planet also "preserveth them fro[m] ye assaults of their enemies" (Maplet, 52r). The children of Jupiter are articulate rhetoricians. Physically, they have light complexions, "white colour & faire, medled with rednesse." Their bodies are strong and well-proportioned, with "faire eyen and teeth, and faire haire, faire beard and round" (Batman, 130r).

Jupiter rules the abdomen and middle of the body: "the wombe, and navell, the shorte rybbes...the bowelles...the vaynes, Raynes, backe, and buttocks"; he also has dominion over "the naturall spirite" (due to his association with air) and "the ryghte hande and the left eare" (Askham, *Treatyse*, B1v). His sanguine reign is usually auspicious for the curing of acute diseases, for medical interventions, and for husbandry; Jupiter "geveth the temperature, benefete, shap, and fasshyon, and ayrie humour and smell" to all growing things (Askham, *Treatyse*, A3v).

Friday: Venus

> *Venus* is cold and moist, temperate, Phlegmatick, Feminine, of the night, of good nature, and is called the lesser fortune.
>
> (Dariot, 16)

Like her namesake, the goddess of love, the sanguine planet Venus is associated with pleasure. Her children are "Gentle Lovers of delights" (Dariot, 23), who enjoy romance, leisure, sociability, and festive entertainments. Good-natured Venus, who is cold and moist, rules Taurus and Libra; she is especially effective at tempering the influence of hot, dry Mars. This feminine planet is auspicious for most medical interventions.

In Figure 3.2.7 from the *Kalender of Shepherds*, the children of Venus can be seen participating in the activities typical for their ruler, as two lovers in a lavish bath are serenaded by musicians next to a lovely outdoor picnic. "Those that be borne under Venus," Maplet writes, "are amiable, and of merry & smylinge Looke or Countenaunce, greate laughers, very wanton, & such as do greatly delight in Musicke" (20v). They are drawn to pleasant pastimes: "they shalbe pleasaunt singers, with sweete voice, & full of wanton toyes, playes, and skoffings, and shal greatly delighte in daucing, and gambauldes, with leaping and springing, and wil use playing at the chesse, and at the cardes, and tables" (*Kalender*, L4r). Physically, the children of Venus are also pleasing, "delicate in gesture" and "elegant" (Hopton, *Concordancy*, 83). Sybarites, they enjoy luxury and are "geven much to the composing and making of sweete Oyntments and Odoures" (Maplet, 20v).

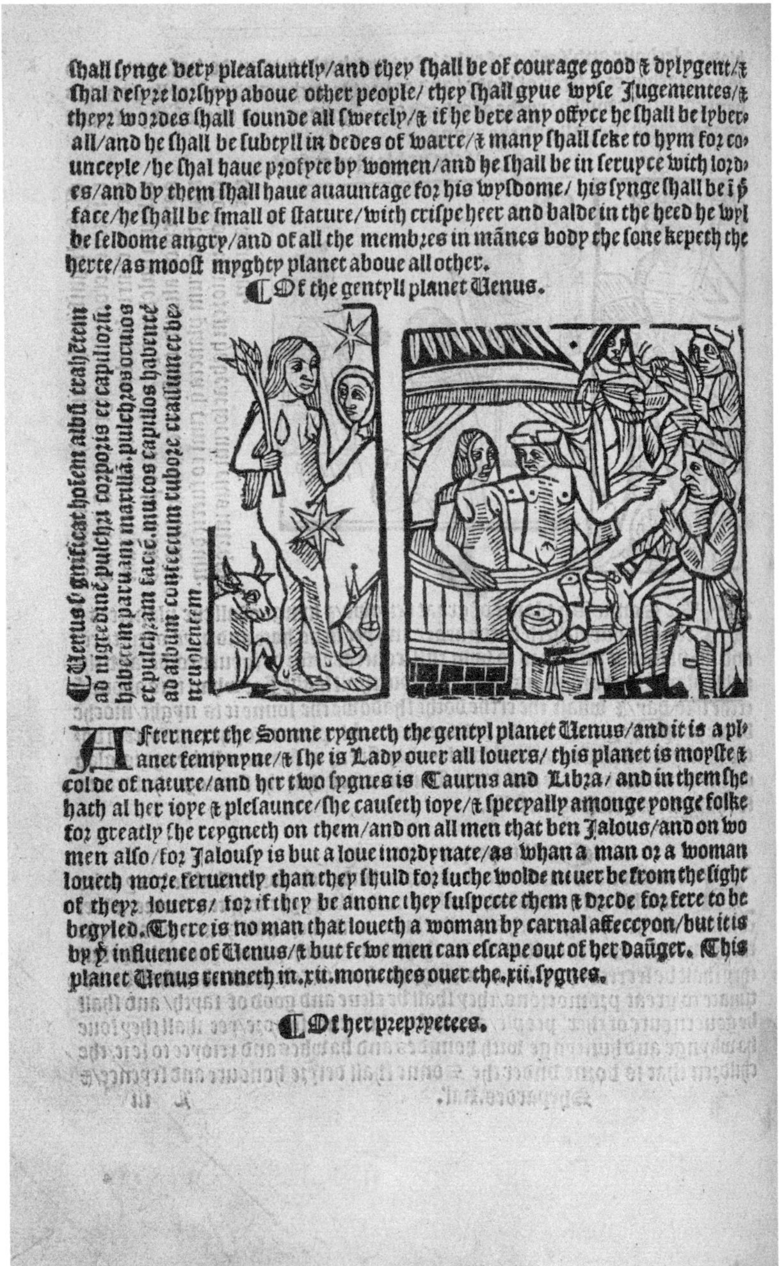

shall synge very pleasauntly/and they shall be of courage good & dylygent/& shal desyre lordshyp aboue other people/ they shall gyue wyse Jugementes/& theyr wordes shall sounde all swetely/& if he bere any offyce he shall be lyberall/and he shall be subtyll in dedes of warre/& many shall seke to hym for coūceyle /he shal haue profyte by women/and he shall be in seruyce with lordes/and by them shall haue auauntage for his wysdome/ his synge shall be i þ face/he shal be small of stature/with crispe heer and balde in the heed he wyl be seldome angry/and of all the membres in mānes body the sone kepeth the herte/as moost myghty planet aboue all other.

¶ Of the gentyll planet Uenus.

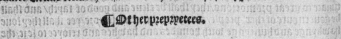

After next the Sonne rygneth the gentyl planet Uenus/and it is a planet femynyne/& she is Lady ouer all louers/ this planet is moyste & colde of nature/and her two sygnes is Taurus and Libra/ and in them she hath al her ioye & plesaunce/she causeth ioye/& specyally amonge yonge folke for greatly she reygneth on them/and on all men that ben Jalous/and on wo men also/ for Jalousy is but a loue inordynate/as whan a man or a woman loueth more feruently than they shuld for suche wolde neuer be from the sight of theyr louers/ for if they be anone they suspecte them & drede for fere to be begyled. There is no man that loueth a woman by carnal affeccyon/but it is by þ influence of Uenus/& but fewe men can escape out of her dauger. This planet Uenus renneth in .xii. monethes ouer the .xii. sygnes.

¶ Of her propryetees.

Figure 3.2.7 Venus, *Here Begynneth the Kalender of Shepardes* ([1518?], STC 22410), L3v. The Huntington Library, San Marino, California, RB 69474.

As this description suggests, the children of Venus are susceptible to seduction by "all vayne pleasure of the world," including "fair and rich clothes, and pearles, and pretious stones" (*Kalender*, L4r). A man overly influenced by this planet can be "effeminate, fearefull, a lover of maids, spending much upon them, without respect of fame or infamy, idle, sluggish, apt to lust...[and] given to jealousie" (Hopton, *Concordancy*, G2r). Venus is not identified with work, as her children are drawn to "Idlenesse and pleasures" (Dariot, 23), and "impatient of labour" (Hopton, *Concordancy*, G2r-G2v). However, some professions are particularly suited to those under Venus' influence, especially those involving the creation of the beautiful things to which the children of Venus are naturally attracted; they might be successful as "lapidaries, Emproyderers, & such like," as well as cooks, poets, or painters (Dariot, 23–24).

Venus is almost entirely beneficial when it comes to medicine and husbandry, although this planet can exacerbate disorders caused by cold and moist humors. The regions of the body ruled by Venus include the abdomen, "Genitals, Pappes, Throat, Loins, Buttocks, Sperm, Liver, Gomorrhes," and diseases of those parts, including "passions of the Matrix, suffocations, the French Scab, the pissing-evil, [and] flux of the stomach" (Dariot, 24). In husbandry, Venus "gyveth the flowers, fayrenes and temperate humour" (Askham, *Treatyse*, A3v).

Saturday: Saturn

> Saturne is cold and dry, Melancholick, an enemy and destroyer of the nature and life of man, of the day, masculine, evill, and the greatest misfortune.
>
> (Dariot, 16)

Evil Saturn, the "enemy to all things that groweth and beareth of life" (*Kalender*), is the most dangerous and reviled of all the seven planets. Saturn is melancholy, cold and dry, and associated with the element of earth. The two Zodiac signs associated with Saturn, Capricorn the goat and Aquarius the water bearer, can be seen tucked into lower corners of the engraving of Saturn from the *Kalender* (Figure 3.2.8). The sodden quality of earth, coupled with the slow pace of this planet's thirty-year journey around the earth, identify Saturn with all things leaden and lumpish, both in the natural world and in the body and character of man. About the best that John Maplet can say of Saturn is that he has "hys place appoynted him there...far of from the earth, where all creatures lyuing make their abode," proof of God's mercy in placing "the cruellest" planet as far away as possible (Maplet, 59v). Nevertheless, Saturn's earthy heaviness accords a measure of strength, stamina, and perseverance that can have positive effects, especially when Saturn's influence is tempered by his neighbor, the good planet Jupiter.

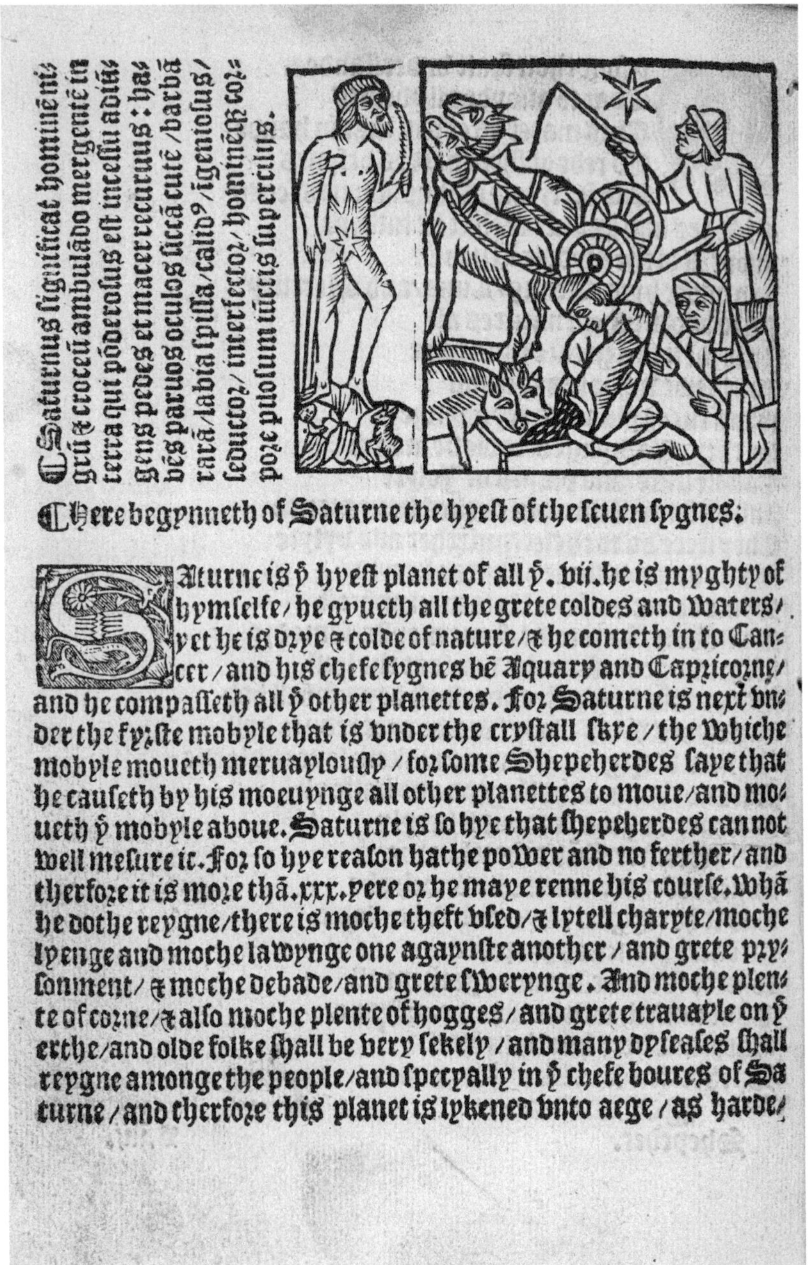

⁋Saturnus significat hominem nigrū & croceū ambulado mergentē in terra qui pōderosus est incessu aditus, gens pedes et macer recuruus: ha= bēs paruos oculos sicca cute, barbā raram, labia spissa, calid9, ignitosus, seductor, intersector, hominēcȝ cor= pore puolum lucris supercilius.

⁋Here begynneth of Saturne the hyest of the seuen sygnes.

Saturne is ẏ hyest planet of all ẏ. vij. he is myghty of hymselfe, he gyueth all the grete coldes and waters, yet he is drye & colde of nature, & he cometh in to Can= cer, and his chefe sygnes bē Aquary and Capricorne, and he compasseth all ẏ other planettes. For Saturne is next vn= der the fyrste mobyle that is vnder the crystall skye, the whiche mobyle moueth meruaylously, for some Shepeherdes saye that he causeth by his moeuynge all other planettes to moue, and mo= ueth ẏ mobyle aboue. Saturne is so hye that shepeherdes cannot well mesure it. For so hye reason hathe power and no ferther, and therfore it is more thā. xxx. yere or he maye renne his course. Whā he dothe reygne, there is moche theft vsed, & lytell charyte, moche lyenge and moche lawynge one agaynste another, and grete pry= sonment, & moche debade, and grete swerynge. And moche plen= te of corne, & also moche plente of hogges, and grete trauayle on ẏ erthe, and olde folke shall be very sekely, and many dyseases shall reygne amonge the people, and specyally in ẏ chefe houres of Sa= turne, and therfore this planet is lykened vnto aege, as harde,

Figure 3.2.8 Saturn, *The Kalender of Shepeherdes* (1528, STC 22411), R4v. The Huntington Library, San Marino, California, RB 69440.

The iconography associated with Saturn is arguably the most complex of all the seven planets, for—as Raymond Klibansky, Erwin Panofsky, and Fritz Saxl established long ago—it overlaps in significant ways with iconography concerning time, death, and melancholy.[1] Saturn's myth replicates the story of Chronus, his Greek prototype, yet the Roman version diverged in significant ways from that original to make Saturn a somewhat more benign figure. The planet Saturn in late medieval and early modern calendars and works of popular astrology, however, is anything but benign. The image in Figure 3.2.8 (from the *Kalender*) includes standard motifs associated with Saturn: husbandry with the ploughman, hogs and prisoners with the criminal in the stocks, physical injury, illness and death. Here (as is often the case) Saturn himself is leaning on a crutch, but lame beggars also figure prominently in images of Saturn. Saturn is also often shown carrying a baby—an image that is threatening, not paternal, given that the Roman myth of the god recounts how Saturn ate four of his children to prevent them from rebelling.

The astrological child of Saturn has "a voyde heart, wicked and bitter as wormwoode" (Godfridus 1585, C6r). Notorious loners, Saturnists are "cold in charitie, and not misericordious and mercifull, but vengeable, and will never be entreated (*Kalender*, L1v). Hopton's list of the faults of the child of Saturn is especially detailed:

> ...he is...abject, squalid, excogitating of base things, a pick-thank and complainer, fearefull, [a]voiding light, loving solitarinesse, sad, envious, stubborne, suspitious, superstitious, untrimmed, malignant, deceiptful, yet fearing deceipt, covetous, austere, slothfull, dull, and a lyar.
>
> (*Concordancy*, 82)

In addition, Saturnists are litigious and great quarrelers and cursers. Physically, in a tradition deriving from Ptolemy, the children of Saturn have "lytle eyen, black hair, great lippes," be "brode shouldred, and shal lke downeward"; they are also "great eater[s] of breade and fleshe," and have "stinkynge breth" (*Kalender*, L1v). They "beare malyce longe in their mynds, and not forget it," and "wyll never forgyve tyll they be revenged of theyr quarrel" (*Kalender*, L1v).

The qualities of retentiveness and dogged tenacity which make Saturnists great holders of grudges also characterize the positive qualities of those under this planet's influence. Though slow to learn, Saturnists retain knowledge well—unlike the children of Mercury, who "doe quickly and redely receiue and take, that whych is red and delyuered unto them, but are on the other side soone forgetfull" (Maplet, 62). The children of Saturn are blessed with stamina for hard labor, and they are "good and strong to doe all thinges that asketh strength only" (Godfridus 1585, C6r). Saturn rules "old men, fathers, Grandfathers, & such like," as well as "beggers" and those engaged in earthy occcupations, including "diggers for metalls or stones, Potters, Curriers, sink-cleansers, & all such base trades" (Dariot, *Dariotus*, 17).

Saturn is an extremely dangerous planet medically, and interventions such as bleeding, purging, or administering medicine are almost always discouraged when Saturn reigns. If an illness begins in a time of day, week, month or year ruled by Saturn, the prognosis is dire; the children of Saturn are prone to early death. Saturn can, however, be useful medically, as his earthiness (and qualities of retention) helps "holdeth and restraineth all maner of fluxes" (Askham, *Litell Treatyse*, A8v). Saturn is especially identified with husbandry, on which he exerts a positive effect: he is the force that "thicketh and kepeth the matter [in] rotes stalkes and leaves together, by the element of earth" (Askham, *Litle Treatyse*, A5v). For this reason, despite Saturn's general hostility to life, his reign is characterized by "much plenty of corne, and also much plenty of hogges" (*Kalender*, L1v). Indeed, the hogs in Figure 3.2.8 appear in most images of Saturn, and the planet is associated with all beasts "whych bee of lumpishe & sluggyshe Nature, and slowe to dryve" (Maplet, 64v).

Note

1 Erwin Panofsky, Raymond Klibansky, and Fritz Saxl, *Saturn and Melancholy* (London: Thomas Nelson and Sons Ltd, 1964).

Plate 9 Labors of the Month, Leaden Font, Church of St. Augustine, Brookland, Kent, UK. Photograph by Phebe Jensen.

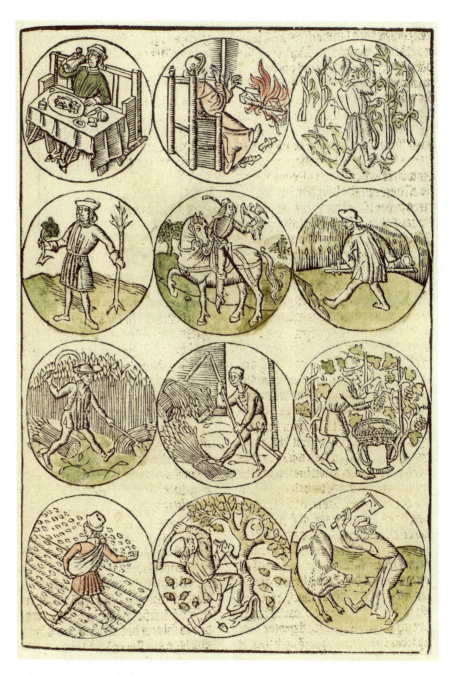

Plate 10 Labors of the Month, Anglicus Bartholomaeus, *Batman vppon Bartholome, His Booke De proprietatibus rerum* (1582), after 141v. The Huntington Library, San Marino, California, RB 447931.

Plate 11 Spring, The Four Seasons Tapestries, Hatfield House, Hatfield, Hertfordshire. Courtesy of the Marquess of Salisbury.

Plate 12 Summer, The Four Seasons Tapestries, Hatfield House, Hatfield, Hertfordshire. Courtesy of the Marquess of Salisbury.

Plate 13 Autumn, The Four Seasons Tapestries, Hatfield House, Hatfield, Hertfordshire. Courtesy of the Marquess of Salisbury.

Plate 14 Winter, The Four Seasons Tapestries, Hatfield House, Hatfield, Hertfordshire. Courtesy of the Marquess of Salisbury.

Plate 15.1 March (Pruning), Wall Painting, Easby Church. Photograph by Phebe Jensen.

Plate 15.2 June, Edmund Spenser, *The Shepheardes Calender* (1586), fol. 22v. Photograph by Phebe Jensen, from the collection of the Folger Shakespeare Library, STC 23091.

Plate 16.1 August (Virgo), Petit-point Silk Panel, Hardwick Hall, 16th century. @ National Trust / Robert Thrift.

Plate 16.2 November (Sowing), Wall Painting, Easby Church. Photograph by Phebe Jensen.

3.3 The twelve months

Introduction

This section of *Astrology, Almanacs, and the Early Modern English Calendar* is a practical reference guide to the agricultural, medical, astrological, religious, and festive associations that were attached to the months in early modern England. This introduction provides an overview of the categories of information and sources used to create the narratives for each of the twelve months of the calendar year.

Labors and agricultural tasks

The iconography of the labors of the months permeated medieval European culture, as Colum Hourihane's *Time in the Medieval World* richly documents.[1] The labors associated with each month were relatively standard, though there were also frequent variations, substitutions, and re-orderings. Examples of the complete cycle can be seen in in Stephen Batman's 1582 edition of Bartholomeus' *De Proprietatibus Rerum* (Plate 10), as well as the leaden font from a church in Brookland, Kent (Plate 9); the standard labors, with variants and Zodiac signs, are listed in Chart 3.3.1.[2] In the early modern period the labors appeared in some printed calendars, almanacs, and prayer books, and some must have survived—as they do to this day—in material form, including wall paintings and domestic decoration.

As an iconographical scheme that idealized rural life, the labors of the months did not define the actual tasks of early modern husbandry, though there were overlaps: March, for example, really was the recommended time for trimming vines and trees. But perpetual and annual almanacs also provided practical advice for farmers, as did the calendrically organized farming guide provided in Thomas Tusser's husbandry manuals, here taken from the 1610 edition, *Five Hundred Points of Good Husbandry*. It seems possible that both the labors, and the actual agricultural tasks, were valued not only for practical use, but because they articulated an idealized vision of rural life with nostalgic appeal.[3]

180 Early modern calendars

	Late Medieval Labors, Figure 1	Variant Labors	Zodiac
January	Dining		Aquarius
February	Sitting by the fire	Bringing home firewood	Pisces
March	Trimming vines	Pruning trees; digging; fixing hedges and ditches	Aries
April	Picking Flowers	Birding	Taurus
May	Birding	Hunting, lovers, outdoor dining with music	Gemini
June	Mowing	Sheep-shearing	Cancer
July	Reaping	Mowing	Leo
August	Threshing	Reaping	Virgo
September	Wine-making	Sowing	Libra
October	Sowing	Wine-making	Scorpio
November	Knocking down acorns; fattening livestock	Cutting down trees	Sagittarius
December	Slaughtering livestock	Feasting; baking bread	Capricorn

Chart 3.3.1 Labors of the Months and Zodiac Signs.

Zodiac, astronomy, and astrology

Each labor of the month was paired with a Zodiac sign, even though the Sun did not enter a new sign until the eleventh, twelfth, or thirteenth day of the month in the Julian calendar, depending partially on the year's position in the leap year cycle. The Zodiac sign associated with each month is the one that began during that month: Aries with March, for example. In the following account for each month, the basic qualities of each Zodiac sign are provided, along with information from perpetual almanacs such as the *Kalender* and Hopton's *Concordancy* concerning the influence of especially important stars, derived from authorities such as Ptolemy, Stadius, or Cardano. These prognostications usually concern the influence of stars when they rise or set cosmical, or at the moment of the Sun's rising, heliacal, just before the Sun rises, or vespertine (also known as achronical), at the moment of the Sun's setting.

The ages of man

The most popular ages of man scheme, following Ovid, identified the human body with the four seasons of the annual year, as discussed in Chapter 3.1 above. But the months had their own scheme for the ages of man which associated each of the twelve months with six years of a man's life. As Bridget Ann Henisch has shown, this tradition appeared in England in late medieval calendars and prayer books, as well as early sixteenth-century printed *horae*, later Marian primers, calendar images, and short poems. Henisch terms this motif the "Calendar Boy" tradition, though the boy grows into a man by Spring. Images illustrating this tradition are taken primarily from illustrations in the early and mid-century primers made for the English market.

Physic

Almanacs usually provide pithy recommendations for diet, medical interventions such as phlebotomy, bathing, and purging, and advice on other Galenic non-naturals (especially exercise, and the quality of the air) for each of the twelve months. This information was distinct from the astrological medical elections based on the phases of the Moon. Generally consistent across almanacs, this advice partly reflects the medical implications of the Sun's location in the Zodiac, but it is also probably the vestige of medieval seasonal recommendations for diet which were then divided into the twelve months of the Julian calendar year. As David Houston Wood has shown, for early moderns such seasonal medical recommendations connected human passions to time and the environment.[4]

The church calendar

Seasons and holy days

Each month includes a general description of the part of the liturgical year that usually falls within that month. Since at least half of each year is affected by the movable feast of Easter and its associated holy days, certain seasons migrate. Their description is given for the month in which they usually fall; Shrovetide and Lent, for example, are described in February, even though they sometimes do not occur until March.

Lectionary

In adapting and reforming the Sarum rite, the Book of Common Prayer established a series of overlapping patterns of prescribed readings of the Bible for every day of the year. The most straightforward cycle concerned the lessons appointed to be read at Morning Prayer—a first reading from the Old Testament, and a second reading from the Gospel—and Evening Prayer—a first reading again from the Old Testament, and a second reading from the Epistles. The chosen readings from the Old Testament would be read through once over the course of one year, while the Gospel and Epistles were each read three times (roughly, in January–April, May–August, and September–December). Divine services on Sundays and holy days included appointed collects—prayers that initiated divine service—and relevant readings from the Gospel and the Epistles that interrupted the daily cycle of readings.

The result of this schedule was a rich tapestry of biblical readings that, through time and repetition, surely became associated with different times of the year. Every year began with Genesis in January; lovely June was the unlikely time to hear the story of Job, and Proverbs dominated July. In an effort to capture some of those associations without providing the overwhelming detail that can be easily found in any post-1559 edition of the Book of Common Prayer, each month below includes a brief description of the readings for that month.

182   *Early modern calendars*

That schedule of readings was not fully established until 1562. Between 1559 and 1561, some of the printed versions of the Book of Common Prayer continued to list the slight variations (especially in the Old Testament selections) from the 1549 prayer book, and it is that older schedule that John Booty included in his otherwise useful modern edition of the 1559 prayer book.[5] The 1549 schedule was printed in the first edition of the Latin prayer book, *Liber Precum Publicarum* (1560). However, one extant 1559 version of the prayer books printed a slightly revised calendar of readings (STC 16292a, prelim. #2), and it was this schedule that became standard in the Book of Common Prayer from 1562 onwards, including (from 1572) the Latin *Liber*. The readings described in the month-by-month calendars below, as well as all quotations from the Book of Common Prayer, reflect this later schedule; they are taken from the 1559 prayer book in which they (apparently) first appeared, STC 16292a, prelim. #2.[6]

Fairs

A standard list of "principal fairs" was included in most perpetual calendars and annual almanacs. This list was not entirely consistent across early modern sources, which included Holinshed's *Chronicles*, Grafton's *Briefe Treatise*, and Hopton's *Concordancy*. A rough estimate of the number of principal fairs in each month, and the most popular saint's days for fairs, is provided below to give readers a general sense of the seasonal cycle.

Law terms

By the sixteenth century, the legal year had been divided into four unequal law terms: Hillary, Easter, Trinity, and Michaelmas. The general parameters of the dates for law terms were summarized in both annual and perpetual almanacs and in prayer books. The dates for Hilary and Michaelmas terms (in January and October) were relatively fixed in the calendar; the dates for Easter and Trinity were tied to the movable feasts of Easter. Within these parameters, the legal calendar was complex. The ecclesiastical courts and some other civil courts were tied to the saints of the pre-Reformation calendar, as they continued to use these names for returns, or dates when suits could be brought or decisions handed down. So, for example, in Michaelmas, the returns in the Court of Arches, the Audience Court of Canterbury, the Court of Consistory, the Court of High Commissioners, and the Court of Delegates were linked to the feasts of St. Faith, St. Edward, St. Luke, Sts. Simon and Jude, All Souls, St. Martin, St. Edmund, St. Katherine, and St. Andrew. Some of these saints, of course, are apostles or evangelists who continued to be commemorated in the Book of Common Prayer. But others are somewhat obscure, their memory kept alive partially by the ecclesiastical courts which, as David Cressy has pointed out, ironically enough were also involved in "enforcing the discipline of the reformed religion."[7]

Festive traditions and pastimes

As Ronald Hutton and David Cressy have shown, one of the most noticeable effects of the Reformation was the curtailment of extra-liturgical pastimes, sports, games, and other activities that had once been associated with the church year.[8] In many cases, these activities ended abruptly in the reign of Henry VIIIth, and though they may have enjoyed a brief resurgence in the Marian reign, were again abolished by the second decade of Elizabeth I's rule. In other cases, activities once celebrated in the church simply moved into the secular realm. In still others, as Cressy's work has particularly shown, religious celebrations were replaced with commemorations that celebrated the English Protestant nation, such as the defeat of the Spanish Armada or the foiling of the Gunpowder Plot.[9] The continuance of traditional calendrical pastimes, or their suppression, was also uneven geographically. Some traditional pastimes linked to the calendar were revived by an Elizabethan nostalgia for merry old England, and later, Jacobean nostalgia, for both those bygone days and the merry world of good queen Bess, though the literary representation of festive pastimes did not always line up with actual practices. For each month, a brief description of those pastimes which appear to have survived the Reformation is provided.[10]

The saints in the calendar

One of the most confusing aspects of early modern almanacs for a modern reader is the inclusion of a large number of Catholic saints who had been excised from the calendar with the Reformation. Most almanacs provide a much longer list of saints than the red- and black-letter saints included in the Elizabethan Book of Common Prayer. The usual rationale for their inclusion was their necessity for dating, as contracts and leases still operated by named saint days. It seems likely that many of the saints in the calendar also had nostalgic, historical, patriotic, or regional appeal, and perhaps for some traditionalists, religious appeal as well.

Each month concludes with a calendar listing the saints that were commemorated in the Book of Common Prayer, and the longer list of saints provided in early modern almanacs. That information is organized into four columns.

Column 1. These are the saints in the 1559 Book of Common Prayer (STC 16292a), abbreviated to *BCP* in parenthetical citations. Red-letter saints are listed in bold type. Movable feasts are, as in all perpetual calendars, omitted.

Column 2. This list is taken from Richard Grafton's *Treatise* (the 1573 edition), as that perpetual calendar seems to have been a standard source for almanac compilers until it was superseded by Hopton's *Concordancy* in 1612. In parentheses after the Grafton entry are variations if these occur in the 1560 edition of the *Liber Precum Publicarum*.

184 *Early modern calendars*

Column 3 and Column 4. In Column 3, the saints in Columns 1 and 2 are listed in modern spelling, with brief biographical information provided for those who can be documented with some degree of certainty. Dates are provided by century for date of death, when known. The dominant source here is David Hugh Farmer's exemplary *Oxford Dictionary of Saints* (F). If the Saint (or his or her identification with a particular date) is not identifiable from Farmer, additional information is provided from the more extensive list in *The Book of Saints*, first compiled by the Benedictine monks of St. Augustine's Abbey, Ramsgate, in 1912 (B), with further clarification if needed from the online *Catholic Encyclopedia* (C).[11] When a Saint's identity, or association with a particular day, cannot be established from one of these three sources, the biography is omitted, and the difficulty noted in the calendars with a bewildered query (?).

A few words of caution are necessary about the information in Column 3. As historians of hagiography well know, any attempt to identify the saints in a calendar is beset with peril. In English post-Reformation calendars, the core set of Reformation saints and holy days in the Book of Common Prayer tend to be firmly fixed to particular dates with little variation. Other popular saints, such as Saint George and Saint Valentine, are similarly fixed in the calendar. For all other saints, however, there are multiple sources of confusion that bedevil the effort to identify them with certainty. These difficulties begin with the basic fact that hagiography repeats stories in which the line between fact and fiction cannot be strictly drawn, and the sources themselves are often conflicting. On one level, it seems ridiculous to attempt to provide an accurate or factual list for biographies for which factual accuracy is not the most important feature. In addition, any saint with even a modest following was often commemorated on multiple dates, including the day of death, birth, other significant biographical or hagiographical event (such as the date for Papal institutions), and translation of relics. Further, from a calendar standpoint, it appears that Saints were often shifted by one or two days to accommodate other holy days; indeed, the calendar is least stable from January to June, the months in which the movable feasts fall, with May as the most chaotic month of all. Finally, saints with similar names are often confused in the calendar. For example, Grafton and Trevelyon both list "St. Sother, virgin" for April 22nd, and the *Liber* endorses this identification with "Sotheris." St. Sother was, apparently, a virgin martyr of Damascus whose remains lie in the Via Appia in Rome. But according to the *Book of Saints*, April 22nd was the date for the commemoration of the second-century Pope, St. Soter. Clearly the similarity in names at some point resulted in confusion over exactly which saint should be commemorated on this particular date. The situation occurs with even greater frequency when the Saint concerned has a more common name, such as Felix, John, or Victor.

For all these reasons, the biographical information in Column 3— except when it concerns well known saints such as the apostles and evangelists—should be considered only as a rough guide. The goal of these calendars is to give modern readers a general sense of the saints who, though exiled from religious observance, survived the Reformation in secular calendars, and brought into Protestant England a cornucopia of legends and religious history that was firmly attached to the country's Catholic past.

January

Labors and agricultural tasks

> Stub Land to make medowes or earable ground,
>   To better thy Bees a new seat must be found:
> Uncover the rootes of thy trees that beare fruit
>   In hope of more plenty to be added unto't.   (Frende 1622, A3r)

As is fitting for a month that begins in the middle of the Christmas feasting season, the labor for January is dining. Sometimes the visual image for January shows a group or couple at a table, often by a fire, with a servant arriving with platters of food, as in the image from Cuningham's 1558 almanac (Figure 3.3.1). Alternatively, the labor might depict a single figure sitting at a laden table (Plate 10). Sometimes that single figure has the double head of Janus "loking with a double face / int[o] ould and new year comming on apace" (Hopton 1607, A3r). An example of the Janus motif survives in one of the labors and Zodiac sign floor tiles in Canterbury Cathedral (Figure 3.3.2).

Figure 3.3.1 January, William Cuningham, *A Newe Almanacke and Prognostication* (1558), Pr.B2v. University of Illinois at Champaign-Urbana, Rare Book and Manuscript Library, 529.5 H484a.

Figure 3.3.2 Janus, January Roundel, Canterbury Cathedral, thirteenth century. Reproduced courtesy of The Chapter of Canterbury.

The Christmas season ends on Epiphany, January 6th, although an older medieval tradition extended it to the Purification on February 2nd. As if reining in his readers after the excessive hospitality of Christmas, Thomas Tusser starts the calendar year by reiterating the virtues of thrift and frugality so central to his books on husbandry: "Who dainties love, / a begger shall prove," he warns; "Who nothing save, / shall nothing have" (Tusser, 157). January is the time to get back to work and, then as now, for self-improvement, especially in a moral or religious sense. "The old yeare's past, the new doth new begin," Ranger writes in 1619, "Put off the old man, abandon deadly sinne" (A3r); Neve in 1607 similarly notes that the "new yeare" is a good occasion to "flee from wicked sinne" (A4v), and Alleyn interprets "Janus" with his "doubled face" as an emblem encouraging man "To shunne sinne present, and to come" (1609, A3r).

For husbandmen recommitting to hard work and thriftiness after the Christmas season, January provides a host of miscellaneous agricultural tasks. Now is the time to "stub" land, or pull up roots in order to make meadows "arable," a task accomplished by servants "with mattocke in hand, / to stub out the bushes, that noyeth the land" (Tusser, 65). As usual, carefully timed fallowing is essential for producing rich land; Tusser also warns the husbandman to "hast not to fallow till March be begun" (66). Oats can be sowed in the newly broken up land, however, "to suck out the moisture" (66), then harvested in May to provide fodder for the cows.

Tending fruit trees is the second most mentioned enterprise for January. Their roots might now be exposed to increase the Summer's yield, or the trees might be taken out all together and new trees set (planted). Tusser's list of those "trees or rootes to be set or removed" this month is extensive, including apple, apricot, cherry, chestnut, bullace (black or white plum), filberts, gooseberry, and huckleberry (59–60). John Woodhouse, who repeats almost all of Tusser's recommendations, adds to that list "Rose trees" and "Peaches" (1633, B6v). Cutting timber and clearing shrubs can also continue in January. This is a perilous time for livestock, who are vulnerable to disease in the lean Winter months; verjuice is often recommended as "A medicine for faint cattel" (Tusser, 62). The husbandman should in January decide which animals to keep for breeding—"The larger of body, the better for breed, / more forward of growing, more better they speed"—and now geld the rest (Tusser, 64). Attention should also be paid to the kitchen garden, hop-yards weeded "if season be drie," the garden-plot "well trenched and muckt," "Runcivall pease" sowed, and rose bushes set (Tusser, 61). Finally, almanac writers (including Alleyn, John Woodhouse, and Frende) frequently repeat Tusser's advice that the careful huswife should inspect the beehive, for if it needs to be moved, January is a good time to do it.

Zodiac, astronomy, and astrology

January's Zodiac sign is Aquarius, the water bearer, visible in the upper left-hand corner of the Cuningham woodcut in Figure 3.3.1. Aquarius is "of the West, masculine, ayrie, and sanguine, and governeth the legges" (Alleyn 1606, B5v).

In some medieval sources, the state of the sky on New Year's Day was considered important in predicting the weather, and though such prognostications are less frequent in the early modern calendars, they do appear, as in Hopton's assertion that "New-yeares day in the morning being red, portends great tempest and warre" (*Concordancy*, 101). Another day believed to predict future weather was the holy day marking the Conversion of Saint Paul on January 25th; the lore went that "if the Sun shine, it is a token of a happy yeare: if raine or snow, indifferent: if musty, great death; but if it thunder, there will be great windes and death that yeare" (*Concordancy*, 102). Other stars such as Orion's girdle, in rising vespertine or cosmical this month, could trouble the air and cause wind and rain.

The ages of man

>The fyrst vi yeres of mannes byrth and atge
>May wel be compared to Janyuere.
>For in this month is no strengt[h] no overage [achievement]
>More than in a childe of the g[r]ece of vi yere. (*This Prymer*, STC 16076, 1556)

The image for January in the monthly ages of man scheme invariably shows a group of children playing with hobbyhorses, kites, spinning tops, balls,

188 *Early modern calendars*

and other toys, often in a state of mayhem suggested by figures sprawled out on the floor. The *Kalender* stresses the similarity between January, when there "is no vertue nor strength, in that season nothing on earth groweth," and the first six years of age, which are "without wit, strength, or cunning" (1631, B1r).

Physic

>   Now if your body in health you'l keepe,
>   Warme meates for it is very meete:
>   Fly Phisicke, Sloath, and Venery,
>   Avoid all Bathes most carefully.   (Neve 1626, A3r)

The diseases incident to the Sun in Aquarius, which rules the legs, are "Fever quartanes, blacke Jaundies, swelling of the legges, and varices [varicose veins]" (Alleyn 1606, B5v). The bitter cold of January should be countered with hot foods and drinks, especially white wine, "spiced meate," and broths (Ranger 1617, A3r). All medical interventions are discouraged in this Winter month, except occasional warm baths, as is venery and oversleeping.

The church calendar

Seasons and holy days

January 1st, the eighth day of Christmas, is also in the Book of Common Prayer a holy day celebrating the Circumcision; the Collect for the day asks that God to "graunt us the true circumcision of the spirite" (*BCP*, C4r). The final four days of the festive season follow, culminating in Twelfth Night (the evening of January 5th) and ending with the second holy day of the month, Epiphany, on January 6th. For that day, the Collect notes that it was "by the leading of a starre" that God "diddest manyfest thy onely begotten sonne to the Gentiles," but that in the present, the faithful "know thee now by faith," not external signs (*BCP*, C5r). The third holy day for January is the Conversion of St. Paul, on January 25th; the Epistle appointed for that day recounts Paul's conversion on the road to Damascus (Acts 9), while the Collect honors the Apostle through whom God "hast taught all the world" (*BCP*, K7r).

After the Christmas season, a series of Sundays after Epiphany follow, the number varying between one and six depending on the date for Easter. The countdown to Holy Week begins on Septuagesima Sunday, the ninth Sunday before Lent; this is sometimes in January, with the earliest possible date January 18th.

In addition to the three official holy days of the month, there are a total of six black-letter commemorations in January, two for women (St. Prisca and St. Agnes), one for an early medieval Pope (St. Fabian), and one for

St. Hilary, the bishop whose longevity in the calendar was probably tied to his importance for delineating the law term that bears his name. St. Vincent, the proto-martyr of Spain, is also commemorated in January, as is a somewhat mysterious martyr of Beauvais, St. Lucian.

Lectionary

The readings for the month for Morning and Evening Prayer begin with Genesis 1 on January 2nd, after the special readings for the feast of the Circumcision. The final reading from Genesis falls in Morning Prayer on the 27th; after this begin a series of readings from Exodus that continue until February 11th. The first cycle of New Testament readings begins in January, though it is put aside (as always) for the intervening special readings for holy days; first up is Matthew, which ends on January 31st. The first Epistle reading is Romans, followed by (on January 19th) First Corinthians, which is read from the first through the twelfth chapters until the end of the month.

Fairs

Unsurprisingly, cold January is the very slowest month when it comes to principal fairs in England and Wales, with approximately ten listed in Hopton's *Concordancy*. Three of these (at Bristol, Churchingford, and Gravesend) fall on the 25th, the day marking the Conversion of St. Paul.

Law terms

Hilary Term begins on St. Hilary's day, January 13th, or the following day if the 13th falls on a Sunday; it continues until the 12th or 13th of February.

Festive traditions and pastimes

The first six days of January continue the traditional celebrations of the twelve-day Christmas season. Activities might include wassailing, feasting, music, games, shows, pageants, and plays. New Year's Day, the feast of the Circumcision, was the traditional day for giving gifts, as is often noted in the almanac poetry: "When as the olde yeeres date doth ende," notes Gray in 1591, "For good new yeere all wish and crave: / And Newyeeres gyftes abrode they sende, / To faythful friendes they hope to have" (A4v). Though plays might be performed at any point in the season, *Twelfth Night* was especially associated with the drama, as well as with Lord of Misrule festivities. The day after Epiphany, Plough Monday, had been celebrated in late medieval England by the blessing of the plough brought into the church. At the Reformation, those celebrations, where they continued, transformed into secular games outside the church, which sometimes involved young men hauling ploughs around villages while soliciting contributions.[12]

January

Day	1 BCP	2 Grafton, (Liber)	3 Identification	4 Source
1	**Circumcision**	Circumcision of Christ	Feast commemorating circumcision of Jesus	F
2		Oct. of S. Stephin	Octave of St. Stephen	
3		Octa. of S. John (Genovasae virg.)	Octave of St. John (St. Genevieve, virgin patroness of Paris, 6th c.)	F
4		Oct. of Innocents	Octave of Holy Innocents	
5		Oct. of Th. Becket (Depo. Edwardi Re.)	Octave of Thomas Becket (St. Edward, King of England, 10th c.)	F
6	**Epiphanie**	Twelfe day.	Feast commemorating the visit of the Magi	
7		Felix [& Ian]	St. Felix and St. Januarius, dates unknown	B
8	Lucian	Lucian	St. Lucian of Beauvais, martyr, dates unknown	F
9		Agapete virgin (Iudoci)	? (St. Judoc, prince of Brittany and hermit, 7th c.)	F
10		Paule first hermit	St. Paul of Thebes, first Christian hermit, 4th c.	F
11		Linus	Possibly St. Linus, Pope, possibly martyr, 1st c. (also September 23rd)	F
12		Arcade martyr	St. Arcadius, martyr in Roman Africa, 4th c.	F
13	Hyllary	Hilari bishop	St. Hilary, Bishop of Poitiers, 4th c.	F
14		Felicia	St. Felix of Nola, priest in Italy, 4th c. (alternately November 15th).	F, B, C
15		Maure (& Isidori)	St. Maurus, monk and abbot, 6th c.; St. Isidore the Egyptian, priest, 5th c.	F, B
16		Marcell	St. Marcellus, Pope, 4th c.	F
17		Anthony (Sulpiti episc.)	St. Antony of Padua, priest and Franciscan, 13th c. (St. Sulpicius, Bishop of Bourges, 7th c.)	F
18	Prisca	Prisca	St. Prisca, early Roman female martyr, dates unknown	F
19		Wolstan	St. Wulfstan, Bishop of Worcester and Benedictine, 11th c.	F
20	Fabian	Sebastian	St. Fabian, Pope and martyr, 3rd c.; St. Sebastian, Diocletian martyr, 4th c.	F

	1	*2*	*3*	*4*
Day	BCP	Grafton, (Liber)	Identification	Source
21	Agnes	Agnes	St. Agnes, virgin martyr in Rome, 4th c.	F
22	Vincent	Vincent	St. Vincent of Saragossa, proto-martyr of Spain and deacon, 4th c.	F
23		Emerence	St. Emerentiania, virgin and martyr in Rome, 4th c.	F
24		Timothe	St. Timothy, disciple of the Apostle Paul, bishop and martyr, 1st c.	F
25	**Conver. Paul**	Conver. of Paul	Conversion of St. Paul, Apostle, 1st c.	F
26		Policarpe	St. Polycarp, Bishop of Smyrna and martyr, 2nd c.	F
27		Agnes second (Jan. 28th in *Liber*) (Iuliani confess.)	Second feast for St. Agnes (see January 21st and 28th) (St. Julian of Le Mans, bishop, 4th c.)	F
28		Valerii	St. Valerius, Prelate of Saragossa, 4th c.	B
29		Theodore (Valerii episcopi)	? (St. Valerius, Bishop of Trier or Treves, Germany, 4th c.)	B, C
30		Batilde	St. Bathild, Anglo-Saxon wife of Clovis II, 7th c.	F
31		Victor (& Saturnine)	St. Saturninus and St. Victor, martyrs in Alexandria, 3rd c.	B

February

Labors and agricultural tasks

>Superfluous branches from trees prune away,
>And suffer not mosse upon them to stay:
>Plash and twist hedges, riff up your lee land.
>Lay quicksets plant roses the Spring is at hand.   (Prid, *Glasse*, A4v)

The labor of the month for February usually shows a single man sitting by a fire, warming his feet which are often (as in the misericord from Worcester Cathedral in Figure 3.3.3) completely bare. An alternate labor for February is tree-pruning; that task is reflected in images in which the man sitting by the fire is interrupted by servants carrying in wood, as in the February labor from a single sheet Gesner almanac for 1555 (Figure 3.3.4).

192 *Early modern calendars*

Figure 3.3.3 February, Misericord, Worcester Cathedral, fourteenth century. ©www.misericords.co.uk 2017

Figure 3.3.4 February, James Gesner, *An Almanacke and Prognostication* (1555), Single Sheet Broadside. Photograph by Phebe Jensen, from the collection of the Folger Shakespeare Library, STC 400.5.

The medical directives for February reflect the labor of the month in their focus on the need for good fires with which to dispel the cold damp of February (exacerbated by the effect of the Sun in Pisces), but the tasks recommended for this month in the agricultural guides and calendar poems mostly look forward to the happy prospect that "Spring is at hand" (Prid, *Glasse*, A4r). February is the time to manure arable land as weather allows, and to sow some early crops in the kitchen garden: "fitches," "beanes," and "peason." The timing is crucial. "Sow runcivals timely, and all that be graie, / but sow not the white, till S. Gregories daie" (Tusser, 68). No sensible farmer would prune or plant without the guidance of the Moon; waxing, it is "a good time to cut quicksets, to plant or set Roses, and all other sortes of trees," but "in the decrease [plant] all kinds of pulse, Oates, Onions & c" (Alleyn 1606, B6v). Other herbs to be sown in February are mustard seed and hempseed (to control nettles). Miscellaneous tasks include mending hedges with "Osiers" or willows, planting yet more willows to provide shade for the cattle in the heat of Summer, setting your "moulecatcher" to work, and buying fish for Lent from "coastman or Fleming" (Tusser, 69–70).

Zodiac, astronomy, and astrology

Pisces, the sign the Sun enters early in February, "is of the North, feminine, waterie, and flegmatique, and ruleth the feete" (Alleyn 1606, B6r). The stars this month predict unpleasant weather. Regulus, the brightest star in Leo, sets at sunrise on the fourth of February, "of whom *Ptol.* saith, the cleare starre in the heart of the Lyon beginning to set, the North wind bloweth, with often raine"; the vespertine setting of "the taile of the dolphin" on the ninth supposedly "bringeth winds and snow" (Hopton, *Concordancy,* 102). Shrove Tuesday—which may fall in February or March—is an important day for traditional weather prognostications by thunder: "thunder upon Shrove-tuesday foretelleth winde and store of fruit, and plentie," and however much the Sun shines on that day "the like he shineth every day in Lent" (Hopton, *Concordancy,* 102).

The ages of man

> The other vi yeres is lyke February.
> In the ende therof begynneth the sprynge.
> That tyme chyldren is moost apt and redy.
> To receyve chastisement / nurture / and lernynge.   (*This Prymer* 1529, STC 15961.5, fol. 4r)

Representing the years from six to twelve, the ages of man image for February almost always shows a schoolroom, usually filled with quiet and industrious pupils like the student in the center of the image from a Marian primer in Figure 3.3.5.

This particular illustration also stresses the "chastysement" that children are especially in need of during these years. Just as "the dayes begin to wax in length, and the Sunne more hotter," in the second six years of life "the child beginneth to grow and serve and learne such as is taught him" (*Kalender* 1631, B1r).

194 *Early modern calendars*

Figure 3.3.5 February, Catholic Church, *This Prymer of Salisbury Use* (Rouen, 1555, STC 16068), A3v. The Huntington Library, San Marino, California, RB 56677.

Physic

> Milke, Fennish fowle, and phisicke flie,
> > Bath, but use not Phlebotomie;
> Take heed of cold, feed warilie,
> > Least agues breed thy miserie. (John Rudston 1615, A3v)

Ruled by watery Pisces, damp February is a time to "eschew all slymie meates, as salt fish, milke, and such like" (Burton 1617, B5v); "foggy fenn fowles, with foode of phlegmatick humor" is "now to be cheefly refused" (Harvey 1589, A3v). The cold damp of February can also be countered with fires, which "purgeth grose ayre" (Harvey 1589, A3v); in this sense, the labor of the month has a medicinal role. Warm clothes can also help one avoid the "strange Agues" which "this moneth are likely to be troublesome" (Burton 1617, B5v), for "The weather cold and apt to snowe, / Distempers bodies here below" (John Johnson 1613, A3v). The sicknesses especially predicted with the Sun in Pisces are "the Gout, scabs, leprosie and Palsie" (Alleyn 1606, B6r).

As for medical interventions, the advice for February varies more than for most months. On the one hand, much of the calendar poetry recommends complete abstinence from physic; as Neve advises in 1606, "This Moneth as yet no Phisicke use, / For feare that you your selfe abuse: / Bleed not nor bath, be ruld by me, / Except upon necessity" (A5v). Rudston, however, takes a more moderate position, recommending baths, but not medicine or phlebotomy (1615, A3v), and Bretnor defers to the recommendation of the physician: "Tis not amisse to purge to bath or bleede, / if learned counsell see thou stand in neede" (1616, A6r). As the liminal month between the absolute prohibition of medical interventions in the Winter, and their recommended use in Spring, February appears to have provoked a range of opinions on these questions.

The church calendar

Seasons and holy days

February is often associated with Shrovetide and Lent, though Ash Wednesday can actually fall as late as March 10th.

The feast of the Purification (also known as Candlemas) on February 2nd is the first of several Lady Days for the year; the Collect for the day in the Book of Common Prayer includes no mention of that ceremony, but instead, recalls Jesus' presentation in the temple. Because both these events are recounted in Luke 2, which is also the Gospel for the day, the early modern celebration of the Purification is a particularly clear example of the way in which after the Reformation all the Lady Day celebrations were oriented away from Mary to her son.

196 *Early modern calendars*

However, with these and other significant changes, Lady Days continued to be commemorated in early modern England. The Sarum Rite had recognized Marian holidays with various levels of liturgical commemoration:

February 2nd, the Purification
March 25th, the Annunciation
July 2nd, the Visitation of Mary to Elizabeth
August 15th, the Assumption
September 8th, the Nativity
December 8th: the Conception

Two of these were holy days in the reformed English prayer book: the Purification on February 2nd and the Annunciation on March 25th. Three others were retained in the post-1562 Book of Common Prayer as black-letter remembrances: the Nativity, the Visitation of Mary to Elizabeth, and the Conception. This left the Assumption on August 15th out of official remembrance altogether in both English and Latin versions of the prayer book, but that day was invariably noted in the secular calendars, and it continued to function as an important calendrical marker. Husbandry directives sometimes suggest that tasks such as sowing or reaping take place between the two Lady Days of late Summer and early Autumn (in August and September), and fairs that were held on all the Lady Days appear to have also been held on August 15th.

The second holy day in February was St. Matthias' Day, which celebrated the Apostle who was chosen by Jesus, as the Collect for the day notes, "in the place of the traitor Judas" (*BCP*, K8v). The Epistle for the day, Acts 1, recounts how St. Matthias also bested a second candidate (Joseph), by lots.

St. Matthias' Day was a somewhat mobile holiday because of its relationship to leap year. Before 1662, the intercalated day added to February every four years was inserted as February 24th; afterwards, it was added as February 29th. In leap years, then, St. Matthias' Day was pushed one day forward, and it is perhaps for this reason that the Book of Common Prayer lists it on February 25th, unlike most other early modern calendars (including the Latin *Liber*). The rule in the Sarum rite was that St. Matthias Day had to occur four days after St. Peter's Chair, counting inclusively in the Roman fashion; that would land it on February 24th in a leap year and February 25th on all other years.

February, of course, is the month to commemorate (on February 14th) the mysterious but popular St. Valentine long associated with romance. It also includes the second (or in some calendars, the third) commemoration of St. Agatha, on February 5th. The Sarum saint from Armenia, St. Blaise, is noted for February 3rd.

Lectionary

On February 1st, the Old Testament reading in the Book of Common Prayer is Exodus 11; selections from Exodus continue until February 10th.

After that, the Old Testament readings move to excerpts from Leviticus, Numbers, and Deuteronomy. The New Testament begins with Mark 1 on February 1st; that book is finished on February 17th and followed by Luke (1–11). The Epistle picks up with 1st Corinthians 13, moving to Second Corinthians on February 6th, Gallatians on February 19th, and Ephesians on February 25th.

Fairs

The Lady Days were traditional times for fairs, and the Purification on February 2nd is no exception: Hopton notes eight principal fairs for that date. Another four fall on February's second official holy day, St. Matthias. Including these, there are only a total of approximately eighteen fairs fixed in the calendar in cold, damp February. But depending on the date for Easter, the many fairs tied to the movable feasts may begin this month. The most popular day for the pre-Lenten season is Ash Wednesday (with a total of ten), though there were also fairs held on Shrove Monday (Newcastle-under-Lyme), and the first Monday, Tuesday, and Thursday in Lent, at Winchester, Chertsey in Surrey, Bedford, and Banbury.

Law terms

Hilary term, which begins on January 13th or 14th, ends on February 12th or 13th, regardless of the date of Lent or Easter.

Festive traditions and pastimes

Candlemas

The hallowing of candles for Candlemas, and the candle-lit processionals that in late medieval England filled the church with light on this dark early day of February, were outlawed at the Reformation. There appears to have been some pushback against that prohibition, especially in more religiously conservative areas of the country. As Hutton notes, the tradition that birds chose their mates on St. Valentine's Day appears in both Chaucer and Gower; certainly, the association of St. Valentine's with lovers was well established by the sixteenth century, and references appear throughout the literature of the period.[13]

Shrovetide

The three days before Ash Wednesday comprised Shrovetide: Shrove Sunday, Collop Monday, and Shrove Tuesday. As the last chance for fun and feasting before the forty days of Lent, this period was celebrated with games, wrestling, football, and cock fights, and among the elite, with pageants,

198 *Early modern calendars*

shows, or plays. Some towns also hosted Shrovetide celebrations and entertainments. London especially became known for marauding apprentices who could become violent. But the central and most consistent tradition of Shrove Tuesday was feasting, especially on pancakes filled with the meat that was soon to be prohibited, a feast that began, as in Thomas Dekker's *The Shoemaker's Holiday*, with the ringing of church bells.[14]

February

	1	2	3	4
Day	BCP	Grafton, (Liber)	Identification	Source
1		St. Briget	St. Brigid of Ireland, Abbess of Kildare, 6th c.	F
2	**Purifi. Mary**	Purifi. of our Lady	Lady Day, Purification in the Temple of the Virgin Mary	
3	Blasii	Blasé	St. Blaise, Bishop of Sebaste in Armenia, dates unknown	F
4		Gilbert	St. Gilbert of Sempringham, priest and founder of Gilbertine Order, 12th c.	F
5	Agathe	Agathe	St. Agatha, virgin and martyr, dates unknown	F
6		Vedasti & Amandi	St. Vedast, Bishop of Arras, 6th c.; St. Amand, Abbot of Elnon, monk in Flanders, 7th c.	F
		(Dorothy virgin)	(St. Dorothy, virgin and Diocletian martyr, 4th c.)	
7		Anguli bishop	St. Augulus, Bishop and (possibly) Diocletian martyr in London, 4th c.	B
8		Paule bishop	St. Paul of Verdun, Bishop of Verdun, 7th c.	B
9		Apelin	St. Apollonia, Deaconess of Alexandria and martyr, 3rd c.	F
10		Scholastica	St. Scholastica, first Benedictine nun and sister of St. Benedict, 6th c.	F
11		Eustrasii	Possibly St. Austraberta or Eustraberta, virgin martyr of France, 7th c. (also February 10th)	B, C
12		Eulalie	St. Eulalia of Barcelona, Diocletian martyr, 4th c.	B, C
13		Wolstan (Ulfranni, Pharmuthi)	Possibly St. Wulfstan, Benedictine and Bishop of Worcester, (also January 19th, June 7th), 8th c. (?)	F
14	Valentine	Valentine	St. Valentine, Roman martyr (possibly Bishop of Terni), 3rd c.	F

The twelve months

Day	BCP	Grafton, (Liber)	Identification	Source
	1	2	3	4
15		Faustine & Jonite	St. Faustinus and St. Jovita, brothers martyred in Brescia, Lombardy, 2nd c.	B
16		Julian virgin	St. Juliana, virgin and martyr in Italy, 4th c.	F
17		Policron	St. Polychronius, possibly Bishop of Babylon, 4th c.	B
18		Simion (Hugh)	St. Simon, Bishop of Jerusalem, kinsman of Jesus mentioned in Matthew 13th, 2nd c. (?)	B
19		Sabini	St. Gabinus, Roman Christian, father of St. Susanna, 3rd c.	B
20		Mildred	St. Mildred, Abbess and daughter of the King of Mercia, 8th c.	B
21		L xix martirs	?	
22		Cathedra s. Petri	Feast of St. Peter's Chair, St. Peter, Apostle, 1st c.	F
23		(Polycarpe)	St. Polycarp, bishop of Smyrna and martyr, 2nd c.	F
24		Mathy (February 25th in *BCP* and *Liber*)	St. Matthias, apostle, 1st c. (leap years)	F
25	St. Mathias	S. Pauli	?	F
26		Nestor (Alexandri episcopi)	St. Nestor, bishop in Pamphylia, Asia Minor, and martyr, 3rd c. (?)	F
27		Augustine	Possible additional commemoration for St. Augustine of Canterbury (May 26) or St. Augustine of Hippo (August 28th)	
28		Oswolde	St. Oswald, Bishop of Worcester and Benedictine monk, 10th c.	F

March

Labors and agricultural tasks

    Set Pumpeons and Citurels, March counselleth so,
    With Rosemary, Rew, Sage and many hearbs moe:
    Close cover the rootes of the trees thou mad'st bare,
    And cariage for compost let next be thy care.   (Frende 1622, A4r)

Figure 3.3.6 March, William Cuningham, *A Newe Almanacke and Prognostication* (1564), Pr.A6r. The Huntington Library, San Marino, California, RB 59329.

The traditional agricultural labor for March is trimming tree branches and vines, as can be seen in *Batman upon Bartholome* (Plate 10), the leaden font at Brookland (Plate 9.2), and the medieval wall-painting for March from Easby Church (Plate 15.1). As usual, almanacs stress the importance of astrological timing for these tasks: "in the new of the Moone cut your Vynes, quicksets, and hedges, Grafte, set Vines and Quicksets" (Burton 1617, B6v). Figure 3.3.6, from a Cuningham 1564 almanac, depicts the mending of hedges (quicksets) and fences.

The actual agricultural tasks in England in the first month of Spring were more extensive, of course, as Thomas Tusser's long list of herbs and vegetables to be sown in March attests (72–74). Most often mentioned in the calendar poetry are melons (pumpeons and citurels) and cucumbers, as well as "Rosemarie, Rue, Sage, Isope [hyssop], and such like," which should be set at "the full of the Moone" (Alleyn 1607, B6r). Now is the time to cover up tree roots, and also to graft and plant fruit trees. The husbandry poems in Prid's *Glasse of Vain-glorie* and elsewhere identify March as the time to plough "barly land," as well as to "sow beans otes & peason" (A5r). Tusser and others often stress the need to tend the all-important hop this month: "Grant hop great hill," writes Alleyn in 1607, "to grow out at will" (B8v). For tasks associated with animal husbandry, Tusser and early modern almanac compilers identify March as the time to repair the damage wreaked by restless horses on stone walls over the Winter, to geld lambs, to guard geese and ducks lest they escape, to tend doves in dovecotes, and to kill avian pests such as "crow, pie, and cadow, rooke, buzzard, & raven" (Tusser, 78).

Zodiac, astronomy, and astrology

The Sun enters the first point of Aries the Ram on March 10th–12th in the sixteenth-century Julian calendar, a sign that "is of the East, masculine, fierie and cholerick" (Alleyn 1606, B6v); its ruling planet is Mars (Figure 3.3.7). The major stars associated with the start of Spring are the Pleiades.

The ages of man

> March betokeneth the vi yeres folowynge
> Arayeng the erthe wt pleasaunt verdure.
> That season youth careth for nothynge.
> And without thought dooth his sporte and pleasure.   (*Thys Prymer*,
> 1538, STC 16008.3, fol. 4v)

Covering the years of youth from twelve to eighteen, March in the ages of man scheme is represented by scenes of "sporte and pleasure," usually hunting with hounds or birding (on foot or horseback). For this reason, the March images sometimes anticipate the labors of the month motifs for April and May, and they reflect standard elements of the iconography for Spring. The *Kalender* provides a more serious understanding of this age, in which "the child…waxeth big to learne doctrine & science, and to be faire and honest" (1570, A6rr).

Figure 3.3.7 Aries, Richard Roussat, *Arcandam* (Paris, 1542), K1r. Photograph by Phebe Jensen, from the collection of the Folger Shakespeare Library, 183–794q.

Physic

> Now doeth great humors in man breede,
> Of former surfets take good heede:
> Now bleede you may with modesty,
> And bath and pur[g]e if that neede be.   (Neve 1606, A6v)

Medically, the most significant aspect of March is the sudden increase in humors (especially blood) that reflects the coursing of the elements in nature with the revivals of Spring. Increased humors could create the need for purging, as Alleyn explains:

> In this month, the humours of mans bodie beginne to moove and increase, and nowe grosse feeding breedeth grosse blood, & grosse humours, wherefore (in milde or warme weather) it is very good to purge, and clense the blood, by potions, bathings, and blood-letting.
> (1606, B7r)

Yet those interventions should be practiced with moderation ("with modesty," as Neve puts it), least too robust flows prove fatal.

As with general prescriptions for Spring, a major medical concern in March (also reflected in Neve's poem) is that earlier surfeiting (in the slow Winter months) may now manifest as disease. Invariably, calendar poetry recommends "Victuals light and pure" (Dauncy 1614, A4r); "More health is gotten by observing diet" in this month, notes Bretnor in 1616, "then pleasure tane by vaine excesse & ryot" (A7r). Aries "governeth the head, face, eyes, and eares"; diseases incident to this Zodiac sign, and so to March, are "the Appoplexie, Mania: woundes and spots in the face, abortions, and other impiteous diseases, Ring-wormes, and Morphewes [blisters]," including blisters caused by scurvy (Alleyn 1606, B6v).

The church calendar

Seasons and holy days

March invariably includes Lent, which can begin as late as March 10th. Conversely, the earliest date for Maundy Thursday (the last day of Lent) is March 19th, and the earliest possible day for Easter is March 22nd. The month of March, then, sometimes includes Holy Week (approximately ten out of every thirty-five years).

The single red-letter fixed holy day for March in the Book of Common Prayer is the Annunciation on March 25th, the second of the Lady Days. The Annunciation is noted in the Collect of the day as a time to reflect not on Mary herself, but on Christ's incarnation. This date was one of multiple days identified as the demarcation for the *anno domini*. Though March 25th remained the start of the legal year officially until 1752, that practice was confusing, as almanac makers often noted. In the early modern period, dates between January 1st and March 25th were sometimes noted with a split date (1597/1598). March 25th was also the date that Julius Caesar had originally fixed for the Vernal Equinox, though that equinox had migrated approximately two weeks earlier in the calendar by the sixteenth century.

Six black-letter saints are commemorated in the Book of Common Prayer for March: St. David, the patron saint of Wales (March 1st), St. Chad, the seventh-century Bishop of Lichfield in Mercia (March 2nd), St. Perpetua, the third-century Carthaginian martyr (March 7th), the medieval Pope, St. Gregory the Great (March 12th), St. Edward, the tenth-century English King and martyr (March 18th), and St. Benedict, founder of the Benedictine Rule (March 21st).

Lectionary

On March 1st, the Old Testament readings for Morning and Evening Prayer continue in Deuteronomy (beginning with Chapter 16), progressing to Joshua on March 9th, Judges on March 15th, Ruth on March 26th, and 1 Kings begins on March 28th. The Gospel reading for March 1st is Luke 12; the readings then progress through Luke before moving to John on March 14th. The first Epistle reading for March is Ephesians 5, followed by Colossians 1, Thessalonians, Timothy, Titus, Philippians, and Hebrews 2.

Fairs

In keeping with the general tradition of holding fairs on Lady Days, there are approximately nine set in the calendar for March 25th, the feast of the Annunciation. In addition, about four fairs were held on St. Gregory's Day, and another three on St. David's Day (all in Wales). In this month as in April, however, most fairs were tied to the movable holidays, with fairs indicated for "Mid-lent Sunday," the fifth Sunday in Lent, the Wednesday before Palm Sunday, and the Wednesday before Easter (Hopton, *Concordancy*, 170). The most popular days for fairs in the lead-up to Easter, however, were Palm Sunday Eve, Palm Sunday itself (ten), and, perhaps surprisingly given the austerity of the religious commemoration for that day, Good Friday (seventeen).

Law terms

March represents a gap in the legal calendar, since Hilary Term ends in February, and the earliest possible day for the Easter term to begin, fifteen days after Easter Sunday, was April 6th. However, as already noted, the Annunciation was a crucial day in the legal calendar as it marked the start of the regnal year, and was a day in which quarterly "rents and contracts fell due."[15] The Annunciation was often paired with Michaelmas (September 29th) in annual early modern calendars, as the two were separated by almost exactly six months, and both were dates in which leases (especially agricultural leases) turned over.

Festive traditions and pastimes

March is not a particularly festive month, as it invariably includes at least part of Lent. For festivities associated with the pre-Lenten Shrovetide season, see February; for festivities associated with Easter, see April.

Lent

In this season, the Church of England encouraged prayer, reflection, sobriety, and fasting, though there was opposition against strict Lenten restraints from different directions: by the godly who saw no justification for its keeping in the Bible, and by the less godly who complained about its gloominess. Nicholas Breton, for example, paints a miserable picture of "Solitarinesse and Melancholy" that in this month "breed the hurt of Nature"; Lent is an "uncomfortable season, the Heavens frown, and the Earths punishment" (D2v-D3r). For much of the early modern period, marriage was prohibited during Lent from Septaguisima Sunday until the Octave of Easter. The Elizabethan and Jacobean regimes kept up the late medieval prohibition against eating meat in Lent (permitting white meats, such as chicken, eggs, and cheese and other dairy), though this was no longer justified by religion, but by "new, and more secular, arguments that it encouraged self-discipline and helped the fishing industry."[16] It is perhaps worth puzzling over the fact that the recommendations for physic in February almost invariably warn against eating fish or "Fennish fowle" this month (Rudston 1615, A3v), due to the weather and the watery influence of Pisces—recommendations that seem in direct conflict with the law.

March

	1	2	3	4
Day	BCP	Grafton, (Liber)	Identification	Source
1	David	David	St. David, Welsh monk and bishop, 6th c.	F
2	Chad	Chad	St. Chad, Bishop of Mercia (Litchfield), 7th c.	F
3		Martine (Marinus & Asterius)	? (St. Marinus and St. Asterius, Roman martyrs, 3rd c.)	(F)

The twelve months 205

	1	2	3	4
Day	BCP	Grafton, (Liber)	Identification	Source
4		Adrian	St. Adrian, missionary (possibly Irish), 9th c.	F
5		Eusebii & Foce	St. Eusebius of Cremona, Italian Abbot (Bethlehem), 7th c.	B, C
6		Victor	St. Victor, St. Victorinus, and Companions, martyrs in Nicomedia, date unknown	B
7	Perpetue	Perpetue	St. Perpetua, Carthage martyr, 3rd c.	F
8		Felix	St. Felix of Dunwich, Bishop of the East Angles, 7th c.	F
9		XL Martyrs	Forty Martyrs, Sebaste (now Sivas, Turkey), 4th c.	F
10		Agapete	Possibly St. Agapitus, Bishop of Ravenna, 3rd c. (usually March 16th)	B
11		Quirion	?	
12	Gregory, Epi. Rome	Gregory	St. Gregory the Great, Pope, 7th c. (see Sept. 3rd)	F
13		Theodore	?	
14		Candide (Petri martyris)	? (Possibly St. Peter, martyr in Africa with Aphrodosius, 5th c. (also March 13th; see March 22nd).	(B)
15		Longius	St. Longinus, soldier who pierced the side of Jesus, 1st c. [see August 15th]	F
16		Boniface bish., (Hylarii & Tacoani)	Possibly St. Curetan Boniface, Bishop of Ross, 7th c. (usually March 14th); or St. Boniface, bishop and Carthusian monk, 13th c. (usually March 13th). (St. Hilary and St. Tatian, Bishop and Deacon of Aquileia, martyrs, 3rd c.)	B (C)
17		Patrike	Bishop and Patron Saint of Ireland, 5th c.	F
18	Edward, Regis	Edward	St. Edward, English King and martyr, 10th c.	F
19		Joseph	St. Joseph, husband of Mary, 1st c.	F
20		Cutbert	St. Cuthbert, English monk and Bishop of Lindisfarne, 7th c.	F
21	Benedict	Benet	St. Benedict, Italian abbot and author of the Benedictine Rule, 6th c.	F
22		Aphrodosii	Possibly St. Aphrodosius, Diocletian martyr in Africa with St. Peter (usually March 14th)	B

(*Continued*)

206 Early modern calendars

	1	2	3	4
Day	BCP	Grafton, (Liber)	Identification	Source
23		Theodore	Possibly St. Theodore of Canterbury, archbishop, 7th c. (usually March 26th)	F
24		Agapite	Possibly St. Agapius, Diocletian martyr with Timolaus, 4th c.	
25	**Annunciation**	Annunciation of our Lady	Also known as Lady Day	
26		Castoris, Martir	Possibly St. Castulus, Diocletian martyr, 3rd c., or St. Castor (usually March 28th)	C
27		Resurrect. Domini		
28		Dorothe	St. Castor and St. Dorotheus, martyrs in Tarsus, date known	C
29		Quintin (Victorini)	? (?)	
30		Quirine	St. Quirinus, Roman martyr, 2nd c.	B, C
31		Adeline	?	

April

Labors and agricultural tasks

> When Nyghingales are tunyng of their notes,
>> And every Byrde with chearefull voyce doth syng.
> And Trees, and Shrubbes beginnes to change their cootes,
>> To each ones mynde, much comfort doth it bryng. (Gray, 1588, A4v)

The labors for the months of April and May eschew agricultural occupations for outdoor pleasures that reflect the joys of renewal in Spring. The iconography of these two months is often interchangeable in the calendars of the sixteenth century. April is usually associated with flowers, as in the misericord of a single female figure from St. Mary's, Ripple (Figure 3.3.8); flowers in the April images may be held by a single man or woman, but more often by a pair of lovers pictured in a garden or a landscape (as in the Hatfield House tapestry for Spring, Plate 11.) Such imagery reflects the understanding of April as the "Moneth that flourisheth with flowers, / And to the earth yeeld pleasant showers" (Neve, 1606, A7v). Of course proverbially, flowers are also associated with May, as in Tusser's version of the familiar saying, "Sweet Aprill shewers, / Do spring May flowers" (79). Conversely, although birds and birding are a primary motif in images of May, they often show up in April calendars too.

Figure 3.3.8 April, Misericord, St. Mary's, Ripple, Worcester, fifteenth century. ©www.misericords.co.uk 2017

Of course April, like March, was in reality a busy time for agricultural tasks, as the calendar poetry stressed:

In land that is stubborne in tilling and tough,
    Your Barley this moneth may be sow'd well inough:
Your Garden with good seeds see well that you fraught,
    And sow Hemp and Flaxe now, else all
    will prove naught.   (Frende 1622, A4v)

Ploughing was the main heavy labor of April, its precise timing dependent on the weather. Tusser stresses the pitfalls and benefits of ploughing when the weather was either too wet or too dry, the need to remove old hillocks and stones, the key benefits of April "fallowing" (plowing fields in April to be left fallow in May), and the importance of providing rich provender for cattle and other livestock this month, especially given possible overgrazing in common areas. The "hopyard" needed continued attention in April, as this was the time to put in the poles, "Three poles to a hillock," as Tusser directs (80). Other tasks involved chopping and trimming wood to sell to the tanner or shipyard, and the ongoing planting of kitchen gardens: hemp, flax, artichokes, cucumbers, melons, citrons, pulse, etc.

"From April beginning, till Andrew be past / so long with good huswife, her dairy doth last," Tusser observes in his notes on husbandry for this month (81). In early modern England, cows were usually bred to calve between February and March, meaning that cow's milk began to be available for human consumption in late March or early April. April, then, traditionally initiated an eight-month dairy season. Women mostly oversaw the

208 *Early modern calendars*

dairy, which included the all-important tasks of collecting milk and cream and producing butter and cheese. Calendrical literature is sprinkled with conventional images of dairymaids, some rosy-cheeked and appealing, others slatternly and wasteful, like Tusser's "Slut Cisly untaught," who produces "whitemeat naught" (79). Butter production lasted throughout the season—cheese too, though that task was more associated with the Autumn months and final preparations for Winter. The production of enough butter and cheese to last the nine months during which the dairy cows were gestating was crucial to the economy of households, large and small.

Zodiac, astronomy, and astrology

The Sun enters the sign of Taurus the Bull on approximately the eleventh day of April in the Julian calendar; that sign "is of [the] South, feminine, earthie, and melancholique, and governeth the necke, throte, and voyce" (Alleyn 1606, B7v). In the middle of April (the 17th), the Pleiades begin to rise at dawn, "causing West Winds"; on the 22nd, a star in Scorpio, Lucida Lancis, sets just at dawn, "often provoking showers of raine" (Hopton, *Concordancy*, 104).

The ages of man

> The next vi yere maketh foure and twenty
> And fygured is to joly Apryll.
> That tyme of pleasures man hath moost plenty
> Fresshe and lovyng his lustes to fulfyll.   (*This Prymer*, 1531,
>   STC 15973, A5v)

April is the young adult time of life, and the iconography associated with it stresses the "pleasures" of love and courtship. The images for April in this scheme often show two lovers, as in the example from a 1531 prayer book produced in Rouen for the English market (Figure 3.3.9); here (as is often the case) the lovers walk outside and enjoy the blossoms of April, accompanied by a chaperone.

With the emphasis on love comes moral perils, of course; the eighteen to twenty-four year old who can now "gather the swete flowers of hardynes" must also "beware [that] the colde wyndes and stormes of vyces beate not downe the flowers of good maners" (*Kalender*, 1570, A7r).

Physic

> This moneth all things their strength renewe,
>   by letting of blood you shall not rewe:
> The powres are open and blood abounds:
>   of purging also no harme redounds.   (Mathew 1612, A4v)

The twelve months 209

Figure 3.3.9 April, Catholic Church, *This Prymer of Salisbury Use* (Rouen, 1531, STC 15971), [A4v]. Photograph by Phebe Jensen, from the collection of the Folger Shakespeare Library, STC 15971.

"Of all times in the yeere," April is "the best to prevent sicknesses likelie to ensue, or for speedie remedie in extremities," for in this month "Nature herselfe renueth strength through all the bodie, so that where sicknesse hapneth, shee soone unburdeneth herself thereof by meanes of Physicke" (Alleyn 1606, B7v-B8r). For that reason, April (like May) is a particularly good time for the key medical interventions of purging, bleeding, and bathing. The troublesome "surfeits old" engendered in the Winter, and not yet overcome by the efforts of physic in March, can now be dispersed: "Now *Galens* sonnes are set on worke, / For griefes that in our body lurke" (Ranger 1619, A4v). Exercise is also recommended; it's especially "good to hunt, to ride and run, / so that extreames heerein thou ever shun" (Bretnor 1616, A8r).

The diseases ruled by Taurus, and so to be especially feared in April, include "Squinances [tonsillitis], Scrophules [enlargement of the lymph nodes], Catharres, and hoarsenes" (Alleyn 1606, B7v).

The church calendar

Seasons and holy days

Easter and the associated customs of its immediate aftermath, including Easter Week, often fall in April, as the last possible date for Easter Sunday in the Julian calendar is April 25th. The week before Easter was marked with additional divine services, including special Collects for Monday, Tuesday, Wednesday, and Thursday, as well as for Good Friday and Easter Eve. The Sunday after Easter was popularly known as Low Sunday, though that name does not appear in the official prayer book.

The single fixed red-letter saint's day in April celebrates St. Mark the Evangelist on April 25th; the Collect thanks God for "the heavenly doctrine of thy evangelist S. Mark," and prays that the Gospel will keep the faithful from being "caried away with every blast of vaine doctrine" (*BCP*, L2r). Four black-letter saints were commemorated in April in the Book of Common Prayer: St. Richard, the thirteenth-century Bishop of Chichester (April 3rd); St. Ambrose, a fourth-century Bishop of Milan (April 4th); St. Alphege, the tenth-century Bishop of Winchester (April 19th); and one of the most beloved and thoroughly celebrated saints in the calendar, the patron saint of England, St. George (April 23rd).

Lectionary

On April 1st, the Old Testament reading is from 1 Kings 6, and the lessons progress through 1, 2, and 3 Kings for the rest of the month (ending with 3 Kings 8 on April 30th.) Meanwhile the Gospel reading in Morning Prayer picks up with John 19 on March 1st, and continues for the rest of the month. The Epistle starts in Hebrews 3, moving to James (April 12th), 1 and 2 Peter (April 17th), and 1 and 2 John (April 25th).

Fairs

The most popular fixed day for fairs in April was St. George's day (thirteen), followed by St. Mark the Evangelist (seven). The rest of the month saw only nine fairs, scattered through the calendar and around the country. However, April usually included a number of the movable affairs attached to Easter, either those at the end of Lent, or those in Easter Week, the week following Easter Sunday. Three fairs, at Bickleworth, Evesham, and Newcastle-under-Tine, were scheduled for the Monday following Low Sunday.

Law terms

Since Easter term was, like Trinity, tied to the movable feasts, its dates varied widely from year to year. As Grafton writes, Easter term begins on "the mondaie being the 15 daie after (Grafton, *Treatise*, A3v). It usually ends on the day (or possibly the third day, according to Grafton) after Ascension Day. This means that Easter Term could begin as early as April 6th, or as late as May 9th.

Festive traditions and pastimes

Easter

The Reformation curtailed the more elaborate ceremonials of the week preceding Easter, including foot-washing (of the poor by the rich or royal) on Maundy Thursday, and the blessing of palms on Palm Sunday. Good Friday was still a fast, but as Nicholas Breton describes it in *Fantasticks*, also a day of great anticipation for the end of the austere season, as "Butchers now must wash their Boords, make cleane their Aprons...and cut out their meat for Easter Eve market," poulterers must "make ready their Rabbets," and "Cookes have their Ovens cleane, and all for Pies and Tarts against the merry Feast" (D3r).

April

	1	2	3	4
Day	BCP	Grafton, (Liber)	Identification	Source
1		Theodore (Gildarde)	St. Theodora, Roman martyr, 2nd c. (St. Gildarde, see June 8th)	C, B B
2		Mary Egypt	St. Mary of Egypt, Egyptian martyr, 4th c.	F
3	Richard	Richard bishop	St. Richard of Chicester, bishop, 13th c.	F

(*Continued*)

212 *Early modern calendars*

	1	2	3	4
Day	BCP	*Grafton*, (Liber)	Identification	Source
4	Ambrose	Ambrose	St. Ambrose, Bishop of Milan, 4th c.	F
5		Martian	?	F
		(Vincentius)	(St. Vincent Ferrer, Dominican friar, 15th c.)	F
6		Sixtus bishop	St. Sixtus, Pope, 2nd c.	F
7		Egisippus (April 8th in *Liber*)	St. Hegessipus, Roman historian, 2nd c.	F
		(Euphemie)	(St. Euphemie, French virgin martyr, 4th c.)	F
8		Perpetuus (April 9th in *Liber*)	St. Perpetuus, Bishop of Tours, 5th c.	F
9		Passion of the vii Virgins (April 10th in *Liber*)	?	
10		Tiburci & Valer. (April 14th in *Liber*)	St. Tiburtius and St. Valerian, Roman martyrs, companions of St. Cecilia, date unknown	F
11		July bishop (Appoline)	St. Guthlac, hermit of Crowland, 8th c. (?)	F
12		Oswold archbishop (April 15th in *Liber*)	St. Oswald, Benedictine monk and Bishop of Worcester, 10th c. (see February 28th)	F
13		Zenoni (April 12th in *Liber*) (Eusemie)	St. Zeno, African Bishop of Verona, 4th c. (usually April 12th) (?)	F
14		Olife	?	
15		Leonard	?	
16		Isidore	Possibly St. Isidore, Archbishop of Seville, 7th c. (usually April 4th)	F
17		Cosmy (Aniceti episcopi Ro.)	? (St. Anicetus, Syrian Pope of Rome, 2nd c.)	(B)
18		Quintine (Eleutherius & Anthi.)	? (St. Eleutherius, Bishop of Illyria, and his mother, St. Anthia, 3rd c.)	(F)
19	Alphege	Alphe	St. Alphege, Bishop of Winchester, 10th c.	F
20		Victor martyr	St. Victor, Zoticus and companions, martyrs in Nicomedia, 4th c.	B

	1	2	3	4
Day	BCP	Grafton, (Liber)	Identification	Source
21		Simon bishop	St. Simeon, bishop, and companions, martyrs in Mesopotamia, 4th c.	B
22		Sother virgin	St. Soter, Pope, 2nd c.	B
23	St. George	George martyr	St. George, patron saint of England, 4th c.	F
24		Wilfride bishop	St. Wilfrid, Northumbrian bishop, 8th c.	F
25	*Mark, Evangelist*	Mark Evangelist	St. Mark, Evangelist, 1st c.	F
26		Clete bishop	St. Cletus, Bishop of Rome, 1st c.	F
27		Anastast bishop	St. Anastatius, Pope, 5th c.	B
28		Vitalis martir	St. Vitalis, Italian martyr, 3rd c.	F
29		Peter Mediolencis	St. Peter of Verona, Dominican friar and priest, patron saint of Inquisitors, 13th c.	F
30		Erkenwalde	St. Erkenwald, Bishop of London, 7th c.	F

May

Labors and agricultural tasks

> I May from all extorte suborned grace,
>   That views my sweet and Paradice-like face:
> Flora hath cloath'd me with her Tapestry,
>   Wrought by Dame Nature fine and curiously.   (Hawkins 1624, A54)

As in Figure 3.3.10 from Buckminster's 1567 almanac, the visual iconography of May is almost entirely concerned with pleasure: dining *al fresco*, flirting, making music, birding, picking flowers, and wandering in the pleasantly burgeoning fields. As Hawkins' calendar poem for 1624 suggests through the personified May with her "Paradice-like face," this is the most idealized of the twelve months, a time "wherin Nature hath her fill of mirth, and the Senses are filled with delights" (Breton, *Fantasticks*, C2r).

The actual tasks of husbandry for May include tending bees, which are now "ready to swarm" (Tusser, 87), planting kitchen gardens, fallowing fields, and weeding. The herbs and vegetables most often recommended for sowing this month include "parsly and onions, corainder and leekes" as well as "Smailage," a kind of celery, and "basill" (Prid, A6r), "sweete Marjerom"

Figure 3.3.10 May, Thomas Buckminster, *A New Almanacke and Prognostication* (1567), A8r. University of Illinois at Champaign-Urbana, Rare Book and Manuscript Library, 529.5 H484a-1567.

and "Sommer saverie" (Alleyn 1606, B8v), "Leeks, Onyons, Purselan" and "Gourds, Cucumbers and Mellons" (Frende 1622, A5r, B7r), "pescods," and "Good flaxe & good hemp" (Tusser, 86). Women were encouraged to work the still to produce "Aquavitae, and other stilled waters" (Alleyn 1606, B8v). To these busy planting tasks in May, Tusser adds copious advice about the care of livestock. The time to separate lambs from their mothers was "Phillip and Jacob," the first of May, if the husbandman "thinkest to have any milke of their dams" (84); milking of sheep was to be stopped at Lammas, the first of August. Calves should this month be let out to pasture with their mothers. Weeding continues apace in May, which is also a good time to mend thatched roofs and hire children to rid fields of stones.

Zodiac, astronomy, and astrology

The Sun enters the sign of Gemini, the Twins, on May 11th (Figure 3.3.11). Gemini "is of the West[,] masculine, ayrie and sanguine" (Alleyn 1606, B8r). Sirius or Canis Major, the Dog Star that will wreak havoc in July and August, now sets in the evening, and "if the full Moone happen within two daies before or after, it prognosticates blasting to corne and other flowers" (Hopton, *Concordancy*, 105). Hopton reports a number of potential hazards to crops depending on the interplay between stars and the Moon this month, lore drawn from Stadius, Ptolemy, and Cardano. For example, if the Moon is new or full on the 23rd when Aquila (the Eagle) rises at dawn, then "all fruites bee hurt with wormes and Caterpillers." If the Sun shines on May 25th, "Some say…wines shall prosper well" (105). Rain on Ascension Day—which was usually in May, more rarely on April or June depending on the date of Easter—"it doth betoken scarcitie of all kinde of foode for cattell, but being faire, it signifieth plenty" (Hopton, *Concordancy*, 104).

Figure 3.3.11 May, Catholic Church, *Hore Beate Virginis Marie* (Paris, 1520, STC 15926), [A4v]. Photograph by Phebe Jensen, from the collection of the Folger Shakespeare Library, STC 15926.

The ages of man

> As in the month of maye all thyng is in myght.
> So at xxx yeres man is in chyef lyking.
> Pleasaunt and lusty/ to every mannes sight
> In beaute & in strength / to women pleasyng.   (*Thys Prymer*, 1538, STC 16008.3, fol. 6v)

The lovers who often figured in the May labor of the month are also prominent in the twelve-month ages of man scheme, which identifies this month with the years between thirty and thirty-six. As in April, illustrations for May often feature courting couples: on horseback, perambulating or sitting in enclosed gardens, and cavorting in woods or fields. Just as May itself "is bothe fayre and pleasaunte," so a man in this time of year is "moste joyfull and pleasant…and seketh playes, sportes, and lusty pastyme" (*Kalender*, A7r).

Physic

> Now art thou bid by gentle May,
>   Purge, vomit, bath and bleed:
> Leave bed, walke fieldes in morne, use meanes,
>   Of Health to sowe the seede.   (Dauncy 1614, A5r)

May is a particularly good month for health, auspicious for all medical interventions including purging, bathing, and bleeding. The almanacs especially encourage taking physic this month, as it must be avoided—"except necessitie inforce thee" (Alleyn 1606, B5v)—during the hot months of June, July, and August. "Now whosoever doth desire, / Of learned skill the helpe to finde," Johnson advises, "Delay not time for durt or mire, / For Phisicke will soone be out of kinde" (1613, A5r). Other general recommendations are to rise early and take exercise if able-bodied, especially by walking in "the fields, that smell most fragrantly" (Rudston 1613, A5r). Hawkins does warn that the bounteous flowers of May with their "various colours," each "of different power," can sicken as well as heal: "some of them can / Give health in sickenesse, others killeth man" (1627, A4r). Eating lightly (but not fasting) is recommended for this month; healthful drinks include "clarified whay, with coole herbs" (Burton 1617, B7v), especially Sage (Rudston 1613, A5r).

Diseases governed by Gemini and prevalent in May include "Flegmous" (phlegmatic) inflammations such as cellulitus, "Farnuculus" (faruncles, or boils), and other diseases involving swelling, especially in the shoulders, arms, and hands (Alleyn, 1606, B8r).

The church calendar

Seasons and holy days

Since the latest possible date for Easter is April 25th, May usually includes at least some of the important movable feasts that follow that holy day. The Easter season stretches on, usually (though not always) into June. Immediately following Easter Sunday, divine services held on Monday and Tuesday include special Collects reinforcing the message of sacrifice. The next Sunday is often called Low Sunday, or the First Sunday in Easter; it is followed by the Second, Third, and Fourth Sundays after Easter. The Thursday after the Fifth Sunday—Rogation Sunday—is Ascension Day, forty days after Good Friday. Next up is Ascension Sunday, on the sixth Sunday after Easter; this is followed by Whitsunday. The latter ushers in the festive week of Whitsuntide. The next Sunday—now eight Sundays after Easter—is Trinity Sunday; Corpus Christi falls on the Thursday afterwards. The earliest date for Corpus Christi is May 21st, and the latest is June 24th.

In the calendar of fixed holy days, May 1st is the single red-letter saint's day for the month: Philip & Jacob, commemorating the Apostle Philip (who is named in the Collect of the Day), and the Apostle James the lesser, who is remembered in the readings for divine service by the first of his four Epistles.

Two medieval English clerics are commemorated with black-letter notice in the Book of Common Prayer for May: St. Augustine, the eighth-century missionary and later Archbishop of Canterbury (May 26th), and St. Dunstan (May 19th), who was successively Abbot at Glastonbury,

Bishop of Worcester, and Archbishop of Canterbury in the tenth century. The Book of Common Prayer also notes the Invention of the Cross (previously called the Exaltation of the Holy Cross in Roman missals), on May 3rd, a holy day marking the discovery of the true cross by St. Helen (the mother of Constantine the Great) during a pilgrimage to Jerusalem in the fourth century. Finally, May 6th is one of two annual feasts commemorating St. John the Apostle and Evangelist, known as "Port Latin" from the name of the gate of Rome by which he was tortured in a pot of boiling oil; he is also celebrated in a red-letter holy day on December 27th.

Lectionary

In May the Old Testament readings continue in Kings, finishing 2 Kings, 3 Kings, and on May 29th, 4 Kings; that evening, the reading progresses to the first book of Hester (Esdras). May marks the start of the second annual reading of the Epistles and Gospel, with Romans 1 on May 2nd and Matthew 1 on May 3rd. As in the first cycle, the Epistle readings progress from Romans 1 (May 2nd to May 16th) to 1st Corinthians (May 18th–31st). In the Gospel readings, the book of Mark begins on May 31st.

Fairs

This month, the most popular day for fairs in the fixed calendar is the feast of Philip & Jacob (May 1st) with seventeen, followed two days later with about fifteen fairs on the day celebrating the Invention of the Cross (May 3rd). Approximately three fairs were permanently fixed on St. John's Day, May 6th, with an additional seven or so the next day, commemorating the eighth-century Bishop of York, St. John of Beverly. One of these fairs was, unsurprisingly, at Beverly itself. Four fairs were held on St. Dunstan's Day, May 19th, and a dozen others scattered through the month, for a total of forty-three fairs on fixed calendar dates.

Yet this number in no way represents the total fair activity for May, since the lion's share of annual fairs were attached to the movable feasts that followed Easter. These usually began in May, except when Easter was very late. The first set of fairs after Easter Week occurred following Rogation Sunday, five weeks after Easter, the week that included Ascension Thursday: two for the Tuesday, two for Ascension Eve, seventeen for Ascension Day, and another three for the following week, for a total of twenty-four. Next up was Whitsunday, the seventh Sunday after Easter, the busiest fair week of the year with a total of ninety-two, including twenty-seven (the most for any day of the year) on Whitsun Monday, and eighteen on Whitsun Tuesday. The following Sunday was Trinity Sunday, followed the next Thursday by Corpus Christi Day; that week included thirty principal fairs, thirteen of them on Corpus Christi Day itself. All told, the number of principal fairs held in England during the four weeks between Rogation Sunday and the first Sunday after Trinity was close to 150, a number that does not include any of the fixed fairs that also happened to occur during this season.

Law terms

Both Easter and Trinity terms are tied to the dates of Easter. Easter term begins on the Monday that falls fifteen days after Easter Sunday, which is also known as the Easter *quindene*. This term lasts twenty-six days, ending on the Monday following Ascension Day. After Easter Term there is a break of eighteen days, then Trinity Term begins twelve days after Whitsunday, on the day after Corpus Christi. For this reason, May might include parts of both Easter and Trinity terms, or the eighteen-day gap in between.

Festive traditions and pastimes

May is a traditional month for revelry and pastimes, no doubt because the weather is finally warm enough for outdoor gatherings, and there is a lull in agricultural tasks between sowing in March and April, and mowing and haymaking in June. The festive feeling in May must also have been heightened by the extraordinary number of fairs held this month.

Whitsuntide and May Games

In late medieval England, Whitsuntide had been a popular time to hold church ales, the festive celebrations which raised money for church reparations. As Hutton has shown, church wakes and church ales were on the decline in Elizabethan England, under pressure from Protestant reformers.[17] Yet in some regions of the country they continued, and even in the absence of church ales some of the activities associated with those celebrations persisted. These activities were not necessarily tied to particular dates, but they had a strong cultural association with the merry month of May. These festivities included Morris dancing, Robin Hood shows, pageants, mock battles, and May poles, which once erected could stand for weeks (or even months) and become focal points for locals to gather, dance, drink, and carouse (or so detractors claimed). May celebrations among the aristocracy could involve riding out into the countryside, outdoor feasting, and dancing. On May 1st, May Day, the feast of Philp and Jacob, the gathering of the May involved retreating into nearby woods to bring back flowers and greenery into villages or towns. May Day might also see the appointment of Summer lords and ladies, perhaps including a Queen of the May. Parades could also be part of May festivities, as in the Wells May Shows of 1607. These and more Summer pastimes are derisively described by the reformer Philip Stubbes in *The Anatomie of Abuses*.[18] Though they were controversial and under attack from Reformers, the festive pastimes of May, which often continued into June, apparently did persist in the early modern period.[19]

Rogations

The Reformation was effective in ending the Rogation processionals, which had traditionally occurred on the Monday, Tuesday, and Wednesday between Rogation Sunday and Ascension Thursday. On the eve of the Reformation, and again in Marian England, these processionals involved priests in liturgical robes leading their flocks around the parish, carrying crosses and the consecrated host under a canopy, sometimes with garlands and decorated banners with images of Christ and the saints. A rogation processional takes pride of place on the front cover of Foxe's *Acts and Monuments* as an example of popish religious error. The compromise under Elizabeth was to turn the rogation processional into a tour of parish boundaries, accompanied by the reading of psalms and a rogation homily, with bells, crosses, garlands, or other vestiges of popish superstition strictly forbidden.[20]

May

	1	2	3	4
Day	BCP	Grafton, (Liber)	Identification	Source
1	**Philip & Jacob**	Philip and Jacob	St. Philip and St. Jacob, Apostles, 1st c.	F
2		Athanast Bishop	St. Athanasius, Bishop of Alexandria, 4th c.	F
3	Invention of the Crosse	Inven. of the crosse	Commemorates the Jerusalem pilgrimage of St. Helena, mother of Constantine the Great, 4th c.	
4		Festum coronis spine (Florian)	The Feast of the Holy Crown (of Thorns) (St. Florian, Roman Diocletian martyr, 4th c.)	(B)
5		Godard	St. Godard, Bishop of Hildesheim in Saxony, 11th c. (also May 4th)	B
6	John, Evangelist	John Port latin	St. John, Apostle and Evangelist, 1st c.	F
7		John of Beverley	St. John of Beverley, Bishop of York, 8th c.	F
8		Appara S. Michaeli	St. Michael, Archangel	F
9		Trans. of S. Nichol	St. Nicholis, Bishop of Myra, 4th c.	F
10		Gordian & Epemachy	St. Gordian and St. Epimachus, Roman martyrs, 3rd c.	F
11		Antonie	St. Antoninus of Florence, Archbishop, 15th c. (usually May 10th)	F
12		Acheley	St. Achilleus, Roman martyr with St. Neureus, 2nd c. (see May 31st)	F
13		Sarvatius	St. Servatus, Bishop of Tongres, Belgium, 4th c.	C

(Continued)

220 *Early modern calendars*

	1	2	3	4
Day	BCP	Grafton, (Liber)	Identification	Source
14		Boniface	St. Boniface, Bishop of Ferentino, Italy, 6th c.	B
15		Isidore Martir	St. Isidore the Farmer, patron saint of Madrid, 12th c.?	F
16		Brandon	St. Brendan the Navigator, Abbot of Clonfert, 6th c.	F
17		Trans. of Barnard		
18		Diascori martyr	St. Dioscorus, Egyptian martyr, 4th c.	F
19	Dunstane	Dunstan	St. Dunstan, Benedictine monk and Archbishop of Canterbury, 10th c.	F
20		Barnardine	St. Barnardine of Siena, Franciscan, 15th c.	F
21		Elen queene	St. Helen, empress, mother of Constantine the Great, 4th c.	F
22		Julian virgin	St. Julia of Carthage, 5th c.	B
23		Desiderii martir	St. Desiderius, Bishop of Langres, 5th c.	B
24		Trans. of S. Frauncis		
25		Adelme bishop	St. Aldhelm, Abbot of Malmesbury, 8th c.	F
26	Augustine	Augustine of Engl.	St. Augustine of Canterbury, Archbishop and missionary to England, 7th c.	F
27		Bede presbiteri	The Venerable Bede, monk of Jarrow and 1st English historian, 8th c.	F
28		Germane	St. Germanus of Paris, abbot, 6th c.	F
29		Coronis martyr	St. Cauranus, Roman preacher, 5th c. (usually May 28th)	C
30		Felix	St. Felix, Pope and martyr, 3rd c.	B
31		Petronil	St. Petronilla, martyr, supposed daughter of St. Peter, 1st c.	F
		Nerii	(Possibly St. Nereus, Roman martyr with St. Achilleus, 2nd c., usually May 12th)	F

a **Note on May Saint's Days:** Grafton's *Treatise* misaligns the May saints for the second half of the month, listing St. Boniface for May 13th—one day earlier than the date in the *Liber* and other early modern Protestant prayer books. All subsequent saints for May 14th to May 31st are listed one day earlier in Grafton's calendars than in official sources (though some errors are corrected in the 1599 edition of the *Treatise*). Those errors have been corrected above, to align the dates with the official prayer books. Because almanac compilers often used Grafton to construct their calendars, the almanacs reflect considerable confusion surrounding the dates of the saints in the second half of May, with some following the incorrect calendar in Grafton's *Treatise*, even though those conflicted with the Book of Common Prayer.

June

Labors and agricultural tasks

> The simple Sheepe for Shepheardes care,
> Now payes him home with Lambe and wool.
> But some so greedy make no spare,
> Both Fell and Fleece at once to pull.   (Gray 1591, B1v)

June is a month where the idealized labors also happen to reflect the standard agricultural tasks in England. The most frequently represented is sheep-shearing (Figure 3.3.12), followed closely by mowing (as in the image for June in Spenser's *The Shepheardes Calender*, Plate 15.2), though in the English calendars the latter task is often associated with July. Sheep-shearing and mowing are both top agricultural tasks for this month. Tusser provides detailed advice on shearing, recommending that husbandmen begin by washing the sheep in a clear stream and letting them "drie in the sunne" (89), that the task be completed within two days, and that fleecing not take place before the middle of June. Farmers should be careful not to cut too close, as "such ungentlenes" will make the sheep run away or "pine" (90). Gray's calendar poem for June 1591, above, reiterates Tusser's concern that greedy farmers should avoid the "fell." Mowing also begins in June, with a careful eye toward "the weather, the wind and the skie": "By little and little, thus doing ye win, / that plow shall not hinder, when harvest comes in" (Tusser, 90). Generally the advice is to begin mowing low-lying fields this month, leaving higher pastures (and haymaking) until July.

Another primary task for farmers and their wives for June is to prepare for the fall harvest by mending hay carts, shoring up hovels, and generally

Figure 3.3.12 June, William Prid, *The Glasse of Vaine Glory* (1600), A6v. Photograph by Phebe Jensen, from the collection of the Folger Shakespeare Library, STC 931.

ensuring there is enough dry "barn-roome" and "yard-room" for housing corn so the harvest is protected from "mouse" and "raine" (Tusser 91). Tusser recommends using gorse bushes—"whins or...furzes"— to repair outbuildings and thatch, and to prepare firewood, using "tall-wood" for kindling and "billet" for thicker logs (91). June is a recommended time to "sette Rosemarie, and Gilloflowers," sow radishes, and make use of the blooming roses by making "oyle of Roses, syrope of Roses, and still Rose water" (Alleyn 1606, C1r).

Zodiac, astronomy, and astrology

Cancer the crab, the Zodiac sign for June, "is of the North, feminine, waterie, and flegmatique, and ruleth the breast, ribbes, pappes of women, lunges, liver and Spleene" (Alleyn 1606, B8v). Hopton's *Concordancy* records various astral influences on the weather and crops for this month. The Sun's entry into Cancer causes "Wine and Olives" to "flourish." On the 16th, the air is made "intemperate" by the dawn rising of Arcturus; on the 21st the west winds begin to blow when "the left side of Orion" rises at dawn. If there is a full moon when the "lesser Dogge" (Canis Minor) sets in the evening, it presages harm to "fruits" and "sweet flowers and vines, by reason of his burning heate." If it raines on the 24th, "Hazell-nuts do not prosper" (Hopton, *Concordancy*, 106).

The ages of man

> In June all thyng falleth to rypenesse
> And so dooth man at xxxvi yere olde.
> And studyeth for to acquyre richesse.
> And taketh a wyfe to kepe his housholde.   (*This Prymer*, 1532, STC 15978, B8r)

June, the month that marks a man's age from thirty-six to forty-two, rounds off the courting and cavorting of April and May with the coming-of-age ritual of marriage. Wedding ceremonies dominate the imagery, as in a page from a 1529 Regnault prayer book made for the English market (Figure 3.3.13).

In this calendar tradition, marriage is invariably described as a function of thrift, rather than romance: entering middle age, a man should take a wife who will "kepe his housholde" as part of a larger strategy by which he will "acquyre rychesse." This time represents the apogee of a man's life, "for then hath nature gyven hym beauty and strengthe at the full, and rypeth the sedes of parfyte understandynge" (*Kalender*, A7v).

Physic

> The time for Physicke now is past,
> Coole hearbs in whay to drinke now vse:
> And Venus sports now will thee waste
> Restraine therefore from hatefull stewes.   (Johnson 1624, A5v)

The twelve months 223

Figure 3.3.13 June, Catholic Church, *This Prymer of Salysbury Use* (Paris, 1529, STC 15961.5), B2v. Photograph by Phebe Jensen, from the collection of the Folger Shakespeare Library, STC 15961.5.

Whereas the Spring months were spent balancing the humors thrown off by Winter surfeiting, in June, as Alleyn writes, "thy humors now dispersed be," and all medical interventions stop, unless absolutely essential (Alleyn 1607, A5v). If necessity demands, physic should be administered only by a learned practitioner, and only "early in the morning, that it may have wrought before the heate of the day doe come" (Alleyn 1606, C1r). The prohibition on purging, bleeding, bathing (up to a point) and taking medicine continues through the three hot months of Summer. Vigorous physical activity, including sex, is considered perilous in the increasing heat: "From violent exercise now abstaine, / Except thou wilt in trouble remaine" (Neve 1605, B1v), though pleasant outdoor recreation is still recommended, as it was for Spring: "Now hunt the Hare, the fearfull Buck pursue / bid idlenesse and Venus sports adieu" (Bretnor 1616, B2r). The delights of the flowers and blossoming fields is often remarked in the calendar poetry, especially those roses that yield rose oil, rose syrup, and rose water, as in this appropriately overblown verse by George Hawkins:

> No way inferiour to the flowers of May,
>   Are the dew-dropping Roses, I display:

With other flowers, exquisitely rare,
Whose odiferous scent perfumes the aire.   (Hawkins 1625, A5v)

For diet, calendar poetry for June encourages "a light and thinne diet, for the stomacke is not nowe so well able to digest as in Winter, or some other of the former months" (Alleyn 1606, C1r). The most frequently recommended drink is whey—the skim milk left after the fat has been removed for cheese production—often flavored with herbs. Aside from recommending whey and salads, the diet directives mostly stress what should be avoided: strong or sweet drinks (including wine), spices, and meat. The particular sicknesses associated with Cancer and June include "Alopesia" (alopecia, or sudden hair loss), "waterie eyes, coughes, Rewmes, Scabbes, and Leprosie" (Alleyn 1606, B8v).

The church calendar

Seasons and holy days

The long series of post-Easter holidays usually end in June, as the latest possible date for Corpus Christi (the Thursday after Trinity Sunday) is June 24th.

There are two holy days fixed in the calendar for June in the Book of Common Prayer. The first commemorates John the Baptist on June 24th; the second, St. Peter on June 29th. In the Sarum rite, June 29th was the feast of St. Peter and St. Paul, and that double commemoration remains in many calendars; St. Paul is also given black-letter notice the following day, June 30th, though the red-letter commemoration for the saint marks his conversion on January 25th.

The first black-letter saint in the Book of Common Prayer for June is St. Nichomedes, an early Roman martyr. Although in the Sarum rite and all other early modern calendars (including the Latin *Liber*) his date is June 1st, the Book of Common Prayer somewhat unaccountably moves him to June 3rd. June 5th is a feast of St. Boniface, an Anglo-Saxon monk from Devon who became Archbishop of Mainz; June 20th commemorates the translation of the relics of St. Edward, King and Martyr.

Lectionary

June is the month of Job, which is read in the first lessons for Morning and Evening Prayer from June 3rd (following the last few chapters from the Book of Hester), and continuing until the 23rd. The last week of the month the Old Testament readings start in on Proverbs. Meanwhile the Gospel readings, now in their second annual run-through, begin with Mark 2–16 (June 1st–June 16th), then turn to Luke 1–12

(June 17th–30th). The Epistle progresses from First Corinthians, Second Corinthians, and Galatians into Ephesians.

Fairs

The busy season for fairs continues in June. In addition to the large numbers attached to the movable holidays after Easter, some of which invariably fall this month, there are another ninety or more principal fairs attached to the fixed calendar. These include approximately thirty-one on the feast of St. John the Baptist (June 24th), twenty-four on St. Peter's Day (June 29th), and eight on the evening before St. Barnabas' Day, which in the Julian calendar always fell near or on the longest day of the year.

Law terms

Since Trinity Term begins twelve days after Whitsunday on the Friday after Corpus Christi Day and lasts for nineteen days, part of this law term falls in June.

Festive traditions and pastimes

Sheep-shearing

Some evidence, most of it literary, suggests an informal tradition whereby farmers feasted workers on the occasion of the June shearing of sheep, though feasting in the calendar literature is more clearly associated with the successful return of the harvest in August.

Midsummer

Midsummer—like the Annunciation and Michaelmas—was an important calendar marker for quarterly dating. According to George Gascoigne in *The noble arte of venerie or hunting* (1575), for example, the "Harte & Bucke" is in season "from Midsomer untill Holyroode day"; the hare from Michaelmas till Midsummer; and the otter from "Shrovetide untill Midsomer" (238). The Midsummer watches—military exercises, famously described in John Stowe's *Survay of London* (1598)—had been curtailed at the Reformation, and so were (to a lesser extent) the magnificent communal bonfires of Midsummer Eve. But other miscellaneous lore about the day continued, such as the information in Thomas Lupton's book of secrets, *A Thousand Notable Things, of Sundry Sorts* (London, 1579), that "on Mydsomer Eve...there is founde under the roote of Mugwoort a cole, which preserves or kepes them safe from Plague, the carbuncle, lightning, the Quarteyn ague, and from burning, that beares the same upon them" (15).

226 *Early modern calendars*

June

	1	2	3	4
Day	BCP	Grafton, (Liber)	Identification	Source
1		Nichomed martyr	St. Nichomedes, Roman martyr, dates unknown	F
2		Merceline & Pet.	St. Marcellinus and St. Peter, Roman martyrs, 4th c.	F
3	Nichomede[a]	Erasme martyr	St. Erasmus [St. Elmo], bishop in Syria, 4th c. (also June 2nd)	B
4		Petroci conf.	St. Petroc, abbot in Cornwall, 6th c.	F
5	Boniface	Boniface bishop	St. Boniface, Anglo-Saxon monk (Devon) and Archbishop of Mainz, 8th c.	F
6		Wolston (Melonis archiepisc.)	St. Wulfstan, Benedictine monk and Bishop of Worcester, 11th c. (usually June 7th) (?)	F
7		Medard & Gil.	St. Médard, Bishop of Vermandois, 6th c.;	F
8		William conf.	St. William of York, archbishop, 12th c.	F
9		Trans. of Edm.	St. Edmund of Abingdon, Archbishop of Canterbury, 13th c.	F
10		Innocent conf.	?	
11	Barnarb.	Barnard	St. Barnabas, Apostle, 1st c.	F
12		Basill	St. Basilides, Roman martyr, dates unknown	F
13		Antony	St. Antony of Padua, Franciscan friar, 13th c.	F
14		Basill bishop	St. Basil the Great, Bishop of Caesarea, 4th c.	F
15		Vite Modeste	St. Vitus and St. Modestus, martyrs, 4th c.	F
16		Trans. S. Richard	St. Richard of Chichester, Bishop, 13th c. (also April 3rd)	F
17		Botolph	St. Botulf, East Anglian bishop, 7th c.	F
18		Marceline (Marci & Marcelliani)	St. Mark and St. Marcellian, Roman martyrs, 3rd c.	F
19		Gervasii & Pro.	St. Gervase and St. Protase, protomartyrs of Milan, dates unknown	F
20	Edwarde	Trans. S. Edward	St. Edward, English King and martyr, 10th c. (see also March 18th)	F
21		Walburge virgin	Possibly St. Walburga, Anglo-Saxon abbess and virgin martyr, 8th c. (usually May 1st)	F

	1	2	3	4
Day	BCP	Grafton, (Liber)	Identification	Source
22		Albany martyr	St. Alban, protomartyr of Britain, 3rd c.	F
23		Audre (Etheldredae virg.)	St. Audrey/Etheldreda, queen and abbess of East Anglia and abbess, 7th c.	F
24	John the Baptist	John the Baptist	St. John the Baptist, 1st c.	F
25		Trans. of Eligii	St. Eloi, Bishop of Noyon (France), 7th c.	F
26		John & Paule	St. John & St. Paul, Roman martyrs, 4th c.	F
27		Crescentis martir	St. Crescens, disciple of St. Paul, bishop and martyr, 2nd c.	B
28		Leo bishop	St. Leo, Pope from Sicilia, 7th c.	B
29	Peter, Apostle	Peter & Paule	St. Peter and St. Paul, Apostles, 1st c.	F
30		Com. of Paule	St. Paul, Apostle	F

a Nichomedes is listed for June 3rd in the English Book of Common Prayer (1559 and after), though he is listed by the correct date (June 1st) in Grafton, the *Liber*, and most other early modern English calendars.

July

Labors and agricultural tasks

> With tossing and raking, and setting in cox,
>   grasse lately in swathes, is meat for an Oxe:
> That done goe and cart it, and have it away,
>   the battel is fought, ye have gotten the day.   (Tusser, 93)

Though mowing began in June and is also sometimes represented in the labor for that month, mowing and haymaking were the more common labors for July in English calendars. The most recognizable attribute for mowers is the long-handled scythe, along with pitchforks (or sometimes rakes), as in the stained-glass roundel from Cassioberry now in the Victoria and Albert Museum (Figure 3.3.14). Another typical visual motif is the hay cocks, shown in the Cassioberry glass and in the June labor from *Kalender*, (Plate 15.2). Long-handled scythes also feature prominently in a misericord representing the month of July (or possibly June) in Worcester Cathedral (Figure 3.3.15).

Bucolic though stylized images of haymaking may be, the agricultural guides stress the enormous amount of hard, hot work involved. Tusser imagines haymaking as a "battell," urging husbandmen to "muster thy servants, be captaine thy selfe, / providing them weapon and other like pelfe,"

228 *Early modern calendars*

Figure 3.3.14 July, Glass Roundel, ca. 1450–1475. © Victoria and Albert Museum, London.

Figure 3.3.15 July, Misericord, Worcester Cathedral, fourteenth century. ©www.misericords.co.uk 2017

and emphasizing the "feare" and "danger" of work in the hot fields (93). "[T]urne idlenesse out of your Hay-medowes," Burton warns, "as an enemie to the Time following" (1617, B8v). Once the month is "well nigh out worne" harvesting may begin (Prid, A7r), though that enterprise is usually associated with August: "Ere July be cleane gone, to harvest you may, /

with sickle be doing in wheate and in Rie" (Alleyn 1607, C2v). Aside from the task of mowing July is an even quieter month agriculturally than June, and Tusser's July poem is shorter than that for any other month. Accordingly, now is the time to catch upon those tasks that were "forgotten month past" (Tusser, 93). Other recommended activities include harvesting green beans, hemp, and flax, and gathering wormwood "to save against March, to make flea to refraine" (Tusser, 94). Breton's *Fantastickes,* aside from noting how the "heat parcheth the earth, and burnes up the grasse on the mountaines," identifies July with thunderstorms and a profusion of smelt and lamprey (C3r).

Zodiac, astronomy, and astrology

The Sun enters Leo on July 12th; the sign is "of the East, masculine, fierie, and chollericke" (Alleyn 1606, C1r-v). By far the most significant astronomical phenomenon for July is the Dog Days. The start and end date and duration of the Dog Days varied according to how exactly they were calculated: whether by the time of the rising of the Great Dog Star (Sirius) or the Little Dog Star (Procyon), and whether that rising was calculated as heliacal (just before sunrise) or cosmical (at sunrise). For example, in Hopton's *Concordancy,* the Dog Days begin on July 19th and end on August 29th, but in the 1559 Book of Common Prayer the Dog Days begin on July 6th and end on September 5th. The almanacs also vary in their calculations.

During the Dog Days, the stars in Canis Major and Canis Minor are thought to exacerbate the influence of fiery Leo, and all almanacs and medical books agree it is a perilous time both for individual bodies and general peace. As Philippa Berry has shown, Shakespeare deliberately situates the action of *Romeo and Juliet* in this part of the year to enhance the sense of choleric danger; as Benvolio fruitlessly warns Mercutio: "For now, these hot days, is the mad blood stirring" (3.1.4).[21] In the weather lore for the month, July 2nd is a "Criticall day," according to Hopton, because of the rising of "Orions Girdle"; "for if it raine this day it doth continue so often for 4 weeks" (*Concordancy*, 106). Another weather platitude claims that "if it be faire 3 Sundayes before S. James Day, [July 26th] corne will be good: but wet, corne withereth" (Hopton, *Concordancy*, 107).

The ages of man

> At xl yere of aege or elles never
> Is ony man endewed with Wysdome.
> For than for thou his myght fayleth ever
> As in July dooth every blossome.   (*Thys Prymer,* 1538, STC
>   16008.3, A8v)

230   *Early modern calendars*

July, which represents the years from forty to forty-six, is a turning point in the life of the calendar man, whose vigor begins to subside just as blossoms fade in July, for now "the sonne begynnethe a lyttle for to dyscende downewarde: so man then goth fro[m] youth towarde age" (*Kalender* 1570, A7v). Following the weddings of June, in July the central figure is usually represented with children and servants.

Physic

> Godnight bludlettinge, that cures many phantasies, and griefes:
> In lieu of medicines, let cooling victualles, and bathes,
> Used with discretion suffize: play and sleepe moderately:
> Dogg, and Lyon, raigne lyke Vulcane, hott as a Furnace.   (Harvey 1589, A6r)

Generally the medical advice in July repeats what was said in June, with even more serious warnings against overindulgence, overexertion, and medical interventions. "As Iune before, so Iuly more," writes Watson in 1600, "forbiddeth lust, hot spice, and wine" (B2v). Though purging, bleeding, and taking medicine is still discouraged, "coole baths" are recommended, especially in rivers: "Now in July Dogge dayes begin, / The rivers are best to bathe in" (Neve 1605, B2v). The other main advice is to "sleep not much in July" (Neve 1609, A7r). Hopton warns against "suddaine colds, for nothing sooner breedeth the plague: and therefore to drinke being hot, is naught" (*Concordancy*, 107).

Leo rules "the heart, stomacke, backe, sides, and the midriffe, with Virgo"; sicknesses associated with the sign and the month of July are "*Cardiaca passio*, or troubling of the hart, and often sounding [swooning]" (Alleyn 1606, C1v). Medical recommendations stress the dangers of the choleric Dog Days, when the hot star Sirius and the hot planet Leo reign—especially for young people and naturally choleric temperaments.

Church calendar

Seasons and holy days

By July the post-Easter holy days have at last ended, and the calendar is in the long stretch of Pentecost Sundays after Trinity, which continue until Advent. The single red-letter saint's day in July commemorates St. James the Apostle on July 26th.

July includes another one of the seven medieval Marian feast days, demoted to black-letter status in the Book of Common Prayer: the Visitation of the Virgin Mary to St. Elizabeth. Although the Sarum Rite, the *Liber*, and all other calendars put the Visitation on July 2nd, the Book of Common Prayer moves it to July 1st. Three other female saints are commemorated with black-letter observances this month: St. Margaret (on the 20th); St. Mary Magdalen (the 22nd), and St. Anne (the 26th). In addition, the Book of Common Prayer commemorates St. Martin on July 3rd—diverging once again from all other sources, including the *Liber* and the Sarum Rite, which puts that feast day on July 4th. The other black-letter saint is St. Swithin, the ninth-century Bishop of Winchester, on July 15th.

Lectionary

By July 1st the Old Testament readings have progressed to Proverbs 12, which is followed by Ecclesiastes (beginning in Evening Prayer on the 11th). Jeremiah begins on July 16th and continues into August. The Gospel starts off in Luke 13, progressing to John on July 13th. The Epistles read this month are Philip, Colossians, Thessaonians, Timothy, Titus, and Hebrews.

Fairs

The Summer fair season continues in full swing in July, with a total of approximately 105 fairs. The most popular date for fairs in this part of the year is July 25th, the feast of St. James, with about forty. Other busy fair days include the Feast of St. Mary Magdalen on the 22nd, with approximately nineteen, and the feasts of St. Thomas (July 7th) and St. Margaret (July 20th), each with about twelve. The Visitation is the set day for only six principal fairs.

Law terms

Usually Trinity Term is over before July begins, but when Easter is late, the term drags into July. The latest date on which it can end is July 11th.

Festive traditions and pastimes

Rushbearing

Another late medieval custom that met the wrath of Protestant reformers was rushbearing: the practice of bringing into town—often into the church—rushes collected from the woods to use as floor coverings in poorer households or civic buildings. Disallowed by Grindal's visitation articles, the practice was later "explicitly legalized" by James Ist's Book of Sports.[22] It appears occasionally in literary representations; "A Countrey *Rush-bearing,* or Morrice Pastorall" is the preferred "festivall" for Pedlars in Richard Brathwaite's *Whimzies,* for example (19).

July

Day	BCP	Grafton, (Liber)	Identification	Source
	1	2	3	4
1	Visitati. Mary[a]	Oct. of S. John Baptist	See June 24th	
2		Visitation of our Lady	Medieval Marian feast day commemorating the Visitation of the Virgin Mary to St. Elizabeth	F
3	Martin	Trans. of S. Tho. Apost.	St. Thomas, Apostle, 1st c.	F
4		Trans. of S. Martin	St. Martin of Tours, monk and bishop, 4th c.	F
5		Zoe virgin & martyr	St. Zoe, Roman martyr, 3rd c.	BC
6	Dogge dayes	Octa. Peter	See June 29th	
7		Trans. of S. Thomas	St. Thomas Becket, Archbishop and martyr, 12th c.	F
8		Deposition of Grim.	St. Grimbald, monk and Dean of New Minster, Winchester, 10th c.	F
9		Cirilli bishop	?	
10		vii bretherne martirs	Seven Brothers, Roman martyrs, 2nd c.	F
11		Trans. of S. Benet	St. Benedict, abbot and author of the Benedictine Rule, 6th c.	F
12		Nabor & Felix	St. Nabor and St. Felix, Diocletian martyrs, 4th c.	B
13		Private	?	
14		Revel	?	
15	Swithune	Trans. of S. Swithine (Sociori)	St. Swithin, Bishop of Winchester, 9th c. (?)	F
16		Osmonde	St. Osmund, Bishop of Salisbury, 11th c.	F
17		Kenelme kyng	St. Kenelm, Prince of Mercia, 9th c.	F
18		Arnulph bishop	St. Arnulf, Bishop of Metz, 7th c.	F
19		Rufine & Justine	St. Justa and St. Rufina, sisters, potters, and martyrs at Seville, 3rd c.	F
20	Margaret	Margaret virg.	St. Margaret of Antioch, martyr, dates unknown	F
21		Praxade virgin	St. Praxedes, virgin martyr of Rome, 2nd c.	F
22	Magdalen	Mary Magdalen	St. Mary Magdalen, follower of Jesus, 1st c.	F

	1	2	3	4
Day	BCP	Grafton, (Liber)	Identification	Source
23		Apolin bishop	St. Apollinaris, Bishop of Ravenna, martyr, date unknown	F
24		Christine vir.	St. Christina, virgin and martyr, possibly 4th c.	F
25	James, Apostle	James Apostle	St. James, Apostle, 1st c.	F
26	Anne	Anne	St. Anne, mother of the Virgin Mary, 1st c.	F
27		vii Sleepers	The Seven Sleepers of Ephesus, martyrs, dates unknown	F
28		Sampson bishop	St. Samson, Welsh Bishop of Dol, 6th c.	F
29		Felix & his felowes	Possibly St. Felix, martyr with St. Julia and St. Jucunda, dates unknown (usually July 27th). July 29th is also the commemoration for Felix II, Pope and Martyr, 4th c.	B, C
30		Abdon & Seni.	St. Abdon and St. Sennen, Roman martyrs, 4th c.	F
31		Germany bishop	St. Germanus of Auxerre, bishop, 5th c.	F

a   The Visitation—July 2nd in almost all calendars of the period—is listed by July 1st in the English Book of Common Prayer.

August

Labors and agricultural tasks

> Be blithe to see sweet Ceres store,
> Fayre cut, fast bonnd, and home conuayde,
> Let scattered corne be glean'd by poore,
> And Haruest creatures, dewly paide.   (Gray 1604, A6)

Harvesting the corn—wheat, rye, barley, oats—is the standard labor for August, sometimes in combination with threshing (also a labor for September). The primary harvesting tool is the short-handled sickle, prominent in the labor from the 1555 primer in Figure 3.2.16. Usually the field laborers include women as well as men, as in the couple harvesting in a misericord from St. Mary's, Ripple (Figure 3.3.17).

August indeed was the primary month for the enormously important and all-consuming work of the harvest, though in some areas that enterprise began in July. The calendar poetry repeatedly cheers on the laborers,

Figure 3.3.16 August, Catholic Church, *Hereafter Followeth the Primer* (1555, STC 16071), B1v. Photograph by Phebe Jensen, from the collection of the Folger Shakespeare Library, STC 16071.

Figure 3.3.17 August, Misericord, St. Mary's, Ripple, fifteenth century. ©www.misericords.co.uk 2017

reminding them of the importance of the harvest to prepare for the coming Winter. Tusser provides extensive advice on both the harvest itself, and the proper treatment of work crews. It is wise to pay the "harvest-lord more, by a peny or two" (98) as he must motivate the field hands; it's a good idea to provide reapers with gloves and keep them happy with evening feasting: "In harvest time harvest folke, servants and all / should make altogether, good cheere in the hall: / And fill out the black bol, of bleith to their song, / and let them be mery all harvest time long" (100). Tusser's poem for August also stresses the importance of timing the harvest, completing the job quickly, and tithing the corn (no matter what one thinks of the local priest). As the calendar poetry also often suggests, it is important to allow the poor to "go and gleane" what's left in the field after the harvest; then, farmers might release their cattle onto the fields, "to mouth it up cleane" (Tusser, 100).

Although harvesting is the main agricultural task for the month, there is other work to be done in August, some of it falling to maids and housewives: paring saffron, or perhaps shifting the saffron to a new field, gathering and drying mustard seed, harvesting or covering peas so the doves and magpies don't get them, manuring and smoothing fields that have lain fallow over the Summer, gathering and stacking wood for the Winter, and harvesting hops. It is apparently never too early to get on one's horse and procure the "Ling, Salt-fish and Herring" for Lent (101).

Zodiac, astronomy, and astrology

The Sun enters the sign of Virgo, the Virgin, on August 14th, "being of the South, feminine, earthy, and melancholique," governing "the belly, guttes, and midrife with Leo" (Alleyn 1606, C1v). Virgo is often seen holding a strand of wheat, as in Figure 3.3.16, and the embroidered valence of the twelve months from Hatfield House (Plate 15.1). Though the Dog Days begin in July, the full fury of Sirius is felt in August: "at the rising of this starre all living creatures bee troubled; and ... it is scarce possible that drynesse and sicknesse should not be" (Hopton *Concordancy*, 107). According to Stadius (via Hopton), "many more enormities" occur in August as a result of the influence of Sirius, "as troubling of Wine in Cellars, dogges going mad, fluxes of the Seas & waters, death of fishes, with the extremitie of heat" (*Concordancy*, 107–108).

The ages of man

> The goodes of the erthe is ga[th]red evermore.
> In august so at xlviii yeres
> Man oughth to gather some goodes in store
> To softeyne aege that than draweth nere.   (*This Prymer* 1556,
>   STC 16076, B1r)

This month the calendar poetry concerning the ages of man metaphorically equates the annual gathering of the harvest with the time of life, from forty-eight to fifty-six, when a man should gather goods in store for his old age, "when he may nother gette nor wyn" (*Kalender*, A7v). The central figure is usually depicted in rich robes, surrounded by the bounty of the harvest.

Physic

> Dog daies being come the burning heate,
>   Mens bodies out of frame doth bring:
> The helpe of medicines is not greate,
>   Therefore take heed in everie thing.   (Johnson 1613, A6v)

August, the last month of Summer, concludes the three-month period of the year in which all medical interventions should be avoided, along with wine, meat, and sexual activity. The calendar poetry looks forward with a sense of relief to the end of the Summer season—"The roaring Lion, and the mad Dogges rage, / This moneth doth terminate and their heate asswage"—but in the meantime men would do well to shun *"Aesculapius, Bacchus,* [and] *Venus,"* and instead, "Embrace thou cooling drinkes, vse slender diet, / If long on earth thou mean'st to liue in quiet" (Booker 1631, A6v). Excessive sleep should still be avoided, especially after the midday meal, as well as all baths—even in the cool rivers recommended in July. There is great danger in August of "taking colde after heats" (Alleyn 1606, C2r), which can cause "pleiorisies most hard to cure" (Johnson 1612, A6v). Generally, the illnesses associated with the Sun in Virgo are digestive: "Illiaca" or obstruction in the small intestine, "Collica passio" or disturbance in the colon, "oppilations" or obstructions of the spleen, and "black Jaundies," or obstruction in the bile duct. Sleeping in the afternoon heat also causes "head-ach, Catharres, and makes one very unlustie" (Alleyn 1606, C2r).

The Church calendar

Seasons and holy days

August falls in the long season of Pentecost or Sundays after Trinity. The single red-letter saint's day in August is August 24th for St. Bartholomew, the Apostle who was "geven grace...truly to beleve, and to preach" the word of God (*BCP*, L6v).

The first black-letter holy day noted in the Book of Common Prayer is Lammas, August 1st, a harvest festival with Anglo-Saxon origins notable for a large number of fairs. August 6th was the Feast of the Transfiguration, and the next day, August 7th, the Feast of the Name of Jesus: how exactly those two vestigial Catholic feasts were celebrated in the early modern period is unclear. August 10th noted the Roman third-century martyr, St. Laurence, August 28th St. Augustine of Hippo, and August 29th was a second commemoration for John the Baptist, celebrating the date of his beheading.

Lectionary

The Old Testament readings for August begin in Jerome, moving from there to Lamentations, then excerpts from Ezekiel, the Book of Daniel, and Hosea. Meanwhile, the Gospel reading completes John on August 2nd; Acts follows until the 30th, with its accompanying Epistle readings of Hebrews, James, Peter, John, and Jude. On the last day of the month, the third cycle of the annual gospel begins again with Matthew and Romans 1.

Fairs

As harvest gets underway the fair season continues in full swing. The most popular days for fairs in August are traditional holy days, with Lammas leading on August 1st, with twenty-six. Other popular days are St. Laurence's Day, August 10th (twenty-five), and the fourth Lady Day of the year, the Assumption, August 15th (twenty). On St. Bartholomew's Day, August 24th, there were approximately nineteen principal fairs scheduled, including the famous Bartholomew Fair in Smithfield.

Law terms

The law courts are not in session in August, since Trinity Term ends on July 11th at the very latest, and Michaelmas does not begin until October.

Festive traditions and pastimes

Harvest fairs appear to have continued following the Reformation. The festivity associated with the harvest has left more records in literary than historical sources, though as we have seen Tusser recommends harvest feasting and "good cheare in the hall" (100). "Oh, 'tis the merry time," Nicholas Breton claims, "wherein honest neighbours make good cheere, and God is glorified in his blessings on the earth." According to Breton, that "good cheere" might include crowning "Captaine of the Reapers" with a "Garland of Flowers," as well as music, dancing, and feasting: the "Pipe and the Tabor is now lustily set on worke, and the Lad and the Lasse will have no lead on their heeles: the new Wheat makes the Gossips Cake" (*Fantasticks*, C3v).

August

	1	2	3		4
Day	BCP	Grafton, (Liber)	Identification		Source
1	Lammas	Peter vinc. Lamas	St. Peter's Chains, marking the dissolution of the Apostle's chains in prison. Lammas, festival (Anglo-Saxon in origin) celebrating the harvest		F
2		Steven martyr	St. Stephen, Pope and (by legend) martyr, 3rd c.		F
3		Invent. S. Steph	St. Stephen, proto-martyr, 1st c.		F

(*Continued*)

238 Early modern calendars

Day	1 BCP	2 Grafton, (Liber)	3 Identification	4 Source
4		Justine	?	
5		Oswald	St. Oswald, King of Northumbria and martyr, 7th c.	F
6	Transfigura	Transfiguracion	Feast celebrating the transfiguration of Jesus Christ	
7	The name of Jes.	The feast of Jesu	Feast of the Name of Jesus	
8		Ciriake & Socii	?	
9		Romane martyr	St. Romanus, Roman martyr, 3rd c.	F
10	Laurence.	Laurence martyr	St. Laurence, Roman deacon and martyr, 3rd c.	F
11		Tiburcius martyr	St. Tibertius (usually with St. Susanna), Roman martyr, 3rd c.	F
12		Clare virgin	St. Clare, founder of the Poor Clares, 13th c.	F
13		Hipoliti & So.	St. Hippolytus, Roman priest and martyr, 3rd c.	F
14		Eusebii	St. Eusebius, martyr in Palestine, 3rd c.	B
15		Assump. of our Lady	Feast celebrating the assumption of the Virgin Mary	
16		Rocke	St. Roch, hermit born in Montpellier, 14th c.	F
17		Octa. of Laurence	St. Laurence (see August 10th)	
18		Agapite martyr	St. Agapitus, martyr of Praesneste, dates unknown	F
19		Magnus	St. Magnus, Earl of Orkney and martyr, 12th c.	F
20		Lewes bish.	St. Louis of Toulouse, Franciscian friar and bishop, 13th c. (usually August 19th)	F
21		Barnard	St. Bernard, Cistercian monk and Abbot of Clairvaux, 12th c. (usually August 20th)	F
22		Oct. Assump	See August 15th	F
23		Timothe	St. Timothy, Diocletian martyr, 4th c.	F
24	**Barthol. Apo.**	Barthol. Apostle	St. Bartholomew, Apostle, 1st c.	F
25		Lewes king	St. Louis, King Louis IX of France, 13th c.	F
26		Severine	St. Zephyrinus, Pope, 3rd c.	F
27		Ruffe martyr	St. Rufus of Capua, martyr, date unknown	F
28	Augustine	Justine (Augustine)	? St. Augustine of Hippo, patristic writer and doctor of the Church, 5th c.	F

	1	2	3	4
Day	BCP	Grafton, (Liber)	Identification	Source
29	Behead of Jo	Decola. of S. John	St. John the Baptist, beheading, 1st c.	F
30		Felix and Judact.	St. Felix and St. Adauctus, Roman martyrs, 4th c.	F
31		Cuthburge virgin (Paulini episcopi)	St. Cuthburga, 1st Abbess of Wimborne, 8th c. ?	F

September

Labors and agricultural tasks

> Sow timely thy white wheat, sow Rie in the dust,
>   let seed have their longing, let soile have her lust:
> Let Rie be partaker of Michaelmas spring,
>   to beare out the hardnesse, that winter doth bring.   (Tusser, 32)

Sowing is a standard labor for September in many English calendars; it is also the most extensive and important agricultural task for the month on the early modern English farm. Sowers in calendar imagery usually scatter seeds from a basket or sling, as in the Easby Church wall-painting in Plate 16.2 and the illustration from Buckminster in Figure 3.3.18; in the latter, the sower works (as was typical) alongside another laborer creating furrows with a plow. Sometimes the calendar images for September represent a related task: scaring away birds to prevent them from eating the seeds, a job often given to "mother or boy" who are "armed, with sling or

Figure 3.3.18 September, Thomas Buckminster, *A New Almanacke and Prognostication* (1567), B5r. University of Illinois at Champaign-Urbana, Rare Book and Manuscript Library, 529.5 H484a-1567.

with bow, / to scare away pigeon, the rooke and the crow" (Tusser, 32). The labors for September and October are somewhat interchangeable; sometimes wine making is identified with September and sowing with October, as in the standard medieval scheme (Plate 10). For example, the labor for September is wine-making in Cuningham's 1558 almanac; when the exact same woodcuts are reused for Buckminster's 1567 almanac, however, sowing is moved to September, and wine-making to October.

Michaelmas—the feast of St. Michael the Archangel celebrated on September 29th—is an especially important date for husbandry, as it marks the start and end of annual farm leases. Tusser begins his description of September with recommended strategies for the "new farmer" who is taking over farms and the "old farmer" who is preparing to vacate a site (28). Calendar poetry for September sometimes notes the renewal of leases and perfidy of landlords: "Now Landlordes laugh, and shewe a smyling grace," Gray notes in his 1588 almanac, "And Tenauntes poore, do pynch to spare theyr pence" (A7r).

Many other husbandry tasks were recommended for September in early modern calendars. This is the month for harvesting fruit, though the calendar poetry urges caution against consuming it in excess: "Come you that planted," the personified September tells the farmer in Hawkins' 1627 almanac, "I will satisfie / your expectation with fruites from each tree" (A7r). Hemp should be harvested, then washed in clean water. Now is the time to "[s]et or sowe seedes for your winter herbes," and to "set Artichokes, Roses, Apples, Barberries, Wardens, Cherries, Strawberries, Quicksets, and Gilloflowers" (Alleyn 1606, C3r). "Mast" (acorns) is gathered in September, though that is more frequently the labor of the month for November: in early modern usage, "acorn" referred to all hard fruit from trees (not only oaks). To harvest honey, husbandmen should now smoke the hives. Kindling and rushes can be gathered from brakes to mend thatch and stoke kitchen fires through the Winter. Felled trees might be turned into lumber for use or sale; rams should be gelded, and hogs ringed. Finally, the careful husbandman must watch out for "runabout prowlers" who are especially active around the time of the harvest: "Hew make shift" Tusser derisively names them, the thieves of sheets, firewood, mast, farm equipment, or even food on the wing or hoof: "fat goose and the capon, duck, hen, and the pig" (35).

Zodiac, astronomy, and astrology

The Sun enters the sign of Libra, the scales, in the second week of September; that sign "is of the West, masculine, ayrie and sanguine, and ruleth the loynes, navell, reines, buttockes, and the bladder with Scorpius" (Alleyn 1606, sig. C2r). This date marks the start of Autumn as the Sun crosses the equator on its way to the Tropic of Capricorn in the southern hemisphere. According to Hopton the first of September is a "criticall" day: "if it do not raine then, the rest of Autumne is like to be dry" (Hopton, *Concordancy*, 109). The "cosmicall" rising of Arcturus on the 12th often brings rain, and two days later, "Swallowes leave to bee seene," signaling the end of Summer (Hopton, *Concordancy*, 109). On the 17th the star Lucida Coronae "rises cosmicall," which causes the "windes [to] turne, troubling the seas with winterly wether" (Hopton, *Concordancy*, 109). Another piece of weather lore reported by Hopton claims that the age of the Moon on Michaelmas, September 29th, provides the number of "flouds [that] will happen that Winter" (*Concordancy*, 109). Michaelmas Spring or Michaelmas Summer are terms used in the almanacs to describe the warm weather that often returns in September, before the first frost.

The ages of man

> Lete no man thynke for to gather plenty
> > yf at liiii yere he have none
> Nomore than yf his barne were empty
> > In Septembre whan all the corne is gone.   (*Hore Beatissime*,
> > > 1530, STC 15968, ✠ 6r)

September covers the ages from forty-eight to fifty-four, and as in August, the emphasis is on gathering "plenty" to see a family through both the literal Winter and the individual, metaphorical Winter that is old age. Just as this month "wynes be made, and the fruites of trees be gathered," so does man "gather and kepe as much as shulde be sufficient for him in his olde age" (*Kalender*, A7r). The calendar imagery often provides a cautionary tale of what can happen without such preparations.

Figure 3.3.19 provides a typical example in its image of a tattered vagabond who, having failed to fill his own barn, is chased away by a dog from the full barrels put up by the thrifty, which he perhaps plans to pilfer, like Tusser's "Hew make shift" (35).

Physic

> Now maist thou Phisicke lately take,
> And bleede and bath for thy healths sake:
> Eate Figges and Grapes, and spicery,
> For to refresh thy members dry.   (Neve 1605, B4v)

In September the summerlong prohibition against medical interventions—bathing, purging, bleeding, and taking medicine—is lifted, as the Dog Days release their dangerous grip. As always, however, almanac compilers steer patients towards "the learned" and away from quacks. Diet can now become more varied after the bland, cool food of Summer; "spice you may use with your meate" (Thomas Rudston 1613, A7r). Though readers are

242 *Early modern calendars*

Figure 3.3.19 September, Catholic Church, *Enchiridion, Preclare Ecclesie Sarum* (Paris, 1530, STC 15965), B1v. Photograph by Phebe Jensen, from the collection of the Folger Shakespeare Library, STC 15965.

encouraged to eat the fruit harvested this month, including "Figges and Grapes" (Neve 1605, B4v), since "Raw fruites and new, makes many rue" (Watson 1600, B4v), caution and moderation is encouraged: "Take heed of surfet, naughty fruits forbeare, / if thou intends to live another yeare" (Bretnor 1616, B5r). The illnesses associated with the Sun in Libra are "dimnesse of sight, stopping of the urine, the stone in the reynes, and the collicke," appropriate to the sign's control over the belly, loins, and bladder (Alleyn 1606, C2v).

The Church calendar

Seasons and holy days

September continues the long season of Pentecost, or Sundays after Trinity. The first of two red-letter saint's days, September 21st, commemorates St. Matthew, who was called "from the receipt of custome to be an Apostle and Evangelist" (*BCP*, L7r). The second celebrates St. Michael the Archangel; the collect for that day thanks God for having "ordeyned & consituted the services of all Aungels & men in a wonderful order" (*BCP*, L7v).

Four medieval saints are commemorated with black-letter holy days for September: St. Giles, the seventh-century hermit venerated in Provence, St. Lambert, Bishop of Maastricht, the Antioch martyr Cyprian (but not his traditional companion, St. Justine), and the theologian St. Jerome. In addition, the Nativity of Mary (fourth of the medieval Marian holidays) is recognized on September 8th, and the Exaltation of Holy Cross on September 14th. The latter recalls the discovery of the cross in Jerusalem by St. Helena, the mother of Constantine (whose feast day is August 18th).

Lectionary

The Gospel and Epistle readings (now in their third cycle for the year) begin with 2 Matthew and 2 Romans on September 1st. The Book of Mark commences on September 28th, and the Epistle reading progresses to First Corinthians on September 16th. In September, the Old Testament readings range through some of the shorter and lesser known books: Hosea, Joel, Amos, Obadiah, Jonah, Micah, Nahum, Habakkuk, Zephaniah, Haggai, Zechariah, Toby, and Malachi.

Fairs

As the harvest season begins to wind down in September, fair activity continues robustly: there are approximately 109 principal fairs in the fixed calendar for this month. These cluster, predictably, on the month's holy days, with about thirty on St. Michael's Day (the 29th), twenty-three on St. Matthew's Day, and fourteen on the feast of the Holy Cross

244 Early modern calendars

(September 14th). The other big day for fairs, with approximately thirty, is September 7th, the eve of the feast of the Nativity of Mary.

Law terms

The law courts are never in session in September, since Trinity Term ends in July (at the latest) and Michaelmas begins in October. However, one of the most important days for the legal calendar is Michaelmas itself, September 29th, the feast of St. Michael the Archangel. As Cressy notes, Michaelmas was "most important of the annual, half-yearly or quarterly days for payments of rents and dues," including the farm leases discussed above. Michaelmas was also the start of the annual fiscal year for many parishes, and the date on which local elections were held.[23]

Festive traditions and pastimes

Aside from the intermittent harvest festivals that might continue in September (see August, above), September is not a month particularly known for festive cheer or traditional pastimes.

September

	1	2	3	4
Day	BCP	*Grafton*, (*Liber*)	*Identification*	Source
1	Gyles	Egidii	St. Giles (Egidio), hermit and monk in Provence, 7th c.	F
2		Anthoni	St. Antonius, martyr, 2nd c.	B
3		Gregory	St. Gregory the Great, Pope, 6th-7th c.	F
4		Trans. of S. Cutbert	Cuthbert, monk and Bishop of Lindisfarne, 7th c.	F
5	Dog days end	Bertin	St. Bertin, Abbot of Sithiu, 7th c.	F
6		Eugenius	?	
7		Gorgon	St. Gorgonius, Roman Martyr (usually September 9th), dates unknown	F
8	Nati. of Mary	Nativitie of our Lady	Virgin Mary, Nativity	
9		Silvius	?	
10		Protho and Jasincti (September 11th in *Liber*)	St. Protus and St. Hyacinth, Roman martyrs, dates unknown	F
11		Marcian	?	
12		Maurily	?	
13		Amancie	Possibly St. Amatus of Sion (Switzerland), bishop, 7th c.	B

	1	2	3	4
Day	BCP	Grafton, (Liber)	Identification	Source
14	Holy crosse.	Exalt. crucis	Exaltation of the Holy Cross	
15		Oct. of Mary	Octave of September 8th, Nativity of the Virgin Mary	
16		Edith	St. Edith, Virgin from Wilton, Kent, 10th c.	F
17	Lambert	Lambert	St. Lambert, Bishop of Maastricht, patron of Liege, 8th c.	F
18		Victor (& Coronae)	Possibly St. Victor and St. Corona, married couple martyred in Syria, 2nd c. (usually May 14th)	B
19		Januarii martyr	St. Januarius, Bishop of Benevento and martyr, 4th c.	F
20		Eustacius	St. Eustace, Roman martyr, dates unknown	F
21	St. Mathewe	Mathew apost.	St. Matthew, Apostle, 1st c.	F
22		Mauris (& Sociorii)	St. Maurice and companions, martyrs, 3rd c. ?	F
23		Tecle virgin	St. Tecla of England, Benedictine nun and abbess, 8th c.	F
24		Andoche martyr	St. Andochius, priest of Smyrna, 2nd c.	B
25		Firmini martyr	St. Firmin, bishop and martyr in Amiens, 4th c.	F
26	Ciprian	Ciprian and Justine	St. Cyprian and St. Justina, martyrs of Antioch, 3rd-4th c.	F
27		Cosine and Damian	St. Cosmas and St. Damian, martyrs in Cyrrhus, dates unknown	F
28		Exupere	?	
29	St. Michael	Michael Archangel	St. Michael, Archangel	F
30	Hierom	Jerome	St. Jerome, monk and theologian from Dalmatia, 5th c.	F

October

Labors and agricultural tasks

> Good Husbands now, in sowing busie are,
>   whilst like the Devill some are sowing Tare:
> Some seeke to sow sedition all about,
>   but God soone roots such Caterpillers out.   (Hopton 1613, B6v)

246 *Early modern calendars*

Wine-making is the traditional image for October in the early modern English printed calendars, with the alternative—sowing—more often attached to September. Vines were not significantly cultivated in early modern England, though the physic directives encouraged wine-drinking this month after the abstemiousness of Summer and early Autumn. Perhaps because of the absence of wineries in England, the calendar poetry stresses other agricultural tasks. Hopton's calendar poem for his October 1613 almanac, like many others, discusses sowing, using that task as a metaphorical springboard for a religious warning about remaining spiritually vigilant.

In addition to sowing, October was a time to gather acorns and hastings, to plant some trees—"Acorns, Filberts, Smal nuts, and Walnuts"—and to remove or prune others—"Apples, Peares, Quinces, and Wardens, &c" (Alleyn 1606, C3v). Before the Autumn rains set in, the husbandman was also advised by Tusser to gather firewood, stack and store wheat and rye straw, make malt, and "Brew now to last, / till winter be past" (37). The fruit harvested in September might be processed in October, into either perry (a wine made from pears), cider, or verjuice. Anticipating the slaughter of livestock in December, agricultural guides provide extensive advice about the care of cattle, "hog, sow, or...bore": how to fatten them properly, cull sick animals from a herd, and treat common diseases (Tusser, 42).

Zodiac, astronomy, and astrology

On about October 12th, the Sun enters the sign of Scorpio, the scorpion (seen in the upper right corner of Figures 3.3.20 and 3.3.21). This Zodiac sign is "of the North, feminine, waterie, and flegmatique, governing the

Figure 3.3.20 October, William Prid, *The Glasse of Vaine-Glorie* (1600), A8v. Photograph by Phebe Jensen, from the collection of the Folger Shakespeare Library, STC 931.

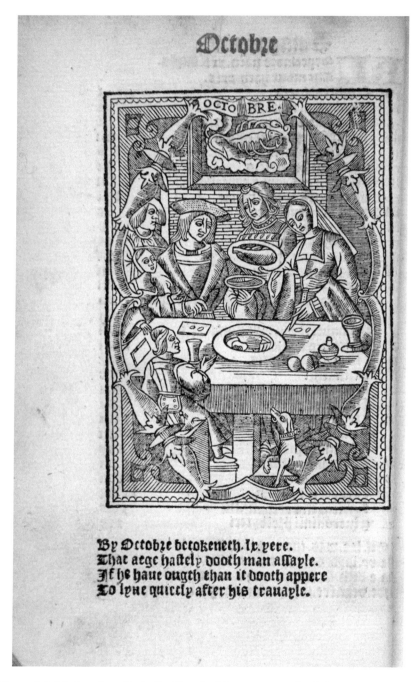

Figure 3.3.21 October, Catholic Church, *This Prymer of Salisbury Use* (Rouen, 1556, STC 16076), B3v. Lambeth Palace Library, ZZ1556.04

secrete members, the fundament and the bladder, with Libra" (Alleyn 1606, C3r). After the 15th, when "the Dragons Taile setteth vespertine," one "must expect no more warmnesse," according to Hopton (*Concordancy*, 110). Another important date for weather prediction this month is October 26th, when "the left foot of Orion setteth with the 12th degree of Scorpio, causing often great rain" (Hopton, *Concordancy*, 110).

The ages of man

>By October betokeneth lx yere.
>That aege hastely dooth man assayle.
>Yf he have ought / than it dooth appere.
>To lyve quyetly after his travayle.   (*Hore Beatissime* 1530, STC 15968, ✠6v)

The October images in the ages of man scheme, representing the years sixty to sixty-six, usually show a husbandman who has successfully gathered in the harvest of his life in preparation for old age—providing a contrast to the tattered prodigals of September (Figure 3.3.19).

Figure 3.3.21 shows a characteristic scene of a man dining with his family, attended by a servant. For this month the *Kalender* reveals its Catholic orientation, suggesting that in this phase of life, man must "do penaunce and good workes," so that after his death "he may gather and have [the] spiritual profyte" that is metaphorically associated with the gathering of corn and "other maner fruytes" in the agricultural year (A7v).

Physic

>Go hunt, drinke Wine thats olde, and good:
>Use exercise for health:
>Now mayst thou take good stoore of food
>Which hath good store of wealth.   (Frende 1593, B5v)

By October, all of the strictures against excessive eating, drinking, and sleeping give way. As the cold weather comes on, "hote meates and drinkes, will doe the good"; it is important to dress warmly and stay dry to avoid "agues... / Which breed infection in the bloud" (Johnson 1613, A7v). The calendar poetry for October stresses the advantages held by the wealthy as Winter comes on, echoing the theme of the standard ages of man motif for the month. Exercise is recommended, usually the higher-status sports of "hawking and hunting" (Browne 1620, B5v) for those who can afford such pastimes; "Good sport abroad for such as keepen hounds," Bretnor notes in 1615, "but best at home for him yt hath no grounds" (B6r). From a medical point of view, the cold month of October is good for conspicuous consumption and rest: "Now maist thou eate and drinke and sleepe, / That swimmest in thy wealth" (Dauncy 1614, A7v).

The Church calendar

Seasons and holy days

The "phisition" evangelist St. Luke, "whose praise is in ye gospell, to be a phisition of the soul," is commemorated in the Book of Common Prayer for October 18th (*BCP*, L8r). The second holy day for the month, October 28th, celebrates the apostles St. Simon and St. Jude; the collect for those saints emphasizes the establishment of modern congregations "upon the foundacion of the Apostles & Prophets," with "Jesu Christ himselfe being the head cornerstone" (*BCP*, L9r).

St. Etheldreda, an Anglo-Saxon queen (October 17th), St. Crispin and Crispinian, the patron saint of shoemakers (October 24th), and St. Faith, the third-century virgin martyr from Gaul (October 6th), are all given black-letter commemorations in the October Book of Common Prayer, along with a sixteenth-century Bishop of Reims (St. Remigius on October 1st) and St. Denys or Dennis, the patron saint of Paris (October 9th). In addition, October 13th marks the translation of St. Edward, St. Edward the Confessor.

Lectionary

The Gospel and Epistle readings for October repeat the pattern for June and July, beginning with Mark and First Corinthians, and progressing to Luke and Colossians. Old Testament readings include Judith, The Book of Wisdom, and Ecclesiastes.

Fairs

There are approximately ninety-one principal fairs in October, a dozen or so less than September. The most popular days for fairs this month are the feasts of St. Luke on the 18th, the feast of the actress and penitent St. Pelagi on the 8th, and the feast of Sts. Simon and Jude on the 28th, each with approximately thirteen or fourteen.

Law terms

Though named for Michaelmas (September 29th), Michaelmas term actually begins on the 9th or 10th of October. The longest law term of the year, it continues until the 28th or 29th of November.

Festive traditions and pastimes

As Cressy has noted, the religious celebrations once associated with All Hallow's Eve on October 31st were in some cases transformed into traditions of local "civic or parochial ceremonies," such as dinners or (at St.

250 *Early modern calendars*

Andrew by the Wardrobe in London) gifts of firewood to the poor.[24] There may have been some residual bell-ringing or candle-lighting in more conservative areas left over from medieval traditions, though those activities were certainly on the wane in the Elizabethan period. Otherwise, October, like its fellow Autumn months, is not known for communal festivity, outside of the intermittent harvest festivals which have left little trace on the historical record.

October

	1	2	3	4
Day	BCP	*Grafton* (Liber)	*Identification*	Source
1	Remige	Remigii bishop (& Bauonis)	St. Remigius, Bishop of Reims, 5th-6th c. (St. Bavo, hermit from Brabant, 7th c.)	F
2		Leodegarii bishops	St. Leger, Bishop of Autun and martyr, 7th c.	F
3		Candidi martir	St. Candidus, Roman martyr, dates unknown	B
4		Fraunces confessor	St. Francis of Assisi, founder of the Franciscan Order, 13th c.	F
5		Apolinarie	St. Apollinaris of Valence, Bishop of Valence, France, 6th c.	B
6	Fayth	Faythe	St. Faith, virgin martyr in Gaul, 3rd c.	F
7		Marci & Marcil.	Possibly St. Mark and St. Marcellian, Roman martyrs, 3rd c. (usually June 18th)	B,
8		Pelagi	St. Pelagia, actress of Antioch and penitent, 5th c.	F
9	Dennis	Dionice	St. Denys, patron saint of France and Bishop of Paris, 3rd c.	B
10		Gerion and Victor	St. Gereon (and companions), martyrs of Cologne, 4th c.	B
11		Nicasius	St. Nicasius, Bishop of Rouen, 3rd c.	B
12		Wilfride virgin	St. Wilfrid, bishop from Northumbria, 8th c.	F
13	Edwarde	Transf. of Edward	St. Edward the Confessor, King of England and martyr, 11th c.	B
14		Calixt	St. Callistus, Pope and martyr, 2nd c.	F
15		Wolfran	St. Wulfram, Archbishop of Sens, 7th c.	F
16		Michaelis in mente	St. Michael, Archangel (see September 29th)	F
17	Etheldrede	Transf. of Etheld	St. Etheldreda, queen and Abbess of Ely, 7th c. (see June 23rd)	F

	1	2	3	4
Day	BCP	*Grafton* (Liber)	*Identification*	Source
18	**Luke**	Luke Evangelist	St. Luke, Evangelist, 1st c.	F
19		Phrideswide virgin	St. Frideswide, virgin patron of Oxford, 8th c.	F
20		Austrebert virgin	Possibly St. Austreberta, French abbess, 8th c. (also February 10th)	B
21		xi M. virgins	The 11,000 Virgins, martyrs and companions of St. Ursula, 4th c. (see Oct. 26th)	F
22		Mary Salome	St. Mary Salome, mother of St. James and St. John the Evangelist, 1st c.	B
23		Maglorie (Oct. 24th in *Liber*) (Romani episcopi)	St. Maglorius, Irish abbot, 6th c. (St. Romanus, Bishop of Rouen, 7th c.)	F
24	Crispine	Crispin & Crispini (Oct. 25th in *Liber*)	St. Crispin and Crispinian, martyrs and patrons of shoemakers, 3rd c.	F
25		Trans. of John Be.	St. John of Beverley, Bishop of York, 8th c. (see May 7th)	F
26		Ursula (Euaristae episco. Ro.)	St. Ursula, virgin martyr, 4th c. (also October 21st) (St. Evaristus, Pope, 1st-2nd c.)	B
27		Florence	St. Florentius of Trechateaux, martyr in France, 3rd c.	B
28	**Simon & Jude**	Simon and Jude	St. Simon and St. Jude, Apostles, 1st c.	F
29		Narcissus bishop	St. Narcissus of Jerusalem, bishop from Greece, 2nd-3rd c.	B
30		Germane bishop (and Capuiai)	St. Germanus of Capua, bishop in Italy, 6th c. (?)	B
31		Quintine	St. Quentin, martyr, dates unknown	F

November

Labors and agricultural tasks

> This moneth men seeke to fatt ther swyne wt foode
> they strike downe mast and gettith woode to burne
> providing so to avoyd rough winters moode
> And feede ther folke till Spring tyde do returne.[25]

Knocking down acorns from trees to fatten livestock (and particularly hogs) is usually the labor for the month for November, as in the misericord

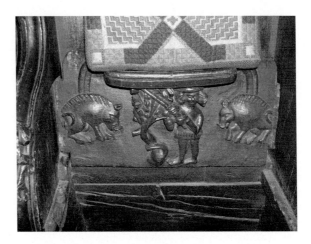

Figure 3.3.22 November, Misericord, Great Malvern Priory, fifteenth century. ©www.misericords.co.uk 2017.

Figure 3.3.23 November, William Cuningham, *A Newe Almanacke and Prognostication* (1558), B5r. University of Illinois at Champaign-Urbana, Rare Book and Manuscript Library, 529.5 H484a.

from Great Malvern Priory in Figure 3.3.22. A common alternate labor, chopping down trees (Figure 3.3.23), also appears in the calendar poetry.

November is the best month to "Fell downe all your Timber at wane of the Moone" and to "Cut ashes to furnish your Harrow and Plough" (Frende 1622, A8r). Otherwise, the agricultural activities that began in the previous Autumn months continue as the fruits of the harvest are processed and the farm made ready for Winter. Primary among these is threshing. "Let the Thresher take his flayle," writes Nicholas Breton, "and the ship no more sayle" (D1r), due to the increasingly inclement weather. Tusser and others refine that general advice, suggesting that strategic threshing will allow the corn to last: some corn should be threshed immediately to make malt, some winnowed and used for seed, but it's mostly best to thresh "as need shall require" over the course of the Winter (44). Cows, Tusser insists, prefer their corn "fresh threshed for stover" or cattle feed; farmers should "forbeare" from threshing some of the corn "till Candlemas comming, for sparing of hay," and also wait to thresh wheat to be sold to the baker, which should remain "unthrheshed till March, in the sheafe let it lie" (44).

Tending fruit trees continues from September, as November is a good time "to set Crabbe-tree stockes, to remove Trees, as in the last moneth in the increasing of the Moone," and to "uncover the rootes of your Apple-trees, and so let them rest till March" (Hopton, *Concordancy*, 111). "Hallontide" is also the time to sow "Greene peason or hastings," whereas the farmer should hold off on sowing "Gray peason or runcivals" for three months, until Candlemas in February (Tusser, 45). Hallowtide is also when "slaughter time entereth in," though the actual killing of the animals is usually represented in December. At "Martalmas," the careful husbandman should "hang up a beefe," so that over the Winter, "thy folke shall looke cheerely, when others looke thin" (Tusser, 44–45). Other miscellaneous tasks include ploughing headland or other small parcels of land, trenching the kitchen garden, stabling horses, and cleaning the privy and the chimney. As in September, Tusser warns in November about theft: the "pilfering thresher" who "will carrie home corne," or the wandering thief who "in his bottle of leather so great / will carrie home daily, both barly and wheat" (46).

Zodiac, astronomy, and astrology

The Zodiac sign for November is Sagittarius, the archer visible in Figure 3.3.23, who is "of the East, masculine, fierie and chollericke, governing the thighs and hyps" (Alleyn 1606, C3v). On November 5th the Dog Star, Sirius, sets as the Sun rises, which predicts "southernly wether" (Hopton, *Concordancy*, 110). Frost and rain are created partly by the cosmical setting of the star Hyades on the 10th, and the Pleiades two days later: "if then the heaven bee cloudy, it denunciates a wet Winter: if dry, a sharpe Winter" (Hopton, *Concordancy*, 110–111).

The ages of man

> Whan man is at lxvi yere olde.
> Whiche lykened is to bareyne Novembre.
> He wereth unweldy / sekely / and colde.
> Than his soule helth is tyme to remembre.　　　*(Thys Prymer*, 1538,
> 　　　　　　　　　　　　　　　　　　　　　　　　STC 16008.3, 12v)

The age represented by "barayne Novembre," from sixty-six to seventy two, is a period of physical decline but spiritual regeneration. The images in the primers for this month sometimes show a rich man in a melancholic

254   Early modern calendars

pose, while nearby a doctor examines his urine. Similarly, in a John Securis almanac for 1562 that appears to reuse French woodcuts—a rare example of the use of the ages of man motif in an annual almanac for the English market—the everyman figure prays before a life-size crucifix (C3r).

Physic

> Olde wines and sweete, are thought most meete,
>   to breede good blood, and warme thee,
> From lust abstaine, all bathes refraine,
>   sweete spice now little harme thee.   (Watson 1600, B6v)

The illnesses prevalent with the Sun in Sagittarius are "hote Feavers, Opthalmia, bleared eyes, and falls from hie places, and from horses, & c." (Alleyn 1606, C3v). Hot meats, hot drinks (including wine) to "nourish the blood" (Alleyn 1606, C4r), "Spicery" in one's "cates" (John Rudston 1615, A8r), and warm clothing are recommended as the weather cools. A surprising number of almanacs are careful to recommend the (surely obvious) advantage of going "dry shod" in order to fend off the "rewme and pose," or head colds (Alleyn 1606, C4r). The descriptions of climate and medical dangers for the month stress the unremitting rain, cold winds, and chill "Ayre": "In summe," Nicholas Breton writes, "with a conceit of the chilling cold of it…I hold it the discomfort of Nature, and Reasons patience" (*Fantastickes*, D1r-v). Because of these meteorological conditions, "November breeds rhumes that troubles the head" (Mathew 1612, A8r). It is a transitional month when it comes to physic, the last safe month in which to take medicine until March, "except necessitie doe compell" (Alleyn 1606, C4r). The calendar poetry also cautions against phlebotomy and baths, though they are not entirely forbidden, and the always (it seems) perilous dangers of "lust" are especially grave this month (Watson 1600, B7v).

The church calendar

Seasons and holy days

Advent Sunday is the fourth Sunday before Christmas; it falls on November 27th–December 3rd, depending on the day of the week of Christmas each year. The Advent season ends on Christmas Day. Although the Book of Common Prayer is primarily structured around the Julian Calendar—the cycle of readings begins each January 1st—the schedule of Sunday and Holy Day collects and readings begins with Advent, which is the official start of the liturgical year.

   The two red-letter holy days for November fall on the first and last days of the month. For November 1st, All Saint's Day, the collect avoids any whisper of this holy day's medieval importance by de-emphasizing prayers for the dead or adoration of the saints, acknowledging instead the saints as models that Christians should "folowe... in al vertues, and godly living" (*BCP*, L9v). November 30th, St. Andrew's Day, often (though not always) falls within the season of Advent, and sometimes on Advent Sunday itself; that Apostle is especially notable because he "redeley obeied the calling of thy sonne Jesus Christ, & followed him without delay" (*BCP*, K6r).

Nine saints are commemorated in the Book of Common Prayer for this month; two are virgin martyrs: the famous St. Katherine who was tortured on a wheel, on November 25th, and the lesser known Roman martyr St. Cecilia on November 22nd. Four are bishops: St. Martin (November 11th) and St. Brice (November 13th), both of Tours, St. Hugh of Lincoln (November 17th), and St. Malo or Machute, possibly a Welsh bishop active in Brittany (November 15th). The hermit St. Leonard was commemorated on November 6th, and the Pope St. Clement on the 23rd. Finally, the translation of the popular St. Edward, Anglo-Saxon King and Martyr, was noted on November 20th.

Lectionary

November's Gospel readings are in Luke and John, with the Epistle repeating the third cycle (last read in July) from Colossians through Hebrews. The Old Testament readings come from Ecclesiastes, Barnabus, and Isaiah.

Fairs

The number of principal fairs in November, around ninety, roughly equals that for October, though in this month, they are spread widely through the calendar. The most popular days include St. Andrew's Day, November 30th, with approximately twenty-one, St. Leonard's Day, November 6th, with thirteen, St. Martin's Day, November 11th, with ten; and St. Clement's Day, November 23rd, with nine.

Law terms

November is the month of Michaelmas Term, which begins on the 9th or 10th of October, and continues until the 28th or 29th of November.

Festive traditions and pastimes

November 1st, All Saint's or All Hallow's, was part of a three-day Hallowtide season that had historically been a Christian feast celebrating the dead. That commemoration included the traditions for All Hallow's Eve on October 30th (described above, in October), All Saint's itself, and All Soul's, on November 2nd. In the late middle ages, a rich set of traditional activities for this period developed, which included dressing in mourning attire, marking All Soul's Day with bonfires and food (cakes and wine), and most importantly, ringing the church bells all night on

256 *Early modern calendars*

All Saint's Night. These activities were greatly curtailed at the Reformation in light of the Protestant denial of both purgatory and the notion that the activities of the living could succor the souls of the dead.[26]

November is also host to two English political holidays: November 17th, Accession Day, commemorating Elizabeth's accession to the throne in 1558, and after 1605, November 5th, known in the period as Gunpowder Day (and later as Guy Fawkes), marking the deliverance of King James and other members of his government from the Gunpowder conspiracy. Both came to be traditionally marked with bonfires.

November

	1	2	3	4
Day	BCP	*Grafton* (Liber)	Identification	Source
1	**All Saintes**	All Saincts	All Saints' Day or All Hallow's, commemorating all Christian saints	
2		All Soules	All Souls' Day, remembering the dead	
3		Wenefride virgin	St. Winifred, Welsh virgin, 7th c.	F
4		Amancius (& Vitalis)	St. Amantius, patron saint of Tiphernum near Perugia, 6th c.	B
5		Lete pres.	St. Laetus, priest in the Diocese of Orleans, 6th c.	B, C
6	Leonarde	Leonarde	St Leonard, hermit, 6th c.	B
7		Wilfride arche.	St. Willibrord of Yorkshire, Archbishop of Utrecht, 8th c.	F
8		Quatuor corona	Four Crowned Martyrs, martyrs in Rome, 4th c.	F
9		Theodore martir	St. Theodore, Roman soldier and martyr, 4th c.	B
10		Martin bishop of R.	Possibly St. Martin I, Pope, 7th c. (usually November 12th)	C
11	St. Martin	Martin bishop	St. Martin of Tours, monk and bishop, 4th c.	F
12		Paternie	St. Paternus, monk in Sens, dates unknown	B
13	Bryce	Brice	St. Brice, Bishop of Tours, 5th c.	F
14		Trans. of Erkin	St. Erkenwald, Bishop of London, 7th c.	F
15	Machute	Machute	St. Malo, bishop in Brittany, 7th c.	F
16		Edmond arche.	St. Edmund of Abingdon, Archbishop of Canterbury, 13th c.	F
17	Hugh	Init. Reg. Elizabeth (Hugonis episcopi)	Coronation of Queen Elizabeth 1. (St. Hugh of Lincoln, Carthusian monk and bishop, 13th c.)	F F

The twelve months 257

Day	1 BCP	2 Grafton (Liber)	3 Identification	4 Source
18		Oct. s. Martin.	See November 11th	
19		Sainct Elizabeth	St. Elizabeth of Hungary, queen, 13th c.	F
20	Edmund king	Edmund king	St. Edmund, King of East Anglia and martyr, 9th c.	F
21		Presenta. of Mary	Commemorating the presentation of the Virgin Mary in the Temple	
22	Cycelie	Cecili virgin	St. Cecilia, Roman martyr, 3rd c.	F
23	Clement	Clement	St. Clement, Pope and martyr, 1st c.	F
24		Grisogoni martir	St. Chrysogonus, martyr of Aquileia, 4th c.	F
25	Katherine	Katherine virgin	St. Catherine of Alexandria, 4th c.	F
26		Lini	?	
27		Agricoli (& Vitalis)	St. Agricola, martyr in Bologna with St. Vitalis, 3rd c.	F
28		Rufi	St. Rufus (and companions), Roman martyrs under Diocletian, 3rd c.	F
29		Saturne	St. Sernin, Bishop of Toulouse and martyr, 3rd c.	F
30	**Andrew Apo.**	Andrew Apost.	St. Andrew, Apostle, 1st c.	F

December

Figure 3.3.24 December, Detail, Four Seasons Tapestries, Hatfield House, Hatfield, Hertfordshire. Courtesy of the Marquess of Salisbury.

258 *Early modern calendars*

Labors and agricultural tasks

> Provide (good husbands) Brawne and Souse,
> Fat Beefe and Mutton for the house:
> With other Cates for Christmas cheere,
> Because it comes but once a yeere.   (Vaux 1622, A8v)

The primary labor for the month of December in both the late medieval and early modern English calendars is slaughtering livestock—usually hogs, sometimes cattle—which had been carefully fattened up with mast through September, October, and November. Usually, as in this detail from the Winter tapestry from Hatfield House (Figure 3.3.23) and the December thumbnail from Prid's calendar (Figure 3.3.25), a woman assists the male butcher by catching blood in a vessel.

December was a relatively slow month on the early modern farm, a time (according to Tusser) for small jobs such as making kindling with "beetle and wedge," sharpening tools with grindstones, feeding the bees, and watching out for cattle to make sure none become "myriad" (48). Care must be taken that the smaller calves get enough to eat; the fear is that they would be "lurched," or deprived of food by wily older animals (Tusser, 49). St. Steven's Day on December 28th was the traditional day to "let blood" from one's horse (Tusser, 50). Other tasks include cutting down timber, digging out the garden, and caring for fruit trees.

The slaughtering of animals represented in the labor for December was often directly tied to the true obsession in December calendars: the Christmas season. Even Tusser, who for the other eleven months of the year

Figure 3.3.25 December, William Prid, *The Glasse of Vaine-Glorie* (1600), A9v. Photograph by Phebe Jensen, from the collection of the Folger Shakespeare Library, STC 931.

harps incessantly on thrift, now emphasizes the importance of giving freely in this season. Christmas is the time to "Leave husbandry sleeping," for "What ever is sent thee by labour and paine, / a time there is lent thee, to rend[e]r it againe" (51). The goal of housekeeping and the riches attained by thrift is to "use and bestow it, as Christ doth us bid" through hospitality to "The neighbor, the stranger, and all that have need" (Tusser, 53). The main activity at Christmas, then, is to "banket, the rich with the poor" (53), dispensing all the plenty that had been so scrupulously gathered all year:

> Good bread and good drinke, a good fire in the hall,
>   brawne, pudding, and souse, & good mustard withall:
> Beefe, mutton, and porke, shread pies of the best,
>   pig, veale, goose, and capon, and turkey well drest,
> Cheese, apples, and nuts, iolly carols to heere,
>   As then in the countrye is counted good cheere.
> What cost to good husband is any of this?
>   Good household provision onely it is.   (Tusser, 55)

Tusser's emphasis on feasting "thy needy poore neighbour" (54) at Christmas is reiterated in the almanac calendar poetry. "You that are rich," Balles encourages his readers in a 1631 almanac, "with love the poore remember / Be open-hearted in this cold December, / Shew forth your faith by workes of charity, / And you shall live with Christ eternally" (A8v). Frende notes that when "cold December is come in, / and poore mans back is cloathed thin," it is the duty of the more fortunate to "Feed and cloath him, then as you may / for God threefold will it repay" (1616, A8v).

Zodiac, astronomy, and astrology

Capricorn, the goat, the Zodiac sign for December, is a sign "of the South, feminine, earthy, and melancholique"; it rules the knees (Alleyn 1606, C4r). The mythical halcyon days, a period of calm in the depth of Winter, are said (by Hopton, citing Cardanus and Stadius) to occur in the first half of December, near the Winter Solstice (approximately December 12th), though they are also sometimes calculated to begin a week or so earlier. The "South-windes" supposedly blow on the 26th, the result of "the faire starre Arcturus" setting "vespertine." Hopton also recounts the lore that "if Christmas day come in the new Moone, it is a token of a good yeare, and so much the better, by how much it is nearer the new Moone: the contrary happeneth in the decrease" (*Concordancy*, 111).

The ages of man

> The yere by Decembre taketh his ende
> And so dooth man at threscore and twelve.

260 *Early modern calendars*

>Nature with aege will hym on message sende
>The tyme is come that he must go hyms selve.   (*This Prymer* 1556,
>STC 16076, B5v)

December in the ages of man scheme inevitably shows a deathbed scene, often with a priest, a grieving wife, and children or other bystanders, and medical paraphernalia such as urine glasses (Figure 3.3.26).

The Catholic primer images often include candles, crosses, and ointment jars for extreme unction. By the age of seventy-two a man's "heare" is "whyte and gray, and his body croked & feble, & then he leseth his perfyte understanding" (*Kalender*, A7v). If he lives any longer than this, it is a reflection of "his good gydynge and dyetynge in his youth" (A8r).

Physic

>Warm clothes and fire prepare you must
> Yet use thou not excesse in lust:
>Good Christmas keepe, such pastime take,
> As may in Christ thee mery make.   (Hopton 1606, A8v)

Medical problems common under Capricorn are "ache in the knees, deafnesse, losse of speech and sight, itch, scabbes, and foulenesse of the skinne"

Figure 3.3.26 December, Catholic Church, *Enchiridion, preclare ecclesie Sarum* (Paris, 1530, STC 15965), B4v. Photograph by Phebe Jensen, from the collection of the Folger Shakespeare Library, STC 15965.

(Alleyn 1606, C4r). On the bright side, the enforced leisure, dining, and good company that characterize the long twelve days of feasting and conviviality at Christmas accord with the recommendation for physic: "In this month be quiet, and use good diet, let them be thy Phisitions. Let thy kitchin be thine Apothecarie, let warme clothing be thy nurse, merry company thy keepers, and good hospitalitie thine exercise" (Alleyn 1606, C4v). All warm things are good: "Hot meat, sweet wine, & fire of fragrant wood, / the spirits raise, and help to chear the blood" (Bretnor 1615, B8r). "December loves warme Potions," as Frende's 1593 almanac notes, as well as good shoes against the damp, and warm clothes (B7v). Medicine is still to be avoided, and other interventions discouraged, though not with the violence of the Summer prohibitions against phlebotomy and baths.

The church calendar

Seasons and holy days

Advent begins on Advent Sunday, the fourth Sunday before Christmas, which can be as early as November 27th or as late as December 4th; that season ends on Christmas Day. The Book of Common Prayer and other calendars note December 16th as the day in which the seven or eight "O Sapientia" antiphons were introduced into the liturgy, continuing a medieval tradition though with Protestant revisions. The first red-letter holy day for the month is the feast of St. Thomas (December 21st), remembered for being "doubtful in thy sonnes resurrection," a lesson for the faithful to "without al doubt...beleve in thy son Jesus Christ, that our faith in thy sighte never be reproved" (*BCP*, K6v).

Christmas Day ushers in four consecutive red-letter holy days. On the 25th, thanksgiving is offered to God for having "given us thy only begotten sonne to take our nature upon him, and this daye to be borne of a pure virgin" (B7v). On the 26th, the martyr St. Stephen is said to teach by example how "to learne to love our enemies," as he himself "praied for his persecutors to thee" (C1v). St. John, the Apostle and Evangelist, is noted on the 27th for his "doctrine" which helped "cast thy bryghte beames of light upon thy church" (C2r). On the 28th, the slaughter of the "Innocentes" by Herod is presented as a model for the faithful to "mortifie and kill all vices in us" (C2v).

Three saints are commemorated with black-letter notice in the Book of Common Prayer for December. The first is St. Nicholas, the sixth-century bishop in Gaul. The second, St. Lucy, was a Roman Virgin, whose feast day on December 13th is sometimes the shortest day of the year, hence amplifying the symbolism of the candles associated with her commemoration. The third is St. Silvester, a fourth-century Pope. December also includes the last Lady Day of the year, the Conception, given black-letter observance on December 8th.

The veneration of St. Thomas à Becket, the Archbishop murdered in Canterbury Cathedral, was outlawed by proclamation in 1538, as the many annotations in late medieval primers and books of hours striking out his name attest. Although banished from the Book of Common Prayer, St. Thomas is still noted on the day of his martyrdom (December 29th) in most early modern almanac calendars.

Lectionary

In December, the Gospel reading begins in Acts 2, and by the end of the month, the third and final cycle of Gospel readings for the year is completed. The Epistle readings start on December 1st with Hebrews 7, continuing through James, Peter, and John. The readings in the Old Testament for this month are entirely in Isaiah.

Fairs

As would be expected, December is a thin month for fairs, with a total of only approximately twenty-five. About eight of these are on St. Nicholas' Day, December 6th, and nine are on the final Lady Day of the year, December 8th, celebrating the Conception. The rest are scattered throughout the calendar, with the three for December 29th, the feast of St. Thomas à Becket, perhaps the vestige of the more extensive commemorations of this saint in late medieval England.

Law terms

The law courts are not in session in December, as the month falls in the gap between Michaelmas and Hilary terms.

Festive traditions and pastimes

The elaborate religious ceremonies of Christmas in late medieval England were curtailed at the Reformation, but social, cultural, and above all gastronomical traditions associated with the season continued. Christmas Eve was a fast that prepared for the twelve days of excessive eating and drinking that followed, during which almost no one was expected to work. Though more extreme Protestant reformers objected to Christmas as a pagan celebration without clear biblical justification, and Christmas was outlawed in Scotland in the sixteenth century, in New England in the seventeenth century, and briefly in England itself during the Commonwealth years, the majority of English men and women (including the godly) kept Christmas in early modern England.[27]

The major cultural expectation for the twelve days was generosity and hospitality, as is reflected in calendar poetry stressing the importance of feeding underlings and the poor. The offered hospitality varied depending on social rank. At the top of the social world, royal and noble households hosted sumptuous feasts, and gentry hosted neighbors, but even householders with modest means were expected to provide food and entertainment. Traditional Christmas dishes included plum pudding (beef broth with currants, raisins, and plums), minced pie (meat and fruit baked in a pastry coffin), roast meats (especially beef and brawn), and hot spiced ale. But other dishes abound. "[T]he Beasts, Fowle, and Fish, come to a generall execution," as Breton colorfully explains, and there might also be "stolne Venison," "a fat Coney," and "small Birdes" such as woodcocks on the table (*Fantastickes*, D2r). Music was often part of the entertainment, with hired musicians in wealthier households and carols sung in more modest venues; the "youth must dance and sing," while "the aged sit by the fire" (*Fantastickes*, D1v). Other pastimes and traditions included the hobbyhorse, the wassail bowl, cards and dice, and mumming or wearing masks, though as Hutton has shown, the idea that mumming plays were part of Christmas celebration in medieval and early modern England is an invention of nineteenth-century folklorists. The twelve days of Christmas were indeed a traditional time for pageants, shows, and plays, especially on Twelfth Night. The practice of decking churches with greenery—yew, box, holly, and ivy—seemed to have declined in the sixteenth century, but it was still at least intermittently practiced in the 1590s.[28]

December

	1	2	3	4
Day	BCP	Grafton, (Liber)	Identification	Source
1		Loye	St. Eloi, Bishop of Noyon and goldsmith, 7th c.	F
2		Libane	?	
3		Deposi. Osmond (December 4th in *Liber*)	St. Osmund, Bishop of Salisbury, 11th c.	F
4		Barbara virgin (Dec. 3rd in *Liber*)	St. Barbara, virgin martyr, date unknown	F
5		Sabba abbot	St. Sabas of Jerusalem, abbot, 6th c.	F
6	Nicholas	Nicholas bish.	St. Nicholas, Bishop of Gaul, 6th c.	F
7		Oct. S. Andrew	See November 30th	
8	Concept. Ma.	Conception of our Lady	Conception, Virgin Mary	F
9		Ciprian abbot	St. Cyprian, monk of Perigueaux, 6th c.	B
10		Eulalia virgin	St. Eulalia of Merida, virgin martyr, 4th c.	F

(*Continued*)

264 *Early modern calendars*

	1	2	3	4
Day	BCP	Grafton, (Liber)	Identification	Source
11		Damass.	St. Damasus, Pope from Spain, 4th c.	F
12		Paule bish.	?	
13	Lucie	Lucie vir.	St. Lucy, Roman virgin and Diocletian martyr, 4th c.	F
14		Othile virgin	St. Othilia, virgin of Alscace, 8th c.	B
15		Valery bishop	St. Valerian, Bishop of Abbenza, 5th c.	B, C
16	Osapienc.	O Sapientia	Feast marking the liturgical inception of antiphons leading up to Christmas	
17		Lazarus bishop	St. Lazarus, raised from the dead by Jesus, 1st c.	B
18		Gracian bishop	St. Gatian or Gratian, Bishop of Tours, 4th c.	B, C
19		Venesi (virgin)	?	
20		Julian	St. Julius, Thracian martyr, dates unknown	B,C
21	**Thomas Apo.**	Thomas Apostles	St. Thomas, Apostle, 1st c.	F
22		30 Martirs	Thirty Diocletian martyrs, 4th c.	C
23		Victor virgin	St. Victoria, Roman martyr and virgin, 3rd c.	B
24		Cauldy (Sanctarum virg. 40)	? ?	
25	**Christmas**	Christmas day	Nativity of Jesus	
26	**St. Stephen**	Stephyn	St. Stephen, protomartyr, 1st c.	F
27	**St. John**	John Evangelist	St. John, Evangelist and Apostle, 1st c.	F
28	**Innocentes**	Innocents day	Commemoration of the Slaughter of the Innocents	
29		Thomas Becket	St. Thomas, Archbishop of Canterbury and martyr, 12th c.	F
30		Trans. of James	St. James the Great, Apostle, 1st c.	F
31	Silvester	Silvester bishop	St. Sylvester, Pope, Roman, 4th c.	F

Notes

1 Colum Hourihane, *Time in the Medieval World: Occupations of the Months and Signs of the Zodiac* (Princeton, NJ: The Index of Christian Art, distributed by Penn State University Press, 2007). See also J.C. Webster, *The Labours of the Months in Antique and Medieval Art to the End of the Twelfth Century*

(Princeton, NJ: Princeton University Press, 1938); Henisch, *The Medieval Calendar Year*, and J. Fowler, "On the Medieval Representations on the Months and Seasons," *Archaeologia* 44 (1873): 137–189. There are some examples in the (limited) survivals of church wall painting; see E.W. Tristram, *English Medieval Wall Painting: The Thirteenth Century* (Oxford: Oxford University Press, 1950), 26; and Matthew Reeve, *Thirteenth Century Wall Painting of Salisbury Cathedral: Art, Liturgy, Reform* (Woodbridge, Suffolk: Boydell, 2008), 99–100.

2 For labors in early modern printed books see Luborsky and Ingram, *Guide To English Illustrated Books*, Appendix 2, no. 2: 95–102.
3 Roger S. Wieck, *Time Sanctified: The Book of Hours in Medieval Art and Life* (New York: George Brazillier 1988), 37.
4 Wallis, "Medicine," 113. See David Houston Wood's study of the implications for early modern identity of the connection between time and environment in humoral medicine, *Time, Narrative, and Emotion in in Early Modern England* (London: Routledge, 2009), especially 26–31.
5 John Booty, ed., *The Book of Common Prayer 1559: The Elizabethan Prayer Book* (Washington, DC: The Folger Shakespeare Library, 1976).
6 Pollard and Redgrave, *STC*, 93; Brian Cummings, *The Book of Common Prayer: The Texts of 1549, 1559, and 1662* (Oxford: Oxford University Press, 2013), lii–lv.
7 Cressy, *Bonfires and Bells*, 11.
8 Hutton, *Stations of the Sun*, and *Rise and Fall*; Cressy, *Bonfires and Bells*; Martin Ingram, "Ridings, Rough Music and the 'Reform of Popular Culture'" in Early Modern England," *Past and Present* 105 (1984): 79–113; Phebe Jensen, *Religion and Revelry in Shakespeare's Festive World* (Cambridge: Cambridge University Press, 2008).
9 Cressy, *Bonfires*, 110–129 and 141–155. See also Alison Chapman, "The Politics of Time," and "Whose Saint Crispin's Day Is It? Shoemaking, Holiday Making, and the Politics of Memory in Early Modern England," *Renaissance Quarterly* 54, no. 4 (2001): 1467–1494.
10 For fuller accounts of the history of festive pastimes in England see Hutton, *Stations of the Sun*, and Hutton, *Rise and Fall, passim*.
11 David Hugh Farmer, *The Oxford Dictionary of Saints* (Oxford: Oxford University Press, 5th edition, 2010); The Benedictine Monks of St. Augustine's Abbey, Ramsgate, *The Book of Saints* (London: A&C Black, Ltd, 1921); Catholic Online, https://www.catholic.org/saints/. See also Alison A. Chapman, *Patrons and Patron Saints in Early Modern English Literature* (London: Routledge, 2013).
12 Hutton, *Stations*, 126–128.
13 Ibid., 146–150.
14 Cressy, *Bonfires*, 18–19; Hutton, *Stations*, 152.
15 Cressy, *Bonfires*, 20.
16 Ibid., 170.
17 Hutton, *Rise and Fall*, 87–119, and *Stations*, 244–257.
18 Philip Stubbes, *The Anatomie of Abuses* (1583), 92r–97v.
19 See the longer description of May pastimes and the controversies surrounding them in Hutton, *Stations*, 226–276 and 295–303, and Jensen, *Religion and Revelry*, 26–53.
20 Hutton, *Stations*, 282-83.
21 Philippa Berry, "Between Idolatry and Astrology: Modes of Temporal Repetition in Romeo and Juliet," in Dympna Callaghan, ed., *A Feminist Companion to Shakespeare* (Oxford: Wiley-Blackwell, 2001), 378–392.
22 Hutton, *Stations*, 324.
23 Cressy, *Bonfires*, 29.

266　Early modern calendars

24 Ibid., 30.
25 Thomas Fella, *His Booke of Diverse Devices and Sorts of Pictures*, a manuscript book in the Folger Shakespeare Library edited by Martin Sanford and John Blatchly (Dorchester: The Dorset Press, 2012). Fella's manuscript includes a twelve-month calendar with calendar poems and illustrations of labors of the month.
26 Bell-ringing on All Saint's Night, though frowned upon and directly prohibited in some visitation articles, appears to have persisted into the Elizabethan period, especially in more conservative areas of the country such as Lancashire.
27 Hutton, *Stations*, 112–123.
28 Ibid., 35–36; Cressy, *Bonfires*, 32.

3.4 Sample calendars, 1518–1640

January

The perpetual calendars in the often-reprinted *Kalender of Shepherds* reflect the mingling of astrological and religious information typical of the pre-Reformation English *horae* (Figure 3.4.1). Though the calendar pages varied in the century of the *Kalender's* popularity, most of them conform more or less to the layout in this example, which is from a blended edition of the *Kalender* now in the Huntington Library. This particular calendar is from an edition printed c. 1518 by Julian Notary.

The calendar includes an illustration for the labor of the month—feasting—at the top left, and a conventional Latin month poem that provides standard medical and dietary advice. The saints follow the Sarum rite. The numbers and letters enable readers to turn this perpetual calendar into an annual one: they provide the golden number, the time of day for new and full Moons for each year in the Metonic cycle (with black ink for morning and red ink for afternoon hours), the dominical letter, and keys to other tables in the *Kalender* that allow for the calculation of movable feasts for any given year. The thumbnail images on the right margin represent holy days, here the Circumcision, the Epiphany, St. Maurus (a sixth century Abbot and follower of Benedictine), St. Suplicius, and at the bottom of the column, St. Paul, whose conversion was celebrated on January 25th.

February

The French physician and prophet Michel de Notradame or Nostradamus first published his gnomic utterances in annual almanacs, several of which were printed in England beginning in the late 1550s (Figure 3.4.2). This February calendar is from a 1559 Nostradamus almanac printed in London. The calendar includes standard almanac information: the day of the month, the dominical letter, the saint's day (following the Sarum Rite), the time for new and full Moons, and the Moon's location in the Zodiac. The most unusual feature of this calendar is the cryptic prophecies for

268 *Early modern calendars*

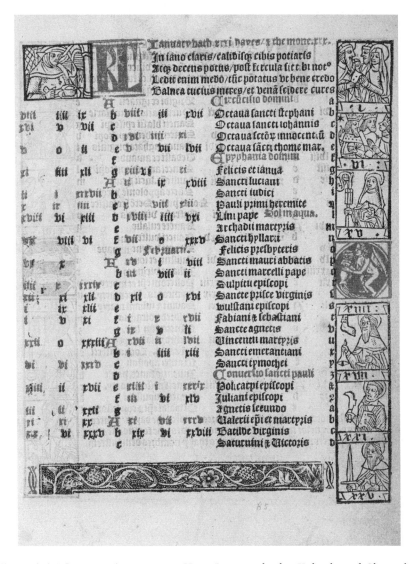

Figure 3.4.1 January, Anonymous, *Here Begynneth the Kalender of Shepardes*, ([1518?], STC 22410), B5r. Huntington Library, San Marino, California, RB 69474.

which Nostradamus was famous. The headings for each month eschew the usual poems on weather or physic, presenting instead short prophecies. Each day is attached to an even more compressed prognostication, some politically ominous—"Churches pilled," "*Mors mulieris magnae*"—some quotidian or banal—"wine & salt delivered," "colde and drye."

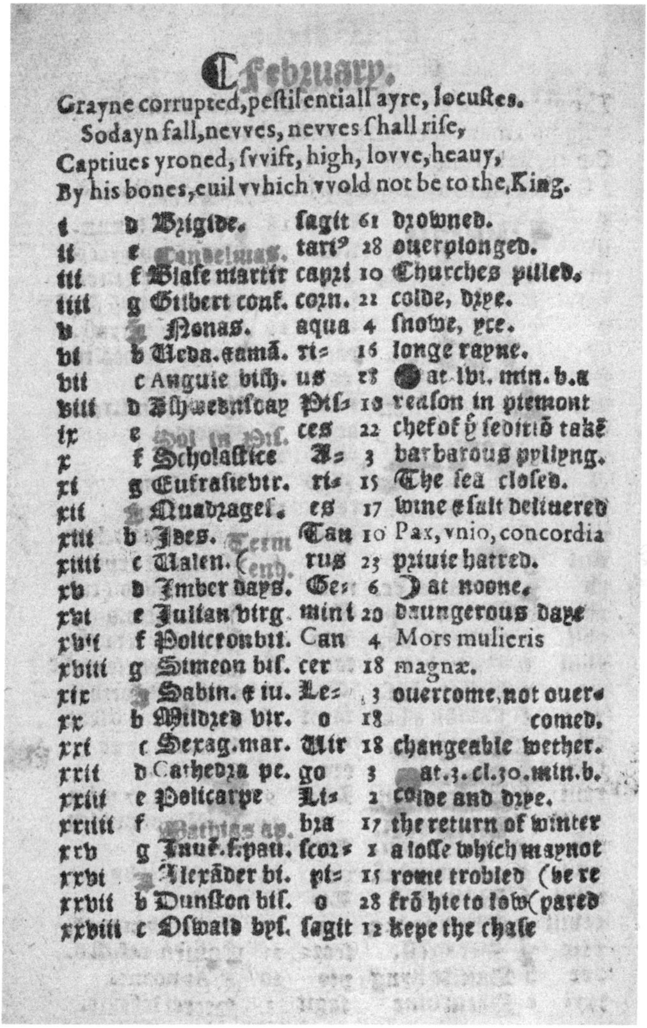
Februarý.

Grayne corrupted, pestilentiall ayre, locustes.
Sodayn fall, nevves, nevves shall rise,
Captiues yroned, svvift, high, lovve, heauy,
By his bones, euil vvhich vvold not be to the King.

i	d	Brigide.	sagit	61	drowned.
ii	e	Candelmas.	tari⁹	28	ouerplonged.
iii	f	Blase martir	capri	10	Churches pilled.
iiii	g	Gilbert conf.	corn.	21	colde, drye.
v	A	Nonas.	aqua	4	snowe, yce.
vi	b	Veda.eamā.	ri-	16	longe rayne.
vii	c	Anguie bish.	us	13	● at.ibi. min. b.a
viii	d	Ashwednsday	Pis-	18	reason in pyemont
ix	e	Sol in Pis.	ces	22	chefof ye seditiō takē
x	f	Scholastice	A-	3	barbarous pyllyng.
xi	g	Eufrasievir.	ri-	15	The sea closed.
xii	A	Quadrages.	es	17	wine & salt delivered
xiii	b	Ides. Term	Tau	10	Pax, vnio, concordia
xiiii	c	Valen. (end.	rus	23	priuie hatred.
xv	d	Imber days.	Ge-	6	☽ at noone.
xvi	e	Julian virg.	mini	20	daungerous daye
xvii	f	Polcronvii.	Can	4	Mors mulieris
xviii	g	Simeon bis.	cer	18	magnæ.
xix	A	Sabin. & iu.	Le-	3	ouercome, not ouer-
xx	b	Mildred vir.	o	18	comed.
xxi	c	Sexag.mar.	Vir	18	changeable wether.
xxii	d	Cathedra pe.	go	3	● at.3.cl.30.min.b.
xxiii	e	Policarpe	Li-	2	colde and drye.
xxiiii	f	Mathias ap.	bra	17	the return of winter
xxv	g	Inuē.s.pau.	scor-	1	a losse which maynot
xxvi	A	Alexāder bi.	pi-	15	rome trobled (be re
xxvii	b	Dunston bis.	o	28	frō hite to low(pared
xxviii	c	Oswald byf.	sagit	12	kepe the chase

Figure 3.4.2 February, Michael Nostradamus, *An Almanacke for the Yeare of Oure Lorde God, 1559,* A2v. Huntington Library, San Marino, California, RB 52428.

March

Thomas Buckminster produced annual almanacs from 1566 until his death in 1599, making him one of the most prolific Elizabethan almanac compilers (Figure 3.4.3). Buckminster was also a physician and clergyman, the Rector of St. Mary Woolnoth (on Lombard Street in London) from 1572 until his death. This octavo almanac follows a layout typical for almanacs

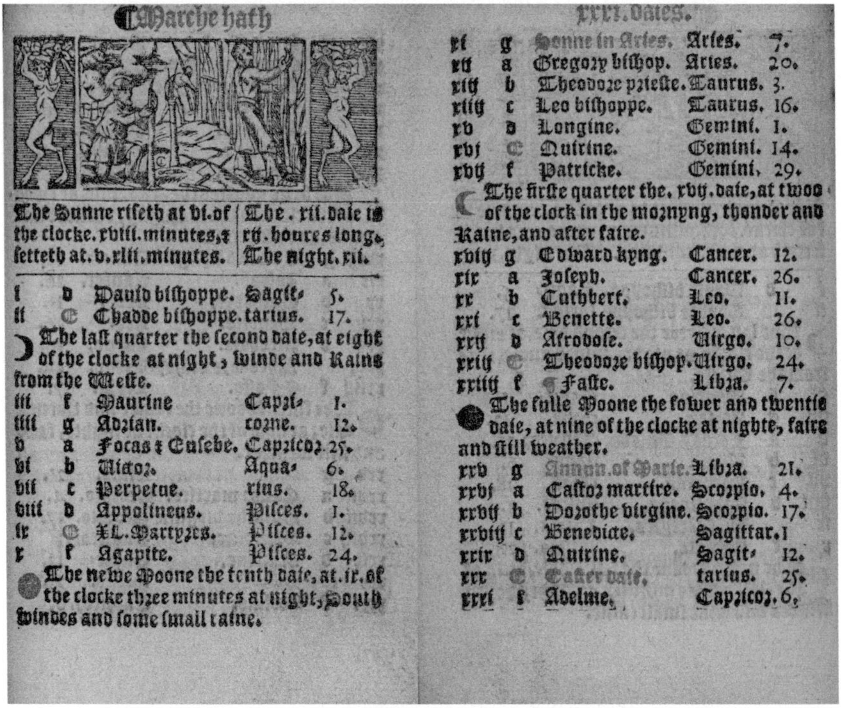

Figure 3.4.3 March, Buckminster, *A New Almanacke and Prognostication* (1567), A7r-A7v. University of Illinois at Champaign-Urbana, Rare Book and Manuscript Library, 529.5 H484a-1567.

published in the 1550s and 1560s. The layout is similar to that in early almanacs by Cuningham (Figure 2.5), though Buckminster provides slightly less information on the calendar pages—only the location of the Moon, the exact time for the changes of the Moon, weather predictions for the four lunar quarters, and the length of the day and night at the time of the Sun's entry into Aries. The woodcuts for the labors of the month previously appeared in the prognostication portion of Cuningham's 1558 almanac.

April

The physician John Securis, trained at Oxford and the University of Paris, compiled almanacs for approximately twenty years, from 1562 to 1581. These were calculated for Salisbury, where Securis (who adopted the Latin version of his English name, Hatchett) was born and lived after his education.[1] As described in Chapter 1.4, Securis was one of the compilers attacked by Nicholas Allen in *The Astronomers Game* in 1569. He defended himself, his profession, and the astrological arts vigorously against these and other disparagements in his almanacs throughout his career.

Sample calendars, 1518–1640   271

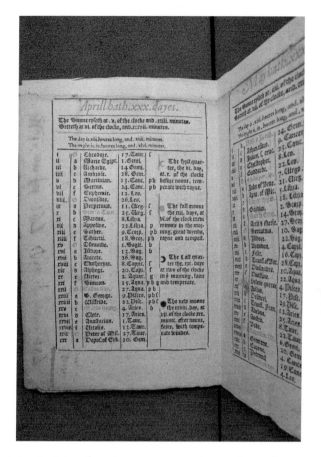

Figure 3.4.4 April, John Securis, *1576. An Almanacke and Prognostication*, A3v. Photograph by Phebe Jensen, from the collection of the Folger Shakespeare Library, STC 512.3.

Before the Watkins and Roberts monopoly of 1571 Securis almanacs were printed by John Walley, Thomas Marsh, and William Powell, in formats that included broadside, 16°, and 8°. This April calendar from Securis' last surviving almanac, the edition of 1581, is typical of the format after the genre had become standardized in the Watkins and Roberts years. The top of the page provides basic information about the time of sunrise and sunset, and the length of daylight and nighttime hours at the start of the month. The rest of the calendar is presented in vertical columns with (1) the date in Roman numeral, (2) the dominical letter, (3) the saint's day and entry of the Sun into a new Zodiac sign, (4) the location of the Moon in the Zodiac, (5) symbols indicating good and evil days for elections such as purging and bleeding, and (6) times for the new, quarter, half, and full moon, along with the briefest of weather forecasts for that hour.

272 *Early modern calendars*

May

This calendar is from a single sheet almanac for 1572 by Thomas Hill, a rare survival of a popular format that was evidently designed for pinning

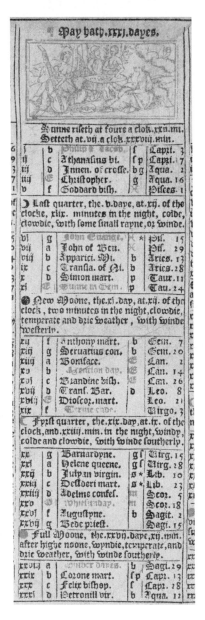

Figure 3.4.5 May, Thomas Hill, *A New Almanack* (1572), Single Sheet Almanac, Detail.

on walls (Figure 3.4.4). Hill, a Cambridge educated mathematician, compiled multiple almanacs and published books on dream interpretation, astronomy, astrology, physic, and gardening, including the popular *Profitable Arte of Gardening* (first published in 1568).[2] The thumbnail labor at the top of the calendar roughly replicates the composition of the labor in Buckminster's 1567 almanac. (See a similar grouping in the Pieter van der Heyden engraving after Bruegel, Figure 3.1.3.) Such broadside or single sheet almanacs provided in condensed form much of the information in the longer almanacs and prognostications, including prognostications for eclipses; the keys to the symbols in the calendar (and a small version of Zodiac Man) appear in the lower edge of the sheet (see Plate 2).

June

J.D. was probably John Dade, a physician who compiled almanacs from 1589 to 1614 (Figure 3.4.6). His name lived on in almanacs published by William Dade (possibly his son), then on and on in almanacs that bore the Dade name into the second half of the seventeenth century.

This triple almanac suggests the degree to which the Gregorian reforms of 1582 provoked interest in the calendar. Many almanacs become double, in order to keep track of the eleven-day discrepancy between the Julian and

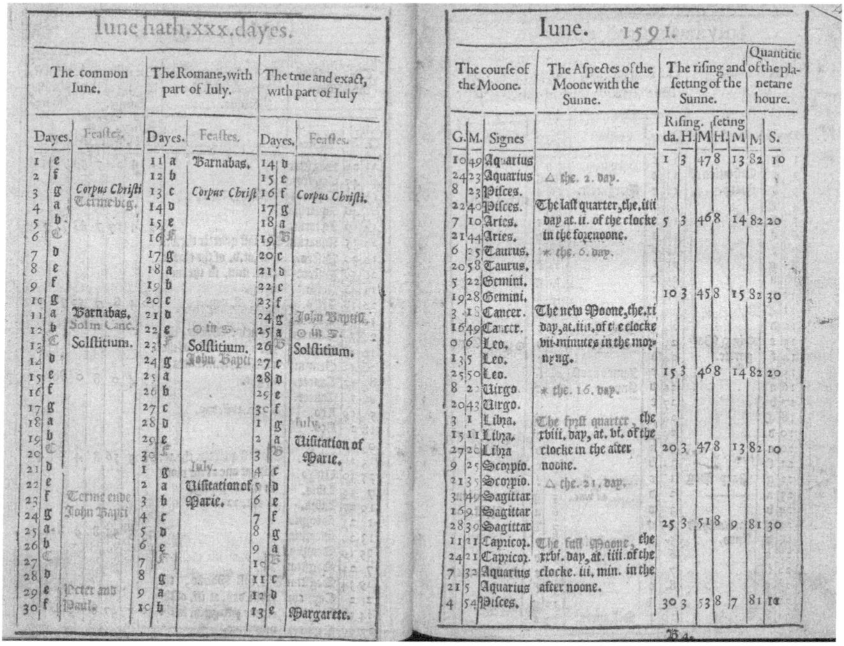

Figure 3.4.6 June, J.D. *A Triple Almanacke for the yeere of our Lorde 1591*, B3v-B4r. Cambridge University Library, Syn.7.59.22.

274 *Early modern calendars*

Gregorian calendars, and the significant differences in dates for movable feasts. Dade, however, goes one step further, creating this "Triple almanacke." Though he praises the Gregorian reforms for accurately situating Easter in the twelve-month calendar in relation to the equinox, Dade laments that they have not positioned Christmas as the shortest day of the year, as should be the case. To accomplish this, Dade's calculations put his calendar three days behind the Gregorian calendar (and so eight days ahead of the Julian calendar). This innovation was never adopted.

Dade's calendar is also atypical in format. Spreading across two pages, it includes a minimum number of saints—only those in the Book of Common Prayer. It provides standard information about the phases of the Moon and its location in the Zodiac, and precise data for the rising and setting of the Sun. It also calculates for readers the length of the planetary (or unequal) daylight hours, which were not frequently included in almanacs until the early seventeenth century.

July

This calendar was added to the 1593 and 1600 editions of W. Prid's popular Protestant prayer book, *The Glasse of Vaine-Glorie, Translated out of S. Augustine*, originally printed in 1585 (Figure 3.4.7). Its reformist bent is suggested by the list of holy days. Included here are only the saints noted by the Book of Common Prayer (both red- and black-letter). But in the far right column, Prid notes important dates in Reformation history, including the names of some English Protestant martyrs of the sixteenth century, and miscellaneous information from the Bible. The January calendar, for example, notes that "Martine Luther first writ against the Pope, the yere 1517, and continued to the yeare 1546" (A4r). In this calendar for July, Prid includes three Henrician and Marian martyrs, attaching them to the correct dates for their martyrdoms instead of relying on the jumbled calendar of Foxe's *Acts and Monuments*, as in William Beale's calendar of 1631 (Figure 3.4.11). Yet Prid also includes a wealth of nonreligious calendar material: the traditional labors of the month, given in both woodcuts and the four-line verses on husbandry taken from a William Seres 1580 primer, the length of the day and night for calculating planetary hours, information on calendars ("thirtie daies hath September..."), and advice on medical interventions.

August

Thomas Trevilian or Trevelyon compiled and illustrated three magnificent manuscript miscellanies: one in the Wormsley Library (1616), a more recently discovered miscellany now in the library at University College, London (c. 1603), and the Trevelyon manuscript of 1608 in the Folger Shakespeare Library, edited by Heather Wolfe, and represented by the August calendar in Figure 3.4.8.[3]

Sample calendars, 1518–1640 275

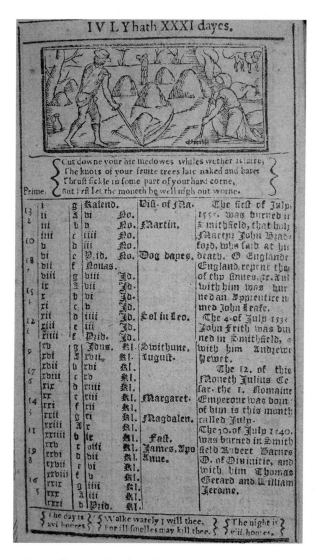

Figure 3.4.7 July, William Prid, *The Glasse of Vaine-Glorie* (1600), A7r. Photograph by Phebe Jensen, from the collection of the Folger Shakespeare Library, STC 931.

Trevelyon was clearly fascinated with calendars; all three manuscripts include elaborate calendars, and all pull a range of material from annual and perpetual almanacs and other sources, including almanacs by Thomas Buckminster, Thomas Bretnor, Edward Pond, and Henry Alleyn, and material from Thomas Tusser's *Five Hundredth Points of Good Husbandry*, Leonard Digges' *Prognostication Everlasting*, and Richard Grafton's

The Prime	Dayes	Dominicall letter	The saynts dayes in this mooneth:	houre and minute of Sunne setting	Euill dayes	Good dayes	August. 31. dayes	Epact
	1	C+	Lammas day.	7. 27.	o	G	Though long, yet at length	18
8	2	D	Steuen mart.	7. 20.	o	G	the same againe:	19
16	3	E	Inuen. of Stuen.	7. 18.	B	o	Looke about thee:	19
5	4	F	Iustine priest.	7. 16.	o	G	Vaunt spoyles all.	20
	5	G+	Festum niues. k James. p. 14.	B	o	Desperat and deadly	21
13	6	A	Transf. of Christ.	7. 12.	B	o	A haggard no hawke	22
2	7	B	Feast of Jesus.	7. 11.	o	G	Betime or not:	23
	8	C	Ciriac. and his fel.	7. 9.	o	G	pleasant and profitable	24
10	9	D	Roman mart.	7. 7.	o	G	the same againe:	25
	10	E+	Laurence mart.	7. 6.	B	o	A malitious bayte:	26
18	11	F	Tiburt. mart.	7. 4.	o	G	Scarse currant:	27
7	12	G	Clare Virgin.	7. 2.	o	G	the same againe:	28
	13	A+	Sun. in Virgo.	7. 0.	o	G	Nothing impossible.	29
15	14	B	Eusebius.	6. 58.	o	G	the same againe:	111.
4	15	C+	Assump. of Mary	6. 56.	o	G	the same a gaine:	1
	16	D	Roch mart.	6. 54.	B	o	Borse then ahalter	2
12	17	E	Octa Lawrenc.	6. 52.	o	G	Open harted:	3
1	18	F	Agapite. mart.	6. 50.	B	o	Franticke humours.	4
	19	G	Magnus. mart.	6. 48.	B	o	the same againe:	5
9	20	A	Lewes byshop.	6. 46.	o	G	A mendes for all:	6
	21	B	Barnarde.	6. 44.	o	G	the same againe:	7
17	22	C	priuatus.	6. 42.	o	G	the same againe:	8
6	23	D	Timothe. fast.	6. 40	o	G	Borke, or win not	9
	24	E+	Barthol. apostle.	6. 38.	B	o	Great boast small roast	10
14	25	F	Lews. kyng.	6. 37.	o	G	Too, too familiar.	11
3	26	G	Seuerine.	6. 35	B	o	Cautous. carousing:	12
	27	A+	Dog dayes ende.	6. 33.	B	o	the same againe	13
11	28	B	Augustine byshop.	6. 31.	o	G	A good match in hand	14
	29	C+	John beheaded.	6. 30.	o	G	the same againe:	15
19	30	D	Felix and Audac.	6. 28.	o	G	the same againe:	16
8	31	E	Cuthburge Virgin.	6. 26.	B	o	Beware the next:	17

Figure 3.4.8 August, Trevelyon Miscellany, Manuscript, Folger Shakespeare Library, V.b.232, fol. 11r, 1608. Used by permission of the Folger Shakespeare Library.

Treatise.[4] The saints in the calendars in the 1608 manuscript appear to combine the lists from Grafton's *Treatise* and Bretnor's annual almanacs. Each calendar in the Folger manuscript is presented opposite a page that includes an illustrated labor of the month, calendar poetry for the month, and other standard almanac information such as the length of the hours of night and day. Trevelyon's creative merging of different sources, his use of traditional calendars updated with Tudor imagery, and his inclusion of

Sample calendars, 1518–1640 277

information typical of most almanacs—dates for Easter, parameters of the law terms, how to find the age of the Moon, the dates for principal fairs, equivalences for measurement, directions, and historical chronology—suggest he was steeped in the calendar culture of the time.

September

Aside from the calendars in almanacs, the most widely distributed calendars from the start of the Elizabethan reign until the middle of the seventeenth

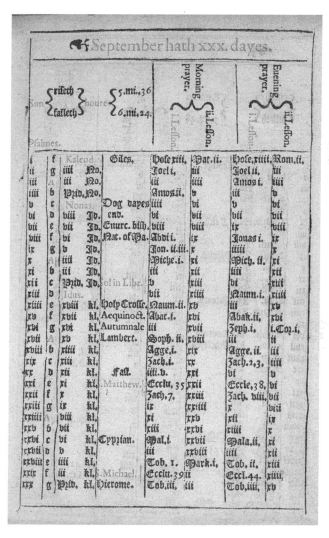

Figure 3.4.9 September, Church of England, *The Booke of Common Prayer* (1611), A6r. The Huntington Library, San Marino, California, RB 438000:367.

278 Early modern calendars

century (and later) were the perpetual calendars included in the printed Book of Common Prayer (Figure 3.4.9). These were printed in great numbers and every possible size, from folio to 24°.[5] Each Book of Common Prayer included a perpetual calendar, such as this one from a 1600 Robert Barker Folio edition of the Book of Common Prayer, with the day of the month, the dominical letter, the Roman *kalends*, and the red- and black-letter saint's days. Limited astronomical information is also included in this and other Book of Common Prayer calendars: here, the "Dog-dayes end" on September 5th–6th, and the Sun enters Libra on September 12th (information which is not as exact as that in the annual almanacs). The most significant aspect of this calendar, though, is the tethering of every day to a particular biblical reading, a practice that infused the annual calendar with the word of God.

October

Thomas Bretnor, a physician, mathematician, and teacher in London, compiled almanacs from 1607 to 1618.[6] He became a byword for almanacs generally; Middleton goes after him by name in *No Wit No Help like a Woman's*. This October calendar with blanks (Figure 3.4.10),

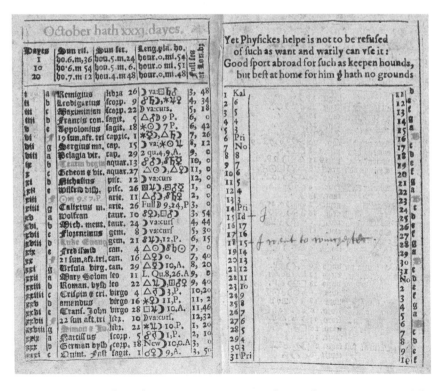

Figure 3.4.10 October, Thomas Bretnor, *A New Almanacke* (1616), B4v-B5r. The Huntington Library, San Marino, California, RB 46191.

from a Bretnor 1616 almanac, survives in a series of bound almanacs in the Huntington Library owned by a relative of Chief Justice Sir Henry Montague, whose institure is recorded correctly for November 18th, 1616. The entries are sparse. October includes one unfinished entry (for the 15th), and the single notation of a journey for the 18th: "I went to Winchester."

This 1616 calendar captures the way in which the amount of astrological information in the annual almanacs gradually increased in the seventeenth century. Beneath the first heading on the left-hand page, Bretnor includes standard information on the rising and setting of the Sun—adjusted every ten days—and the length of the planetary hours. The calendar itself provides the day of the month, dominical letter, saint's day with law terms, and location of the Moon in the twelve signs, but also (in the penultimate column) the aspects of the seven planets: conjunctions, oppositions, triunes, quadratures, etc. The final column adds information on high tide at London Bridge on each day. The second page of the almanac lists on the left the day of the month and the Roman *kalends*, and, to the right, the day of the month in the Gregorian calendar, with the associated dominical letter. The astronomical and astrological information in Bretnor's calendar is perfectly at home with the conventional calendar poem at the top of this page, which reminds readers that medical interventions are acceptable in October, if necessary and used with caution, and this month is a good time for outdoor exercise fitting one's social station.

November

Most early modern calendars included a full complement of late medieval saints. There are occasional signs of Protestant resistance to this inclusion—resistance which would increase in the 1640s. A 1631 almanac by William Beale, academic and later the master of St. John's College, Cambridge, provide an early example of such resistance (Figure 3.4.11).[7] Beale has replaced the usual saints—both the black-letter saints in the Book of Common Prayer, and the longer list of late medieval saints—with the calendar from Foxe's *Acts and Monuments:* "the names of many Martyrs with the year wherein they Suffered for the testimony of the truth" (A1r). The calendar does include, in red-letter, a notation for the Gunpowder Plot on November 5th, which was added to most annual calendars after 1605. Beale also puts some annual information for 1631 into red-letter: the start of Advent on November 27th, which also marked the start of a period when weddings were prohibited, and the end of Michaelmas term on November 28th. The astronomical information in Beale's calendar is limited: he provides an overview of the phases of the Moon in the headnote, and in the far-right column, the time for sunset. However, the prognostication portion of Beale's almanac includes standard almanac information, including an unusually detailed guide to the impact of planetary aspects on the sublunar world.

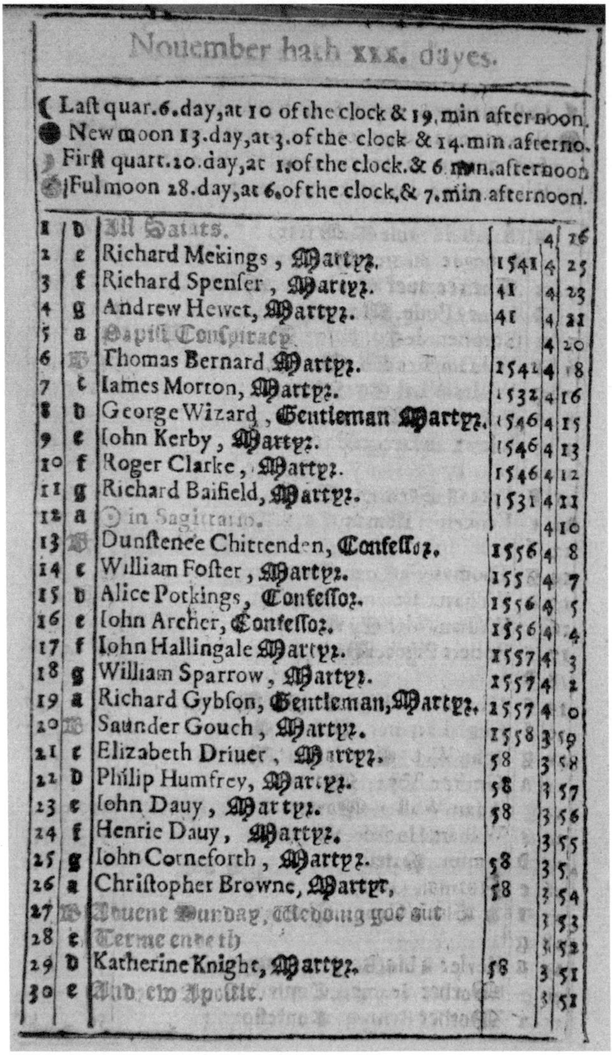

280 *Early modern calendars*

> November hath xxx. dayes.
>
> (Laſt quar.6.day,at 10 of the clock & 19.min afternoon.
> ● New moon 13.day,at 3.of the clock & 14.min.afterno.
>) Firſt quart.10.day,at 1.of the clock.& 6.mwn.afternoon
> ◐ Fulmoon 28.day,at 6.of the clock,& 7.min.afternoon.

1	d	All Saints.		4	26
2	e	Richard Mekings, Martyr.	1541	4	25
3	f	Richard Spenſer, Martyr.	41	4	23
4	g	Andrew Hewet, Martyr.	41	4	22
5	a	Papiſt Conſpiracy		4	20
6	b	Thomas Bernard Martyr.	1541	4	18
7	c	Iames Morton, Martyr.	1532	4	16
8	d	George Wizard, Gentleman Martyr.	1546	4	15
9	e	Iohn Kerby, Martyr.	1546	4	13
10	f	Roger Clarke, Martyr.	1546	4	12
11	g	Richard Baifield, Martyr.	1531	4	11
12	a	☉ in Sagittario.		4	10
13	b	Dunſtence Chittenden, Confeſſor.	1556	4	8
14	c	William Foſter, Martyr.	1556	4	7
15	d	Alice Potkings, Confeſſor.	1556	4	5
16	e	Iohn Archer, Confeſſor.	1556	4	4
17	f	Iohn Hallingale Martyr.	1557	4	3
18	g	William Sparrow, Martyr.	1557	4	2
19	a	Richard Gybſon, Gentleman,Martyr.	1557	4	0
20	b	Saunder Gouch, Martyr.	1558	3	59
21	c	Elizabeth Driver, Martyr.	58	3	58
22	D	Philip Humfrey, Mar.yr.	58	3	57
23	e	Iohn Dauy, Martyr.	58	3	56
24	f	Henrie Dauy, Martyr.		3	55
25	g	Iohn Corneforth, Martyr.	58	3	5
26	a	Chriſtopher Browne, Martyr.	58	3	54
27	b	Aduent Sunday, Wedding goe out		3	53
28	c	Terme endeth		3	52
29	D	Katherine Knight, Martyr.	58	3	51
30	e	And ew Apoſtle.		3	51

Figure 3.4.11 November, William Beale, *Beale 1631, A Almanacke*, A8r. Lambeth Palace Library, [YY751.27].

December

The astrological autodidact John Booker, originally a member of the Company of Haberdashers, first published almanacs in 1631, then went on to become one of the leading astrologers associated with the Parliamentarian cause in the middle of the seventeenth century (Figure 3.4.12).[8] Booker's almanacs are among the most astrologically detailed of the period, though in his almanacs from the mid-1640s onward the prognostications became

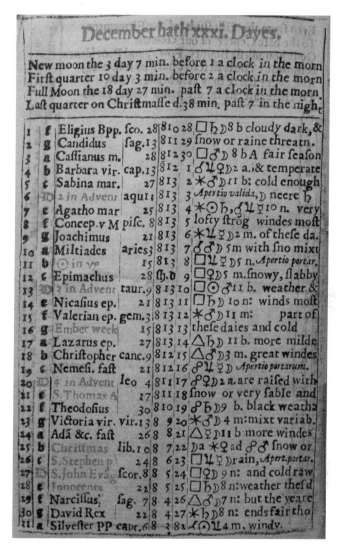

Figure 3.4.12 December, John Booker, *M.D.C. XL Almanack Et Prognostication* (1640), B7v. Photograph by Phebe Jensen, from the collection of the Folger Shakespeare Library, STC 419.9.

entirely focused on political factionalism. That detail is reflected in this calendar page for December 1640, where Booker provides the time of sunrise to the second, as well as planetary aspects and their implications for the weather. Eschewing the usual notes on physic and agriculture, and the moralizing ditties of most almanac poetry, Booker's almanacs sometimes include poems that summarize the astrological prediction for the month, described in more detail in Chapter 1.4.

282 Early modern calendars

Notes

1 N. Moore & S. Bakewell, "Securis [Hatchett], John (fl. 1550–1580), physician," *Oxford Dictionary of National Biography*. 23 September 2004; Accessed 10 Sep 2019.
2 John Considine, "Hill, Thomas (c. 1528-c. 1574), pseud. Didymus Mountaine] (c. 1528–c. 1574), Writer and Translator," *Oxford Dictionary of National Biography*. 23 Sep. 2004; Accessed 1 Dec. 2019.
3 On these three manuscripts see Heather Wolfe, "A third manuscript by Thomas Trevelyon/Trevilian." The Trevilian manuscript in the Wormsley library is partially reprinted in facsimile in Nicolas Barker, ed., *The Great Book of Thomas Trevilian: A Facsimile from the Manuscript in the Wormsley Library* (London: The Roxburghe Club, 2000); the Folger Trevelyon/Trevilian manuscript is reproduced in its entirety in Wolfe, ed., *The Trevelyon Miscellany*. The third Trevelyon/Trevilian miscellany is University College Library MS Ogden 24.
4 Wolfe, "Introduction," *The Trevelyon Miscellany*, 16–17.
5 See the description and chart of editions from 1549 to 1641 in Pollard and Redgrave, *Short-Title Catalogue*, 2.87–2.90.
6 Bernard Capp, "Bretnor, Thomas (1570/71–1618), astrologer and medical practitioner," *Oxford Dictionary of National Biography*. 23 Sep. 2004; Accessed 10 Dec. 2020.
7 Nicholas W. S. Cranfield, "Beale, William (d. 1651), college head." *Oxford Dictionary of National Biography*. 23 Sep. 2004; Accessed 9 Sep. 2019.
8 Capp, "Booker." See the longer discussion of Booker's career as an astrologer in Chapter 1.3.

Bibliography

Primary bibliography

Texts and citations

Orthography

Early modern printed works are transcribed with original spelling, except that abbreviations have been silently expanded, and some orthography emended (v to u, f to s, j to i). Following early modern conventions that reflect early modern cosmology, the names of the seven classical planets—including the Sun and Moon—are capitalized throughout, as are the four seasons (Spring, Summer, Autumn, Winter), twelve months, days of the week, "Earth" when it refers to the planet, and "Zodiac."

Early modern printed books, excluding almanacs

Primary material is cited in-text by author, title, date and page number or signature on first citation, and author-page on subsequent references. STC numbers are given parenthetically for volumes that are difficult to distinguish, including English primers. Unless otherwise noted, the place of publication is London.

Titles for all early modern printed works (including almanacs) follow Pollard & Redgrave, with some emendations and additions from facsimile editions in *Early English Books Online*, the online English Short Title Catalogue (ESTC), and for almanacs, the invaluable bibliography in Bernard Capp's *Astrology and the Popular Press*.

Unless otherwise noted:

- Citations to the Kalender of Shepherds (*Kalender* in parenthetical citations) are taken from the 1570 edition (STC 22415).
- Citations to the Book of Common Prayer (*BCP* in parenthetical citations) are taken from the edition now listed as STC 16292a, which bears a 1559 date but might not have been printed until 1561.
- Citations to Claude Dariot's astrological primer (Dariot in parenthetical citations) are taken from the 1653 edition, *Dariotus Redivivus* (Wing D257).
- Citations to Tusser's husbandry manual (Tusser in parenthetical citations) are taken from the 1610 edition, *Five Hundred Points of Good Husbandry* (STC 24388).
- Citations to Hopton's *Concordancy of Years* are taken from the 1615 edition (STC 13779).

284 Bibliography

Early modern printed annual almanacs and prognostications

Citations to annual almanacs and prognostications are given in-text by author-date when the compiler is known, and by STC number for anonymous works.

In standard annual almanacs by named compilers titles vary, but only slightly. This bibliography provides the title for the earliest cited edition (unless there is significant variation in subsequent editions), as well as, below, the year and STC or Wing number for all other cited editions.

Very few almanacs indicate the year of imprint, but in those that do the date is the same as the year for which the almanac is calculated, even though almanacs must have been printed in the last months of the previous year. Following Pollard & Redgrave, Capp's *Astrology*, the ESTC, and EEBO, almanac publication dates below are the same as the year for which the almanac was calculated.

Manuscripts

Anonymous. *Almanac*, Containing Table of Dominical Letters and Golden Numbers. 16th century. British Library, Add MS 17367.

Anonymous. Book of Magic, with Instructions for Invoking Spirits. *Ca. 1577–1583*. Folger Shakespeare Library, V.b.26 (1).

Heydon, Sir Christopher. A Meteorological Dyary and Prognostication for this Present Yeare of our Lord. 1609–1620. The Huntington Library, MSS HM 80396, 28.

Trevelyon, Thomas. Trevelyon Miscellany. *1608*. Folger Shakespeare Library, V.B. 232.

———. Miscellany. University College, London, MS Ogden 24.

Published public records

Great Britain. *Calendar of Patent Rolls, Preserved in the Public Records Office*. Vols. 5 and 7. Nendein, Lichetenstein: Kraus Reprint, 1976.

Great Britain. *Calendar of State Papers, Domestic Series, of the Reign of Elizabeth, 1598–1601*. Edited by Mary Anne Everett Green. London: Longmans, Green, and Co., 1869.

Almanacs

Anonymous almanacs

A Blancke and Perpetuall Almanack, Serving as a Memorial. 1556. STC 401.
Almanack for Twelve Years. 1508. STC 387.
Almanacke for.xv Yeres. [1522.] STC 389.
Almanacke for xiiii Years. [1539.] STC 392.2.
Almanacke for, xv, Yeres. 1524. STC 390.
An Almanack and Pronosticacion of M.CCCCC.XX[XIX]. 1539. STC 392.3.
An Almanacke Moste Exactly Sette Foorth for the Terme of xiiii Yeres. [1544.] STC 393.
The City and Countrey Chapmans Almanack. 1685. Wing A1403A.
The Money Monger. Or, The Usurers Almanacke. 1626. STC 24209.5.
A Perfyte Pronostycacion Perpetuall. 1566. STC 406.3.
The Treasurers Almanacke. 1627. STC 24210.

Named compilers, annual and multi-year almanacs, and prognostications

Adkin, M. *Adkin. An Almanacke for the Yeare of our Lord MDCXL*. Cambridge. 1640. STC 406.5.

Allestree, Richard. *Allestree. 1617. A New Almanacke and Prognostication*. STC 407.
    1619, STC 407.2.   1639, STC 407.22.
    1620, STC 407.3.

Alleyn, Henry. *Alleyn. 1606. An Almanack and Prognostication*. STC 408.
    1607, STC 408.2.   1609, STC 408.5.
    1608, STC 408.4.

Askham, Anthony. *An Almanacke and Prognostication*. 1552. STC 410.4.

Balles, Thomas. *Balles. 1631. A New Almanacke and Prognostication*. STC 411.

Barham, William. *W. Barham. 1639. An Almanack for the Yeere of our Lord and Saviour Christ*. STC 411.5.

Beale, William. *Beale. 1631. An Almanacke, for the Yeere of our Lord God*. 1631. STC 412.

Bogaert, Arnould. *A Pronostication for Divers Yeares*. [1553.] STC 3204.

Booker, John. *A Bloody Irish Almanack*. 1646. Wing B3723A.

———. *Bowker. 1631. A New Almanack and Prognostication*. STC 419.
    1632, STC 419.1.   1640, STC 419.9.
    1633, STC 419.2.

———. *M.D.C. XL Almanack Et Prognostication*. 1640. STC 419.9.

Boorde, Andrew. *A Pronostycacyon or an Almanacke for the Yere of our Lorde, M. CCCCC.xlv*. 1545. STC 416.5.

Bourne, William. *An Almanacke and Prognostication for Three Years*. 1567. STC 417.

———. *An Almanacke and Prognostication for X Yeeres*. 1571. STC 418.

Bretnor, Thomas. *Bretnor. 1607. A Newe Almanacke and Prognostication*. STC 420.
    1610, STC 420.3.   1615, STC 420.8.
    1611, STC 420.4.   1616, STC 420.9.
    1612, STC 420.5.   1617, STC 420.10.
    1618, STC 420.11.   1619, STC 420.12.
    1620, STC 420.13.

Browne, Daniel. *Browne. 1620. A New Almanacke and Prognostication*. STC 421.5.

1624, STC 421.9.

Buckminster, Thomas. *A New Almanacke and Prognostication*. 1567. STC 422.
    1568, STC 422.3.   1571, STC 422.5.
    1589, STC 423.3.   1590, STC 423.5.

Burton, Gregory. *Burton. 1617. An Almanacke and Prognostication*. STC 426.5.

Butler, Robert. *Butler. 1629. A New Almanacke and Prognostication*. STC 427.
    1630, STC 427.2.   1631, Cambridge, STC 427.3.
    1632, Cambridge, STC 427.4.

Carre, James. *Carre. 1593. An Almanacke and Prognostication*. STC 428.

Chamberlaine, Joseph. *Chamberlaine. 1631. A New Almanacke and Prognostication*. STC 429.7.

Clark. *Clark. 1633. A New Almanack and Prognostication*. Cambridge. STC 430.2.

286 Bibliography

Coverdale, Miles. *A Faythful and True Pronostication*. [1547.] STC 20423.
Coxe, Francis. *A Prognostication Made for ye Yeere of our Lorde God 1566*. STC 431.7.
    1567, STC 401.3.
Cuningham, William. *A Nevve Almanacke and Prognostication*. 1558. STC 432.
    1564, STC 432.5.   1566, STC 433.
D. J. *A Triple Almanacke for the Yeere of our Lorde God 1591*. STC 433.7.
Variant, 1591, STC 433.
Dade, John. *Dade. 1602. An Almanack and Prognostication*. STC 434.14.
    1607, STC 434.19.
Dauncy, Gervase. *Dauncy. 1614. His President for the Starres, or the Almanacke of Prognostications, for This Yeere of Our Redemption*. STC 425.31.
    1615, STC 435.33.
Digges, Leonard. *Almanacke and Prognostication*. 1556. STC 435.37.
Dove, Jonathan. *Dove. 1627. A Prognostication for This Yeare of our Lord God*. Cambridge. STC 436.
    1639, Cambridge, STC 436.11.
Einer, N. *Einer. 1626. An Almanacke and Prognostication*. STC 438.7.
Evans, John. *Evans. 1613. A New Almanacke and Prognostication*. STC 441.5.
Farmer, William. *The Common Almanacke or Kalender, Drawen Foorth for This Yeere. 1587*. STC 443.
———. *Farmer. 1612. His Prognosticall Almanacke for this Bissextile Yeere*. Dublin. STC 443.5.
Frende, Gabriel. *A New Almanacke and Prognostication for the Yeere of our Lord God. M.D. LXXXIX*. 1589. STC 444.4.
    1590, STC 444.4.   1598, STC 445.4.
    1591, STC 444.7.   1616, STC 445.11.
    1593, STC 444.10.   1620, STC 445.15.
    1595, STC 445.   1622, STC 445.17.
    1597 STC 445.2.
Gesner, James. *An Almanacke and Prognostication*. 1555. STC 447.7.
Gilden, George. *Gilden. 1616. A New Almanacke and Prognostication*. STC 448.
    1620, STC 448.5.   1622, STC 448.7.
    1621, STC 448.6.
Gossene, George. *A Newe Almanacke and Prognostication*. 1571. STC 449.
Grammar, Abraham. *Grammar. 1628. A New Almanacke*. STC 450.3.
Gray, Walter. *An Almanacke and Prognostication, made for the Yeere of our Lord. M.D.LXXXVIII*. 1588. STC 451.
    1591, STC 451.4.   1604, STC 451.14.
    1593, STC 451.6.
H., T. *An Almanack Published at Large, in Forme of a Booke of Memorie*. 1571. STC 454.
Hartgill, George. *The Prognostication for this Yeere of our Lord God*. 1581. STC 454.5.
Harvey, John. *An Almanacke, or Annuall Calendar, With a Compendious Prognostication*. 1585. STC 455.3.
    1589, STC 455.7.
———. *Leape Yeere. A Compendious Prognostication for the Yeere of our Lorde God. M.D. LXXXIIII*. 1584. STC 455.

Hawkins, George. *Hawkins. 1624. A New Almanacke, and Prognostication.* STC 456.
    1625, STC 456.3   1627, STC 456.7.
Heuring [or Huring], Simon. *An Almanacke and Prognostication for the Yeare of our Lorde. M.D.L.I.* 1551. STC 464.
———. *An Almanacke and Prognosticatyon, for the Yeare of Our Lorde, M.D.LI.* 1551. Worcester. STC 464.3.
Hewlett, William. *Hewlett. 1627. A New Almanacke.* STC 457.3.
    1628, STC 457.4.   1629, STC 457.5.
Hill, Thomas. *A New Almanack for the Yeare of our Lorde God M.D.LXXII.* 1577. STC 459.
Holden, Mary. *The Womans Almanack for the Year of our Lord, 1688.* Wing A1827.
Hopton, Arthur. *Hopton. 1606. An Almanack and Prognostication.* STC 461.
    1607, STC 461.2.   1613, STC 461.8.
    1608, STC 461.3.
Hubrigh, Joachim. *An Almanacke and Prognostication, for the Year of our Lorde God. 1568.* STC 462.7.
Jinner, Sarah. *An Almanack and Prognostication for the Year of our Lord, 1659.* Wing A1845.
Johnson, John. *Johnson 1612. An Almanacke and Prognostication.* STC 465.1.
    1613, STC 465.2.   1624, STC 465.12.
Johnson, Thomas. *Johnson. 1602. An Almanacke and Prognostication.* STC 466.4.
    1604, STC 466.6 (broadside)   1604, STC 466.7.
Kidman, Thomas. *Kidman, 1631. A New Almanack and Prognostication.* Cambridge. STC 469.
Kinde, John. *Kinde. 1625. A New Almanacke or Prognostication.* STC 469.9.
Laet, Gaspar (the Elder). *[Prognostication for the Year] M.CCCCC.xvii.* Antwerp. STC 470.3.
Laet, Gaspar (the Younger). *Almynack and Pronostication of the Yere of Oure Lord, M. CCCCC. and XXX.* 1530. Antwerp. STC 471.
———. *[An Almanack and Pronostication.]* 1545. STC 477.
———. *The Pronosticacion Calculed by Mayster Jaspar Laet of Andwarpe.* 1533. [Antwerp?] STC 471.5.
Langley, Thomas. *Langley. 1639. A New Almanack and Prognostication.* STC 479.5.
Lloyd, Evans. *An Almanacke and Prognostication for the Yeere of our Lord M.D.LXXXII.* 1582. STC 480.3.
Low, Henry. *1554. An Almanack and Prognostication, for the Yere of our Lorde M.D.LIIII.* STC 481.
    1569, STC 482.9.   1574, STC 482.12.
———. *A Prognostication for the Yeare of oure Lorde God. M.D.LX.* STC 482.3. 1564, STC 482.7.
Mathew, William. *Mathew. 1612. A New Almanacke and Prognostication.* STC 483.10.
    1602, STC 483.
Moore, Philip. *A Fourtie Yeres Almanacke, with a Prognostication.* 1567. STC 484.
Mounslowe, Alexander. *An Almanacke and Prognostation for this Present Yeare of our Lorde, 1561.* STC 488.1.

288 Bibliography

    1576, STC 488.3.   1581, STC 488.7.
    1579, STC 488.5.
Neve, Jeffery. *Neve. 1605. A New Almanacke and Prognostication.* STC 489.2.
    1606, STC 489.3.   1609, STC 489.8.
    1607 (broadside), STC 489.4.   1612, STC 489.11.
    1607 (8°), STC 489.5.   1621, STC 489.23.
Neve, John. *Neve. 1626. A New Almanacke, and Prognostication.* STC 490.
Nostradamus, Michael. *An Almanacke for the Yeare of Oure Lorde God, 1559.* STC 492.
    1559 (variant edition), STC 492.2.   1564, STC 492.11.
    1562, STC 492.7.   1566, STC 493.
    1563, STC 492.9.   1567, STC 493.3.
    1563 (variant edition), STC 492.10.   1568, STC 493.7.
―――. *The Prognostication of Maister Michael Nostredamus, Doctour in Phisick.* Antwerp, 1559. STC 492.3.
Osborne, George. *Osborne. 1622. A New Almanacke and Prognostication.* STC 494.
Perkins, Samuel. *Perkins. 1625. A New Almanacke and Prognostication.* STC 495.
    1634, STC 495.9.
Pond, Edward. *Ponde. 1602. A New Almanacke and Prognostication.* STC 501.2.
    1606, STC 501.6.   1612, STC 501.12.
Ranger, Philip. *Ranger. 1617. An Almanacke.* STC 502.3.
    1619, STC 502.5.   1629, STC 503.6.
Rede, William. *Almanach Ephemerides in Anno Domini M d. vii.* 1507. STC 504.
Rivers, Peregrine. *Rivers. 1627. A New Almanacke and Prognostication.* Cambridge. STC 505.2.
Rivers, William. *Rivers. 1628. A New Almanacke and Prognostication.* Cambridge. STC 505.17.
Rudston, John. *Rudston. 1615. An Almanacke and Prognostication.* STC 506.7.
    1616, STC 506.8.
Rudston, Thomas. *Rudston. 1607. A New Almanacke and Prognostication.* STC 507.2.
    1613, STC 507.8.
Scute, Cornelys. *A Pronostication for the Yere of our Lord God M.CCCCC.xliiii.* 1544. STC 508.5.
Securis, John. [*An Almanacke and Prognostication.*] 1562. STC 510.
    1568, STC 511.   1576, STC 512.3.
    1574, STC 512.   1581, STC 512.11.
Smith, Reinold. *Smith. 1622. A New Almanacke, and Prognostication.* STC 514.5.
    1625, STC 514.7.
Sofford, Arthur. *Sofford. 1621. A New Almanacke, and Prognostication.* STC 515.4.
    1633, STC 515.16.   1639, STC 515.22.
Swallow, Thomas. *Swallow. 1628. A New Almanacke.* Cambridge. STC 517.
Tapp, John. *The Sea-mans Kalender.* 1602. STC 23679.
Thibault, Jean. *Pronosticacyon of Maistre John Thibaulte.* 1530. STC 517.10.
    1533. STC 517.12.
Turner, Thomas. *Turner. 1633. An Almanack.* Cambridge. STC 518.
True, Patrick. *True. 1636. A New Almanack and Prognostication.* Dublin. STC 517.16.

Bibliography 289

Twyne, Thomas. *1579. [Almanac.]* STC 518.8.
1585, STC 518.10.
Upcote, Augustine. *Upcot. 1614. An New Almanack and Prognostication.* STC 519.
Vaughan, Lewes. *A New Almanacke and Prognostication, Collected for the Yeare of our Lord God. M.D.L.IX. 1559.* STC 520.
Vaux, John. *Vaux. 1622. A New Almanacke and Prognostication.* STC 522.2.
1624, STC 522.4. 1628, STC 522.8.
Waters, Fr. *Waters. 1627. A New Almanacke.* Cambridge. STC 524.
Watson, Robert. *A Doble Almanacke or Kalender Drawne for this Present Yeere 1600.* STC 525.4.
———. *Watson. 1598. A New Almanacke and Prognostication.* STC 525.2.
1602, STC 525.7.
Westhawe, Robert. *Westhawe. 1594. An Almanacke and Prognostication.* STC 526.
White, John. *White. 1619. A New Almanack and Prognostication.* STC 527.8.
1633, STC 527.23.
Winter, Fr. *Winter. 1633. An Almanack.* Cambridge. STC 530.
Woodhouse, John. *Woodhouse. 1633. A New Almanacke and Prognostication.* STC 531.24.
Woodhouse, William. *Woodhouse. 1602. An Almanacke and Prognostication.* STC 532.

Primers, bibles, and prayer books (listed chronologically)

Catholic Church. *Enchiridion, Preclare Ecclesie Sarum.* Paris, 1530. STC 15965.
———. *Hore Beate Virginis Marie.* Paris, 1520. STC 15926.
———. *Hore Beatissime Virginis Marie.* Paris, 1530. STC 15968.
———. *Hore Presentes Ad Usum Sarum.* Paris, 1498. STC 15887.
———. *The Primer in English and Latin, after Salisburie Use.* 1556. STC 16073.
———. *This Prymer of Salisbury Use is Se Tout along with Houtonyser Chyng.* Rouen, 1556. STC 16076.
———. *This Prymer of Salysbury Use.* Paris, 1529. STC 15961.5
———. *This Prymer of Salysbury Use.* Paris, 1530. STC 15965.
———. *This Prymer of Salysbury Use.* Paris, 1531. STC 15971.
———. *This Prymer of Salysbury Use.* Paris, 1532. STC 15978.
———. *An Uniforme and Catholyke Prymer in Latin and Englishe.* 1555. STC 16060.
Church of England. *A Goodly Prymer in Englyshe, Newly Corrected.* 1535. STC 15988.
———. *A Goodly Prymer in Englysshe, Newely Corrected.* [1538?] STC 15998.
———. *The Manual of Prayers, or the Prymer in Englyshe & Laten.* 1539. STC 16009.
———. *The Manuall of Prayers or Primer in Englysh.* [1540.] STC 16017.
———. *A Primer and a Catechisme.* 1570. STC 20377.3.
———. *The Primer and Catechisme Set Forth at Large.* [1560?] STC 16090.
———. *A Primer or Boke of Private Praier.* 1560. STC 20375.
———. *The Primer, Set Foorth by the Kynges Maijestie and His Clergie.* 1545. STC 16034.
———. *A Primmer, or Boke of Private Prayer.* 1553. STC 20374.

———. *A Prymer in Englyshe, with Certeyn Prayers & Godly Meditations*. 1534. STC 15986.
———. *A Prymmer or Boke of Private Prayer*. 1553. STC 20373.
———. *Thys Primer in Englyshe and in Laten*. Paris, 1538. STC 16008.3.

The book of common prayer

Church of England. *The Booke of the Common Prayer and Administracion of the Sacramentes*. 1549. STC 16267.
———. *The Booke of Common Prayer, and Adminiystracion of the Sacramentes*. 1552. STC 16288.
———. *The Boke of Co[m]mon Prayer, and Administracio[n] of the Sacramentes*. 1553. STC 16290.5.
———. *The Boke of Common Praier, and Administration of the Sacramentes*. 1559. STC 16291.
———. *The Booke of Common Praier, and Administration of the Sacramentes*. 1559. STC 16292.
———. *The Booke of Common Prayer, and Administration of the Sacramentes*. 1559 [1561?]. STC 16292a.
———. *Liber Precum Publicarum*. 1560. STC 16424a.
1572, STC 16426.

Bible and psalter

The Bible: Translated According to the Ebrew and Greek. 1599. STC 2173.
Church of England. *The Psalter, or, Psalmes of David*. 1563. STC 2384.5.

The Kalender

Anonymous. *Here Begynneth the kalender of Shepardes*. [1518?] STC 22410.
———. *The Kalender of Shepeherdes*. 1528. STC 22409.
———. *The Shepardes Kalender*. 1570. STC 22415.
———. *The Shepherds Kalender*. 1631. STC 22423.

Early modern printed books

Allen, Nicholas. *The Astronomers Game*. 1569. STC 361.3.
Allott, Robert. *Englands Parnassus*. 1600. STC 379.
Anonymous. *Compotus Manualis ad Usum Oxoniensium*. Oxford, 1519. STC 561.3.
———. *Here Begynneth the Compost of Ptholomeus*. [1530?]. STC 20480.
———. *The Husbandmans Practise*. 1550. STC 14009.
———. *A Mery Pronosticacion for the Yere of Chrystes Incarnacyon a Thousande Fyve Hundreth Fortye & Foure*. 1544. STC 394.5.
———. *Prognostycacion, and Almanacke of Two Shepherdes*. [1556.] STC 399.7.
———. *A Table Declaring What Planet Dooth Raigne Every Day and Houre Enduring for Ever*. 1598. STC 23634.5.
———. *Wryting Tables, with a Necessarie Calender for XXV. [Yea]res*. 1577. STC 26049.2.

Aristotle. *De Cursione Lune.* 1528. STC 768.
———. *Here Begynneth the Difference of Astronomy.* 1555. STC 770.7.
———. *Here Beginneth the Nature, and Dysposytyon of the Dayes of the Week.* 1554. STC 769.5.
———. *The Secrete of Secretes, Containing the Most Excellent and Learned Instructions of Aristotle the Prince of Philosophers.* 1572. STC 770.3.
———. *[Thus Endeth the Secrete of Secretes of Arystotle.]* 1528. STC 770.
Askham, Anthony. *A Litell Treatyse of Astronomy.* 1550. STC 857a.5.
———. *A Lytell Treatyse of Astronomy.* [1552.] STC 857a.
Batman, Stephen. *Batman upon Bartholome, His Booke De Proprietatibus Rerum.* 1582. STC 1538.
Blagrave, John. *The Mathematical Jewel.* 1585. STC 3119.
Blundeville, Thomas. *M. Blundevile His Exercises.* 1594. STC 3146.
Boorde, Andrew. *The Breviary of Healthe.* 1552. STC 3374.
———. *The Pryncyples of Astronamye.* 1547. STC 3386.
Bourne, William. *The Art of Shooting in Great Ordinance.* 1578. STC 3419.7.
———. *A Regiment for the Sea.* 1574. STC 3422.
———. *Treasure for Traveilers.* 1578. STC 3432.
Brathwaite, Richard. *Whimzies: or, a New Cast of Characters.* 1631. STC 3591.
Breton, Nicholas. *Fantasticks, Serving for Perpetuall Prognostication.* 1626. STC 3650.
Calvin, John. *An Admonicion against Astrology Judiciall.* 1561. STC 4372.
Carleton, George. *Astrologomania: The Madnesse of Astrologers.* Oxford, 1624. STC 4630.
Chamber, John. *A Treatise against Judicial Astrologie.* 1601. STC 4941.
Cogan, Thomas. *The Haven of Health.* 1584. STC 5478.
Coxe, Francis. *A Short Treatise Declaring the Detestable Wickednesse of Magicall Sciences.* 1561. STC 5950.
———. *The Unfained Retraction of Fraunces Cox.* 1561. STC 5951.
Cuningham, William. *The Cosmographical Glasse.* 1559. STC 6119.
Dariot, Claude. *A Breefe and most Easie Introduction to the Astrological Judgement of the Stars.* 1583. STC 6275.
    1598, STC 6276.
———. *Dariotus Redivivus, or, A Briefe Introduction Conducing to the Judgement of the Stars.* 1653. Wing D257.
Daw, Jack. *Vox Graculi, or Jacke Dawes Prognostication.* 1623. STC 6386.
Dekker, Thomas. *The Ravens Almanacke.* 1609. STC 6519.2.
Digges, Leonard. *An Arithmeticall Militare Treatise, named Stratioticos.* 1579. STC 6848.
———. *A Boke named Tectonicon.* 1561. STC 6849.5.
———. *A Geometrical Practice, named Pantometria.* 1571. STC 6858.
———. *A Prognostication Everlasting of Ryght Good Effecte.* 1556. STC 435.39.
———. *A Prognostication of Right Good Effect.* 1555. STC 435.55.
Elyot, Thomas. *The castel of helth gathered and made by Syr Thomas Elyot.* 1539. STC 7643.
Erra Pater. *The pronostycacyon for ever of Erra Pater.* 1540. STC 439.3.
    1605, STC 439.19.   1609, STC 439.21.

292   Bibliography

Fella, Thomas. *Thomas Fella: His Book of Divers Devices and Sorts of Pictures.* Edited by Martin Sanford and John Blatchly. Dorchester: The Dorset Press, 2012.

Field, John. *Ephemeris Anni.* 1557. STC 443.9.

———. *Ephemerides Trium Annorum. 58. 59. et 60.* 1558. STC 443.11.

Fine, Oronce. *The Rules and Righte Ample Documentes, Touching the Use and Practise of the Common Almanackes.* 1558. STC 10878.7.

Foulweather, Adam. *A Wonderfull, Strange and Miraculous, Astrologicall Prognostication for this Yeer of our Lord God 1591.* STC 11209.

Foxe, John. *Acts and Monuments of Matters most Speciall and Memorable.* 1632. STC 11228.

Fulke, William. *Antiprognosticon Contra Inutiles Astrologorum Praedictiones.* 1560. STC 11419.

———. *Antiprognosticon That Is to Saye, an Invective agaynst the Vayne and Unprofitable Predictions of the Astrologians.* 1560. STC 11420.

Gascoigne, George. *The Noble Arte of Venerie or Hunting.* 1575. STC 24328.

Godfridus. *Here begynneth the Boke of Knowledge of Thynges Unknowen Aperteynynge to Astronomy.* 1554. STC 11930.7.

———. *The Knowledge of Things Unkowne Apperteyning to Astronomy.* 1585. STC 11932.

Grafton, Richard. *A Briefe Treatise Conteinyng many Proper Tables and Easie Rules.* 1573. STC 12155.
1585, STC 12158.5.

———. *A Litle Treatise, Conteyning Many Proper Tables and Rules Very Necessary for the Use of All Men.* 1571. STC 12153.
1572, STC 12154.

Greene, Robert. *Planetomachia: Or the First Parte of the Generall Opposition of the Seven Planets.* 1585. STC 12299.

Harrison, William. *The Description of England: The Classic Contemporary Account of Tudor Social Life.* Edited by Georges Edelen. Ithaca, NY: Cornell University Press, 1968.

Hartgill, George. *Calendaria: Sive, Tabulae Astronomicae Universales.* 1594. STC 12895.

———. *Generall Calenders Or, Most Easie Astraonomicall Tables.* 1594. STC 12896.

Harvey, John. *An Astrologicall Addition.* 1583. STC 12907.

Harvey, Richard. *An Astrological Discourse upon the Great and Notable Conjunction of the Two Superiour Planets, Saturne & Jupiter.* 1583. STC 12155.

Hesiod. *The Georgicks of Hesiod.* Translated by George Chapman. London, 1618. STC 13249.

Heth [Heath], Thomas. *A Manifest and Apparent Confutation of an Astrological Discourse.* 1583. STC 13255.

Heydon, Sir Christopher. *A Defence of Judiciall Astrologie.* 1603. STC 13266.

Hill, Thomas. *The Proffitable Arte of Gardening.* 1568. STC 13491.

Holinshed, Raphael. *The First Volume of the Chronicles of England, Scotland, and Irelande.* 1587. STC 13569.5.

Hopton, Arthur. *A Concordancy of Yeares.* 1612. STC 13778.
1615. STC 13779.

Howard, Henry, Earl of Northampton. *A Defensative against the Poyson of Supposed Prophesies.* 1583. STC 15838.

Hutchinson, Roger. *The Image of God, or Laie Mans Booke.* 1550. STC 14019.
I., A. *A Perfyte Pronostycacion Perpetuall.* [1556?] STC 406.3.
Indagine, John. *Briefe Introductions, Bothe Naturall, Pleasaunte, and also Delectable, unto the Art of Chiromancy.* 1558. STC 14075.
James 1st, King of England. *Daemonologie in Forme of a Dialogue.* 1597. STC 14364.
Jonson, Ben. *The Comicall Satyre of Every Man Out of his Humor.* 1600. STC 14767.
Lilly, William. *Christian Astrology.* 1647. Wing L2215.
Lupton, Thomas. *A Thousand Notable Things, of Sundry Sortes.* 1579. STC 16955.
Magnus, Albertus. *The Boke of Secretes of Albertus Magnus.* 1560. STC 258.5.
Maplet, John. *The Diall of Destiny.* 1581. STC 17295.
Markham, Gervase. *The Second Booke of the English Husbandmen.* 1614. STC 17356.
———. *Verus Pater.* 1622. STC 24693.
de Mediolano, Joannes. *Regimen Sanitatis Salerni.* 1528. STC 21596.
Melton, John, *Astrologaster, or, The Figure-Caster.* 1620. STC 17804.
Middleton, Thomas. *No Wit No Help like a Womans.* London, 1657. Wing, M1985.
———. *The Owles Almanacke.* London, 1618. STC 6515.
de Montulmo, Antonius. *A Ryghte Excellente Treatise of Astronomie.* 1554. STC 483.14.
Moulton, Thomas. *This is the Myrour or Glasse of Helthe.* [Before 1531.] STC 18214a.
Ovid. *Ovids Festivalls, or Romane Calendar.* Cambridge, 1640. Trans. John Gower. STC 18948.5.
———. *The xv Bookes of P. Ovidius Naso, Entytuled Metamorphosis.* Translated by Arthur Golding. 1567. STC 18956.
Overbury, Sir Thomas. *Sir Thomas Overburie his Wife.* 1616. STC 18909.
Perkins, William. *Foure Great Lyers.* 1584. STC 19721.7.
Pliny, the Elder. *The Historie of the World.* 1601. Translated by Philemon Holland. STC 20029.
Plot, Robert. *The Natural History of Stafford-shire.* 1686. Wing P2588.
Prid, William. *The Glasse of Vaine-Glorie: Translated out of S. Augustine.* 1600. STC 931.
Record, Robert. *The Castle of Knowledge.* 1556. STC 20796.
Roussat, Richard. *Arcandam Doctor Peritissimus ac Non Vulgaris Astrologus.* Paris, 1542.
———. *The Most Excellent, Profitable, and Pleasant Booke of the Famous Doctor and Expert Astrologien Arcandam or Aleandrin.* [1562?] STC 724.
Scot, Reginald. *The Discoverie of Witchcraft.* 1584. STC 21864.
Searle, John. *An Ephemeris for Nine Yeeres.* 1609. STC 22142.
Simotta, George. *A Theater of the Planetary Houres for All Dayes of the Yeare.* 1631. STC 22561.
Spenser, Edmund. *The Shepheardes Calender.* 1586. STC 23091.
Stow, John. *Summarie of the English Chronicles.* 1566. STC 23325.4.
———. *A Survay of London.* 1598. STC 23341.
Stubbes, Philip. *The Second Part of the Anatomie of Abuses.* 1583. STC 23380.5.
———. *The Anatomie of Abuses.* 1583.
Tanner, Robert. *"A Mirror for Mathematiques."* 1587. STC 23674.5.
———. *A Prognosticall Judgement of the Great Conjunction of the Two Superiour Planets.* 1583. STC 23676.

Trevelyon, Thomas. *The Trevelyon Miscellany of 1608: A Facsimile Edition of Folger Shakespeare Library MS V.b.232*. Edited by Heather Wolfe. Washington, DC: Folger Shakespeare Library, 2007.

Trevilian, Thomas. *The Great Book of Thomas Trevilian: A Facsimile from the Manuscript in the Wormsley Library*. Edited with an Introduction by Nicolas Barker. The Roxburghe Club, 2000.

Tusser, Thomas. *Five Hundred Points of Good Husbandry*. 1614. STC 24389. 1610, STC 24388.

Verstegen, Richard. *A Restitution of Decayed Intelligence: In Antiquities*. Antwerp, 1605. STC 21361.

Virgil. *The Bucoliks of Publius Virgilius Maro*. 1589. Trans. Abraham Fleming. STC 24817.

W.W. *A New, and Merrie Prognostication*. 1623. STC 24921.

Whitney, Geffrey. *A Choice of Emblemes*. 1586. STC 25438.

Secondary bibliography

Allen, Don Cameron. *The Star-Crossed Renaissance: The Quarrel about Astrology and its Influence in England*. Durham: Duke University Press, 1941.

Ambrose, Laura Williamson. "Travel in Time: Local Travel Writing and Seventeenth-Century English Almanacs." *Journal of Medieval and Early Modern Studies* 43, no. 2 (2013): 419–443.

Anderson, Jennifer, and Elizabeth Sauer, eds. *Books and Readers in Early Modern England: Material Studies*. Philadelphia: University of Pennsylvania Press, 2002.

Arber, Edward, ed. *A Transcript of the Registers of the Company of Stationers 1554–1640 A.D.* London and Birmingham: privately printed, 1875–1894.

Aston, Margaret. "The Fiery Trigon Conjunction: An Elizabethan Astrological Prediction." *Isis* 61.2, no. 207 (1970): 159–187.

Barker, Nicholas, ed. *The Great Book of Thomas Trevilian*. London: The Roxburghe Club, 2000.

Barnes, Robin B. *Astrology and Reformation*. Oxford: Oxford University Press, 2016.

Bauckman, Richard. "Science and Religion in the Writings of Dr. William Fulke." *British Journal for the History of Science* 8, no. 1 (1975): 17–31.

The Benedictine Monks of St. Augustine's Abbey, Ramsgate. *The Book of Saints*. London: A&C Black, Ltd, 1921.

Berry, Philippa. "Between Idolatry and Astrology: Modes of Temporal Repetition in *Romeo and Juliet*." In *A Feminist Companion to Shakespeare*, edited by Dympna Callaghan, 378–392. Oxford: Wiley-Blackwell, 2001.

Bezza, Giuseppe. "Representation of the Skies and the Astrological Chart." In *A Companion to Astrology to the Renaissance*, edited by Brendan Dooley, 59–86. Leiden: Brill, 2014.

Birchenough, Edwyn. "The Prymer in English." *The Library*, Series 4, no. 18 (1938): 177–194.

Blagden, Cyprian. "The Distribution of Almanacks in the Second Half of the Seventeenth Century." *Studies in Bibliography* 11 (1958): 107–116.

———. "The English Stock of the Stationers' Company." *The Library: The Transactions of the Bibliographical Society* 10, 5th Series (1955): 163–185.

———. "The English Stock of the Stationers' Company in the Time of the Stuarts." *The Library: The Transactions of the Bibliographical Society* 12, 5th series (1957): 167–186.

———. *The Stationers Company: A History, 1403–1959.* Cambridge, MA: Harvard University Press, 1960.

Blayney, Peter. *The Stationers Company and the Printers of London, 1501–1557.* 2 vols. Cambridge: Cambridge University Press, 2013.

Bober, Harry. "The Zodiacal Miniature of the Tres Riches Heures of the Duke of Berry: Its Sources and Meaning." *Journal of the Warburg and Courtauld Institutes* 11 (1948): 1–34.

Bodley, Sir Thomas. *Letters to Thomas James, Keeper of Bodleian Library.* Oxford: Clarendon Press, 1926.

Boorst, Arno. *The Ordering of Time: From the Ancient Computus to the Modern Computer.* Trans. Andrew Winnard. Chicago: University of Chicago Press, 1993.

Booty, John, ed. *The Book of Common Prayer 1559: The Elizabethan Prayer Book.* Washington, DC: The Folger Shakespeare Library, 1976.

Bosanquet, Eustace F. *English Printed Almanacks and Prognostications: A Bibliographical History to the Year 1600.* London: Chiswick Press, 1917.

———. "Notes on Further Addenda to English Printed Almanacks and Prognostications to 1600. *The Library*, 4th series, 18 (1937): 39–66.

Braswell, Laurel. "The Moon and Medicine in Chaucer's Time." *Studies in the Age of Chaucer* 8 (1986): 145–156.

Brouscon, Guillaume. *Sir Francis Drake's Nautical Almanack, 1546.* London: Nottingham Court Press, in association with Magdalene College, Cambridge, 1980.

Burnett, Charles. "The Twelfth-Century Renaissance." In *The Cambridge History of Science, Volume 2*, edited by David C. Lindberg and Michael H. Shank, 365–384. Cambridge: Cambridge University Press, 2013.

Burrow, J.A. *The Ages of Man: A Study in Medieval Writing and Thought.* Oxford: Oxford University Press, 1988.

Butterworth, Charles C. *The English Primers, 1529–1545.* Philadelphia: University of Pennsylvania Press, 1953.

Callaghan, Dympna. "Confounded by Winter: Speeding Time in Shakespeare's Sonnets." In *A Companion to Shakespeare's Sonnets*, edited by Michael Schoenfeldt, 104–118. Oxford: Blackwell Publishing, 2007.

Camden, Carroll. "Astrology in Shakespeare's Day." *Isis* 19 (1933): 26–73.

———. "Elizabethan Almanacs and Prognostications." *The Library* 12 (1931): 83–108 and 194–207.

———. "Elizabethan Astrological Medicine." *Annals of Medical History* 2 (1930): 217–226.

———. "The Wonderful Year." In *Studies in Honor of Dewitt T. Starnes*, edited by Thomas P. Harrison, Archibald A. Hill, Ernest C. Mossner, and James Sledd, 163–179. Austin: The University of Texas Press, 1967.

Capp, Bernard. *Astrology and the Popular Press: English Almanacs, 1500–1800.* Ithaca, NY: Cornell University Press, 1979.

———. "Booker, John (1602–1667), Astrologer." *Oxford Dictionary of National Biography.* 23 September 2004. Accessed 19 November 2019.

———. "Bretnor, Thomas (1570/71–1618), astrologer and medical practitioner." *Oxford Dictionary of National Biography*. 23 September 2004; Accessed 10 December 2020.

Carey, Hilary M. "Astrological Medicine and the Medieval Folded Almanac." *Social History of Medicine* 16 (2004): 345–363.

———. *Courting Disaster: Astrology at the English Court and University in the Later Middle Ages*. New York: St. Martin's Press, 1992.

———. "Henry VII's Book of Astrology and the Tudor Renaissance." *Renaissance Quarterly* 65, no. 3 (2012): 661–710.

———. "What is the Folded Almanac?" *Social History of Medicine* 16, no. 3 (2003): 481–509.

Carlebach, Elisheva. *Palaces of Time: Jewish Calendar and Culture in Early Modern Europe*. Cambridge, MA: Harvard University Press, 2011.

Catholic Church. Catholic Online. https://www.catholic.org/saints/.

Chapman, Alan. "Astrological Medicine." In *Health, Medicine, and Mortality in the 16th Century*, edited by Charles Webster, 275–300. Cambridge: Cambridge University Press, 1979.

Chapman, Alison A. "Marking Time: Astrology, Almanacs and English Protestantism." *Renaissance Quarterly* 60, no. 4 (2007): 1257–1290.

———. "Now and Then: Sequencing the Sacred in Two Protestant Calendars." *Journal of Medieval and Early Modern Studies* 33, no. 1 (2003): 91–123.

———. *Patrons and Patron Saints in Early Modern English Literature*. London: Routledge, 2013.

———. "The Politics of Time in Edmund Spenser's English Calendar." *Studies in English Literature* 42, no. 1 (2002): 1–24.

———. "Whose Saint Crispin's Day Is It? Shoemaking, Holiday Making, and the Politics of Memory in Early Modern England." *Renaissance Quarterly* 54, no. 4 (2001): 1467–1494.

Cheney, C.R. *Handbook of Dates for Students of English History*. Cambridge: Cambridge University Press, 1995.

Church of England. *The Calendar of the Prayer-Book Illustrated, with an Appendix of the Chief Christian Emblems*. Oxford and London: James Parker and Co, 1866.

Clegg, Cyndia Susan. *Press Censorship in Elizabethan England*. Cambridge: Cambridge University Press, 1997.

———. *Press Censorship in Jacobean England*. Cambridge: Cambridge University Press, 2001.

Coates, Alan Edward, Nigel F. Palmer, and Silke Schaeper, eds. *A Catalogue of Books Printed in the Fifteenth Century Now in the Bodleian Library*. Oxford: Oxford University Press, 2005.

Considine, John. "Hill, Thomas [pseud. Didymus Mountaine] (c. 1528–c. 1574), Writer and Translator." *Oxford Dictionary of National Biography*. 23 Sep. 2004; Accessed 1 Dec. 2019.

Cooper, Helen. "Pastoral and Georgic." In *The Oxford History of Classical Reception in English Literature*, edited by Norman Vance and Jennifer Wallace, 201–224. Oxford: Oxford University Press, 2015.

Copenhaver, Brian P. "Astrology and Magic." In *The Cambridge History of Renaissance Philosophy*, edited by C.B. Schmitt, Quentin Skinner, Eckhard Kessler, and Jill Kraye, 264–300. Cambridge: Cambridge University Press, 1988.

———. "Natural Magic, Hermeticism, and Occultism in Early Modern Science." In *Reappraisals of the Scientific Revolution*, edited by David C. Lindberg and Robert S. Westman, 261–302. Cambridge: Cambridge University Press, 1990.

Coyne, G.V., S.J, M.A. Hoskin, and O. Pedersen, eds. *Gregorian Reform of the Calendar*. Rome: Pontificia Academia Scientiarum, 1983.

Craig, Hardin, ed. *The Works of John Metham*. London: Kegan Paul, Trench, Trubner, & Co., for The Early English Text Society, 1916.

Crane, Mary Thomas. *Losing Touch with Nature: Literature and the New Science in Sixteenth Century England*. Baltimore: Johns Hopkins University Press, 2014.

Cranfield, Nicholas W. S. "Beale, William (d. 1651), college head." *Oxford Dictionary of National Biography*. 23 September 2004; Accessed 9 September 2019.

Craven, William G. *Giovanni Pico della Mirandola: Symbol of his Age*. Geneva: Librarie Droz, 1981.

Cressy, David. *Bonfires and Bells: National Memory and the Protestant Calendar in Elizabethan and Jacobean England*. Berkeley: University of California Press, 1989.

Cross, Claire. "Gilby, Anthony (c. 1510–1585), Religious Writer and Church of England Clergyman." *Oxford Dictionary of National Biography*. 23 September 2004. Accessed 3 March 2019.

Cummings, Brian. *The Book of Common Prayer: The Texts of 1549, 1559, and 1662*. Oxford: Oxford University Press, 2013.

Curry, Patrick. *Prophecy and Power: Astrology in Early Modern England*. Princeton, NJ: Princeton University Press, 1989.

Curth, Louise. "The Commercialisation of Medicine in the Popular Press: English Almanacs 1640–1700." *The Seventeenth Century* 17, no. 1 (2002): 48–69.

———. *English Almanacs, Astrology and Popular Medicine*. Manchester: Manchester University Press, 2007.

Daly, Peter M. "The Sheldon 'Four Seasons' Tapestries at Hatfield House: A Seventeenth-Century Instance of Significant Emblematic Decoration in the English Decorative Arts." *Emblematica* 14 (2005): 251–296.

Das, Nandini, ed. *Robert Greene's Planetomachia (1585)*. Aldershot: Ashgate, 2007.

Dawson, Mark. "Astrology and Human Variation in Early Modern England." *The Historical Journal* 56, no. 1 (2013): 31–53.

Dempsey, Charles. *The Portrayal of Love: Botticelli's Primavera and Humanist Culture at the Time of Lorenzo the Magnificent*. Princeton, NJ: Princeton University Press, 1992.

Dohrn-van Rossum, Gerhard. *History of the Hour: Clocks and Modern Temporal Hours*. Chicago: Chicago University Press, 1992.

Dooley, Brendan, ed. *A Companion to Astrology in the Renaissance*. Leiden: Brill, 2014.

Driver, Martha W. "Ideas of Order: Wynkyn de Worde and the Title Page." In *Texts and Their Contexts: Papers from the Early Book Society*, edited by Julia Boffey and V. J. Scattergood, 87–149. Dublin: Four Courts, 1997.

———. "The Illustrated de Worde: An Overview." *Studies in Iconography* 17 (1996): 349–403.

———. *The Image in Print: Book Illustration in Late Medieval England and its Sources*. London: The British Library, 2004.

———. "When is a Miscellany Not Miscellaneous? Making Sense of the 'Kalender of Shepherds.'" *The Yearbook of English Studies* 33 (2003): 199–214.

———. "Woodcuts and Decorative Techniques." In *A Companion to the Early Printed Book in Britain, 1476–1558*, edited by Vincent Gillespie and Susan Powell, 95–124. Woodbridge, England: Brewer, 2014.

Duffy, Eamon. *Marking the Hours: English People & their Prayers, 1240–1570*. New Haven, CT: Yale University Press, 2006.

Eade, J.C. *The Forgotten Sky: Astrology in English Literature*. Oxford: Oxford University Press, 1984.

Eamon, William. "Astrology and Society." In *A Companion to Astrology*, edited by Brendan Dooley, 141–191. Leiden: Brill, 2014.

Early English Books Online. "About EEBO and the Text Creation Partnership," eebo.chadwyck.com.

Eisner, John, ed., *The Kalendarium of Nicholas of Lynn*. Athens: The University of Georgia Press, 1979.

Erler, Mary. "The Laity." In *A Companion to the Early Printed Book in Britain, 1476–1558*, edited by Vincent Gillespie and Susan Powell, 134–149. Cambridge: D. S. Brewer, 2014.

———. "The *Maner to Live Well* and the Coming of English in Francois Regnault's Primers of the 1520s and 1530s." *The Library* 6 (1984): 229–243.

Faracovi, Ornella. "The Return to Ptolemy." In *A Companion to Astrology*, edited by Brendan Dooley, 87–98. Leiden: Brill, 2014.

Farmer, David Hugh. *The Oxford Dictionary of Saints*. Oxford: Oxford University Press, 5th edition, 2010.

Fissell, Mary. "Readers, Texts, and Contexts: Vernacular Medical Works in Early Modern England." In *The Popularization of Medicine, 1650–1850*, edited by Roy Porter, 72–96. London: Routledge, 1992.

Fleming, Juliet. *Graffiti and the Writing Arts of Early Modern England*. Philadelphia: University of Pennsylvania Press, 2001.

Fleming, Juliet, William H. Sherman, and Adam Smyth, eds. "The Renaissance Collage: Toward a New History of Reading." *Journal of Medieval and Early Modern Studies* 45, no. 3 (2015).

Ford, Margaret Lane. "Importation of printed books into England and Scotland." In *The Cambridge History of the Book*, edited by Lotte Hellinga and J. B. Trapp, 179–201. Cambridge: Cambridge University Press, 2008.

Fowler, J. "On the Medieval Representations on the Months and Seasons." *Archaeologia* 44 (1873): 137–189.

Friedman, John B. "Harry the Hawarde and Talbat His Dog: An Illustrated Girdlebook from Worcestershire." In *Art Into Life: Collected Papers from the Kresge Art Museum Medieval Symposia*, edited by Carol Garrett Fisher, Scott Fisher, and Kathleen L. Scott, 115–153. East Lansing: Michigan State University Press, 1995.

Garin, Eugenio. *Astrology in the Renaissance: The Zodiac of Life*. Trans. Carolyn Jackson and June Allen. London: Routledge and Kegan Paul, 1983.

Geneva, Ann. *Astrology and the Seventeenth Century Mind: William Lilly and the Language of the Stars*. Manchester: Manchester University Press, 1995.

George, David. "Weather-Wise's Almanac and the Date of Middleton's 'No Wit No Help like a Woman's.'" *Notes and Queries* 211, no. 13 (1966): 297–301.

Grafton, Anthony. *Cardano's Cosmos: The Worlds and Works of a Renaissance Astrologer*. Cambridge, MA: Harvard University Press, 2000.

———. *Commerce with the Classics*. Ann Arbor: University of Michigan Press, 1997.

Grafton, Anthony, and Daniel Rosenberg. *Cartographies of Time: A History of the Timeline*. Princeton, NJ: Princeton Architectural Press, 2010.

Grafton, Anthony, and William R. Newman. *Secrets of Nature: Astrology and Alchemy in Early Modern Europe*. Cambridge, MA: MIT Press, 2011.

Grant, Edward. "Cosmology." In *The Cambridge History of Science, Volume 2: Medieval Science*, edited by David C. Lindberg and Michael H. Shank, 436–455. Cambridge: Cambridge University Press, 2013.

———. *Planets, Stars, and Orbs: The Medieval Cosmos, 1200–1687*. Cambridge: Cambridge University Press, 1994.

Greenblatt, Stephen, ed. *The Norton Shakespeare, Based on the Oxford Edition*. By William Shakespeare. Third edition. New York: WW Norton, 1998.

Gross, Joseph. "Hartgill, George (b. in or before 1555, d. in or before 1597), Astronomer and Astrologer." *Oxford Dictionary of National Biography*. 23 September 2004. Accessed 19 December 2018.

Gumbert, J. P. *Bat Books: A Catalogue of Folded Manuscripts Containing Almanacs or Other Texts*. Turnhout: Brepols, 2016.

Halio, Jay, ed. *The Tragedy of King Lear*. By William Shakespeare. Cambridge: Cambridge University Press, 1992.

Hamling, Tara. *Decorating the Godly Household: Religious Art in Post-Reformation Britain*. New Haven, CT: Yale University Press, 2010.

Harkness, Deborah. *The Jewel House: Elizabethan London and the Scientific Revolution*. New Haven, CT: Yale University Press, 2008.

Hellinga, Lotte, and J. B. Trapp. *The Cambridge History of the Book in Britain, Volume 3, 1400–1557*. Cambridge: Cambridge University Press, 2008.

Heninger, S.K. *A Handbook of Renaissance Meteorology*. Durham: Duke University Press, 1960.

Henisch, Bridget Ann. *The Medieval Calendar Year*. University Park: The Pennsylvania University Press, 1999.

Hetherington, Norriss S. "Almanacs and the Extent of Knowledge of the New Astronomy in Seventeenth Century England." *Proceedings of the American Philosophical Society* 119, no. 4 (1975): 275–279.

Hodnett, Edward. *English Woodcuts 1480–1535*. Oxford: Oxford University Press, 1973.

Horrocks, Thomas A. *Popular Print and Popular Medicine: Almanacs and Health Advice in Early America*. Amherst: University of Massachusetts Press, 2008.

Hoskins, Edgar. *Horae Beatae Mariae Virginis or Sarum and York Primers with Kindred Books*. London: Longmans, Green, and Co., 1901.

Hourihane, Colum. *Time in the Medieval World: Occupations of the Months and Signs of the Zodiac*. Princeton, NJ: The Index of Christian Art, distributed by Pennsylvania State University Press, 2007.

Hunt, Arnold. "Book Trade Patents, 1603–1640." In *The Book Trade and its Customers 1450–1900: Historical Essays for Robin Myers*, edited by Arnold Hunt, Giles Mandelbrote, and Alison Shell, 27–54. Winchester: St. Paul's Bibliographies, 1997.

Hunt, Maurice. "Climacteric Ages and the Three Seasons of *The Winter's Tale*." *Renascence* 69, no. 2 (2017): 69–80.

Ingram, Martin. "Ridings, Rough Music and the 'Reform of Popular Culture' in Early Modern England." *Past and Present* 105, no. 1 (1984): 79–113.

Jackson, William A. "Variant Entry Fees of the Stationers' Company." *The Papers of the Bibliographical Society of America* 51, no. 2 (1957): 103–110.

Jensen, Phebe. "Astrology in the Long Reformation: 'Doctor *Faustus* in Swadling Clouts.'" *Reformation* 24, no. 2 (2019), 92–106.

———. "Causes in Nature: Popular Astrology in *King Lear*." *Shakespeare Quarterly* 69, no. 4 (2018): 205–227.

———. *Religion and Revelry in Shakespeare's Festive World*. Cambridge: Cambridge University Press, 2008.

Johnson, A.F. "Title-pages: Their Forms and Development." In *Selected Essays on Books and Printing*, edited by Percy H. Muir, 288–297. Amsterdam: Van Gendt & Co, 1970.

Johnson, Francis R. *Astronomical Thought in Renaissance England: A Study of the English Scientific Writings from 1500 to 1645*. Baltimore, MD: The Johns Hopkins Press, 1937.

Johnston, Stephen. "Digges, Leonard (c. 1515–c. 1559), Mathematician." *Oxford Dictionary of National Biography*. 23 September 2004. Accessed 20 November 2019.

Jones, Norman L. "Elizabeth, Edification, and the Latin Prayer Book of 1560." *Church History* 53, no. 2 (1984): 174–186.

Jones, Peter Murray. "Medicine and Science." In *The Cambridge History of the Book in Britain Volume III: 1400–1557*, edited by Lotte Hellinga and J.B. Trapp, 433–448. Cambridge: Cambridge University Press, 1999.

Jowett, John. "The Writing Tables of James Roberts," *The Library* 20, no.1 (2019): 64–88.

Juste, David, and Hilbert Chiu. "The 'De Tonitruis' Attributed to Bede: An Early Medieval Treatise on Divination by Thunder Translated from Irish." *Traditio* 68 (2013): 97–124.

Kassell, Lauren. "Almanacs and Prognostications." In *The Oxford History of Popular Print Culture, Volume I, Cheap Print in Britain and Ireland to 1660*, edited by Joad Raymond, 431–442. Oxford: Oxford University Press, 2011.

———. "Maplet, John (d. 1592), writer on natural philosophy." *Oxford Dictionary of National Biography*. 23 September 2004. Accessed 19 June 2019.

———. *Medicine and Magic in Elizabethan London: Simon Forman: Astrologer, Alchemist, and Physician*. Oxford: Clarendon Press, 2005.

Kathman, David. "Roberts, James (b. in or before 1540, d. 1618?), Bookseller and Printer." *Oxford Dictionary of National Biography*. 23 September 2004. Accessed 20 November 2019.

Kendrick, A. F. "The Hatfield Tapestries of the Seasons." *The Annual Volume of the Walpole Society* 2 (1912–1913): 89–95.

Kibre, Pearl. "'Astronomia' or 'Astrologia' Ypocratis." In *Studies in Medieval Science, Alchemy, Astrology, Mathematics, and Medicine*, XIV 133–156. London: The Hambledon Press, 1984.

Kiefer, Frederick. *Shakespeare's Visual Theatre: Staging the Personified Characters*. Cambridge: Cambridge University Press, 2003.

Klein, H. Arthur. *Graphic Worlds of Peter Bruegel the Elder*. New York: Dover Publications, 1963.

Landes, David. *Revolution in Time: Clocks and the Making of the Modern World.* Cambridge, MA: Harvard University Press, 1983.
Langeslag, Paul S. *Seasons in the Literatures of the Medieval North.* Woodbridge, Suffolk: D.S. Brewer, 2015.
Larkey, Sanford V. "Astrology and Politics in the First Years of Elizabeth's Reign." *Bulletin of the Institute of the History of Medicine* 3, no. 3 (1935): 171–186.
Lawrence-Mathers, Anne. "Domesticating the Calendar." In *Women and Writing, c. 1340-c. 1650,* edited by Anne Lawrence-Mathers and Phillipa Hardman, 34–61. York: York Medieval Press, 2010.
Le Goff, Jacques. *Time, Work and Culture in the Middle Ages.* Trans. Arthur Goldhammer. Chicago: University of Chicago Press, 1980.
Lindberg, David C., and Michael Shank, eds., *The Cambridge History of Science, Volume 2: Medieval Science.* Cambridge: Cambridge University Press, 2013.
Luborsky, Ruth Samson, and Elizabeth Morley Ingram. *A Guide to English Illustrated Books, 1536–1603.* 2 vols. Tempe, AZ: Medieval & Renaissance Texts & Studies, 1998.
Marston, John. *Jacke Drums Entertainment.* In *The Plays of John Marston in Three Volumes, Volume Three,* edited by H. Harvey Wood. Edinburgh: Oliver and Boyd, 1939.
McCluskey, Stephen C. *Astronomies and Cultures in Early Medieval Europe.* Cambridge: Cambridge University Press, 1998.
McKerrow, Ronald Brunlee, and F. S. Ferguson. *Title Page Borders used in England & Scotland, 1485–1640.* London: Printed for the Bibliographical Society at the Oxford University Press, 1932.
McRae, Andrew. *Literature and Domestic Travel in Early Modern England.* Cambridge: Cambridge University Press, 2009.
Means, Laurel Braswell. *Medieval Lunar Astrology: A Collection of Representative Middle English Texts.* Lewiston, NY: Edwin Mellen Press, 1993.
Mooney, Linne R. "English Almanacs from Script to Print." In *Texts and their Contexts: Papers from the Early Text Society,* edited by John Scattergood and Julia Boffey, 11–25. Dublin: Four Courts Press, 1997.
———. "A Middle English Verse Compendium of Astrological Medicine." *Medical History* 28, no. 4 (1984): 406–419.
Mooney, Linne R., ed. *The Kalendarium of John Somer.* Athens: The University of Georgia Press, 1999.
Moore, N., and Bakewell, S. "Securis [Hatchett], John (fl. 1550–1580), physician." *Oxford Dictionary of National Biography.* 23 September 2004; Accessed 10 September 2019.
Moreton, Jennifer. "John of Sacrobosco and the Calendar." *Viator* 25 (1994): 229–244.
———. "Robert Grosseteste and the Calendar." In *Robert Grosseteste: New Perspectives on his Thought and Scholarship,* edited by James McEvoy, 77–88. Turnhout: Brepols, 1996.
Morgan, Paul. "George Hartgill: An Elizabethan Parson-Astronomer and his Library." *Annals of Science* 24, no. 4 (1968): 295–311.
Murphy, Donna. *The Mysterious Connection Between Thomas Nashe, Thomas Dekker, and T.M.: An English Renaissance Deception?* Cambridge: Cambridge Scholars Publishing, 2013.

Nicholson, Marjorie. "English Almanacs and the 'New Astronomy.'" *Annals of Science* 4, no. 1 (1939): 1–33.
North, John D. "Astronomy and Astrology." In *The Cambridge History of Science, Volume 2: Medieval Science*, edited by David C. Lindberg and Michael H. Shank, 456–484. Cambridge: Cambridge University Press, 2013.
———. "Celestial Influence: The Major Premise of Astrology." In *Astrological Hallucinati: Stars and the End of the World in Luther's Time*, edited by Paolo Zambelli, 44–100. Berlin: De Gruyter, 1986.
———. *Horoscopes and History*. London: University of London, 1986.
———. "Medieval Concepts of Celestial Influence: A Survey." In *Astrology, Science, and Society: Historical Essays*, edited by Patrick Curry, 5–17. Woodbridge: Boydell and Brewer, 1987.
O'Boyle, Cornelius. "Astrology and Medicine in Later Medieval England: The Calendars of John Somer and Nicholas of Lynn." *Sudhoffs Archiv* 89, no. 1 (2005): 1–22.
Panofsky, Erwin. *Studies in Iconology: Humanistic Themes in the Art of the Renaissance*. Oxford: Oxford University Press, 1939.
Panofsky, Erwin, Raymond Klibansky, and Fritz Saxl. *Saturn and Melancholy: Studies in the History of Natural Philosophy, Religion and Art*. London: Thomas Nelson and Sons, 1964.
Parr, Johnstone. "Edmund's Nativity in *King Lear*." *The Shakespeare Association Bulletin* 21 (1946), 181–185.
———. *Tamburlaine's Malady and Other Essays on Astrology in Elizabethan Drama*. Tuscaloosa: University of Alabama Press, 1953.
Parry, Glyn. *The Arch-Conjuror of England: John Dee*. New Haven, CT: Yale University Press, 2011.
Pearsall, Derek, and Elizabeth Salter. *Landscapes and Seasons of the Medieval World*. Toronto: University of Toronto Press, 1973.
Pollard, Alfred W., and G. R. Redgrave. *A Short-Title Catalogue of Books Printed in England, Scotland, & Ireland*. London: Bibliographical Society, 1976–1991.
Poole, Robert. *Time's Alteration: Calendar Reform in Early Modern England*. London: UCL Press Limited, 1998.
Prescott, Anne Lake. "Getting a Record: Stubbs, Singleton, and a 1579 Almanac." *Sidney Journal* 22, nos. 1–2 (2004): 131–137.
Principe, Lawrence. *The Scientific Revolution: A Very Short Introduction*. Oxford: Oxford University Press, 2011.
Ptolemy. *Ptolemy: Tetrabiblos*. Edited and translated by F.E. Robbins. Cambridge, MA: Harvard University Press, 1940.
Rabin, Sheila J. "Pico and the Historiography of Renaissance Astrology." *Explorations in Renaissance Culture* 36, no. 2 (2010): 170–180.
Raymond, Joad. "Pond, Edward (d. 1629), Almanac Maker." *Oxford Dictionary of National Biography*. 23 September 2004. Accessed 7 December 2018.
Raymond, Joad, ed. *The Oxford History of Popular Print Culture, Volume I, Cheap Print in Britain and Ireland to 1660*. Oxford: Oxford University Press, 2011.
Reeve, Matthew. *Thirteenth Century Wall Painting of Salisbury Cathedral: Art, Liturgy, Reform*. Woodbridge, Suffolk: Boydell, 2008.
Rhodes, Neil, ed. "The Owl's Almanac." In *Thomas Middleton: The Collected Works*, edited by Gary Taylor and John Lavagnin, 1271–1302. Oxford: Oxford University Press, 2007.

Richards, E. G. *Mapping Time: The Calendar and Its History.* Oxford: Oxford University Press, 1998.
Robbins, F.E., ed., and trans. *Ptolemy: Tetrabiblos.* Cambridge, MA: Harvard University Press, 1940.
Robbins, Rossell Hope. "English Almanacks of the Fifteenth Century." *Philological Quarterly* 18 (1939): 321–331.
———. "Medical Manuscripts in Middle English." *Speculum* 45, no. 3 (1970): 393–415.
Rusche, Harry. "Edmund's Conception and Nativity in *King Lear*." *Shakespeare Quarterly* 20, no. 2 (1969), 161–164.
Rutkin, H. Darrel. "Astrology." In *The Cambridge History of Science, Volume 3: Early Modern Science*, edited by Katherine Park and Lorraine Daston, 541–561. Cambridge: Cambridge University Press, 2008.
———. "Mysteries of Attraction: Giovanni Pico della Mirandola, Astrology and Desire." *Studies in History and Philosophy of Biological and Biomedical Sciences* 41 (2010): 117–124.
———. *Sapientia Astrologica: Astrology, Magic and Natural Knowledge, ca. 1250–1800.* Cham, Switzerland: Springer, 2019.
———. "Understanding the History of Astrology (and Magic) Accurately: Methodological Reflections on Terminology and Anachronism." *Philosophical Readings* 7, no. 1 (2015): 42–54.
Sanford, Martin, and John Blatchly, eds. *Thomas Fella: His Book of Divers Devices and Sorts of Pictures.* Dorchester: The Dorset Press, 2012.
Schaffer, Simon. "Science." In *The Oxford History of Popular Print Culture, Volume I, Cheap Print in Britain and Ireland to 1660*, edited by Joad Raymond, 398–416. Oxford: Oxford University Press, 2011.
Shakespeare, William. *Romeo and Juliet.* Edited by René Weis. London: Bloomsbury Arden, 2012.
Sherman, William H. *John Dee: The Politics of Reading and Writing in the English Renaissance.* Amherst: University of Massachusetts Press, 1995.
———. *Used Books: Marking Readers in Renaissance England.* Philadelphia: University of Pennsylvania Press, 2008.
Shinn, Abigail. "'Extraordinary Discourses of Unnecessarie matter': Spenser's *Shepheardes Calender* and the Almanac Tradition." In *Literature and Popular Culture in Early Modern England*, edited by Andrew Hadfield and Matthew Dimmock. Farnham, Surrey: Ashgate, 2009.
Simmons, R. C. "ABCs, Almanacs, Ballads, Chapbooks, Popular Piety and Textbooks." In *The Cambridge History of the Book in Britain, Volume 3, 1400–1557*, edited by Lotte Hellinga and J.B. Trapp, 504–513. Cambridge: Cambridge University Press, 2008.
Siraisi, Nancy G. *Medieval and Early Renaissance Medicine: An Introduction to Knowledge and Practice.* Chicago: University of Chicago Press, 1990.
Slack, Paul. "Mirrors of Health and Treasures of Poor Men." In *Health, Medicine, and Mortality in the Sixteenth Century*, edited by Charles Webster, 237–273. Cambridge: Cambridge University Press, 1979.
Smith, Margaret M. "Red as a Textual Element during the Transition from Manuscript to Print." In *Textual Cultures: Cultural Texts*, edited by Orietta Da Rold and Elaine Treharne, 187–200. Cambridge: D.S. Brewer, 2010.

Bibliography

———. *The Title-Page: Its Early Development, 1460–1510*. London: The British Library & Oak Knoll Press, 2000.

Smoller, Laura Ackerman. *History, Prophecy, and the Stars: The Christian Astrology of Pierre d'Ailly, 1350–1420*. Princeton, NJ: Princeton University Press, 1994.

Smyth, Adam. "Almanacs and Ideas of Popularity." In *The Elizabethan Top Ten: Defining Print Popularity in Early Modern England*, edited by Andy Kesson and Emma Smith, 125–133. London and New York: Routledge, 2013.

———. *Autobiography in Early Modern England*. Cambridge: Cambridge University Press, 2010.

———. *Material Texts in Early Modern England*. Cambridge: Cambridge University Press, 2017.

Sommer, H. Oskar. *The Kalender of Shepherdes: The Edition of Paris 1503 in Photographic Facsimile*. London: Kegan Paul, Trench, Trubner & Co., 1891.

Sondheim, Moriz. "Shakespeare and the Astrology of his Time." *Journal of the Warburg Institute* 2, no. 3 (1939): 243–259.

Stallybrass, Peter, Roger Chartier, J. Franklin Mowery, and Heather Wolfe. "Hamlet's Tables and the Technologies of Writing in Renaissance England." *Shakespeare Quarterly* 55, no. 4 (2004): 379–419.

Stark, Ryan J. "The Decline of Astrology in the Jonathan Dove Almanac Series." *Renaissance and Reformation / Renaissance et Reformation* 30, no. 2 (2006): 43–66.

The Stationers Register. "The Stationers Register Online." Accessed January-July, 2019, https://stationersregister.online/.

Stubbings, Frank. "A Cambridge Pocket-Diary, 1587–1592. *Transactions of the Cambridge Bibliographic Society* 5, no. 3 (1971): 191–202.

Taavitsainen, Irma. *Middle English Lunaries. A Study of the Genre*. Helsinki: Memoires de la Societe Neophilologique de Helsinki, 1988.

Talbot, C.H. "A Mediaeval Physician's *Vade Mecum*." *Journal of the History of Medicine and Allied Sciences* 16, no. 3 (1961): 213–233.

Taylor, E.G.R. *The Mathematical Practitioners of Tudor & Stuart England*. Cambridge: Cambridge University Press, 1967.

Thomas, Keith. *Religion and the Decline of Magic*. New York: Scribner, 1971.

Thorndike, Lynn. *A History of Magic & Experimental Science*. 8 vols. New York: MacMillan, 1923–1958.

Trevisan, Sara. "The Impact of the Netherlandish Landscape Tradition on Poetry and Painting in Early Modern England." *Renaissance Quarterly* 66, no. 3 (2013): 866–903.

Tristram, E.W. *English Medieval Wall Painting: The Thirteenth Century*. Oxford: Oxford University Press, 1950.

Turner, Gerard L'Estrange. *Elizabethan Instrument Makers: The Origins of the London Trade in Precision Instrument Making*. Oxford: Clarendon, 2000.

Tuve, Rosamond. *Seasons and Months: Studies in a Tradition of Middle English Poetry*. Totowa, NJ: D.S. Brewer, 1933.

Vanden Broecke, Steven. *The Limits of Influence: Pico, Louvaine, and the Crisis of Renaissance Astrology*. Leiden: Brill, 2003.

Veldman, Ilja. "Seasons, Planets and Temperaments in the Work of Maarten van Heemskerck: Cosmo-Astrological Allegory in Sixteenth-Century Netherlandish Prints." *Simiolus* 11, nos. 3–4 (1980): 149–176.

Walker, Katherine. "'Daring to Pry into the Privy Chamber of Heaven': Early Modern Mock-Almanacs and the Virtues of Ignorance." *Studies in Philology* 115, no. 1 (2018): 129–153.

———. "Early Modern Almanacs and the Witch of Edmonton." *Early Modern Literary Studies* 18 (2015): 1–25.

Wallis, Faith. "Medicine in Medieval Calendar Manuscripts." In *Manuscript Sources of Medieval Medicine*, edited by Margaret R. Schleissner, 105–143. New York: Garland Publishing, 1995.

———. "Michael of Rhodes and Time Reckoning: Calendar, Almanac, Prognostication." In *The Book of Michael of Rhodes: A Fifteenth Century Maritime Manuscript, Volume 3, Studies*, edited by Pamela Long, 281–319. Cambridge, MA: MIT Press, 2009.

Wallis, Faith, trans. and ed. *The Reckoning of Time, by The Venerable Bede*. Liverpool: University of Liverpool Press, 1999.

Webster, Charles, ed. *Health, Medicine, and Mortality in the Sixteenth Century*. Cambridge: Cambridge University Press, 1979.

Webster, J.C. *The Labors of the Months in Antique and Medieval Art to the End of the Twelfth Century*. Princeton, NJ: Princeton University Press, 1938.

Wedel, Theodore Otto. *The Medieval Attitude toward Astrology, Particularly in England*. New Haven, CT: Yale University Press, 1920.

Wells-Cole, Anthony. *Art and Decoration in Elizabethan and Jacobean England: The Influence of Continental Prints, 1558–1625*. New Haven, CT: Yale University Press, 1997.

Westman, Robert S. *The Copernican Question: Prognostication, Skepticism, and Celestial Order*. Berkeley: University of California Press, 2011.

———. "The Melanchthon Circle, Rheticus, and the Wittenberg Interpretation of the Copernican Theory," *Isis* 66, no. 2 (1975): 164–193.

White, Helen C. *The Tudor Books of Private Devotion*. Madison: University of Wisconsin Press, 1951.

Wieck, Roger S. *Time Sanctified: The Book of Hours in Medieval Art and Life*. New York: George Brazillier, 1988.

William A. Jackson. *Records of the Court of the Stationers Company 1602 to 1640*. London: The Bibliographical Society, 1957.

Wilson, William. *Shakespeare and Astrology: From a Student's Point of View*. Boston, MA: Occult Publishing Company, 1903.

Wolfe, Heather. "A Third Manuscript by Thomas Trevelyon/Trevilian." *The Collation: Research and Exploration at the Folger*. December 7, 2012. https://collation.folger.edu/2012/12/a-third-manuscript-by-thomas-trevelyontrevelian/. Accessed 19th June 2019.

Wolfe, Heather, ed. *The Trevelyon Miscellany: A Facsimile Edition of Folger Shakespeare Library MS V.b.232*. Washington, DC: Folger Shakespeare Library, 2007.

Wood, David Houston. *Time, Narrative, and Emotion in Early Modern England*. London: Routledge, 2009.

Yates, Frances A. *Giordano Bruno and the Hermetic Tradition*. London: Routledge and Kegan Paul, 1964.

Index of Saints and Holy Days

Abdon & Sennen 233
Achilleus 219
Adauctus & Felix 239
Adeline 206
Adrian 205
Advent 230, 254–255, 261
Agapete 190
Agapitus, bishop 205
Agapitus, martyr 238
Agapius &Timolaus 206
Agatha 196, 198
Agnes 188, 190–191
Agricola 257
Alban 227
Aldhelm 220
All Hallow's 249, 251–252, 254–256
All Saint's 254–256
All Soul's 255–256
Alphege 210, 212
Amand 198
Amantius 256
Amatus 244
Ambrose 210, 212
Anastatius 213
Andochius 245
Andrew 182, 207, 250, 257, 263
Anicetus 212
Anne 231, 233
Annunciation of Mary 48, 202–204, 206
Anthony of Padua 190
Antoninus of Florence 219
Antonius 244
Antony of Padua 226
Aphrodosius 205
Apollinaris of Ravenna 233
Apollinaris of Valence 250
Apollonia 198
Arcadius 190
Arnulf 232

Assumption of Mary 237–238
Asterius & Marinus 204
Athanasius 219
Audrey or Etheldreda 227, 249–250
Augulus 198
Augustine of Canterbury 199, 216, 220
Augustine of Hippo 199, 236, 238
Austraberta, martyr 198
Austreberta or Eustraberta, abbess 250

Barbara 263
Barnabas 226
Barnardine 220
Bartholomew 236–238
Basil 226
Basilides 226
Bathild 191
Bavo 250
Bede 220
Benedict 198, 203, 205, 232
Bernard 238
Bertin 244
Blaise 196, 198
Boniface, Archbishop of Mainz 226
Boniface, Bishop of Ferentino 220
Boniface, Bishop of Ross 205
Boniface, Carthusian monk 205
Botulf 226
Brendan 220
Brice 255–256
Brigid 198

Callistus 250
Candidus 250
Castulus & Dorotheus 206
Catherine of Alexandria 257
Cauldy 264
Cauranus 220
Cecilia 212, 255, 257
Chad 203–204

308 *Index of Saints and Holy Days*

Christina 233
Chrysogonus 257
Cirake 238
Circumcision 190
Cirilli 232
Clare 238
Clement 255, 257
Cletus 213
Conception of Mary 261–263
Conversion of Paul 191
Cosmas & Damian 245
Cosmy 212
Crescens 227
Crispin & Crispinian 249, 251
Cuthbert 205, 244
Cuthburga 239
Cyprian & Justina 245
Cyprian of Perigueaux 263

Damasus 264
Damian & Cosmas 245
David 203–204
Denys 249–250
Dioscorus 220
Dorotheus & Castulus 206
Dorothy 198
Dunstan 216, 220

Edith 245
Edmund of Abingdon 226, 256
Edmund, King of East Anglia 257
Edward the Confessor 250
Edward, King and Martyr 190, 203, 205, 224, 226, 249, 255
Eleutherius 212
Eleven thousand virgins 250
Elizabeth of Hungary 257
Elmo or Erasmus 226
Eloi 227, 263
Emerentiania 191
Epimachus & Gordian 219
Epiphany 48, 114, 186, 188–190
Erasmus or Elmo 226
Erkenwald 213, 256
Etheldreda or Audrey 227, 249–250
Eugenius 244
Eulalia of Barcelona 198
Eulalia of Merida 263
Euphemie 212
Eusebius, abbot 205
Eusebius, martyr 238
Eustace 245

Eustraberta or Austraberta 198
Evaristus 251
Exaltation of the Holy Cross 217, 243, 245
Exupere 245

Fabian 188, 190
Faith 182, 249, 250
Faustinus & Jovita 199
Felix & Adauctus 239
Felix & his fellows 233
Felix & Januarius 190
Felix & Nabor 232
Felix II, pope 233
Felix of Dunwich 205
Felix of Nola 190
Felix, pope and martyr 220
Firmin 245
Florian 219
Forty martyrs 205
Forty virgins 264
Four Crowned Martyrs 256
Francis 220, 250
Frideswide 250

Gabinus 199
Genevieve 190
George 52, 184, 210, 213
Gereon & companions 250
Germanus of Auxerre 233
Germanus of Capua 251
Germanus of Paris 220
Gervase & Protase 226
Gilbert 198
Gildarde 211
Giles 243–244
Godard 219
Gordian & Epimachus 219
Gorgonius 244
Gracian 264
Gregory 203, 205, 244
Grimbald 232
Guthlac 212

Hegessipus 212
Helen 219, 220
Hilary & Tatian 205
Hilary, Bishop 188–190
Hippolytus 238
Holy Crown 219
Holy Innocents 48, 190, 261, 264
Hugh of Lincoln 199, 255–256
Hyacinth & Protus 244

Index of Saints and Holy Days 309

Innocent 226
Invention of the Cross 219
Isidore the Egyptian 190
Isidore the Farmer 220
Isidore, archbishop 212

Jacob & Philip 219
James the Great, Apostle 230–231, 233, 251, 264
James the Lesser, Apostle 216–217, 219; see also Philip & Jacob
Januarius & Felix 190
Januarius 245
Jerome 243, 245
John & Paul, martyrs 227
John of Beverley 219, 251
John the Baptist 224–225, 227, 232, 236, 239
John, Apostle and Evangelist 190, 214, 219, 251, 261, 264
Joseph 205
Jovita & Faustinus 199
Jude & Simon, Apostles 251
Judoc 190
Julia 220
Julian 191
Juliana 199
Julius 264
Justa & Rufina 232
Justina & Cyprian 245
Justine 238

Katherine 186, 255, 257
Kenelm 232

Laetus 256
Lambert 243, 245
Lammas 214, 236–237
Laurence 236, 238
Lazarus 264
Leger 250
Leo 227
Leonard 212
Leonard, hermit 255–256
Libane 263
Lini 257
Linus, pope 190
Longinus 205
Louis of Toulouse 238
Louis, King of France 238
Lucian 189, 190
Lucy 261, 264
Luke 249–250

Maglorius 251
Magnus 238
Malo 255–256
Marcellian & Mark 226, 250
Marcellinus & Peter 226
Marcellus 190
Marcian 244
Margaret 231–232
Marinus & Asterius 204
Mark & Marcellian 226, 250
Mark, Evangelist 210–211, 213
Martian 212
Martin I, pope 256
Martin of Tours 231–232, 256
Martine 204
Mary Magdalen 231–232
Mary of Egypt 211
Mary Salome 251
Matthias 196, 197, 199
Matthew 243, 245
Maurice & companions 245
Maurily 244
Maurus 190
Médard 226
Melonis 226
Michael 219, 243, 245, 250
Mildred 199
Modestus & Vitus 226

Nabor & Felix 232
Name of Jesus 236, 238
Narcissus 251
Nativity of Jesus 261–264
Nativity of Mary 244–244
Nereus 220
Nestor 199
Nicasius 250
Nicholas 261–263
Nicholis 219
Nichomedes 224, 226–227

O Sapientia 261, 264
Olife 212
Osmund 232, 263
Oswald, bishop 199, 212
Oswald, King of Northumberland 238
Othilia 264

Passion of the Seven Virgins 212
Paternus 256
Patrick 205
Paul & John, martyrs 227
Paul of Thebes 190

310   *Index of Saints and Holy Days*

Paul of Verdun 198
Paul, Apostle 227
Paul, bishop 239
Pelagia 250
Perpetua 203, 205
Perpetuus 212
Peter & Marcellinus
Peter of Verona 213
Peter, Apostle 224, 227
Peter, martyr 205
Peter's Chains 199, 237
Petroc 226
Petronilla 220
Pharmuthi 198
Philip & Jacob 216–217, 219
Polycarp 191, 199
Polychronius 199
Praxedes 232
Presentation of Mary 257
Prisca 188, 190
Private 232
Protase & Gervase 226
Protus & Hyacinth 244
Purification of Mary 148, 186, 195, 197–198

Quentin 251
Quintin 206
Quintine 212
Quirinus 206
Quirion 205

Remigius 249–250
Revel 232
Richard 210–211, 226
Roch 238
Romanus, Bishop of Rouen 251
Romanus, martyr 238
Rufina & Justa 232
Rufus of Capua 238
Rufus, Diocletian martyr 257

Sabas 263
Samson 233
Saturninus & Victor 191
Scholastica 198
Sebastian 190
Sennen & Abdon 233
Sernin 257
Servatus 219
Seven Brothers 232
Seven Sleepers 233
Silvius 244

Simeon 213
Simon & Jude, Apostles 182, 249, 251
Simon, Bishop of Jerusalem 199
Simon, martyr 213
Sixtus, pope 212
Sixty-nine martyrs 199
Slaughter of the Innocents *see* Holy Innocents
Socii 238
Sociori 232
Soter 213
Stephen, pope 237
Stephen, proto-martyr 190, 237, 261, 264
Sulpicius 190
Swithin 231–232
Sylvester 261, 264

Tecla 245
Theodora 211
Theodore 191, 205
Theodore of Canterbury 206
Theodore, Roman soldier and martyr 256
Thirty Diocletian martyrs 264
Thomas à Becket (Thomas of Canterbury) 42, 46, 190, 285–286, 261–262, 264
Thomas, Apostle 261, 264
Tibertius, martyr 238
Tiburtius & Valerian, companions of St. Cecilia 212
Timolaus & Agapius 206
Timothy, Diocletian martyr 238
Timothy, disciple of the Apostle Paul 191
Transfiguration 236, 238

Ursula 251

Valentine 46–47, 184, 196–198
Valerian & Tibertius, companions of St. Cecilia 212
Valerian 264
Valerius of Saragossa 191
Valerius, Bishop of Trier 191
Vedast 198
Venesi 264
Victor & Corona 245
Victor & Victorinus, martyrs 205
Victor, Zoticus & companions 212
Victoria 264
Victorini 206
Vincent Ferrer 212

Index of Saints and Holy Days 311

Vincent of Saragossa 189, 191
Visitation 230–233
Vitalis 213
Vitus & Modestus 226

Walburga 226
Wilfrid 213
William of York 226

Willibrord 256
Winifred 256
Wulfram 250
Wulfstan 190, 198, 226

Zeno 212
Zephyrinus 238
Zoe 232

Index

Accession Day 256
Adkin, M. 131–133
Advent 107, 230, 254–255, 261, 279
advertisements, almanacs 133
Aeolus 140, 157–158
ages of man: Four Ages (Ovid) 140–143, 148, 152–153, 156; seven 127; twelve 42, 180, 187–260 passim, 194, 209, 223, 242, 247, 260
Agrippa, Cornelius 6
alchemy 6, 162, 167
All Hallow's 249, 251–252, 254–256
All Saint's 254–256
All Soul's 255–256
Allen, Don Cameron 6, 82, 87
Allen, Nicholas, *The Astronomers Game* 84–86, 119, 270
Allestree, Richard 100, 102, 104–105, 118, 126, 132, *Plate 5.1, Plate 5.2*
Alleyn, Henry 104, 126, 131, 188–260 passim, 275
almanacs and prognostications 57–74: blanks 115–117, 278; combined 97–133; compilers 61–62, 102; epigraphs 104–15, 118; single sheet or broadside 58–59, 97, 192, 272–273, *Plate 3*; size 97–98; title pages 98–102, *Plates 4.1, 4.2, 5.1, 5.2*; rubrication 4, 98–99, 108, 119; *see also* blanks; chronologies; declarations; elections; law terms; Zodiac Man
almanacs and prognostications, manuscript 39–43; *see also* primer calendars
almanacs and prognostications, printing history: censorship and control 62–64; combined with annual prognostications 60–61; university press 70–72; Watkins & Roberts monopoly 64–67; *see also* Company of Stationers; Stationers' Register
almanacs: clog 51–53, *Plate 2.1, Plate 2.3*; mock 71, 88–90, 101, 109; multi-year 43, 57–58; perpetual 43, 75–78, 97; xylographic 30, 51–53, *Plate 2.2*; *see also* prognostications
Anon: *A Blancke and Perpetuall Almanack* 115; *The City and Countery Chapmans Almanack* 129; *The Compost of Ptolemy* 76, 80; *Here Begynneth the Nature, and Dysposycyon of the Days in the Week* 30, 81; *The Husbandmans Practice* 30, 81; *A Mery Prognostication* 2–3, 88–89; *Table Declaring What Planet Dooth Raigne Every Day and Houre* 129; *Wryting Tables, with a Necessarie Calender* 97, 116
Apollo 162–164
Aquarius 22, 114, 155, 175, 180, 187–188
Arcandam see Richard Roussat
Aries 25, 85, 162, 169, 180, *201–202*; astrological influence of 25, *201–202*; first point of 21, *23*, 120, 139–40; and Mars 142
Aristotle, attributed: *De Cursione Lune* 28–29, 81; *Here begynneth the Nature, and Dysposycyon of the Days in the Weke* 30, 150, 154, 157; *Secretum Secretorum* 81, 140, 146–147, 150
Aristotle: cosmology 9, 18–20, 83, 119
Armillary spheres *19*, 99–101, *100*
Artemis 166
Ascension Day 48, 211, 214, 216–219

Askham, Anthony 6, 61, 79, 129; *A Litell Treatyse of Astronomy* 79, 128–129, 163–178 *passim*
Aston, Margaret 85–87
astrological medicine 25–28; *see also* choleric sanguine temperament; melancholic temperament; phlegmatic temperament
astrology 17–28; Babylonian 26, 36, 162; basis for almanac prognostications 62, 120–124; controversies over; 74–74, 82–88; differentiated from astronomy 17–18; natural vs. judicial 7; popular guides 78–82; Protestant reform of 74–75; *see also* eclipses; elections; horoscopes; horary questions; interrogatories; nativities; prognostications; revolutions; seven planets; signs; twelve Zodiac signs; Zodiac
astronomy: Arabic medieval 17, 22, 39, 82; and *compotes* 38; differentiated from astrology 17–18; *see also* astrology; Autumn Equinox; constellations; Copernicanism; eclipses; Ptolemaic universe; Ptolemy; Spring Equinox; Summer Solstice; Winter Solstice
Autumn Equinox 21, 26, 120, 139, 151

Bacchus xxi, 140, 153–154, 236
Bacon, Roger 39
Balles, Thomas 131, 259
Bankes, Richard 60
barber surgeons 25
Barham, William 131, 133
Barnes, Robin B. 6, 82
Bartholomeus, Anglicus: *De Proprietatibus Rerum* 79, 179, *Plate 10*
Batman, Stephen, *Batman upon Bartholome* 79, 167, 171, 173, 179, 200
Bauckman, Richard 83
Beale, William 48, 114, 274; calendar 279–280
Bede, the Venerable 30, 140, 220
bee-keeping *see* husbandry
Beham, Hans Sebald 168, 169, *170*, 171
Berry, Philippa 229
Bible, the 204; almanac epigraphs 104–105; and astrological controversies 87; and astronomy 29, 139–140; lectionary in the Book of Common Prayer 181–262 *passim*

black bile *see* melancholic temperament
Blagrave, John, *The Mathematical Jewel* 18, *19*, 21–22, 79
blanks, almanacs 115–117, 278
blood 20, 25–26; diseases 155; excess in Spring 146–147, 202; and Mars 167; *see also* phlebotomy; sanguine temperament
bloodletting *see* phlebotomy
Blundeville, Thomas, *M. Blundeville His Exercises* 22, 80
Bogaert, Arnould 60
Book of Common Prayer 37, 43, 46–48; calendar 277–278; lectionary 181–184; *Liber Precum Publicarum* 48, 182–183; and saint's days 114; *see also* Bible
Book of Magic, Folger Shakespeare Library 163
Booker, John 6, 8, 120, 127, 141, 236; career 68–70, 114–115; and William Lilly 80; calendar 280–*281*
Boorde, Andrew 61; *The Breviary of Healthe* 141; *The Pryncyples of Astronamye* 79, 127, 129
Bosanquet, Eustace 5
Bourne, William 78, 99, 127, 129, 133
Brahe, Tycho 4, 120, 132
Brathwaite, Richard, *Whimzies* 4, 231
Bretnor, Thomas 90, 141; advertisements 133; calendar 278–279; defense of astrology 119–120; good and evil days 115–116, *121*; husbandry elections 126; law terms *107*; medical elections 202, 210, 223, 243, 248, 261; and mock almanacs 90; and planetary aspects 114; tide tables 131; travel information 131–132; weather predictions 125; and Thomas Trevelyon 275
Breton, Nicholas, *Fantasticks*: Easter 204, 211; months 213, 229, 237, *253*, 254, 263; seasons 149, 154, 158
brontologies 17, 28–30, 80–81
Brouscon, Guilaume *Plate 2.2*
Browne, Daniel 102, 105, 119, 131, 248
Bruegel, Pieter *145*, 273
Buckminster, Thomas 61, 100–101, 105, 119; attack by Allen 84, 86; calendar 269–270; labors woodcuts 213–*214*, 239–240; political prognostications 63–65; on seasons 147, 154–155, 158–159

314   Index

Burton, Gregory 126, 195, 200, 216, 228
Butler, Robert 131, 133
Byddell, John 46
Bynneman, Henry 64

calendar poetry 38–39, 42, 69, 130, 144, 179–264 *passim*; "The Days of the Week Moralized" 75
calendar: Gregorian reforms 50–51, 115, 130, 273–274; Jewish 34; Julian 34–36, 107, 115, 139, 162; Julian tables 38; *see also* almanacs and prognostications, primer calendars
Calvin, John 28, 199; *An Admonicion against Astrology Judiciall* 84–88
Caly, Robert 47
Camden, Carroll 6, 85
Cancer 22, 25, 85, 151, 165, 180, 222; Tropic of 139, 147
Candlemas 148, 186, 195, 197–198
Canterbury: almanacs for 103; Cathedral floor tiles 185–186
Capp, Bernard 2, 5–6, 9, 63, 67–71, 84, 108, 120
Capricorn 22, 42, 66, 121–122, 175, 180; Tropic of 139, 151, 240, 259–60
Cardano, Jerome 75, 180, 214
Carey, Hilary 25, 40
Carleton, George, *Astrologomania* 88
Carre, James 127, 130
Catholic Encyclopedia 184
Ccres xxi, 140, 148, 233
Chamber, John, *A Treatise Against Judicial Astrologie* 5, 87–88
Chamberlaine, Joseph 102, 131
Chapman, Alison xix–xxii, 2, 8, 48, 103
Cheney, C.R. 8
Chiu, Howard 29
choleric temperament 20, 25–26, 43; and Aries 201; and Leo 229; and Sagittarius 253; and Summer 150
choreographies 132
Christmas: prognostications based on date 30, 259; season 42, 185; 188–189, 258–263
chronologies 52, 77–78, 80, 90, 98, 108, 114, *Plate 7.2*
Church of Saint Augustine, Brookland, Kent 200, *Plate 9*
circle of the sun 20, 38, 106, 130
Circumcision 46, 48, 114, 188–190, 267
Clark (almanac compiler) 130

Cogan, Thomas, *The Haven of Health* 141, 146–47, 151, 160
Collaert, Adriaen 142–143, 148–*150*, 153, 157, *Plate 14*
common notes *see* declarations
Company of Stationers 7, 57, 70; and almanacs 62–66, 67–68, 98–100, 105–106; and university press almanacs 70–71; *see also* almanacs and prognostications, printing history; Stationers' Register; James Roberts; Richard Watkins
complexions *see* temperaments
compotus 36–39
conjuring 6, 83–84, 167; *see also* magic
constellations: Canis Major 148, 155, 214, 229; Canis Minor 148, 155, 222, 229; Orion 148, 155, 187, 222, 229, 248; Pleiades 142, 201, 208, 253; *see also* Zodiac
Coronation of Queen Elizabeth I 256
Copenhaver, Brian 6
Copernicanism: and astrology 17; and Thomas Digges 76; in almanacs 80, 120
Copernicus, Nicholas *see* Copernicanism
Corpus Christi 216–218, 224–225
Coverdale, Miles 83
Coxe, Francis 61, 83, 84
Craig, Hardin 30
Cressy, David 8, 182–183, 244, 249
Cuningham, William 6, 61, 187, 240, 270; almanac title pages 99, 103–104, *Plate 4.1*; calendar *112*, 113–115; *The Cosmographical Glasse* 79; prognostication 119–124, 127, 141; attacked by William Fulke 83; labors *185, 200, 252*
Cupid 143
Curry, Patrick 70
Curth, Louise 2, 1, 133

D., J. *see* John Dade
Dade, John 50, 65, 100–101, 105, 119, 127; calendar 273–274; seasons 147, 151, 155, 159
Dade, William 273–274
dairy *see* husbandry
Dariot, Claude 22, 79, 129; and planets 163–178 *passim*
Dauncy, Gervase 118, 127, 202, 215, 248
Daw, Jack, *Vox Graculi* 90

Dawson, Mark 6
Day, John 47
days of the week 36, 162–178; *see also* planets
declarations, almanac 98, 102, 106–107, 115, *Plate 7.1*
Dee, John 6, 20, 50, 75–76
Dekker, Thomas: *The Raven's Almanacke* 4, 71, 89–90; *The Shoemaker's Holiday* 198
Denham, Henry 64
Diana 162, 166
Digges, Leonard 76–78, 77, 81, 275; weather predictions 123–125
Digges, Thomas 50, 76
Dog Days 109, 148, 155, 165, 229–230, 232, 235, 241, 244
dominical letter prognostications *see* Esdras prognostications
Donne, John, *An Anatomie of the World* 101
Dooley, Brendan 6
Dorne, John 58–59
Dove, Jonathan 71, 105, 120
dragon's head and dragon's tail 22–23, 122
Drake, Sir Francis 52–53
Driver, Martha W. 75, 98–99
Droeshout, Martin *156–157*
Duffy, Eamon 40–41

Early English Books Online (EEBO) 4–5, 284
Easby Church 200, 239, *Plates 15.2, 16.2*
Easter 11; in almanac declarations 51, 106; calculating date 36–39, 51, 274; fairs 197, 203, 211, 217–218, 225; feasts and holy days 48, 181, 188, 210–211, 216, 224; law term 182, 203–204, 211, 218; and perpetual calendars 42–43, 58, 75, 7; *see also* compotes; Gregorian reforms; Lent
eclipses 21, 25; in almanacs and prognostications 59–60, 65–66, 68, 78, 123–124, 127; in the Kalender of Shepherds 75; and mock almanacs 88–89; in primer calendars 43; and weather prognostications 123; *see also* astrology; astronomy; horoscopes
Egyptian days 16–17, 30, 39, 80–81, 115

Einer, N. 126, 131
elections 26–28, 109–111; physic 26–29, 109–111, 110, 147; travel 9, 28, 109, 115; *see also* astrology, prognostications
elections, husbandry 27–28, 76, 86, 109, 111–112, 124–126; and the planets 165, 167, 169, 171, 173, 175, 177–178; *see also* astrology, prognostications
Elyot, Sir Thomas, The Castel of Health 146
encyclopedias, medieval 10
English stock *see* Company of Stationers
epact xx, 106, 130
ephemerides 23, 57, 80, 97, 119
Epiphany 48, 114, 186, 188–190
equator 103, 139, 142, 151, 240
equinoxes, precession of the 139
Erra Pater 30, 80, 88
Esdras (dominical letter) prognostications 17–18, 30–31, 80–81
Evans, John 126

fairs 130, 182; April 211; August 237; December 262; February 197; January 189; July 231; June 225; March 203; May 217; November 255; October 249
Faques, Richard 58
Faracovi, Ornella 18
Farmer, David Hugh 184
Farmer, William 50, 103, 130
farming *see* husbandry
Field, John 80
Fine, Oronce, *The Rules and Righte Ample Documentes* 79, 129
Flora 140, 144, 149, 213
Foulweather, Adam, *A Wonderfull, Strange, and Miraculous, Astrologicall Prognostication* 89
Four Seasons tapestries, Hatfield House 142–143, *257*, *Plates 11, 12, 13, 14*
Foxe, John, *Actes and Monuments* 48–49, *49*, 219, 274
Frende, Gabriel: attacked by Nicholas Allen 86; almanac letter to reader 118; almanac title pages 101–102, *Plate 4.2*; epigraphs 105; months 185, 187, 214, 248, 252, 259; posthumous almanacs 103;

prognostication title pages 118;
  prognostications 65, 126; seasons
  144, 147, 150–151, 154–155,
  157–158
Fulke, William, *Antiprognosticon* 5, 63,
  75, 82–85, 88

Gadbury, John 70
Galenic medicine 27, 76, 79, 105, 155;
  cited in almanacs 119; four capacities
  27, 109; and season 140, 146, 155;
  see also choleric temperament;
  melancholic temperament; phlegmatic
  temperament; physic; sanguine
  temperament
Galle, Philips: Autumn 152, 153–154;
  Spring *143*, 143–144; Summer 148,
  149, 150; Winter 156–157, *158*
Gemini 142, 145, 169, 180, 214–215
Gemini, Thomas 76
Geneva, Anne 6, 70
Georgic 105, 126, 140–141, 144, 160
Gesner, James 191–*192*
Gilden, George 68, 102, 108, *125*, 126,
  128, *Plate 7.2*
Godfridus, *Boke of Knowledge of
  Thynges Unknowen* 29–30, 81,
  126, 177
golden number 37–38, 42–43, 51–52,
  58–59, 106, 130, 267
Goltzius, Hendrick *153*, 157, *159*
good and evil days 39, 80, 115–116,
  121, 125
Good Friday 203, 210–211, 216
Gossene, George 127
Gower, John 129
Grafton, Anthony 6
Grafton, Richard 46–47, 58, 61; *A
  Briefe Treatise* 182–184, 190–276
  passim; *A Litle Treatise* 77–78
Grammar, Abraham 120–127
Gray, Walter: calendar poetry 189,
  206, 221, 223, 240; political
  prognostications 65–66; title pages
  100, 104–105
great conjunction (1583) 85–87
Greene, Robert, *Planetomachia* 87
Gregorian reforms 34, 50–51, 115, 130,
  273–4, 279
Gresham, Edward 100, 120
Griefes of the Printers 64
Grosseteste, Robert 39
Gumbert, J. 40
Gunpowder Day (Guy Fawkes) 256

H., T. *see* Thomas Hill
Hackett, Thomas 64
halcyon days 259
Hallowtide 249, 251–252, 254–256
Hamling, Tara 8, 141
Hardwick Hall 142, *Plate 16.1*
Harkness, Deborah 74
Harrison, William, *The Description of
  England* 131
Hartgill, George 80, 99, 104, 119–120
harvest festivals 236–237; *see also*
  husbandry
harvest *see* husbandry
Harvey, John 21–23, *23*, 99–100, 118,
  195, 230; *An Astrologicall Addition*
  86–87
Harvey, Richard, *An Astrological
  Discourse* 85–87
Hatfield House *see* Four Seasons
  Tapestries
Hawkins, George 132, 213, 216,
  223, 240
Heemskerck, Maarten van *143*–144,
  148–*149*, 152, *153*, 156–*158*, *166*,
  171–*172*
Henisch, Bridget Ann 146, 180
Heth (or Heath), Thomas, *A Manifest
  and Apparent Confutation* 86–87
Heuring, Simon 61
Hewlett, William 127–128
Heyden, Pieter van der *145*
Heydon, Sir Christopher 68; *A Defence
  of JudiciallAstrologie* 5, 68, 87–88
Hill, Nicholas 61
Hill, Thomas 82–83, 115, 272–273,
  Plate 3; *An Almanack Published
  at Large, in Forme of a Booke of
  Memorie* 117, 127
Hilsey, John, Bishop 46
Hippocratus 76, 119, 140, 146
Holden, Mary 129
Holinshed, Raphael, *The First Volume
  of the Chronicles* 87, 130–132, 182
Hopton, Arthur, *A Concordancy of
  Years*: months 180–261 passim;
  planets 163–165, 167, 171–173, 175,
  177; seasons 142, 144, 147, 150–151,
  159
Hopton, Arthur, almanacs: 132,
  245–246, 260
horary questions 20, 75, 88, 162
horoscopes: ascendant 120, 122, 142;
  astrological houses 21, 22, 23–24,
  79, 121–122; casting 20–28, 79–80;

charts *23, 116,* 99; horoscope of
the year 121–122; judgment of 7,
65–66, 120–123; *see also* astrology;
elections; horary questions;
interrogatories; nativities; revolutions
Hourihane, Colum 179
Howard, Henry, Earl of Northampton,
*A Defensative against the Poyson of
Supposed Prophecies* 86–87
Hubrigh, Joachim. 117
humors *see* choleric temperaments;
melancholic temperament; phlegmatic
temperaments; sanguine temperament
hunting 144–145, 165, 201, 248
husbandry 111–112, 126; bee-keeping
185, 213, 240, 258; dairy 204,
207–208; fruit trees 111–112, 154,
185–186, 200, 240–243, 246; harvest
152–154, 157, 228–229, 233–237;
hemp 240; pruning and trimming
200, *Plate 15.1*; sheep-shearing
111, 146, 149, 180, 214, 221, 225;
sowing 154, 180, 196, 213, 239–240,
245–246, 253; *see also* elections,
husbandry; labors of the months
Hutchinson, Roger, *The Image of God* 83
Hutton, Ronald 8, 183, 197, 218, 263

I., A. *A PerfytePronostycacionPerpetuall*
30, 42
Indagine, John, *Briefe Introductions*
80–81
Ingram, Elizabeth Morley 108
interrogatories 20–21

James 1st, King of England 67, 256
Janus 186
Jewish months 34
Jinner, Sarah 129
Johnson, John 104, 119, 195, 216,
236, 248
Johnson, Thomas 59, 100, 102, 105
Jones, Peter Murray 59
Jonson, Ben, The ComicallSatyre of
Ever Man Out of his Humor 9–10
Jugge, Robert 61
Julian calendar *see* calendar
Jupiter 19, 43, 163, 171–172, 173;
astrological influence 63, 69, 82–83,
111, 123; conjunction with Saturn
85–87, 100; and planetary hours
27, 129; Roman god 162; day of the
week 36, 162
Juste, David 29–30

Kalender of Shepherds 19, 75–77, 99,
174, 176; calendar 267–268; months
180–260 *passim*; planets 162–178
passim; seasons 141, 147, 155, 158,
160
Kassell, Lauren 6, 74
Kidman, Thomas 127, 133
Kinde, John 125–126
King, John 61
Kingston, John 47, 61, 106
Klibansky, Raymond 140, 177

labors of the month 30, 42, *59,
179–180, Plate 9*; birding 144,
180, 206; dining *157, 185,* 213,
214; hunting *215;* knocking acorns
252; mowing 149, 221, 227,
228; picking flowers *207;* reaping
(harvesting) 149, 196, 228–229, 233,
234, 235–237; and seasons 142,
144–146, 149, 154, 157; sheep-
shearing *149, 221,* 225; sitting by
the fire 157, 191, *192;* slaughtering
livestock *257, 258;* sowing *239,
246;* threshing 233, 251–252, *253;*
trimming hedges 179, *200;* wine-
making 154, 240, 246; in xylographic
almanacs 52–53, *Plate 2.2; see also*
husbandry
Lady Days 195–196; the Annunciation
48, 202–204, 206; the Assumption
237–238; the Conception
261–263; the Nativity 243–244; the
Purification 148, 186, 195, 197–198;
the Visitation 230–233
Laet family, almanac compilers 57,
59–61, 71, 97, 99
Lammas 236–237
Langley, Thomas 105
Lant, Richard 61
latitude *see* pole arctic
Laud, Archbishop William 53,
Plate 2.3
law terms 107, 114, 182–183, 279;
Easter 203, 211; Hilary 189, 203;
Michaelmas 244, 249, 255; Trinity
211, 225
Lawrence-Mathers, Anne 40
leap year 35–36, 38, 42, 50,
102–103, 106; and St. Matthias Day
196
Lent 202–204; diet 193, 204, 235; fairs
197, 203, 211; prognostications for
193

318 *Index*

Leo 85, 108, 163, 180, 193, 229–230, 235
Libra 140, 180, 240–243; and Venus 173; and Autumn 13, 151–152
Lighterfoote, Richard 102
Lilly, William 68, 70, 80
Lloyd, Evans 101, 118
longitude *see* meridian
Low Sunday 210–211, 216
Low, Henry 61–62, 82, 84, 103
Luborsky, Ruth Samson 108
lunar prognostications 28–29
Lupton, Thomas, A Thousand Notable Things 225
Luther, Martin 72, 82, 274

magic 6–7, 17, 162–163; conflated with astrology 82–84, 88
Magnus, Albertus 20–21, 82
Maplet, John, The Diall of Destiny 79, 164–178 passim
Markham, Gervase, The Second Booke of the English Husbandmen 30; Verus Pater 80
Mars 19, 162–3, 167, 168, 169, 173; astrological influence 22, 24, 88, 123, 201; day of the week 36, 162; helmet 100; and planetary hours 27, 129
Marsh, Thomas 61, 62, 271
Marshall, William 46
Marston, John, Jack Drum's Entertainment 4
Mathew, William 128, 208, 254
Matthias' Day, Saint 196, 197, 199
Mayler, John 61
medicine *see* astrological medicine; choleric temperament; elections; medical interventions; melancholic temperament; phlebotomy; phlegmatic temperament; physic; sanguine temperament
Mediolano, Joannes de, Regimen Sanitatis Salerni 141
melancholic temperament 20, 25–26, 43; and Autumn 154–155; and Lent 204; and Mercury 171; and Saturn 175–178; and Taurus 208; and Virgo 235; and Capricorn 259
Melancthon, Philip 17, 84
Melton, John, Astrologaster 88
Mercury 19, 169–170; astrological influence 24, 122–123; cadaecus 100; day of the week 36, 162, 169–170; and planetary hours 27, 128–129; Roman god 162; day of the week 36, 162, 169–170
meridian (longitude) 102–103; prime 23, 76; *see also* pole arctic
Metonic Cycle 37–40, 51, 106, 267
Michaelmas 204, 225, 240–241, 244, 249; Michaelmas spring 239, 241; *see also* law terms
Middleton, Thomas: No Wit No Help like a Woman's 9–10, 90, 278; The Owles Almanac 4, 88, 90
Midsummer 225
Mirandola, Pico della 22, 82, 87
misericords: Great Malvern Priory 251–252; St. Mary's Ripple 206–207, 233–234; Worcester Cathedral 191–192, 227–228
Montague, Sir Henry 104, 279
Montulmo, Antonius de, A RyghteExcellente Treatise of Astronomie 60
Moon, the 19, 20, 25–28, 114–115, 165–167, 166; astrological medicine; 25–28; and compotes 36–39; dragon's head and dragon's tail 22, 122; 166; epact 106; and Julian calendar 34–37; lunar prognostications 28–29; Paschal Moon 37; and weather predictions 126, 241; *see also* Aristotle; De Cursione Luna; eclipses; golden number
Mooney, Linne 29–39
Moore, Philip 63, 78, 103, 126
Moulton, Thomas, This is the Myrour or Glasse or Helthe 79
Mounslowe, Alexander 61, 65, 101, 103
Muller, Harmen Jansz 166, 171–172

Nashe, Thomas 87
nativities, astrological 20–21, 46, 81, 83–84
Nativity: of Christ 46, 48, 264; of Mary 196, 243–245
Neptune 140
Neve, Jeffrey 119, 184, 186; declaration, *Plate 7.1*; months 188, 195, 202, 206, 223, 230, 241, 243; seasons 188
New Year's Day 30–31, 81, 114, 186–187, 189
Newman, William R. 6
Nicholas of Lynn 26, 39–40

Nostradamus, Michel de 61–64, 74, 82–84, 115; calendar 267–269
Notary, Julian 75, 268; *see also* Kalender of Shepherds

Odington, Walter 39
Osborne, George 109, *110–111*, 133
Overbury, Sir Thomas, *Sir Thomas Overburie his Wife* 4, 39
Ovid: almanac epigraphs 140; *Fasti* 142; *Metamorphosis* 140, 142, 148, 152, 156, 180; *see also* ages of man

Palm Sunday 203, 211
Panofsky, Erwin 140, 177
Parr, Johnstone 6
Parron, William 60, 71
Parry, Glyn 6
Paschal tables 38, 42, 58
pastoral 140–141, 144
Pencz, Georg 167–171
Pentecost 230, 236, 241
Perkins, Samuel 102, 131
Perkins, William, *Foure Great Lyers* 86, 88
Petyt, Thomas 47
Phaeton 164
phlebotomy 77, 147; and Egyptian days 59; and lunar medicine 25–29; and the months 181–272 *passim*; rules in almanacs 110–111; and the seasons 146–147, 151, 155, 178; symbols 272; and Vein Man 109, *Plate 8.2*; Zodiac Man 108–109, *Plate 8.1*; *see also* blood
phlegm *see* phlegmatic temperament
phlegmatic temperament 20, 25–26, 43, 157, 195, 216; and Cancer 222; and the Moon 165–166; and Pisces 193–195; and Scorpio 246–247; and Venus 173–174; and Winter 157–158
physic: advice for Autumn 155, 241–242; 248–249; 254; advice for Spring 147, 195, 202, 208–210, 215–216; advice for Summer 151, 178, 202, 222, 230, 241; advice for Winter 157, 181, 254, 260–261; *see also* astrological medicine; blood; choleric temperament; elections, melancholic temperament; phlebotomy; phlegmatic temperament; sanguine temperament
physicians 155, 167, 195; almanac compilers 59–61, 68–69, 102, 119,
269–270, 273, 278; and seasonal medicine 155
Pisces 17, 180, 204; and February 192–193, 195; and Jupiter 171; and Winter 155;180, 204; and Zodiac Man 25, 85
planetary aspects 24, 68–69, 71, 114, 120, 122–123, 125–126, 279, 281
planetary hours 26–27; in almanacs 68, 71, 76, 78–79, 82, 128–129; and days of the week 162–163; and planets 274–279; *see also* astrology
Planetary Man 43, 76
planets 162–178; and astrological medicine 25–27, 76, 109; and days of the week 36, 162–163; and horoscope charts 22–25; qualities 82–83, 127; relative size 76; seven classical 19–20; and weather predictions *125*, 126; woodcuts 100–101; *see also* the Jupiter, Mars, Mercury, the Moon, Saturn, the Sun, Venus
Pliny, the Elder, *The Historie of the World* 126, 160
Plot, Robert, *The Natural History of Stafford-shire* 51
Plough Monday 189
pole arctic *see* meridian
Pond, Edward: advertisements 133; almanacs: 71, 90, 103, 105, 114, 125; calendar history 130–131; chronologies 114; letters to the reader 118–119, 125; title pages 100; and Thomas Trevelyon 275; travel information 131
Pontano, Johanus 119
Poole, Robert 50
Poor Robin almanacs 4
Powell, William 62, 271
prayer-book calendars *see* primer calendars
Prid, William, *The Glasse of Vaine-Glorie* 114, 191–192, 213; calendar 274–275; labors *221, 246, 258*
primer calendars, Church of England 43–49; *The Manual of Prayers* 46; *Thys Prymer in Englyshe and in Laten* (1538) 201, 215, 229, 253
primers calendars, Catholic Church: *Enchiridion* (1530) 242, *260*; *HoreBeateVirginis Marie* (1520) 41, 215; *HoreBeatissimeVirginis Marie* (1530) 241, 248, *Plate 1.2*; *This*

Prymer of Salisbury Use (1529) 193, 222–223; *This Prymer of Salisbury Use* (1531) 208–209; *This Prymer of Salisbury Use* (1532) 42, 44, 45, 47, 193, 222–223; *This Prymer of Salisbury Use* (1555, 1556) 47, 187, 194, 247, 260
Proclus, *Treatise on the Sphere* 81
prognostications, astrological 118–133; annual 59; brontologies 17, 28–30, 80–81, Plate 1.1; controversies over 74–75, 82–88; Egyptian days 16–17, 30, 39, 80–81, 115; Esdras (dominical letter) prognostications 17–18, 30–31, 80–81; lunar 28–29, 81; *see also* almanacs and prognostications; astrology; eclipses; elections; horoscopes; revolutions; weather
Ptolemaeus, Claudius 2, *3*, 4, 99–100, 120; *Almagest* 17, 39; *Tetrabiblios* 17–18, 24, 39, 123
Ptolemaic astrology 17–20, 177, 180, 214; *see also* astrology
Ptolemaic universe 17, *18*, 19
Ptolemy, attributed, *Centiloquium* 26
Purfoote, Thomas 48, 115–116
Pynson, Richard 60
Pythagoras 140

Ranger, Philip 120, 186, 188, 210, 259
Record, Robert, *The Castle of Knowledge* 79
Redman, John 61
Regiomontanus 23, 57, 85, 103
revolutions, astrological 7, 17, 20–21, 25, 65, 78, 81, 124
Rheinhold, Erasmus 80
Richard of Wallingford 39
Rivers, Peregrine 71, 131
Rivers, William 71, 120
Roberts, James 65–66, 98–99, 101, 105, 117, 271; *see also* almanacs and prognostications, printing history
rogations 219
Roman Indiction 106
Roman months 34–35
Roussat, Richard, *Arcandam* 81, *201*
Rudston, John 120, 195, 204, 254
Rudston, Thomas 102, 130, 241, 216, 241
Rusche, Harry 6
Rushbearing 231
Rutkin, H. Darrell 6

Sadeler, Johan 164
Saenredam, Jan 153, 157, *159*
Sagittarius 22, 85, 151–152, 180, 253–254; and Jupiter 171
saints: in almanacs 59–60, 114, 183–185; in Catholic primers 42–43; in Grafton's treatises 77–78; and law terms 182; mnemonic verses 75; in Protestant prayer books 43–48; symbols on clog almanacs 52; xylographic almanacs 52–53; *see also* Index of Saints and Holy Days
sanguine temperament 20, 25–26, 43; 162, 240; and Aquarius 187; and Gemini 214; Jupiter 171–173; and Libra 214; and Spring 146; and Venus 173–175; *see also* blood
Sarum Rite 42–43, 46–48, 77–78, 181
Saturn 19, 175, *176*, 177–178; astrological influence 43, 65, 69, 122–123; conjunction with Saturn 85–87, 100; day of the week 36, 162; and planetary hours 27, 129; scythe 100
Saul, Fritz 140
Savile, Henry 50
Scorpio 53, 151–152, 180, 208, 246–247, 248, Plate 2.3; and Mars 167–169
Scot, Reginald, *The Discoverie of Witchcraft* 84
Scute, Cornelys 60, 199
seasons 139–161
Securis, John 61, *100*, 103; ages of man woodcuts 254; almanac title pages 99–100; attack by Nicholas Allen 84–85, 119; calendar 270, *271*, 272; political prognostications 65, 141
Seres, William 47–48, 61, 274
Seven Sisters *see* Pleiades
Shakespeare, William 2, 7, 141, 229
sheep-shearing *see* husbandry
Shrovetide 193, 197–198
Simotta, George, *A Theater of the Planetary Houres* 79, 129
Smith, Margaret M. 99
Smith, Reinold 131
Smyth, Adam 2
Sofford, Arthur 100–102, 105–106, 111, 120, 125, 133, Plate 6.1
Somer, John 39–40
Sommer, H. Oskar 75
sowing *see* husbandry

Spenser, Edmund 50, 141, 148, 221, Plate 15.2
Sphere of Apuleius 81
Spring Equinox 21, 23, 34, 37, 50, 99, 106, 120, 139
Stadius 180, 214, 235, 259
star tables 127
stars: Arcturus 142, 148, 222, 241, 259; Asellus 151; Hyades 253; Lucida Corona 241; Lucida Lancis 208; Procyon (*Canis Minor*) 148, 151, 155, 229; Regulus 193; Sirius (*Canis Major*) 148, 155, 214, 229–230, 235, 253; *see also* constellations, Zodiac
Stationers' Company *see* almanacs and prognostications, printing history; Company of Stationers
Stationers' Register 62, 64–65, 67–68
Stow, John, *Summarie of the English Chronicles* 131; *Survay of London* 225
Stubbes, Philip, *The Anatomie of Abuses* 84, 218
Summer Solstice 21, 26, 106, 120, 139, 147; and date of Easter 34, 37; and Gregorian Reforms 50–51
Sun, the 19, 163, *164*, 165; and Apollo 162; circle of the sun 38, 106; and first point of Aries 21, 23, 120, 140; and Julian calendar 34–37; and planetary hours 27, 129; *see also* eclipses; circle of the Sun; Metonic cycle
Sutton, Henry 48, 61
Swallow, Thomas 71

Tanner, Robert, *A Prognosticall Judgement* 85–87; *A Mirror for Mathematiques* 79
Taurus 25, 88, 142, 173, 180, 208
temperaments 20, 43, 76, 140; *see also* choleric temperament; melancholic temperament; phlegmatic temperament; physic; sanguine temperament
Thibault, Jean 60, 99
Thomas à Becket (Thomas of Canterbury) 42, 46, 190, 285–286, 261–262, 264
Thomas, Keith 60, 29
Thorndike, Lynn 82
tide tables 76–77, 90, 131
Trevelyon, Thomas (or Trevilian) 30–31, 76, 81, 184, 274–275; calendar 276–277

Trinity Sunday 36, 216–217, 224; *see also* law terms
True, Patrick 127
Turke, J. 61
Turner, Thomas 132
Tusser, Thomas, *Five Hundred Points of Good Husbandry* 8, 126, 129, 180–259 *passim*, 275
Tuve, Rosamond 140
Twelfth Night 118, 188–189, 263
Twyne, Thomas 86

Upcote, Augustine 126

Vanden Broeke, Steven 6
Vaughan, Lewes 61, 63, 83, 103, 119–120
Vaux, John 105, 130, 258
Veldman, Ilja M. 141
Venus 36, *143*, 146, 162, 173–*174*, 175
Verstegan, Richard, *A Restitution of Decayed Intelligence* 51
Virgil 105, 126, 140, 144
Virgo 169, 234–236, Plate 16.1
Vos, Maarten de 142–*143*, 148, *150*, *164*
Vostre, Simon 41, 42, 75
vulgar notes *see* declarations

W.W., *A New, and Merrie Prognostication* 90
Walker, Katherine 2
Walley, John 61, 64
Wallis, Faith 2, 37–38, 140
Waters, Fr[igid] 71
Watkins, Richard 65–66, 98–99, 101, 105, 117, 271; *see also* almanacs and prognostications, printing history
Watson, Robert 100, 106, 125, 230, 243, 254
Wayland, John 47
weather predictions 123–125, *125*, 126; *see also* prognostications
Wells-Cole, Anthony 8, 141–142
Westhawe, Robert 100, 105, 119, 124
Wharton, George 70
White, Edward 105
White, Helen 47
White, John 101–102, 104, 106, 127, *128*, 132, Plate 6.2
Whitney, *Choice of Emblemes* 148
Whitsun 48, 216–218, 225
Winter Solstice 21, 116, 120, 139, 155
Winter, Frig. 71
Wolfe, Heather 274

322 *Index*

Wood, David Houston 181
Woodhouse, John 126, 187
Woodhouse, William 66, 102, 104
Worde, Wynkyn de 43, 58, 78, 99
Wyer, Robert 28, 58, 60, 61, 76, 78–80

yellow bile *see* choleric temperament

Zodiac 19–25; *see also* Aquarius; Aries; astrology; Cancer; Capricorn; Gemini; horoscopes; Leo; Libra; Pisces; Scorpio; Sagittarius; Taurus; Virgo; Zodiac Man
Zodiac Man: in annual almanacs 7, 59, 60–61, 77, 108–19, *Plates 2, 8.1*; and lunar astrological medicine 17, 25–28; in mock almanacs 3, 90, 109; in multi-year almanacs 78; in perpetual almanacs 75–77; in primer calendars 43, 60–61